Chinese
Buddhist
Apocrypha

Chinese Buddhist Apocrypha

EDITED BY

ROBERT E. BUSWELL, JR.

HAWAII

UNIVERSITY OF HAWAII PRESS

HONOLULU

Printed in the United States of America

90 91 92 93 94 95 5 4 3 2 1

Library of Congress Cataloging-in-Publication Data

Chinese Buddhist apocrypha / edited by Robert E. Buswell, Jr.

p. cm.

ISBN 0-8248-1253-0 (alk. paper)

1. Apocryphal books (Tripiṭaka)—Criticism, interpretation, etc. 2. Ta tsang ching—Criticism, interpretation, etc. 3. Buddhist literature, Chinese—History and criticism. I. Buswell, Robert E.

BQ1217.C48 1990 89-20614

294.3'85'0951—dc20 CIP

University of Hawaii Press books are printed on acid-free paper and meet the guidelines for permanence and durability of the Council on Library Resources

Contents

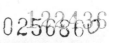

Preface

This volume began to take shape in 1982 among several people at the University of California, Berkeley, who were working in the area of Buddhist apocryphal studies. The volume was conceived as a broad-based survey of the indigenous scriptural literature of the non-Indian traditions of Buddhism, with chapters ranging from East Asian apocryphal sūtras and śāstras, to Tibetan *gter-ma* (treasure) texts and visionary cycles, to Southeast Asian apocryphal *Jātakas*. It was originally planned for the book to appear in the Berkeley Buddhist Studies Series, but with that series now unfortunately moribund, there was little hope that the volume would ever see the light of day. Stuart Kiang, editor at the University of Hawaii Press, was enthusiastic about the project, however, and in 1988 finally convinced me to submit the book to Hawaii. The economic realities of academic publishing in this country, however, demanded that the volume be pared down to more manageable size. After much agonizing, we finally decided to focus on Chinese sūtra materials, while maintaining Davidson's chapter as an appendix. I would like to offer my deepest regrets to several of our original contributors whose works had to be deleted from the final collection, including William Grosnick (La Salle University), Janet Gyatso (Amherst College), Padmanabh Jaini (University of California, Berkeley), Matthew Kapstein (Columbia University), and Alex Wayman (Columbia University). Most of those articles have since appeared elsewhere. I would like to express my gratitude to all the contributors for their patience during the long process of bringing this book to press.

We were extremely fortunate to have had two assiduous readers—Bernard Faure of Stanford and Stephen Teiser of Princeton—who evaluated the manuscript for the Press. Both offered thorough and trenchant critiques of each of the chapters—which went far beyond the call of this often thankless duty—and the volume has benefitted greatly from their many suggestions and advice. I also received many valuable suggestions on the volume and its coverage from Lewis Lancaster and useful comments on my own chapter from Daniel Overmyer. I would also like to thank Victoria Scott, who did a superb job of copyediting the manuscript, and Susan Sugar, who prepared the index to the volume, with funding provided by an Academic Senate Research Grant from UCLA.

ROBERT BUSWELL

Preface

Conventions

Scriptures in the Chinese Buddhist canon are cited according to standard numbers in the *Taishō* printed edition (abbreviated as *T*): *Taishō shinshū daizōkyō,* edited by Takakusu Junjirō and Watanabe Kaikyoku (Tokyo: Daizōkyōkai, 1924–1935). Full citations from the *Taishō* canon are given in the following fashion: title and fascicle number (where relevant); *T*[*aishō*]; *Taishō* serial number; *Taishō* volume number; page, register (a, b, or c), line number(s), e.g., *Ta-fang-kuang fo hua-yen ching* 23, *T* 278.9.542c27–543a1.

Citations from the *Supplement to the Canon* (*Dai-Nihon Zokuzōkyō* [Kyoto: Zōkyō shoin, 1905–1912]) are listed as follows: Title and fascicle number; *ZZ;* series; case; volume; page, column (a, b, c, or d), line number(s), e.g., *Shih-men Hung Chüeh-fan lin-chien lu* 1, *ZZ* 2b, 21, 4 303d13.

Scriptures in the Taoist canon are cited by their number in the *Combined Indices to the Authors and Titles of Books in Two Collections of Taoist Literature,* Harvard-Yenching Institute Sinological Series, no. 25, edited by Weng Tu-chieh (Peking, 1925). This number will be preceded by the initial HY.

To help distinguish indigenous Chinese scriptures from Indian sūtras translated into Chinese, as a general rule we have tried to reserve the term "sūtra" for translated texts. Apocryphal scriptures will be entitled "book," an all-purpose translation of the Chinese term *ching.*

Transliterations of Asian languages follow the systems commonly used in the scholarly community: Wade-Giles for Chinese, revised Hepburn for Japanese, McCune-Reischauer for Korean.

All Buddhist terminology that appears in *Webster's Third New International Dictionary* we consider to have entered the English language and leave unitalicized: e.g., sūtra, śāstra, nirvāṇa. For a convenient listing of a hundred such words, see Roger Jackson, "Terms of Sanskrit and Pāli Origin Acceptable as English Words," *Journal of the International Association of Buddhist Studies* 5 (1982): 141–142.

Introduction

Prolegomenon to the Study of Buddhist Apocryphal Scriptures

ROBERT E. BUSWELL, JR.

It is a sacrosanct belief of the Buddhist traditions that formed outside the homeland of India that their scriptural literatures were translated from Sanskrit or Middle Indic into their native languages. East Asian Buddhists in particular often included a colophon with the scriptures included in their canons, giving the translator's name and the place where, and dates during which, the translation was made. Massive catalogues of these attributions were collected that purported to give accurate accounts of the history of the Buddhist translation effort in China. But despite the seemingly valuable data these ascriptions provide concerning the introduction and diffusion of Buddhist scriptures into new regions of Asia—and, in turn, of those texts' foreign origins—modern scholarship has called much of that information into question. It now appears that many Buddhist scriptures were not "translations" at all, but were composed within the indigenous cultures of Asia and in the native languages of those regions. It is to such scriptures that the term "Buddhist apocrypha" is meant to refer. Because these texts typically reflect their domestic authors' own religious interests and social concerns, which were not directly addressed in translated Indian texts, they are of immense value in any accounting of the development of the non-Indian traditions of Buddhism.

The Multidisciplinary Value of Buddhist Apocrypha

The study of Buddhist apocryphal scriptures has long-neglected implications for scholarship concerning both Buddhism and the native literatures and cultures of Asia. The discipline of Buddhist Studies had its inception in research on doctrinal issues, employing principally the techniques of comparative philology and textual criticism. Today, most Buddhist scholars continue to specialize in one or another of the tenet systems of the religion. Because of Buddhism's Indian origins, philosophical concerns relevant to the schools of the greater Indian tradition have received the lion's share of attention. But even where experts in the non-Indian traditions have examined the contributions of native exegetes to Buddhist doctrine, this has often involved the writings of religious specialists working within such exegetical traditions as the Chinese Fa-hsiang or the Tibetan dGe-lugs schools. The tenets of such learned schools were commonly based on the interpretation of materials assumed to have been originally of Indian origin—that is, scriptures or treatises composed in India (or sometimes Central Asia). As important as such schools may have been for understanding the Chinese or Tibetan response to Indian doctrine, they inevitably place the regional forms of Buddhism within the purview of the greater Indian tradition, treating them as appendages of fundamentally Indological concerns.

Humanities specialists in the non-Indian civilizations of Asia, by contrast, are most concerned with indigenous movements in literature, thought, and history, especially within the élite tradition of classical belles lettres and philosophy. Sinologists in particular have shown only tangential interest in the Buddhist writers and thinkers of China—and this despite the pervasive effect of that originally Indian religion on manifold aspects of Chinese civilization. This cultural defensiveness—or, perhaps, simple hesitancy to deal with the unfamiliar civilization of India—has led many specialists in Chinese humanities to overlook the contributions that the scholar of Buddhism could make to the study of China.

In the case of East Asia, it is only in the last few decades that indigenous Buddhist scriptures have been recognized as a legitimate field of inquiry in either Buddhist Studies or Sinology. Research by scholars such as Yabuki Keiki, Mochizuki Shinkō, and Makita Tairyō[1] has shown that Buddhist apocrypha are an unparalleled source for ascertaining the truly indigenous elements in the sinitic Buddhist traditions. It was these pioneering scholars who first recognized that many of the seminal contributions made by the Chinese to Buddhist culture were, in fact, not results of continually more refined exegeses of translated Indian or Serindian materials. Rather, these contributions occurred in response to indigenous concerns—concerns that are often preserved in Buddhist apocryphal materials and nowhere else. Just as importantly, apocryphal works also offer invaluable corroboration for secular accounts of religious, cultural, and political developments in traditional Asian societies, as Antonino Forte has demonstrated with considerable perspicuity in his monograph *Political Propaganda and Ideology in China at the End of the Seventh Century.*[2] As the point where Buddhist Studies and Sinology converge, the study of apocryphal scriptures will prompt changes in orientation, and expansions in coverage, within both disciplines.

It is to introduce this new field of study that this volume on Chinese Buddhist apocrypha is offered. No pretensions are intended, of course, that the essays collected herein present a comprehensive accounting of sinitic apocrypha. Our attempt is rather to bring together representative samples of the kinds of studies that are possible using apocryphal materials, as examples of the value of these texts in a wide range of scholarship in East Asian humanities. In the process, we hope to facilitate cross-fertilization between those various disciplines. Given the nascent state of research into Buddhist apocrypha, it is not surprising that the contributions are weighted toward studies dealing with textual authenticity and scriptural legitimation. Several of the contributors do, however, broach the role that apocryphal materials can play in documenting the underlying social, political, and cultural forces influencing East Asian civilizations.

The Definition of "Buddhist Apocrypha" and Buddhist Standards of Scriptural Authenticity

Before proceeding to an examination of specific issues raised by the study of indigenous Buddhist scriptures, we would do well to consider the appropriateness of using the Western term "apocrypha" to refer to such works. This question arises because the relationship between canonical scripture and noncanonical apocrypha is considerably different in Buddhism than in the Judeo-Christian tradition, for Buddhism has no corpus of texts distinct from revealed scripture that corresponds to the Apocrypha of Judaism and Christianity.

Etymologically, the word "apocrypha" is derived from the Greek *apokryphos,* referring to writings that are "hidden away" or "secret." Three distinct usages of the term in the early Judeo-Christian tradition have been delineated by R. H. Charles. First, *apokryphos* was applied "in a laudatory signification to writings which were withheld from public knowledge because they were vehicles of mysterious or esoteric wisdom which was too sacred or profound to be disclosed to any save the initiated. Though they insisted on the exclusive canonicity of the twenty-four books [of the Old Testament], they claimed to be the possessors of an oral tradition that not only overshadowed but frequently displaced the written law." Second, the word carried an admonitory sense that "was applied to writings that were withheld from public circulation, not on the ground of their transcendental worth, but because their value was confessedly secondary or questionable." Finally, as the ultimate extension of this meaning, "the word came to be applied to what was false, spurious, or heretical."[3] During Origen's (185?–254?) time, the term was applied to those books now commonly designated as the Pseudepigrapha, which are discussed below. By the fourth century, the Apocrypha came to refer to books read for edification, as distinct from the canonical books, and the adjective "apocryphal" continued to be retained for the Pseudepigrapha. In its present usage, which stems from the age of Jerome (340?–420), "the Apocrypha" refers to the *libri ecclesiastici*—noncanonical, but still edifying, books—as distinguished from the revealed *libri canonici.*[4] The adjective "apocryphal" is retained for works in the former category. Hence, as the term is now understood, "the Apocrypha" designates not "heretical books but books of religious interest which lacked the inspiration and hence the authority of books actually included in the Bible. The criterion is the canon of the Bible; books not contained in an authoritative Bible are apocrypha."[5]

There are several problems involved in applying this usage of the term "apocrypha" to the corpus of native Buddhist literature. The meaning of "apocrypha" is extremely imprecise even in Judeo-Christian circles. The reasons for including some books among the Apocrypha are far from clear and provide no set criteria for determining scriptural authenticity.[6] Unlike the Bible, the Buddhist scriptural collection was an open canon,[7] and until quite late in the history of Buddhism there was no similarly restricted body of scripture that could serve as a standard of comparison through which to ferret out unauthentic writings. In addition, since indigenous Buddhist scriptures were often composed by authors belonging to learned schools in the mainstream of the native traditions, these texts came to be endowed with an authority similar to that of unequivocably canonical sūtras. It therefore is difficult to call a Buddhist scripture "apocryphal" based solely on the supposedly heretical affiliations of its author, as sometimes occurred in the West. These differences make problematic the use of the term "extra-canonical" for Buddhist apocryphal texts.

Sixtus Senensis' neologism "deutero-canonical," meaning canonical books that are of a later date than the earlier texts (which were then termed "proto-canonical"), creates more problems than it resolves by compelling the scholar to assign precise dates to the full range of biblical writings. Such assignments would be all but impossible for Buddhist, and especially Indian Buddhist, texts, for which general eras, let alone precise dates, are rarely known.

The term "pseudepigrapha," or "writings of falsely ascribed authorship," fares somewhat better in a Buddhist context. This term originally referred to Jewish texts accepted only within certain congregations, but it is ambiguous in its Christian usage, "for it is applied arbitarily to only certain Apocryphal books and not to others which are equally deserving of the name."[8] There are, however, many parallels between the literary styles and devices of the Pseudepigrapha and Buddhist apocryphal compositions. For example, the Buddhist scriptures that are considered in this volume commonly attempted to pass themselves off as Indian compositions by adopting the stylistic features, technical terminology (such as Sanskrit transliterations), and Indian evocative elements (Indian proper names and place names) that appeared in translated materials. In fact, the success of an apocryphal scripture was often dependent on its being virtually indistinguishable from a translated sūtra.[9] And just as the Pseudepigrapha are often ascribed to famous saints, so Buddhist apocryphal texts are attributed to the Buddha. But in both cases these ascriptions are more a literary device to enhance the prestige and solemnity of the work than an attempt at deception. Indeed, the rationale for the Protestant rejection of many books of the Apocrypha as being pseudepigraphic seems more ad hoc than logical, for the Apocrypha were equally imaginative and often more imitative of accepted scriptural styles than were pseudepigrapha.

These controversies over the Judeo-Christian usages of these various terms need not detain us further. Were it not for the unwieldiness of the terms "indigenous scriptures" or "original [Chinese] scriptures," these might be preferred to "apocrypha." Still, given the inherent lack of precision in the Western meanings of both "apocrypha" and "pseudepigrapha," either term may be appropriated in a Buddhist usage with little fear of misinterpretation, provided that both are purged of any latent pejorative connotations. As this volume will show, many of the same literary genres found in the Judeo-Christian Apocrypha have their counterparts in Buddhist texts, including the historical, didactic, devotional, and apocalyptic.[10] Both corpora developed in similar social milieus, which witnessed political upheavals, constant threats from the surrounding heterodox community, and explicit messianic expectations.[11] Finally, Chinese exegetes perceived these texts as "spurious books" *(wei-ching)* or "books of doubtful authenticity" *(i-ching),* paralleling one of the meanings of "apocrypha" in the West. Hence, for the purposes of this volume, the term "apocrypha" is used to refer to indigenous Buddhist texts composed outside the Indian cultural sphere, but on the model of Indian or Serindian scripture. Such texts were sometimes written in association with a revelatory experience, but often were intentionally forged using false ascriptions as a literary device both to enhance their authority as well as to strengthen their chances of being accepted as canonical.

This restriction of our coverage to texts composed outside the Indian cultural sphere is important because, in a very real sense, all Mahāyāna sūtras and many Śrāvakayāna scriptures are "apocryphal." Modern scholars know, for example, that most Mahāyāna scriptures were certainly composed after the Buddha's time and represent stages in the adaptation of Buddhism to contemporary social situations and philosophical developments in India. These Indian scriptures were retrospectively attributed to the Buddha for the same reasons as were indigenous Buddhist books composed elsewhere in Asia. Outside India, however, there was little sensitivity to the problem of textual evolution in Indian Buddhism, and any Buddhist scripture of verifiable foreign provenance was typically treated as the authentic Word of the Buddha *(buddhavacana)*. This of course created considerable hermeneutical problems for native exegetes, who were forced to develop complex doctrinal taxonomies *(p'an-chiao)* in order to reconcile the disparate tenet systems described in Indian Buddhist texts, each ostensibly Buddhist, yet each so different. A study of such non-Indian developments may illuminate much concerning the processes by which Indian Buddhist scripture came to be written.

Some of these issues in Indian Buddhist textual criticism are broached in Ronald Davidson's appendix to this volume. As Davidson notes, there were deep-seated structural and interpretative features in the core Indian tradition that ultimately contributed to the production of Buddhist apocrypha. The lack of a critical, linguistic basis for verifying the authenticity of specific sūtras is first noted in the Buddha's own admission that the dharma could be preached "each in his own dialect." Given that there was no single, lineal transmission of the authentic Word of the Buddha to posterity, an elaboration and consolidation of the teachings took place even during the Buddha's own lifetime, which eventually led to dramatic alterations in the doctrinal foundations of the religion. As the definition of the dharma was extended from the teachings of the master himself to the enlightened words of his disciples, finally any sincere description of religious attainment could be considered authentic. At that point, the "inspired speech" *(pratibhā)* of anyone claiming a transcendental vision became the equal of the Buddha's own words, providing a fertile ground for major innovations in Buddhist doctrine through revelation and religious inspiration.

It was the *Abhidharma* treatises that constituted the first major expansion of the scope of the Buddhist canon in India. In their attempts to authenticate their texts, the *Abhidharma* exegetes were compelled to prove either that the Buddha himself had initially taught the system, or that the texts had been compiled by a knowledgeable elder and subsequently recited at the First Council, where the canon was codified. The use of an elaborate mythology to legitimize the Theravāda *Abhidharma* canon was also adopted later by Indian Mahāyānists to validate their own scriptures. These same approaches to authentication were subsequently shared by Vajrayānists in India and ultimately by Buddhists throughout Asia.

Because of their responsibility for establishing the canon, it was the Buddhist cataloguers in particular who were compelled to develop precise criteria for determining textual authenticity, many of which harken back to Indian discussions. Kyoko Tokuno's chapter surveys the assessments of apocryphal scriptures in Chinese Buddhist bibliographical catalogues, a genre of religious writing without counterpart in India. The cataloguers' overriding concern in deciding the canonicity of a text was that there be clear evidence of a sūtra's "Western" provenance. This evidence could consist of either a Sanskrit or Middle Indic original (which would clinch the point that it had indeed been translated into Chinese), or unequivocal signs that the language and style of the text were in accord with those of authentic Indian scripture. Any indications of the presence of such native elements as yin-yang cosmology, local gods and spirits, or Taoist and folk liturgies and rituals (such as those described by Whalen Lai in his chapter) were generally enough to condemn a sūtra as "spurious" *(wei)*.

By no means were the criteria employed by the cataloguers consistent throughout the ages, however, and considerable permutations are noted both in their assessment of what constituted apocrypha as well as in their scriptural typologies. In particular, socio-political necessity frequently overrode historical or doctrinal concerns in the cataloguers' adjudication of a text. Tokuno demonstrates, for example, that the evaluation of condensed scriptures *(ch'ao-ching)* shifted from authentic to spurious because of specific, documentable changes in the social and political fortunes of the Buddhist religion. Converse movements were also true, however, and a number of spurious texts were eventually reclassified as canonical. Among the cataloguers, Fei Ch'ang-fang (fl. late sixth century) is notorious for having arbitrarily assigned to eminent past translators texts previously labeled "anonymous" (*shih-i,* lit., "translator's [name] lost"), and even those considered suspicious or spurious. His actions were apparently prompted by a need to provide a credible textual basis for Buddhism during a time of intense polemical pressure from rival Taoists.

These political concerns were exacerbated by the penchant of the Chinese imperial government for reserving the right to define what was canonical, even to the extent of envisioning itself as the defender of those hallowed texts. Mark Lewis covers such political issues in his chapter. Such a corpus of canonical texts, or *ching,* was considered to be the basis of an orderly society and effective government. After Buddhism was introduced to China, its own scriptures, also labeled *ching,* soon became ensnared in this political definition of canonicity, alternately as an object of polemical derision on the part of rival religious groups and as a new underpinning to the rulership of the barbarian dynasties in the north. As both Lewis and Antonino Forte show for the San-chieh chiao (Three Stages sect), the classification of its scriptural corpus as apocryphal was based more on the contemporary political liabilities of the school than on any compelling historical or hermeneutical considerations.

Issues in the Study of Buddhist Apocrypha

Much of our most fundamental knowledge concerning the historical development of East Asian Buddhism is heavily dependent on a description of the tradition that was maintained principally by the Buddhist cataloguers. However, as Hayashiya Tomojirō first documented in his epochal study of Chinese Buddhist bibliographical catalogues,[12] the information the catalogues provide concerning the dating and translation of presumed Indian scriptures is often inaccurate and sometimes deliberately misleading. This is especially true of the ascriptions appearing in Fei Ch'ang-fang's *Li-tai san-pao chi* (Record of the Three Treasures throughout Successive Generations), which, as mentioned previously, arbitrarily adds translator attributions to several indigenous Chinese compositions. These false ascriptions were later adopted by the T'ang *K'ai-yüan shih-chiao lu* (Catalogue of Śākyamuni's Teachings, Compiled during the K'ai-yüan Era), which became recognized as the definitive Chinese catalogue and thence entered the mainstream of the sinitic Buddhist tradition. Many Buddhist texts that were actually of East Asian origin—including such seminal scriptures as the *Fan-wang ching* (Book of Brahmā's Net; *T* 1484), *P'u-sa ying-lo pen-yeh ching* (Book of the Original Acts that Serve as Necklaces for the Bodhisattvas; *T* 1485), *Shou-leng-yen ching* (*Śūraṃgama-sūtra,* or Book of the Heroic-March Absorption; *T* 945), and *Ta-sheng ch'i-hsin lun* (Treatise on the Awakening of Faith According to the Mahāyāna; *T* 1666)—were in this wise assigned a translator and translation date. Thenceforth they were accepted as authentic renderings of Indian originals, enabling them to play major roles in the subsequent development of East Asian Buddhism.

Considerable ambivalence is also seen in the attitude of Chinese Buddhists toward the judgments of the cataloguers. On the one hand, the Chinese did make a great effort to maintain a "pure" tradition by carefully filtering out unauthentic materials. But on the other hand, Chinese exegetes did not hesitate to accept such spurious materials if they proved useful in elucidating doctrinal points inadequately addressed in the available translated corpus. We find such citations by noted authors like Chih-i (538–597) of the T'ien-t'ai school; Tao-cho (562–645), the important Pure Land exegete; Fa-tsang (643–712), the systematizer of the Hua-yen school; and Ch'eng-kuan (738–840), the traditional fourth Hua-yen patriarch. Their extensive citation of texts that they often knew to be clearly suspicious in origin epitomizes the internal tensions concerning such scriptures that rent Chinese Buddhism throughout its history.[13]

Given this attempted rigor in the Chinese examination of Buddhist textual materials, a number of scriptures that were classified as apocryphal by the cataloguers came to be proscribed and were subsequently dropped from circulation. In the early decades of this century, Yabuki Keiki discovered in the Stein collection of Tun-huang manuscripts at the British Museum several such texts that had long been presumed lost.[14] Most of these scriptures dated from the fourth through early eighth centuries C.E.—the Six Dynasties through mid-T'ang period, which was the formative era of the indigenous schools of Chinese Buddhism—and several illustrated the strong apocalyptic and eschatological bent of the Chinese of that era. What was even more surprising at the time of their discovery, however, was the fact that the content of some of these texts resonated strikingly with that of several scriptures that were part of the mainstream of Chinese Buddhism, scriptures central to the mature Chinese doctrinal synthesis and long accepted by the tradition as authentic. Yabuki's discoveries stimulated a wholesale reevaluation of the canonical corpus, especially by Mochizuki Shinkō. Research by Mochizuki, Hayashiya, Makita, and others showed that catalogue evaluations of canonical texts and traditional views about the evolution of Chinese Buddhist doctrine could no longer be considered reliable. The field of Buddhist apocryphal studies was born.

Several different typologies of sinitic Buddhist apocrypha have been proposed by contemporary scholars, which have implications for the study of this type of scripture throughout Asia. Mochizuki Shinkō has outlined five principal types of apocrypha on the basis of their doctrinal content: (1) scriptures incorporating elements adopted from Taoism and popular religion; this would include such texts as the *T'i-wei Po-li ching* (Book of Trapuṣa and Bhallika; Stein no. 2051; Pelliot 3732; Peking *shuang* 15), *Ching-tu san-mei ching* (Book of the Pure Liberation Absorption; Stein nos. 2301, 4546, 5960, *ZZ* 1.87.4), and *Kuan-ting ching* (Book of Consecration; *T* 1331); (2) texts teaching national protection *(hu-kuo)*, which outline the Mahāyāna precepts and/or the Bodhisattva mārga; this would include such seminal Chinese texts as the *Jen-wang ching* (Book of Benevolent Kings; *T* 245, *T* 246), *Fan-wang ching,* and *P'u-sa ying-lo pen-yeh ching;* (3) texts associated with Buddhist esotericism, focusing specifically on tathāgatagarbha thought; this includes the *Shou-leng-yen ching, Yüan-chüeh ching* (Book of Consummate Enlightenment; *T* 842), and *Chan-ch'a shan-o yeh-pao ching* (Book of Divining the Requital of Good and Evil Actions; *T* 839); (4) the syncretistic *Ta-sheng ch'i-hsin lun,* which Mochizuki places in a class by itself; and (5) śāstras attributed to eminent Indian exegetes like Nāgārjuna; for example, the *Shih Mo-ho-yen lun/Sŏk Mahayŏn-ron* (Treatise Explicating the Mahāyāna; *T* 1668).[15]

Makita Tairyō has proposed a different classification scheme, based on the close associations between Chinese social history and Buddhist apocrypha: (1) texts supporting the views of the ruling élite; this would include scriptures appearing in the second of Mochizuki's classifications, such as the *Jen-wang ching;* (2) writings criticizing the policies of that ruling class, such as are found in the *Hsiang-fa chüeh-i ching* (Book of Resolving Doubts During the Semblance Dharma Age; *T* 2870); (3) works attempting to synthesize or rank differing elements in Chinese traditional thought and religion; this would correspond to texts included in the first of Mochizuki's classifications, for example, the *T'i-wei Po-li ching;* (4) works advocating distinctive ideologies, such as tathāgatagarbha; (5) works that include in their title the name of a presumed living individual, such as the *Shou-lo pi-ch'iu ching* (Book of Śura Bhikṣu; *T* 2873) and the series of scriptures on Prince Moonlight (*Yüeh-kuang t'ung-tzu,* Skt. *Candraprabhākumāra; T* 534, *T* 535); and (6) works dealing with superstitious practices whereby one could cure illness or gain personal fortune.[16]

T'ang Yung-t'ung, in his classic study of early and Six Dynasties Chinese Buddhism, has offered a more eclectic classification of Buddhist apocrypha: (1) texts revealed through divine inspiration; (2) messianic scriptures, such as those devoted to Prince Moonlight, which seem to have been modeled on Confucian prognostication texts *(t'u-ch'en);* (3) works that combine Buddhist doctrines with Chinese folk beliefs, such as the *T'i-wei Po-li ching,* in which the five Buddhist lay precepts are correlated with the five elements and the five directions; and (4) texts written to challenge the Taoist *hua-hu* (converting the barbarians) polemical legend (which claimed that Lao-tzu had been the Buddha's teacher), by positing instead that Lao-tzu was an avatar of the Buddha, sent east to prepare China for the eventual revelation of Buddhism. Other texts extended this last theme to Confucianism as well, claiming that Confucius, his disciple Yen Hui, and even the legendary emperors of antiquity were actually theophanies of great bodhisattvas.[17]

Mizuno Kōgen has alluded to still another possible classification schema for Buddhist apocryphal compositions, based on the motives underlying their composition: (1) texts that relate Buddhism to traditional Chinese folk beliefs; (2) texts that reconcile Buddhism with the indigenous Taoist religion, or that use Taoist terminology and ideas to explicate Buddhist thought; (3) revelatory scriptures that were revealed to their transmitters in a moment of religious inspiration; visionary texts, such as those mentioned in the chapters by Strickmann and Tokuno, and the Tibetan "treasure" *(gter-ma)* texts would be examples of such scriptures; (4) condensed scriptures *(ch'ao-ching),* which compiled extracts from authentic translated sūtras but were labeled apocryphal by the cataloguers because they omitted essential details from the complete scriptures; and (5) texts that attempted to adapt Buddhist doctrines to the indigenous needs of Chinese Buddhists.[18]

There is a unique class of Chinese apocrypha, not mentioned in any of these typologies, that John Brough first revealed—though without ever calling it apocryphal—in his study of the Chinese "translation" of the *Jātakamālā* (Garland of Birth Stories).[19] In this case, the difficulty the Chinese translators had in construing the complex poetic style of the Sanskrit original led them to produce an apocryphal text while having the Sanskrit manuscript right in front of them. This was not simply a matter of a few mistranslations or interpolations. In their despair at rendering the text, the few Sanskrit phrases the Chinese were able to construe served as clues for lifting entire stories verbatim from other texts that contained the same key words: for example, finding the term "tigress" *(vyāghrī)* in their manuscript, they simply wrote out the *Vyāghrī-parivarta,* the last chapter of the *Suvarṇaprabhāsottama-sūtra* (Simile of Golden Light Sūtra; *T* 665). Apart from the titles of a few stories, there is virtually nothing in their Chinese rendering that compares with the original Sanskrit. Compounding their problems, the translators were working without dictionary or grammar and did not have the luxury of an Indian pundit to assist them in construing the text. There is also evidence that they were working under a deadline and were not given time to revise their hurried copy. Even with these caveats, this text must stand as one of the most bizarre products of Chinese translation efforts, and we can only sympathize with the horrific plight of these "translators."

As heuristically valuable as such modern scholarly classifications of sinitic apocrypha may be, I believe their inadequacies reveal precisely why a pluralistic approach to such texts is necessary. The criteria used in developing these schemata vary according to the principal scholarly interests of the writer and are, accordingly, limited by those interests. Where Mochizuki, for example, uses doctrinal filiations as a major criterion in his rankings of apocrypha, Mizuno and T'ang seem more concerned with genre and style, while Makita's categories stem from his interest in social history. To understand the significance of a particular apocryphon, however, we must remain simultaneously aware of its doctrinal content and genre, the motives underlying its composition, its target audience, its resonances with indigenous movements in religion and society, and its long-term effects on the culture as a whole. An accurate classification of Buddhist apocrypha will demand, therefore, a synthesis of the different scholarly interests used in developing various classification schemata.

My own feeling is that attempts to classify apocryphal scriptures are premature at this stage in the development of the field and should be put aside in favor of careful descriptions of the content and background of specific texts. Fortunately, there is considerable information available for many sinitic apocrypha through which to place them in their time and locale. A possible byproduct of centering indigenous sūtras in their Chinese context is that we may in turn be able to extrapolate about the process by which the Indian Mahāyāna canon came to be written. In dramatic comparison to Chinese materials, there is little extant information on the composition of the major Mahāyāna sūtras of India, many of which show elements of syncretism with indigenous Indian culture similar to those which have been found among Buddhist apocrypha in China. Our discoveries concerning the composition of sinitic apocryphal texts may correlate closely with the processes by which the Mahāyāna sūtras were composed in India. Taking such a comparative dimension in our research on Chinese apocrypha may ultimately help to illuminate the textual history of the Indian Buddhist tradition, providing a possible convergence between the study of sinitic apocrypha and still another Asian humanistic discipline—Indology.

Another inevitable fault of such classification schemes is that apocryphal scriptures were often composite texts themselves, which defy subsumption under a single category. For example, the *Chin-kang san-mei ching/Kŭmgang sammae-kyŏng* (*Vajrasamādhi-sūtra,* or Book of Adamantine Absorption; *T* 273), an important East Asian apocryphon with Ch'an admixtures, includes a mārga schema similar to that found in the *Jen-wang ching,* which should require its placement in Mochizuki's second category; however, it includes no national-protection component as does the representative scripture of that class. But the prominent place occupied by tathāgatagarbha thought in the scripture should also be enough to classify it in Mochizuki's third category, along with the *Yüan-chüeh ching.* Finally, the commentators to the *Vajrasamādhi* saw in the text the canonical source for the syncretistic approach of the *Ta-sheng ch'i-hsin lun;* hence, there would be clear justification for placing it in Mochizuki's fourth category. Until a more complete survey of Buddhist apocryphal literature has been made that would allow such texts to be classified with more precision, it seems premature to attempt to develop a comprehensive typology of Buddhist apocryphal literature. Given, too, the variety of perspectives from which such a classification could be made, it is doubtful that any one typology will ever suffice.

Buddhist apocryphal materials may eventually compel a wholesale revision of our assumptions about the development of the Chinese tradition. Indeed, the study of Buddhist apocrypha has already begun to revolutionize our view of the processes governing the evolution of the Chinese Buddhist tradition, particularly of the forces catalyzing innovation in the doctrine and praxis of indigenous learned schools. Buddhism has commonly been portrayed as adapting gradually to the Chinese Weltanschauung, culminating several centuries after its transplantation to its new homeland in the formation of the mature, sinitic schools of T'ang dynasty Buddhism, such as T'ien-t'ai, Hua-yen, and Ch'an. Tokuno's chapter in this volume suggests, however, that the composition of Buddhist apocrypha, which would be an explicit example of such adaptation, may have begun almost simultaneously with the introduction of Buddhism into China, not centuries later.[20] We know that apocryphal texts continued to be written throughout the Six Dynasties and T'ang periods, when the major sinitic schools of Buddhism were formed, and even into the Sung, well after the canon was first codified by the T'ang cataloguers. Although the Six Dynasties through mid-T'ang period (fourth to early eighth centuries) may have been the creative watershed in the writing of apocryphal texts—and indeed, virtually all the texts covered in this volume date from this period—we still must say that the textual history of sinitic apocrypha is all but coextensive with the history of the Chinese Buddhist tradition as a whole. In fact, the composition of apocryphal scriptures is an inevitable byproduct of sinicization, a process of transformation that began with the first translations of Indian texts into Chinese. The monumental task of communicating Indian ideas to a Chinese audience was inevitably informed by indigenous social, political, philosophical, and religious beliefs. Henri Maspero showed long ago that the earliest Chinese translations of Buddhist texts were so heavily laden with Taoist terminology and preconceptions as to make Buddhism and Taoism during the Han dynasty virtually an organic tradition.[21] While a translator—or team of translators—might introduce indigenous philosophical and religious terms into their rendering of an Indian Buddhist text as a way of making the text more intelligible, indigenous sūtras were, in a sense, wholesale rewrites of Buddhist ideas, presenting those ideas in ways that could be more immediately accessible to the Chinese. Hence the composition of Buddhist apocrypha is but one example of a complex process of cultural hermeneutics whereby foreign Indian concepts were transformed into familiar Chinese ideas.

Recent research reveals that many of the most important developments in Chinese Buddhism were not merely reflected in such native scriptures but were actually catalyzed and/or sustained by them. The *Ta-sheng ch'i-hsin lun* is one example of how pervasive an effect an apocryphal composition could have on the indigenous tradition. As Rhi Ki-yong, the major Korean specialist on this treatise, has remarked, regardless of the doubts raised by modern scholars about the Indian provenance of the text, the more than one hundred commentaries written on it by East Asian exegetes attest to its importance to the sinitic Buddhist tradition.[22] For East Asians, suspicions concerning the authenticity of a text paled as its value in explicating Buddhist doctrine and practice became recognized. Hence the Buddhist scholar can no longer hope that a comprehensive view of the development of the religion or a sense of the unique features of the native traditions of Buddhism can be gleaned merely through the study of translated Indian scriptures or of native commentaries to those texts.

As Michel Strickmann points out in his chapter, apocryphal texts written during the Six Dynasties period reveal the strong indigenous influences exerted upon the Buddhism of the period, and demonstrate several of the major factors that underlay the compilation of Buddhist apocrypha: the attempt to popularize Buddhism by producing and circulating a form of literature, based on Buddhist themes, that would be more accessible to the masses; the spread of the eschatological notion of the Final Age of the Dharma *(mo-fa)* among Chinese Buddhists; the close, if often turbulent, relationship between Buddhism and the state; and rivalry with native religious groups. Many of the texts produced during the medieval period soon insinuated themselves into the very fabric of orthodox Chinese Buddhism and came to be accepted by East Asian exegetes as authentic. Indeed, Buddhist religious specialists of a variety of sectarian persuasions were quick to turn to these original Chinese materials (sometimes when clearly sensitive to their domestic provenance, as mentioned above) in order to resolve problematic points even in Indian thought. This shows that indigenous sūtras appealed to the Chinese psyche in a way that Indian texts could not, and demonstrates their central role in the development of a truly native church. Hence, from a number of standpoints, it is apocryphal texts, rather than exegeses of translated Indian scriptures, that often exhibit what is most distinctively Chinese about Chinese Buddhism.

But Buddhist apocrypha also exploit their knowledge of Chinese popular religion and customs to further the cause of Buddhism. One of the most prominent such examples is the *T'ien-ti pa-yang shen-chou ching* (The Divine Spell Book of Heaven and Earth and the Eight Yang; *T* 2897), which has been the subject of important recent work by Daniel Overmyer.[23] This scripture sought to undermine indigenous religious rituals by replacing them with appropriate Buddhist techniques instead. It claims that Buddhist recitation, for example, is more effective at protecting the locality and the household than are the indigenous deities of the popular religion. Even though guarding the local environment, or protecting against arrest, mugging, and wild-animal attack—all services this book offers—might be considered ancillary to the principal soteriological purposes of Buddhism, such efficacious results would further the cause of the religion by demonstrating its superiority to indigenous cults. In more typical Buddhist terms, we might say that such texts are a type of *upāya* or "expedient means" in the service of religious proselytism. Their genius, as Overmyer suggests, is that "they maintain Buddhist superiority while plunging to the depths of Chinese tradition; their authors were evangelists at ground level."[24]

Apocryphal compositions encourage also a reconsideration of the role of local and regional cults in the development of the greater Chinese Buddhist tradition, as Strickmann and Lai suggest in their chapters.

Many scholars of Buddhism have commonly treated Chinese Buddhism as a religion of élite doctrinal specialists, ignoring the important role of the so-called popular Buddhism of the common people in the formation of the indigenous tradition. This rubric "popular" should perhaps be labeled "regional" or "local" Buddhism, as distinct from the Great Tradition of the metropolitan religious élite, who were often patronized by the court. Apocryphal texts may prove instrumental in ascertaining the precise nature of these regional qualities of the larger Chinese tradition.

Provincial religious leaders had political interests that could differ dramatically from those of the Buddhist ecclesia in the metropolitan centers: these local leaders were typically supported by, and were responding to, an audience that was not exclusively Buddhist. Their incorporation of cultic elements into their presentations of Buddhism was an attempt to coopt practices important to the masses, from those of the spirit-medium to those of the diviner. The important role that the temple played in daily life in China made it one of the central institutions of village society. It was obviously to Buddhism's advantage to arrogate to itself local religious practices in its attempt to monopolize popular rites and rituals. The *Chan-ch'a ching,* the text that is the focus of Whalen Lai's chapter, is one of the more blatant examples of this attempt to make the monks into oracles. This scripture depicts the wholesale adoption of local cults and practices into Buddhism; the subsequent reification of those beliefs and practices by Buddhist religious specialists in order to bring them into the mainstream tradition; and, finally, the reintroduction of those practices into the mass culture, now safely clothed in the sanctified raiments of Indian doctrinal terminology. The local tradition would then be able to respond anew to this combination of "popular" and élite. Through this process, Buddhism became rapidly more sinicized and local religion increasingly Buddhicized.

The ritual practices of local cults and the religious rites of such indigenous traditions as early Taoism are related areas in which Buddhist apocryphal compositions provide important documentation. In his chapter, Strickmann treats an important subgroup of Chinese Buddhist apocrypha, the spell-literature, or dhāraṇī-sūtras, of proto-Tantric Buddhism and its progressive acculturation in China. Such sūtras were intended for the final era of Buddhism, a period coterminous with the demise of the world, and partake fully of the eschatological concerns prominent in Chinese Buddhism. Hence dhāraṇī-sūtras are some of the earliest manifestations of this eschatological theme, which would become such an integral part of subsequent Chinese religious history. Recent articles by Sunayama Minoru and Erik Zürcher[25] have also shown the value of Buddhist apocrypha in elucidating the reasons behind social upheavals, such as those which prompted and accompanied the messianic movements of the Six Dynasties period. The symbiosis between the developing indigenous religions of Taoism and sinicized Buddhism is verified by the fact that the great majority of Taoist scriptures composed between the Latter Han and the early sixth century show signs of Buddhist influence, as Zürcher has shown.[26] A specific example of the role played by Buddhist apocryphal texts in the formation of Taoist doctrines is documented by Stephen Bokenkamp in his chapter. There, Bokenkamp suggests that there might have been a symbiotic influence between Buddhism and Taoism in the development of their respective schemata of spiritual development.

The burgeoning importance of eschatological notions in Chinese Buddhism is perhaps best exemplified in the Three Stages teaching (San-chieh chiao), an influential sect of the Six Dynasties church, which receives one of its first extensive treatments in a Western language in chapters in this volume by Mark Edward Lewis and Antonino Forte. Their discussions reveal the value of apocryphal texts in documenting the origins and historical fortunes of such indigenous schools of sinitic Buddhism. The doctrines of Hsin-hsing (540–594), the founder of the school, focused, first, on the teaching of the demise of the dharma, which asserted the inevitable corruption of Buddhism, and second, on his claim that this corruption proved the inefficacy of the teachings and institutions of rival Buddhist schools, which enjoyed official support. Given what Hsin-hsing perceived as the serious degeneration in Buddhism during this Final Age of the Dharma, only the radical doctrines of the Three Stages sect would be able to succor the people of that era. Countering previous theories of the reasons underlying the proscription of the Three Stages sect, Lewis asserts that its suppression by the dowager-empress Wu Tse-t'ien (r. 684–704) did not occur because it actually attempted to subvert the state, but because it refused to acknowledge the authority of the traditional monastic order and the officially sanctioned doctrines and practices of Chinese Buddhism. The sect's rejection of the validity of contemporary Buddhism was indeed an ecclesiastical heresy, but more importantly, the nation and the religion were so intertwined by this time that the state could not but consider Hsin-hsing's challenge to the metropolitan ecclesia as a political issue with direct bearing on the legitimacy of the government itself. Accordingly, the state regarded the texts of the school as politically subversive and called for their proscription.

The vicissitudes in the evaluation of the *Yü-ch'ieh fa-ching ching* (Book of the Yoga Dharma Mirror), a seminal San-chieh chiao text that was itself based on the apocryphal *Hsiang-fa chüeh-i ching,* is treated by Antonino Forte in his chapter. Forte demonstrates that the changes in the cataloguers' evaluation of the *Fa-ching ching* were a direct response to the state's attitude toward the San-chieh chiao, the bibliographers intentionally adapting their judgment to changing political fortunes—a Buddhist Realpolitik. Complementing Lewis' discussion on the suppression of the sect, Forte clarifies that the adjudication of scriptural orthodoxy was frequently a byproduct of decisive social and political conditions rather than the result of objective bibliographical criteria.

It would seem prudent in our consideration of indigenous Buddhist scriptures not to rule out entirely the possibility that some may very well have been emended or even forged outside India or Serindia in Sanskrit or Prakrit before the text was translated into the native languages. In China, as we have already seen, apocryphal compositions are commonly attributed to major foreign translators. Although most of these attributions occurred much later in the history of the transmission of a text, some ascriptions may have begun contemporaneously. Since Indian and Serindian translators often worked in large bureaus together with scores of foreign and Chinese assistants, if a forgery were to be successfully carried out, any alterations of the text would more easily have been made prior to its translation into Chinese—that is, before the manuscript was scrutinized by native collaborators. This possibility is not as farfetched as it might first sound. For example, in his monograph on Buddhism during the Wu Chao usurpation of the T'ang throne, Forte has suggested that, to curry favor with the empress, the Sanskrit manuscript of the authentic *Pao-yü ching* (Rain of Jewels Sūtra) was apparently interpolated by Buddhist monks to include explicit references to a female cakravartin.[27] Forte broaches the possibility that this interpolation was made in the original manuscript and not the translation, since there is no indication that any of the thirty-two Chinese assistants was aware of alterations in the text. Such interpolations may have been ubiquitous in the versions of Indian sūtras made available to the Chinese. Strickmann, for example, speculates in the annotation to his chapter that the famous Chinese translator Fa-hsien may have inserted into his translation of the *Nirvāṇa Sūtra* a reference to oral prophecies concerning the demise of the dharma. If sūtras could be so altered with impunity, then why not entire scriptures?

We may ruminate as to why Sanskrit or Middle Indic recensions of scriptures introduced into China might have been forged by the missionary-translators. The cult of the book was strong in the Chinese church, as it was throughout the domain of the Mahāyāna, and the Chinese greeted with fervent piety translations of previously unknown texts. Numerous are the examples in which the renown of a missionary increased dramatically once he was recognized as a transmitter and/or translator of a new scripture. Indian and Central Asian missionaries would have been in an ideal position to draw upon their own inimitable experiences and training—which the Chinese would have been hard put to question—in composing books carefully adapted to the interests of their Chinese backers. This would have assured increased support for these monks, obviously an important concern to a foreign missionary operating in an alien culture, and would also have enhanced their status in ecclesiastical and political circles. Especially since Indian texts were often transmitted orally, it would have been a relatively simple task for a competent foreign exegete to emend or forge a scripture while reciting the Sanskrit. Without an original-language manuscript against which to check the veracity of the recitation, the authority of the reciter's oral recension would be unassailable. Hence, some texts accepted as authentic by the cataloguers (for whom, after all, the main standard of authenticity was that a text had been brought from the "West") could in fact have been Sanskrit scriptures forged entirely in China or emended by Western missionaries to reflect indigenous Chinese concerns.

Sūtras that may have been composed by Indian or Central Asian missionaries would still be classified as indigenous compositions because they were produced in response to native religious, social, or political verities. The possibility of such foreign authorship should be kept in mind particularly with texts that seem to parallel clearly authentic Indian or Central Asian materials. A number of Chinese indigenous scriptures show few indications of domestic provenance and can be determined to be apocryphal only through close textual research. In a recent article, William Grosnick has proposed that the eminent foreign missionary Paramārtha (499–569) was in an ideal position to write the *Ta-sheng ch'i-hsin lun,* one of the most celebrated of suspected Chinese apocryphal treatises.[28] Indeed, if Grosnick's hypothesis is accepted, it would have important implications for our understanding of Indian Buddhism as well, and would compel us to explore Indian antecedents of what are now regarded as distinctively East Asian innovations, such as the tathāgatagarbha-*ālayavijñāna* synthesis found in the *Ch'i-hsin lun.*

The success or failure of such texts—and ultimately of the foreign missionaries who would have created them—would have been heavily dependent on their reception by Chinese officialdom. As mentioned above, the Chinese government played an inordinate role in deciding the ultimate fate of a new text. Hence, while recognizing the unique calling of missionaries to impart their religion to virgin territories, we must also expect that their motives need not always have been altruistic. We know that there was blatant currying of political favor by Indian and Central Asian missionaries, as we see, for example, in the case of the eminent Indian translator Bodhiruci (572–727 [sic]). Forte's chapter in this volume shows that, in allowing his name to be associated with a sūtra that was clearly apocryphal, Bodhiruci was adapting to the political exigencies of his time, apparently for his own personal aggrandizement. Whatever the higher religious motives that may have prompted missionaries to make the long trek to China, the weaknesses of human character would have led some of the more unscrupulous among them to pursue the worldly fame and fortune that was a byproduct of royal patronage. This is not to suggest that there need necessarily be a broad gap between true religious motivation and a sensitivity to political conditions: indeed, the evidence marshalled in this volume shows that many famous Buddhist figures were profoundly influenced by both kinds of concern.

At the same time that indigenous scriptures have proven to be so valuable in researching the development of sinitic Buddhism, they have also been shown to have important implications for the evolution of secular literature in China. It is now clear that much of the earliest Chinese fiction appeared first in Buddhist-influenced genres—including apocryphal scriptures—that were known throughout Asia. This influence runs in three general directions: from apocryphal texts to the storytelling traditions of vernacular *pien-wen* (transformation texts) and later *pao-chüan* (precious scroll) writings, to Chinese fiction and drama. One of the most important such directions, which has received considerable attention in recent years, is evidenced in the vernacular *pien-wen* texts discovered at Tun-huang along with many apocryphal texts.[29] We find, for example, a large number of *pien-wen* based on the theme of filial piety, drawn from the apocryphal *Fu-mu en-chung ching* (Book of Requiting Parental Kindness; *T* 2887). Similarly, the tale of Maudgalyāyana's visit to hell is adopted by apocryphal compositions like the *Ching-t'u yü-lan-p'en ching* (Book of the Pure Land Ullambana; Pelliot no. 2185), as well as by such *pien-wen* as the *Ta-mu-chien-lien ming-chien chiu-mu pien-wen ping t'u* (The Transformation Text with Illustrations of Mahāmaudgalyāyana Saving His Mother from the Dark Regions; *T* 2858).[30] Hence, scholars of indigenous Chinese literature should find considerable material of value to their own research in a careful study of Buddhist apocrypha.

The impact of Chinese Buddhist apocrypha in such sinicized cultures as Japan is explored by Paul Groner in his chapter dealing with the *Fan-wang ching* (Book of Brahmā's Net). This sūtra is paradigmatic of an important subclass of Chinese Buddhist apocrypha: preceptive scriptures that adapted Indian ethical injunctions to the indigenous social environment. The *Fan-wang ching* was composed in China during the last half of the fifth century and served as the cornerstone of the *Bodhisattva-vinaya* in East Asia. Saichō's (767–822) substitution of its precepts for those of the Indian *Dharmaguptaka-vinaya (Ssu-fen lü),* which had traditionally been followed by the monks of East Asia, was an important step in the development of a genuinely Japanese form of Buddhism. Annen (841–889?), the great systematizer of Tendai Buddhism, discusses these *Fan-wang* precepts and their relationship to the precepts of Esoteric Buddhism. Annen's treatment contributed to the tendency of

Tendai monks to ignore the literal meaning of the precepts and to focus instead on their abstract intent. He incorporated elements from the Esoteric *sanmaya* ordination into the *Fan-wang* counterpart, interpreting the latter ceremony in terms of how it contributed to "the realization of Buddhahood in this very existence." Annen's account of the conditions under which the precepts might be broken, and the ways in which such violations could be expiated, had a profound effect on later Tendai Buddhism and led to the subsequent decline of its monastic discipline. The consequences of Annen's teachings are an excellent example of the results that may sometimes be forthcoming from extreme interpretations of the material in apocryphal scriptures. It is true that indigenous sūtras helped to invigorate the Buddhist tradition by allowing novel teachings to be assimilated into the orthodox tradition; but, as we see with Annen, such permutations sometimes led to unanticipated consequences.

Apocryphal texts also played a major role in the creation of a uniquely Tibetan tradition of Buddhism, and many of the features that characterized Chinese apocryphal compositions have their parallels in Tibet. Tibetologists have long been aware of scriptures that were classified as "hidden" or "treasure" texts *(gter-chos)*—that is, previously concealed scriptures that were hidden away for later revelation. However, the abundance, variety, and influence of these scriptures and the place of their authorized revealers *(gter-ston)* within the tradition have only recently been recognized, rendering such scriptures worthy of study as a genre in their own right. Such Tibetan apocryphal sūtras date from the period of political fragmentation that accompanied the demise of the royal house (ca. 842–975). These texts took two major forms. First were those texts that purported to have been translated at the time of Buddhism's inception in Tibet. Such texts were said to have first been preached by a Buddha in a Pure Land and then transmitted to Indian sages, who finally brought them to Tibet. Second were revelatory scriptures that were said to have been transmitted directly to a human visionary by a member of the Buddhist pantheon. There were two subdivisions within this type: the Pure Visions *(dag-snang),* the spontaneous theophanies of Buddhist deities; and the important *gter-ma,* texts that were buried either physically or psychically sometime after their composition, until a time appropriate for their rediscovery.[31] The traditional models for this latter type of scripture were Indian Mahāyāna sūtras, which the tradition considered to have been stored in the palace of the nāga-king until such time as an eminent sage, such as Nāgārjuna, would rediscover and reveal them.

There were antecedents for buried scriptures in India, as was the case, for example, with the *Pan-chou san-mei ching* (*Pratyutpanna*[*buddha-saṃmukhāvasthita*]*samādhi-sūtra; T* 418; translated into Chinese by Lokakṣema in 179 C.E.), which is described as having been recovered in an underground hiding place.[32] One need only recall the discovery of the *Book of Mormon* by Joseph Smith (1805–1844) for a compelling Western parallel. As Michel Strickmann also mentions in his chapter, the Chinese *Book of Consecration* was perhaps the earliest of such "hidden" Buddhist texts known outside India, being composed in the fifth century, hundreds of years before *gter-ma* appeared in Tibet. Treasure-texts were considered by the later Tibetan tradition to consist principally of scriptures composed or transmitted by the legendary Padmasaṃbhava, the putative founder of the "Old Tradition" (rNying-ma-pa) of Tibetan Buddhism, and buried by his disciples for revelation at a later time. Such scriptures were intended for a limited target audience that was particularly well suited to the message of the text. In earlier times, however, treasure-texts included a large number of scriptures attributed to many eminent teachers, all written in a variety of styles and containing differing doctrines. There is even a chance that some *gter-ma* may have been Chinese compositions, perhaps even apocryphal sūtras. After the defeat of the Chinese monk Mo-ho-yen in his alleged debate with Indian Buddhists at the "Council of Lhasa" (ca. 792–794), some Tibetan records claim that he buried his books as *gter-ma.* Several of the early masters among the rNying-ma-pas trained in China, and with the sudden expulsion of the Chinese Buddhist tradition from Tibet at the end of the eighth century, the texts those masters had brought from China may have gone "underground"—perhaps literally.[33]

As also occurred in East Asia, such "hidden" texts became the foundation of the textual tradition of many of the most influential schools of Tibetan Buddhism. For example, the sNying-thig school of rDzogs-chen—which is regarded as the consummation of the rNying-ma-pa lineage—is founded upon the *Rig-pa rang-shar,* the longest of an eleventh-century compilation of seventeen "hidden" tantras.[34] The same century saw the introduction of another indigenous Tibetan form of scripture, called revelatory cycles *(chos-skor),* which were also raised to canonical status in the rNying-ma school. Janet Gyatso has examined the literary forms such cycles adopted and has explored the means by which they attempted to validate their authenticity. The various texts contained in these cycles were structured according to literary genre, and were generally centered upon a "root," or core, text *(gzhung-rtsa)* that presented the basic Buddhist doctrine revealed in the vision. This core text was supplemented by related commentaries, initiation rituals, and liturgies, and often included a pseudo-historical account of the origins of the cycle and its revelation. These accounts are of particular interest in that their explicit purpose was to present evidence that would authenticate and give authority to the revelation as a whole.[35] Many early Chinese apocrypha were also revealed in a series of cycles, as

Tokuno and Strickmann note in their chapters. These studies broach a topic that has important implications for the study of apocrypha in general: the role of psychic visions in the revelation of scripture and the attitude toward visionary experiences within the indigenous traditions.

Methodological Issues in the Study of Buddhist Apocrypha

Several of the chapters in this volume cover methodological issues and text-critical techniques that may be of use in treating Buddhist apocrypha. We have already referred to the political and social context of apocryphal texts that are frequently mentioned in the chapters collected herein. While such issues are often ignored in Buddhist Studies, they can be of tremendous importance in detailing the significance and contribution of Buddhist apocrypha to the indigenous cultures of Asia.

The very structure of the discipline of Buddhist Studies can actually inhibit the investigation of Buddhist apocrypha. It is most common to conduct research on Buddhism along the lines of the national branches of the religion, and scholars of the tradition are thus typically specialists in Chinese Buddhism, Tibetan Buddhism, Japanese Buddhism, and so forth. The heuristic value of this structure cannot, of course, be denied, especially in studies centering on the contributions of Buddhism to the religious life of a particular geopolitical or cultural region. But as I have pointed out in other contexts,[36] we must be on guard lest such specialization obscure cross-cultural issues that may yield equally important insights concerning the evolution of Buddhism in specific regions. Exclusive focus on national traditions all too easily conceals the manifold points of symbiosis between those traditions, which can be of immense value in detailing both the evolution of the national varieties of Buddhism and the indigenous texts that reflect that evolution. Like the continental approach toward Sinology pioneered by Peter Boodberg,[37] Buddhist Studies must view its subject as the pan-Asiatic religion it has always been.

It is my conviction that this preoccupation with national boundaries has impaired the progress of study on Buddhist apocryphal materials. The very specialization of Chinese Buddhist scholars, for example, has caused most of them to presume that all texts written in Chinese must have been composed in China. But the fact that virtually all East Asian apocrypha are written in literary Chinese is not sufficient proof in itself of those texts' Chinese provenance. Literary Chinese was, after all, the lingua franca of learned communication throughout East Asia. Although China may have dominated creative trends in East Asian Buddhism, this need not imply that doctrinal innovations were not occurring simultaneously in other regions of East Asia, which could have profoundly influenced China as well. In fact, it is becoming increasingly apparent that the role of these neighboring kingdoms—especially Korea, but also Japan, Tibet, and Vietnam—in the development of Buddhism in China cannot be ignored. For example, as far as Korea is concerned, not only did expatriate monks make major contributions to Buddhist ideology and praxis at the major religious centers in China, but the writings of exegetes on the Korean peninsula were influential in the evolution of Buddhism on the Chinese mainland as well. Korea was subject to many of the same dynamics that drove the composition of apocryphal scriptures in China, and Koreans had access to the sources that served as models for Chinese sūtras. The Koreans—like other East Asians—were clearly capable of composing their own original Buddhist scriptures in literary Chinese. And given the close ties between the different East Asian traditions, it would have been a relatively easy matter for such a Korean creation to have been transmitted to China and accepted there as readily as an original Chinese composition.

This was the case, as I have sought to prove elsewhere, with the *Vajrasamādhi-sūtra,* a syncretistic apocryphon containing pronounced Ch'an elements. In a recent book,[38] I compare catalogue evidence about the dissemination of the text with legendary accounts of its recovery to show that it was written in Korea, sometime around 685 C.E., by an early adept of the Korean Sŏn (Zen) tradition. I portray its putative author as a frustrated Sŏn missionary facing an unreceptive, if not downright antagonistic, audience. Distressed over his mission's lack of progress, he finally resorted to textual forgery—the composition of the *Vajrasamādhi*—in order to convey his new teachings. Combining doctrinal elements drawn from several distinct strands in Mahāyāna thought then popular in Korea, he used his sūtra to present Sŏn—and specifically the Tao-hsin line of the early Chinese Ch'an school—surreptitiously to his fellow Silla Buddhists. By placing Sŏn thought in a familiar sūtra framework and drawing heavily from doctrines central to the learned schools of Korean Buddhism, the author ensured that his composition would receive a sympathetic reading from contemporary Korean scholiasts. Introduced some three decades later into China and thence Tibet, the sūtra influenced the subsequent development of the Chinese Ch'an and Tibetan rNying-ma schools. This text thus provides an explicit example of the organicism of East Asian Buddhism, in which a sūtra written outside China could have a considerable impact on the development of Buddhism in China and beyond.

Perhaps the most basic research aid any scholar should use when beginning an evaluation of a suspect East Asian scripture is the Chinese Buddhist bibliographical catalogues. Tokuno's chapter surveys these catalogues and explores the criteria the cataloguers themselves used in adjudicating a text. Her examination clarifies the real value—and the potential shortcomings—of the catalogue data. Forte also discusses the underlying reasons governing the cataloguers' evaluation of a specific scripture and cautions against the tendency of accepting that information at face value. If used critically, however, and their material corroborated independently, the catalogues can serve as invaluable sources of information on the spread and currency of a scripture in different regions and eras, and can prove useful in determining a sūtra's dating, authorship, and provenance.

As another technique of ferreting out apocryphal texts, Lewis Lancaster has discussed the unique terminology that is commonly employed in such compositions—what he terms "apocryphal words."[39] These words seem to have been coined within the Chinese Buddhist community and cannot be directly related either to the non-Buddhist philosophical vocabulary or to any plausible Sanskrit equivalent. The widespread use of such neologisms in Chinese compositions is an apparent indication of the failure of Indian Buddhist terminology to deal with some of the important concerns of Chinese Buddhists, a deficiency that ultimately forced the Chinese to rethink their technical vocabulary. The presence of such peculiarly Chinese terms as *pen-chüeh* (original enlightenment) in a text should alert the scholar to the possibility that the scripture in question may not be a translation at all, but an original Chinese composition.

The different arguments that can be made in support of the Chinese or Central Asian origin of a suspected apocryphon are treated by Kōtatsu Fujita in his chapter on the *Kuan Wu-liang-shou ching* (Book on the Contemplation of the Buddha of Immeasurable Life). His treatment is a classic case study of the types of evidence weighed by philologists in treating a scripture suspected of having been composed outside of India. As Fujita outlines, the Chinese provenance of a text is indicated when the wording is strongly evocative of the vocabulary and style of identifiable Chinese translations. The doctrines included in the text, its terminology, and even the Sanskrit transliterations it adopts will often have striking parallels with other indigenous compositions. Finally, the intrusion of such stereotypically Chinese notions as filial piety may sometimes be sufficient to warrant suspicion about the origins of a scripture. Fujita also points out that the evaluation of a text is often problematic due to the many permutations a scripture might take in its dissemination throughout Asia; hence, caution is always warranted in reaching any final conclusions about the provenance of a specific text and the influences under which it was composed.

Many apocryphal scriptures obviously enjoyed extensive dissemination, as shown by their successive reprintings in the canon, large numbers of indigenous commentaries, frequent citations in expository writings, and the appearance of their principal themes and concerns in later compositions. Such texts had a wide audience and exerted enormous influence on the development of the native tradition. But many other apocryphal texts, such as some of those rediscovered at Tun-huang, were preserved only through a fluke of history and did not exert any long-term effect on the larger tradition. These latter texts have obvious antiquarian interest, but they may also yield valuable insights about regional religious developments during the periods in which they were composed. Perhaps most importantly, the wide variety of indigenous scriptures that we now know to exist in China will compel Buddhist scholars to look beyond the limiting confines of the canon for new sources through which to study Chinese Buddhism. The presence of such texts also demands that scholars begin to place the canon—seen not as a fixed repository but as a fluctuating, tension-filled institution—in its social, historical, and religious contexts. Such a new, more inclusive view of Buddhist textual history will serve to reinvigorate Buddhist Studies and Sinology, to be sure; but it will also suggest how Asian humanistic research in general might benefit from cross-fertilization among its various disciplines.

NOTES

1. Yabuki Keiki, *Sangaikyō no kenkyū* (Tokyo: Iwanami shoten, 1927); idem, *Meisha yoin* (Tokyo: Iwanami shoten, 1930); idem, *Meisha yoin kaisetsu* (Tokyo: Iwanami shoten, 1933); Mochizuki Shinkō, *Bukkyō kyōten seiritsushi ron* (Kyoto: Hōzōkan, 1946); Makita Tairyō, *Gikyō kenkyū* (Kyoto: Jinbun kagaku kenkyūsho, 1976).

2. Antonino Forte, *Political Propaganda and Ideology in China at the End of the Seventh Century: Inquiry into the Nature, Authors and Function of the Tunhuang Document S. 6502 Followed by an Annotated Translation* (Naples: Istituto Universitario Orientale, 1976).

3. R. H. Charles, *The Apocrypha and Pseudepigrapha of the Old Testament in English,* vol. 1 (Oxford: Clarendon Press, 1913), viii. As Bruce M. Metzger also remarks, "From the point of view of those who approved of these books, they were 'hidden' or withdrawn from common use because they were regarded as containing mysterious or esoteric lore, too profound to be communicated to any except the initiated. From another point of view, however, it was held that such books deserved to be 'hidden' because they were spurious or heretical. Thus, the term has had an honorable significance as well as a derogatory one, depending upon those who made use of the word" (Metzger, *An Introduction to the Apocrypha* [New York: Oxford University Press, 1957], 5).

4. See the discussion in W. O. E. Oesterley, *An Introduction to the Books of the Apocrypha* (New York: The Macmillan Co., 1935), 4–5.

5. Moses Hadas, introduction to *The Apocrypha: An American Translation,* Edgar J. Goodspeed, trans. (New York: Random House, Vintage Books, 1959), xvi.

6. "The criteria for discriminating between canonical and Apocryphal docu-

ments may appear to be less than satisfactory, and at times the application of these criteria may seem to have been almost haphazard" (Metzger, *The Apocrypha,* p. 7).

7. See Lewis R. Lancaster, "Buddhist Literature: Its Canons, Scribes, and Editors," in Wendy Doniger O'Flaherty, ed., *The Critical Study of Sacred Texts* (Berkeley: Berkeley Religious Studies Series, 1979), 217–218.

8. Metzger, *The Apocrypha,* p. 6. The Pseudepigrapha includes such works as the book of Enoch, the psalms of Solomon, the books of Adam and Eve, etc.

9. Forte, *Political Propaganda and Ideology,* p. 43.

10. See Metzger, *The Apocrypha,* pp. 4–6, for a discussion on the literary genres commonly employed in Judeo-Christian Apocrypha.

11. The social exigencies of the period during which the Jewish apocrypha were written are documented in Leonhard Rost, *Judaism Outside the Hebrew Canon: An Introduction to the Documents,* David E. Green, trans. (Nashville: Abingdon, 1976), 34–35.

12. Hayashiya Tomojirō, *Kyōroku kenkyū,* vol. 1 (Tokyo: Iwanami shoten, 1941).

13. Quotations from such apocryphal scriptures as the *Jen-wang ching, P'u-sa ying-lo pen-yeh ching,* and *T'i-wei Po-li ching* are ubiquitous in Chinese exegetical writings. In the Chinese Pure Land school, for example, Tao-cho's *An-lo chi* includes extensive citations to apocryphal scriptures; see Satō Ken, "*Anrakushū* to gikyō," *Bukkyō daigaku kenkyū kiyō* 60 (1976): 79–134. In the T'ien-t'ai school, note Chih-i's frequent recourse to apocryphal scriptures in support of his doctrinal positions; see the discussion in Makita Tairyō, "Tendai daishi no gikyō kan," in Sekiguchi Shindai, ed., *Shikan no kenkyū* (Tokyo: Iwanami shoten, 1975), 201–215. Stephen Teiser notes that the learned élite among the Buddhist clergy drew freely from the apocryphal *Ching-t'u yü-lan-pen ching* (Pelliot no. 2185), though with some discretion: they simply did not cite the text by name. See Teiser, *The Ghost Festival in Medieval China* (Princeton: Princeton University Press, 1988), 62. Mizuno Kōgen, in his study of the apocryphal *Dharmapada,* has suggested that "the San-lun, the T'ien-t'ai, the Fa-hsiang, the Hua-yen and other schools attached great importance to the sacred books and depended solely on genuine books. They took no notice of the pseudo-scriptures [i.e., apocrypha]. The pseudo-scriptures made no appeal whatsoever to them" ("On the Pseudo-Fa-ku-king," *Indogaku bukkyōgaku kenkyū* [hereafter *IBK*] 9.1 [1961]: 395). This is clearly mistaken. As only one of what could be numerous examples to the contrary, the apocryphal *Fa-chü ching,* the very scripture Mizuno treats in his study, is cited (though, as is common, without attribution) by Fa-tsang (643–712), the third patriarch of the Hua-yen school, in his *Hsiu Hua-yen ao-chih wang-chin huan-yüan kuan* (viz., *T* 1876.45.637b is taken from the *Fa-chü ching, T* 2901.85.1435a23).

14. As an insight into the struggle scholars sometimes face in their research, I might note the story Yabuki Keiki tells in the epilogue to his *Meisha yoin* (pp. 18–22). According to Yabuki's account, L. D. Barnett, then head of the Oriental Collection at the British Museum, sought to deny Yabuki access to the Stein collection of Tun-huang materials on his visit to London in 1922–1923. The staff relented only after Yabuki threatened to review severely any catalogue on the collection that might be compiled without his help. Yabuki eventually assisted in identifying several of the Buddhist fragments appearing in Lionel Giles' *A*

Descriptive Catalogue of the Chinese Manuscripts from Tun-huang in the British Museum. Photolithographic reprints of the Stein manuscripts examined by Yabuki were first published in his *Meisha yoin,* with an outline of each text and other annotation appearing in his *Meisha yoin kaisetsu* (the apocryphal texts are treated in pt. 1, pp. 178–204; pt. 2, pp. 156–319). Yabuki's earlier work, *Sangaikyō no kenkyū,* introduced a large corpus of apocryphal works affiliated with the Three Stages school. Fifty-six of the texts reproduced in the *Meisha yoin* have been reprinted in vol. 85 of the *Taishō* canon (*T* 2865-*T* 2920).

15. Mochizuki, *Bukkyō kyōten,* pp. 393–694. This classification has been discussed by Makita, *Gikyō kenkyū,* p. 117.

16. Makita, *Gikyō kenkyū,* pp. 40–84, 117–118.

17. T'ang Yung-tung, *Han Wei Liang-Chin Nan-pei-ch'ao fo-chiao shih* (1938; rpt. ed., Taipei: Ting-wen shu-chü, 1976), 2:594–600; summarized in Erik Zürcher, *The Buddhist Conquest of China: The Spread and Adaptation of Buddhism in Early Medieval China* (Leiden: E. J. Brill, 1959), 1:308. For *hua-hu* counterparts in Buddhist literature, see the insightful discussion in Zürcher, *Buddhist Conquest,* pp. 288–320.

18. Mizuno Kōgen, "Gisaku no *Hokkukyō* ni tsuite," *Komazawa daigaku bukkyōgakubu kenkyū kiyō* 19 (1961): 11–14; this study has been summarized in English in his article, "On the *Pseudo-Fa-kiu-king,*" pp. 402–401 [sic].

19. John Brough, "The Chinese Pseudo-Translation of Ārya-Śūra's *Jātakamālā,*" *Asia Major* 11 (1964–1965): 27–53. Brough's study has been summarized, with additional textual sources cited for the stories pilfered by the Chinese translators, in Mizuno Kōgen, " 'J. Brough: The Chinese Pseudo-Translation of Ārya-Śūra's *Jātakamālā*' shōkai," *IBK* 14 (1966): 801–805.

20. Corroboration for this position appears in a different manner in an article by Nakamura Hajime, "The Influence of Confucian Ethics on the Chinese Translations of Buddhist Sūtras," in Ksitis Roy, ed., *Sino-Indian Studies,* Liebenthal Festschrift (Santiniketan, 1957), 156–170. There, Nakamura discusses the influence of indigenous ethical, social, and political ideas on the earliest Chinese translations of Indian Buddhist texts, indicating the adaptation of Buddhism to indigenous concerns even at its incipiency in China.

21. Henri Maspero, *Taoism and Chinese Religion,* Frank A. Kierman, Jr., trans. (Amherst: University of Massachusetts Press, 1981), esp. 37–53, 249–262, and 400–412.

22. Rhi Ki-yong (Yi Kiyŏng), *Wŏnhyo sasang I: Segyegwan* (Seoul: Hongbŏbwŏn, 1967), 14.

23. Daniel Overmyer, "Buddhism in the Trenches: Attitudes Toward Popular Religion in Indigenous Scriptures from Tun-Huang," paper presented at the panel "Rethinking Syncretism," Association for Asian Studies Annual Meeting, San Francisco, March 1988.

24. Idem, personal communication, 13 July 1987.

25. Sunayama Minoru, "Gekkō dōji Ryō Keiki no hanran to *Shura-biku-kyō,*" *Tōhōgaku* 51 (1976): 1–17. Erik Zürcher, "Eschatology and Messianism in Early Chinese Buddhism," in Wilt L. Idema, ed., *Leyden Studies in Sinology,* Sinica Leidensia, vol. 15 (Leiden: E. J. Brill, 1981), 34–56; idem, "Prince Moonlight: Messianism and Eschatology in Early Medieval Chinese Buddhism," *T'oung-pao* 68 (1982): 1–75.

26. Erik Zürcher, "Buddhist Influence on Early Taoism: A Survey of Scriptural Evidence," *T'oung-pao* 66 (1980): 84–147.

27. Forte, *Political Propaganda and Ideology,* pp. 125–136.

28. William Grosnick, "The Categories of *T'i, Hsiang,* and *Yung:* Evidence that Paramārtha Composed the *Awakening of Faith,*" *Journal of the International Association of Buddhist Studies* 12–1 (1989): 65–92.

29. See the recent works by Victor H. Mair, especially *T'ang Transformation Texts: A Study of the Buddhist Contribution to the Rise of Vernacular Fiction and Drama in China* (Cambridge: Harvard University Press, 1989) and *Tun-huang Popular Narratives* (Cambridge: Cambridge University Press, 1983). See also Jaroslav Prusek's classic studies, "The Narrators of Buddhist Scriptures and Religious Tales in the Sung Period," *Archiv Orientální* 10 (1938): 375–389; and "Researches into the Beginnings of the Chinese Popular Novel," *Archiv Orientální* 11 (1939): 91–132.

30. For the *Fu-mu en-chung ching* and *pien-wen* influenced by that scripture, see Michihata Ryōshū, *Bukkyō to Jukyō rinri* (Kyoto: Heirakuji shoten, 1968), 96–114; and Ogawa Kan'ichi, *Bukkyō bunkashi kenkyū* (Kyoto: Nagata Bunshōdō, 1973), 190–203. For *pien-wen* based on the story of Maudgalyāyana, see Ogawa Kan'ichi, "*Mokuren gumo henbun* no genryū," *Bukkyō bungaku kenkyū* 2 (1964); reprinted in his *Bukkyō bunkashi kenkyū* (Kyoto: Nagata Bunshodō, 1973), 157–189. Textual sources for the legend concerning Mu-lien's rescue of his mother include the *Yü-lan-p'en ching* (*T* 685; composed ca. early fifth century) and the *Ching-t'u yü-lan-p'en ching* (Pelliot no. 2185), an early seventh-century apocryphon recovered from Tun-huang. Ogawa asserts that both these texts are of Indian origin (despite the lack of either Sanskrit or Tibetan recensions) because of (1) the large number of translations of Buddhist texts that advocate the veneration of Maudgalyāyana, and (2) the reference in Fa-hsien's travelogue to yearly worship at Mathurā of stūpas dedicated to the Buddha's great disciples, including Maudgalyāyana. Thus he claims that the legend and cult of Mu-lien derived from India and was widely diffused in China chiefly due to its theme of filial piety, which influenced the production of native materials, including the *Mu-lien chiu-mu pien-wen.* Kanaoka Shōkō, "Chūgoku minkan ni okeru Mokuren setsuwa no seikaku," *Bukkyō shigaku* 7–4 (1959): 16–37, discusses the origins and diffusion of the legend of Mu-lien in Chinese popular culture. A detailed outline of the *Mu-lien pien-wen* (Pelliot nos. 2193, 2319) is given in Kenneth Ch'en, *The Chinese Transformation of Buddhism* (Princeton: Princeton University Press, 1973), 25–28. Iwamoto Yutaka, *Jigoku megri no bungaku,* Bukkyō setsuwa kenkyū, vol. 4 (Tokyo: Kaimei shoin, 1979), 35–49, discusses the apocryphal scriptures that were the sources of the various *pien-wen* on Mu-lien. See also Michihata Ryōshū, *Bukkyō to Jukyō rinri* (Kyoto: Heirakuji shoten, 1968), 118–121; Sawada Mizuho, *Jigokuhen* (Kyoto: Hōzōkan, 1968), 137–138 et passim. V. Hrdlickova, "Some Questions Connected with Tun-huang Pien-wen," *Archiv Orientální* 30 (1962): 211–230, also includes some discussion of the theme of filial piety in the *Mu-lien pien-wen;* for extensive references to the *Yü-lan-p'en ching* and the Mu-lien cult, see Stephen F. Teiser's article, "Ghosts and Ancestors in Medieval Chinese Religion: The Yü-lan-p'en Festival as Mortuary Ritual," *History of Religions* 26 (1986): 47–67, and his impressive recent book, *The Ghost Festival in Medieval China.*

31. For Tibetan treasure-texts and their discoverers, see Eva Dargyay, *The Rise of Esoteric Buddhism in Tibet* (Delhi: Motilal Banarsidass, 1977), 63–73; Eva Neumaier-Dargyay, "Einige Aspekte der gTer-ma Literatur der rNying-ma-pa Schule," *Zeitschrift der Deutschen Morgenlandischen Gesellschaft,* Supplementa I, 3 (1969): 849–862; Ramon Pratz, *Contributo allo Studio Biografico dei Primi Gter-ston,* Seminario di Studii Asiatici, Series Minor xvii (Naples: Istituto Universitario Orientale, 1982).

32. "Forty years after the Buddha's Parinirvāṇa the sūtra is copied down, placed in a casket, and buried, eventually to be rediscovered in the 'Last Age' and propagated anew by a faithful core of five hundred Buddhists. . . ." See Paul M. Harrison, "Buddhānusmṛti in the Pratyutpanna-buddha-saṃmukhā-vasthita-samādhi-sūtra," *Journal of Indian Philosophy* 6 (1978): 57 n. 22.

33. See Giuseppe Tucci, *Minor Buddhist Texts, Part II: First Bhāvanākrama of Kamalaśīla,* Series Orientale Roma, 9.2 (Rome: Is.M.E.O., 1958), 44ff., discussed in Dargyay, *Esoteric Buddhism,* pp. 9 and 32.

34. See George N. Roerich, *The Blue Annals* (rpt., Delhi: Motilal Banarsidass, 1976), 192. One of our contributors, Ronald Davidson, is pursuing a major study of this visionary cycle.

35. See Janet Gyatso, "Signs, Memory and History: A Tantric Buddhist Theory of Scriptural Transmission," *Journal of the International Association of Buddhist Studies* 9–2 (1986): 7–35.

36. Robert Buswell, *The Formation of Ch'an Ideology in China and Korea: The Vajrasamādhi-Sūtra, A Buddhist Apocryphon* (Princeton: Princeton University Press, 1989), esp. chap. 1; idem, "Chinul's Systematization of Chinese Meditative Techniques in Korean Sŏn Buddhism," in Peter N. Gregory, ed., *Chinese Buddhist Traditions of Meditation,* Studies in East Asian Buddhism, no. 4 (Honolulu: University of Hawaii Press, 1986), 199–200.

37. Alvin P. Cohen, ed., *Selected Works of Peter A. Boodberg* (Berkeley and Los Angeles: University of California Press, 1979), xii–xiii.

38. Buswell, *The Formation of Ch'an Ideology in China and Korea.*

39. Lewis Lancaster, "The Question of 'Apocryphal' Words in Chinese Buddhist Texts," paper delivered at the Annual Meeting of the American Academy of Religion, Atlanta, Georgia, 24 November 1986.

GLOSSARY

Ch'an 禪
Chan-ch'a shan-o yeh-pao ching 占察善惡業報經
ch'ao-ching 抄經
Ch'eng-kuan 澄觀
Chih-i 智顗
Chin-kang san-mei ching 金剛三昧經
ching 經
Ching-tu san-mei ching 淨度三昧經
Ching-t'u yü-lan-p'en ching 淨土盂蘭盆經
Fa-chü ching 法句經
Fa-hsien 法顯
Fa-tsang 法藏
Fan-wang ching 梵網經
Fei Ch'ang-fang 費長房
Fu-mu en-chung ching 父母恩重經
Hsiang-fa chüeh-i ching 像法決疑經
Hsin-hsing 信行
Hsiu Hua-yen ao-chih wang-chin huan-yüan kuan 修華嚴奧旨妄盡還源觀

hu-kuo 護國
hua-hu 化胡
Hua-yen 華嚴
i-ching 異經
Jen-wang ching 仁王經
K'ai-yüan shih-chiao lu 開元釋教錄
Kuan-ting ching 灌頂經
Kuan Wu-liang-shou ching 觀無量壽經
Kŭmgang sammae-kyŏng 金剛三昧經
Li-tai san-pao chi 歷代三寶紀
mo-fa 末法
Mo-ho-yen 摩訶衍
p'an-chiao 判教
pao-chüan 寶卷
Pao-yü ching 寶雨經
pen-chüeh 本覺
pien-wen 變文
P'u-sa ying-lo pen-yeh ching 菩薩瓔珞本業經
Saichō 最澄
San-chieh chiao 三階教
shih-i 失譯
Shih Mo-ho-yen lun 釋摩訶衍論
Shou-leng-yen ching 首楞嚴經
Shou-lo pi-ch'iu ching 首羅比丘經
Sŏn 禪
Ssu-fen lü 四分律
Ta-mu-ch'ien-lien ming-chien chiu-mu pien-wen ping t'u 大目乾連冥間救母變文并圖
Ta-sheng ch'i-hsin lun 大乘起信論
Ta-yün ching 大雲經
Tao-cho 道綽
T'i-wei Po-li ching 提謂波利經
T'ien-t'ai 天台
T'ien-ti pa-yang ching 天地八陽經
t'u-ch'en 圖讖
wei 偽
wei-ching 偽經
Wu Tse-t'ien 武則天
yin-yang 陰陽
Yü-ch'ieh fa-ching ching 瑜伽法鏡經
Yü-lan-p'en ching 盂蘭盆經
Yüan-chüeh ching 圓覺經
Yüeh-kuang t'ung-tzu 月光童子

The Evaluation of Indigenous Scriptures in Chinese Buddhist Bibliographical Catalogues

Kyoko Tokuno

The Role of Scriptural Catalogues in Chinese Buddhism

Buddhist scriptural catalogues *(ching-lu)* refer to an East Asian genre of Buddhist literature that provides bibliographical listings of scriptural translations and indigenous works.[1] The compilation of catalogues began during the nascency of Chinese Buddhism and continued throughout its history. According to one set of statistics, a total of seventy-six catalogues, including both extant and nonextant compilations, was compiled through the eighteenth century, the majority of which (some fifty-nine catalogues, or 78 percent of the total) date from the T'ang dynasty or earlier. Although this statistic may not be definitive, it does provide clear evidence of the relative amount of bibliographical work undertaken by Buddhist cataloguers during all periods of the dispensation.[2]

Scriptural catalogues are a quintessentially Chinese phenomenon, there being nothing equivalent to them in Indian Buddhist literature.[3] Although their compilation may be considered a natural outgrowth of the Chinese secular bibliographical tradition, which was firmly established by the time Buddhist translation activities began during the latter half of the second century C.E., such indigenous influences account only for their origin.[4] Buddhist catalogues in China developed their own unique coverage, structure, and organization, culminating in a tradition that in many respects surpassed its secular counterpart: they recorded minute facts concerning the translation of a text, including various recensions of a single original and abridgements made from a longer original or translation, as well as precise categorizations of the different types of Buddhist texts circulating in China.[5] A close, comparative examination of these catalogues should yield much information about the processes by which Buddhism evolved in China. As we shall see, Buddhist catalogues are far more than "mere listings" of titles, and deserve our serious attention as crucial source material in studying the textual history of Chinese Buddhism.

What were the motives that prompted Buddhist exegetes to compile catalogues? One answer is provided by Chih-sheng (fl. ca. 730) in the opening lines of his catalogue, the *K'ai-yüan shih-chiao lu* (Catalogue of Śākyamuni's Teachings, Compiled during the K'ai-yüan Era):

> Now as far as the inception of catalogues is concerned, they were intended to distinguish the genuine from the spurious, clarify what is authentic and unauthentic, record the period of the translation, indicate the number of sections and *chüan,* add what was omitted, and eliminate what was superfluous. They sought to make [Buddhist literature in China] correspond to the principles of the orthodox teaching and golden speech [of the Buddha], and bring forward the essentials [of these texts] so that they would be readily observable [through the textual classifications used in the catalogues]. However, since the teachings of the dharma originated in the remote past, as the net of proselytization widened, the datings of the translations were changed and their periods altered, scriptures were often dispersed or lost, and *chüan* were arranged out of order. Moreover, from time to time odd persons added spurious and fallacious [scriptures to the canon], scrambling [the genuine and the spurious] and making it difficult to ascertain their identity. This is why former sages and scholars compiled these catalogues.[6]

To sum up Chih-sheng's statement here, catalogues were essentially a means to keep a comprehensive and accurate record of translations, which could then serve as a guide for ferreting out "suspicious" texts *(i-ching)* and "spurious" texts *(wei-ching)*—namely, indigenous or "apocryphal" compositions that purported to be authentic scripture.[7] Indeed, listings of "suspicious" and "spurious" scriptures have been an integral part of Buddhist catalogues since at least the fourth century, when the earliest extant catalogue was compiled. This proscriptive function of the catalogues is particularly prominent in the earlier periods of Chinese Buddhism when texts were hand-copied, providing ample opportunity for creating new scriptures. The importance of this function also explains the relative profusion of catalogues through the T'ang. Catalogues compiled after the tenth century, when xylographic printing technology came into wide use, were principally descriptive, in that they were designed to serve as indexes to canons already in existence.

The cumulative endeavor of the cataloguers eventually produced the intended result: although the manuscript period witnessed the continuous production of indigenous scriptures, once printing began, virtually all prospects for circulating new indigenous scriptures were eliminated. Those texts proscribed from the canon dropped from circulation and were preserved only because manuscripts were taken to Japan by pilgrims or deposited in the Tun-huang manuscript cache, where they were subsequently discovered at the turn of this century.[8]

Scriptures judged authentic, in contrast, were entered into the canons and transmitted to posterity. Modern scholarship has shown, however, that some of the texts that were accorded canonical status, including many sūtras fundamental to the Chinese Buddhist doctrinal outlook, are or are suspected to be indigenous Chinese compositions.[9] In a very real sense, then, the cataloguers held the key to a scripture's destiny in the Chinese Buddhist textual tradition, regardless of what that text's actual provenance may have been.

Because of the seminal role the cataloguers played in determining the fate of a text, we would do well to consider how they made their decisions and the factors that contributed to their judgments. The goal of this chapter is to examine the treatment of indigenous scriptures in some of the Buddhist catalogues compiled during the Six Dynasties through T'ang period (ca. fourth through eighth centuries) as a means of determining the views, attitudes, and criteria adopted by the cataloguers in their assessments of scriptures.[10] For the reason mentioned earlier, this period saw the most prolific production of Buddhist apocrypha, and Buddhist cataloguers were under particular pressure to cope with issues of authenticity. This examination will also provide insights into the nature of indigenous scriptures themselves. As we shall see, such texts provide valuable sources for the study of Buddhism as accepted, interpreted, and practiced by the Chinese, including both religious specialists and those outside the ecclesiastical élite.[11]

Tsung-li chung-ching mu-lu (Comprehensive Catalogue of Scriptures, by Tao-an; 374)

The first reference to the production of indigenous Chinese scriptures appears in the *Tsung-li chung-ching mu-lu,* compiled by the renowned Chinese cleric Tao-an (312–385). Although the catalogue has not been transmitted in its entirety, most of its contents are preserved in the *Ch'u-san-tsang chi-chi* (see below), the earliest extant catalogue, compiled by Seng-yu (445–518) during the first part of the sixth century.[12] Internal evidence suggests that this catalogue was an attempt to make a comprehensive record of translations made during the nearly two-hundred-year period from the beginning of translation activities in China up to the time of its compilation.[13] Even at this early stage of Buddhism in China, attempts had already been made to "forge" Buddhist scriptures: in the section "Record of Suspicious Scriptures Newly Collected by the Venerable An," a total of twenty-six titles in thirty *chüan* are listed. Judging from the scope of this catalogue's coverage, these numbers probably come close to representing the sum total of all indigenous scriptures written through the end of the fourth century. Tao-an's comments on these texts elucidate the importance of accurate scriptural transmission in Chinese Buddhism and the problem that forgery was creating for the nascent tradition:

> When monks in foreign countries are trained in the teachings [of Buddhism], they kneel down and receive it orally. The teacher confers on his disciples the teachings exactly as he received them from his own teacher by repeating it ten or twenty times. If even one word deviates [from the accepted transmission], it is revised after mutual conference and [the wrong word] is immediately deleted. There is no laxity as far as the monks and the teachings are concerned. It has not been long since the [Buddhist] scriptures reached the land of Chin [viz., China]. But those who delight in this occasion label sand-grains as gold, and believe they have succeeded in such [forgeries]. If no one corrects [such deceptions], then how can we distinguish the genuine from the spurious? If grains and weeds are mixed in farming, Hou Chi would lament over it; if jade and stone are stored [indiscriminately] in a metal chest, Pien He would be ashamed of it.[14] I, An, who dare to undertake this training, see that [the presence of both authentic and spurious scriptures] is like the Ching and Wei rivers merging their flows, or a dragon and a snake proceeding side by side.[15] How could I not be ashamed of this? Now I list what I regard in my mind to be non-Buddhist scriptures *(fei fo-ching)* in order to warn future aspirants, so that they will all know that these scriptures are despicable.[16]

Tao-an suggests that the dissemination of true Buddhist sūtras in China is vitiated by the presence of heterodox, "non-Buddhist" scriptures—an event that, against the background of the presumed accuracy of the Indian transmission, he labels "despicable." Given this state of affairs, which he amply illustrates with similes taken from indigenous Chinese literature, Tao-an declares that strong measures are necessary to safeguard the integrity of the textual foundation of Buddhism and to prevent confusion between authentic translations of Indian texts and heterodox indigenous compositions. Such forged texts must be exposed for what they really are by listing them in this "Record of Suspicious Scriptures." Tao-an thus expresses both his exasperation with those who have corrupted the teachings by forging scriptures, as well as his own sense of responsibility to ensure that the Buddhist teachings be transmitted to Chinese posterity with the same accuracy as they had been in India.

Although Tao-an's statement clearly reveals his concern for, and commitment to, preserving the Indian tradition as it had been transmitted to China, it tells us precious little about the "non-Buddhist" texts themselves and what criteria he used in distinguishing them from authentic scripture. Tao-an says only that he lists as suspicious "what I regard in my mind to be non-Buddhist scriptures." In the absence of any other information, we can only assume that Tao-an evaluated a text solely on the basis of his own knowledge and experience which, to his credit, were no doubt superior to those of most of his contemporary

Buddhists, as is evinced in his numerous commentaries and prefaces to philosophical and meditative scriptures, as well as his firsthand experience with the process of translation.[17] Even so, we remain completely in the dark concerning the exact canons of textual criticism Tao-an may have employed.

Later cataloguers universally praised the pioneering bibliographical achievements of the *Tsung-li chung-ching mu-lu.* Tao-an was credited with having provided critical assessments of dates and translators of works that had previously been unascribed, thereby providing essential information on the history and identification of the scriptures that had been transmitted to China.[18] His attempt to distinguish indigenous scriptures from translated texts was probably the most significant influence exerted by his catalogue. Most of the subsequent catalogues considered in this chapter include a category for *wei* or *i-wei ching,* and reveal the same indignation toward indigenous scriptures and sense of responsibility for the purity of the textual transmission as does Tao-an's. Indeed, Tao-an's catalogue served as a model for his successors to emulate.[19]

Ch'u-san-tsang chi-chi (A Compilation of Notices on the Translation of the *Tripiṭaka,* by Seng-yu; ca. 515)

The *Ch'u-san-tsang chi-chi,*[20] as already mentioned, is the earliest complete catalogue now extant.[21] The section on indigenous scriptures lists a total of twenty titles; we also find twenty-four additional titles in the following section, which Tao-an reserved for commentaries and miscellaneous texts. As Okabe Kazuo has pointed out, this is a result of some textual corruption and these titles should be added to the list of indigenous scriptures, which thus gives forty-four titles—or a total of seventy when we include the twenty-six titles from Tao-an's listing, which is subsumed in this catalogue.[22] Seng-yu's listing, moreover, includes both suspicious and spurious scriptures, but without distinguishing the two types in most cases. This ambiguity was criticized by later cataloguers, as we shall see.

Seng-yu adopts Tao-an's general attitude toward indigenous scriptures, but also introduces specifics that provide some perspective on the phenomenon of scriptural creation. He says that the appearance of "spurious" scriptures was something that the Buddha himself had predicted: the *Ch'ang A-han ching (Dīrghāgama)* contains the Buddha's warning that whatever new teaching (dharma) or code of discipline *(Vinaya)* one might encounter must be verified against scripture; should there be any contradiction, then they should not be taken as the authentic teachings of the Buddha. Furthermore, Seng-yu notes the prediction from the *Ta-pan nieh-p'an ching (Mahāparinirvāṇa-sūtra)* that after the Buddha's demise monks will plagiarize scriptures, causing the dharma to decline.[23] These references to the Buddha's own predictions show that the fabrication of scriptures had been anticipated in the Buddhist tradition since its inception and, if allowed to continue unchecked, was expected to lead to the demise of the true dispensation *(saddharma)*. Since textual forgery might start in China at any time, the cataloguers were expected to maintain vigilance and to prepare for the inevitable.

Seng-yu also advanced beyond Tao-an in providing explicit criteria that could be used in ferreting out spurious and suspect scriptures. These criteria were based on both internal and external evidence. Internal evidence refers to the style and content of a text, which Seng-yu presumed to differ qualitatively in genuine and spurious scriptures. In his view, "The substance and purport of genuine scriptures are eloquent and profound, . . . [whereas] the phraseology of writings pretending [to be genuine] is superficial and coarse." Hence, both genuine and spurious "have no way of escaping from their appearance." The same point is repeated when he says, "As for the above twelve [spurious] scriptures, some deviate [from genuine sūtras] in their meaning and principle, while the prose and verse of others are superficial and base."[24] These comments suggest that Seng-yu viewed indigenous scriptures to be works lacking sophistication in doctrinal presentation and literary artistry. Considering that Chinese translations of Buddhist texts were often the collective products of a group of learned monks and laymen, which passed through several stages of refinement in their accuracy and style, such qualitative differences were—at least in theory—an obvious mark of a text's provenance.[25]

The criteria mentioned thus far are based on general characteristics, but we have indications elsewhere that Seng-yu drew upon more specific, objective evidence. In his annotation to the *Fo-po ching* (Book of Buddha's Bowl), for example, Seng-yu states that this text related "the events of a great deluge that occurred during the *chia-shen* year and the advent of the Bodhisattva Yüeh-kuang." This brief description clearly shows anomalies: Yüeh-kuang's depiction as a bodhisattva-savior deviates from his characterization in Indian Buddhist lore as a pious son who converts his evil father to the Buddhist faith; and the time of his advent, the *chia-shen* year, has Taoist connotations, as it marks the beginning of crisis in the Taoist eschatological scheme. Its deviance from orthodox doctrine and its assimilation of a Taoist idea, then, definitively suggested to Seng-yu the Chinese origin of this text. Moreover, Yüeh-kuang was not merely a common messianic figure during the Six Dynasties period; he also provided ideological justification for uprisings involving Buddhist monks and laymen.[26] Thus Seng-yu's evaluation of this scripture reflects not only his apprehension of heterodoxy, but also the text's potential threat to the ecclesiastical and political establishments.

The external evidence used by Seng-yu in evaluating scriptures refers to proofs of a scripture's provenance. In the case of authentic texts, this meant there was evidence that they had been transmitted from outside of China. Fabricated scriptures are those for which Seng-yu "has neither heard that someone went far into the Outer Regions [viz., India or Serindia, to obtain it] nor witnessed its reception from, and translation by, Western visitors [viz., foreign monks]." Applying these criteria enabled Seng-yu to identify spurious texts, which "were produced at home [viz., China] and gained recognition in the minds [of the people], and which will deceive and mislead future generations."[27] Although these criteria might seem in theory to offer a sound basis for textual evaluation, their application was hampered by the problems of lost or false translator attributions. By Seng-yu's time, there was a large number of scriptures that were already deemed authentic, but that carried neither translators' names nor dates of translation. Even in Tao-an's time, many scriptures were already circulating without any such information.[28] Seng-yu's catalogue itself includes a long listing of "anonymous scriptures" (*shih-i ching;* lit., "translator's [name] lost"), which, according to one estimate, amount to some 72 percent of the total entries in the catalogue.[29] Moreover, even among those bearing attribution, discrepancies were often found, rendering the attributions unreliable.[30] Given this situation, it is extremely unlikely that these criteria would have been of much use in isolating indigenous scriptures. We must therefore presume that, while external criteria may have been perfectly logical in theory, their application was limited in practice. For this reason, internal criteria probably constituted the principal standard of textual evaluation.

One criterion Seng-yu does not mention, but which he obviously used, was whether the authorship of a text by a Chinese was known. Eight entries in his catalogue are accompanied by names of native authors and compilation dates consisting of an emperor's name, reign-title, and year; some also include the general region, or even the specific name of the monastery, where the text was composed.[31] Such detailed information provided sure proof of these texts' Chinese origins, assuring that they would be relegated to the listings of unauthentic texts.

Few of the texts belonging to this category offer any clue as to how such authorship was determined. Fortunately, however, Seng-yu's annotation provides two detailed accounts of the production of indigenous scriptures, both dating from Seng-yu's lifetime. These not only describe Seng-yu's own motives for keeping such minute records, but also provide rare glimpses of the circumstances and motivations under which indigenous scriptures came to be written. For these reasons, they are worth outlining briefly.

The first record concerns a certain Ni-tzu, the daughter of a scholar from the Royal Academy during the Ch'i dynasty (482–502). At the age of nine, she began reciting sūtras that some claimed were from the heavens above and that others called divine revelations. By the time she was sixteen, she had recited some twenty-one scriptures. Her words showed such understanding and intelligence that it was as if she had learned these texts in a former life. Tales of her extraordinary talents spread throughout the capital among Buddhist clergy and lay adherents until the news finally reached the emperor, who summoned her for an audience to inquire about the source of her inspiration. The girl was a fervent Buddhist and, despite her parents' wish to have her marry, she resolved to maintain her practices of poverty *(shao-yü)* and celibacy *(fan-hsing)*. Eventually, she was ordained as a Buddhist nun.

Having narrated the circumstances surrounding these revelations, Seng-yu adds that his own requests for copies of the scriptures were rejected by her family, who secretly hid the texts. Later, they were copied and circulated as genuine scriptures. Seng-yu feared that, once committed to writing, these scriptures would "inevitably remain in the world," and he hoped that, by exposing their Chinese origins, later generations would not be deceived. This apprehension accounts for the wealth of detail Seng-yu provides concerning the origin of these texts.[32]

The second case reported by Seng-yu is said to have occurred in the ninth year of the T'ien-chien reign-era of the Liang dynasty (510). It involved a monk from Ying-chou named Miao-kuang, who falsely claimed sainthood and attracted the attentions of nuns and laywomen. While an ecclesiastical official, Hui-ch'ao, was arranging to have him expelled from the Order, Miao-kuang traveled to the capital and there composed a scripture entitled the *Sa-p'o-jo-t'o chüan-shu chuang-yen ching* (Book of the Adornments of the Family of Sarvajñatā [Omniscience]), which he intended to use as a vehicle for gaining wealth and fame. Miao-kuang had the text copied on a screen covered with dazzling vermilion gauze, which attracted throngs of Buddhist adherents who then made offerings to him. The imperial court became disturbed at the potential for subversion caused by the large crowds of devotees, and eventually ordered Miao-kuang and his collaborator, the calligrapher Lu Yen, arrested and sentenced to death and ten years' exile, respectively. The emperor personally ordered Hui-ch'ao and twenty other eminent monks, including Seng-yu himself, to interrogate Miao-kuang, who admitted his fraud. The monks decided to expel him from the Order, and his confession spared him the death penalty. To prevent any future deceit, however, Miao-kuang was given a lengthy prison sentence, and the screen and all copies of his sūtra were destroyed. Seng-yu concludes by stating that his extensive account was necessary in case some copies of the text had escaped destruction and might mislead posterity.[33]

The story of Miao-kuang reveals that both religious and nonreligious considerations played a role in the evaluation of this text and, indeed, in the handling of the whole incident. Obviously, the false claim of sagehood, which is one of the four gravest offenses *(pārājika)* for a monk, and the fabrication of scripture were intolerable to the Buddhist church and had to be duly censured.[34] But with virtually no discussion on the content of the scripture, the issue of Miao-kuang's offense to religious orthodoxy recedes to the background of the account, while Seng-yu focuses on the wide attention Miao-kuang's claim of sagehood received and the upheaval it created among the populace. Given the emperor's eventual intervention in the case, which Michel Strickmann discusses in his chapter in this volume, we may safely assume that the proscription of Miao-kuang's scripture was largely prompted by the apprehension it prompted among the secular authorities. Such an assumption seems warranted when we realize that Miao-kuang was later identified as a Buddhist rebel by a Taoist polemicist, Fu I (554–639), and that in any given period secular authorities were sensitive to potential sources of socio-political instability.[35]

There is another type of scripture treated in the *Ch'u-san-tsang chi-chi* that is closely associated with indigenous scriptures—the so-called condensed scriptures *(ch'ao-ching)*. According to Seng-yu, the designation *ch'ao-ching* was originally reserved for an abbreviated translation of selected passages from a scripture, which were presumed to convey the text's essential meaning without any superfluous prolixity; this type of scripture had been produced since the time of An Shih-kao (fl. ca. second century) and Chih Ch'ien (fl. ca. late second to mid-third centuries), two of the earliest translators of Buddhist texts in China. Seng-yu reports that people later began to produce their own condensations directly from the Chinese renderings by haphazardly extracting passages, arbitrarily dividing coherent sections, and ungrammatically splitting individual sentences, thereby perverting the original meaning of the scriptures in question. If these practices were to continue, Seng-yu laments, such texts would accumulate through the years and tarnish the dharma-jewel.[36] *Ch'ao-ching* were meant to be accurate synopses of authentic translations that would make more accessible and intelligible to a Chinese audience the difficult, and lengthy, texts of Buddhism. In practice, however, they often deviated from this principle and became something akin to spurious scriptures as far as the cataloguers were concerned.

Despite his apparently harsh criticism of *ch'ao-ching,* Seng-yu was much more tolerant toward such texts than were later cataloguers. He classifies only six *ch'ao-ching* as spurious texts—a relatively small number when compared to the forty-six appearing in the actual listings of *ch'ao-ching,* and to the more than 450 *ch'ao-ching* listed in the section on anonymous translations.[37] This means that in the great majority of cases Seng-yu distinguished *ch'ao-ching* from spurious texts per se, a practice that later cataloguers criticized and altered, as we shall see.[38]

Seng-yu's tolerance for *ch'ao-ching* may be attributed to the academic interests of contemporary Buddhist circles as well as to his perception of the realities that Buddhism faced in China. Thanks to Kumārajīva's exegesis, Chinese scholar-monks of Seng-yu's time had become increasingly aware of the divergent learned traditions of Buddhism and had begun to formulate comprehensive hermeneutical schemata by which to give them coherence. This effort, which would continue through the eighth century, produced elegant classification systems called *p'an-chiao* (analyses of the teachings).[39] At this early stage in the evolution of *p'an-chiao* schemata, *ch'ao-ching* must have served a useful role by providing ready access to the essentials of many lengthy scriptures. Hence, despite the potential abuses to which such condensations might lead, Buddhist scholiasts must have found *ch'ao-ching* indispensable for their systematizing purposes.

Seng-yu also felt that *ch'ao-ching* could play an important role in the survival and spread of the Buddhist religion. Condensed scriptures had been created to replace the voluminous original translations with précis that would be more accessible to a popular audience. By their very nature, such scriptures must have been used to disseminate Buddhism among the less-educated general populace.[40] By classifying most *ch'ao-ching* separately from spurious scriptures, Seng-yu tacitly acknowledged their value in popularizing Buddhism. Moreover, he actively contributed to this process through works compiled with similar aims,[41] thus promoting the survival of the alien religion in the inimical native environment. This was an issue of constant concern to Seng-yu, who discusses his view of the hostile conditions facing Buddhism in his polemical treatise, the *Hung-ming chi* (Anthology on the Dissemination of the Radiance).[42] Thus we may presume that Seng-yu's tolerance for condensed scriptures also derived from a conscious attempt to ensure the vitality of Buddhism.

Chung-ching mu-lu (Catalogue of Scriptures, by Fa-ching, et al.; 594)

The *Chung-ching mu-lu* was compiled under the auspices of the Sui dynasty by twenty leading Buddhist elders, headed by the noted cleric Fa-ching (d.u.), in order to establish a standard listing of canonical scriptures. Compiled after the Sui reunification of China, it was the first comprehensive catalogue created within the Chinese Buddhist tradition, preserving all listings of scriptures recorded in previous catalogues from the Six Dynasties period. Due to its composite character, the number of indigenous scriptures it listed rose sharply, to 197, compared to the seventy given in the *Ch'u-san-tsang chi-chi.*[43] Moreover, indigenous scriptures are found in each of the six rubrics into which the catalogue is organized: sūtras, *Vinaya,* and śāstras of both the Mahāyāna and Hīnayāna branches of Buddhism, respectively.[44] One marked improvement of this catalogue is that it introduces the distinction between "suspicious" scriptures—namely, texts of doubtful authenticity—and the definitively "spurious." In the earlier *Ch'u-san-tsang chi-chi,* these terms had been used interchangeably, indicating that the distinction was either ambiguous or unrecognized.[45]

The compilers' general comments to a list of some twenty-one scriptures of doubtful authenticity suggest that there were two main reasons for classifying texts in this category: divergences in translators' names or translation dates, and/or the suspicious nature of the scriptures' contents. Their comments read:

> In many cases, the colophons to the titles [giving the translator's name, etc.] vary among the various catalogues. The style and doctrine [of these texts] are also ambiguous in nature. It has yet to be established whether they are genuine or spurious. The matter requires further examination.[46]

The texts to which these comments refer include the *Jen-wang ching* (Book of Benevolent Kings), which is considered suspicious because its content and diction do not resemble those of either of the ascribed translators. Other scriptures—such as the renowned *Ta-sheng ch'i-hsin lun* (Treatise on the Awakening of Faith According to the Mahāyāna) and the *Fo-shuo ying-kung fa-hsing ching* (Book of the Religious Practice of the Arhats, Spoken by the Buddha)—show discrepancies between the ascriptions on the manuscripts and those found in the catalogues, the latter of which provide no evidence to support the manuscripts' claimed attributions. The *Chung-ching mu-lu* thus takes a cautious approach in evaluating scriptures that display potential problems and always suggests that further investigation is needed before a definitive conclusion is reached. This call for prudence, however, did not prevail, for some of the suspect texts were arbitrarily dubbed authentic translations by the next cataloguer, Fei Ch'ang-fang, as we shall soon see.

The explicitly spurious scriptures received a decidedly stronger response in this catalogue, as the following general evaluation indicates:

> The preceding eighty-one scriptures all bear the mark of being contrary to what is genuine: some interpolate the golden words [of the Buddha] at the beginning and mention ballad prophecies *(yao-ch'en)* at the end. Others first discuss worldly techniques but later attribute these to the words of the dharma. Still others draw upon yin-yang [cosmology] and good and bad omens, while others explain the fortune and misfortune [caused by] gods and spirits. It is apparent that all such [scriptures] are spurious and fallacious. It is fitting now that their [circulation] be halted, in order to save the world from their peril.[47]

These comments show that the cataloguers of the *Chung-ching mu-lu* used two separate criteria in assessing a text's authenticity: structure and content. Structurally, they note that spurious texts juxtapose genuine and indigenous material. The purpose of this maneuver was, they imply, to lend an air of authenticity to the Chinese compilations. Moreover, the content of such scriptures was characterized by concepts and practices that were pan-Chinese in nature and popular in orientation. Although it is hard to know which spurious titles included which specific indigenous elements, "ballad prophecy" is the exception: we find three such titles that relate the prophecy of the advent of the savior Yüeh-kuang, discussed earlier, and four titles on the coming of Maitreya Buddha in the immediate future—not 576 million years hence.[48]

We have already pointed out that the prophecy of the advent of a messianic figure was considered to be a potential threat to both ecclesiastical and political establishments, an apprehension that became reality several times in Chinese history. That the secular regime was extremely sensitive to this type of material can be deduced from the official interdiction of prophetic texts and Confucian apocrypha *(ch'en-wei)* by successive emperors since the Wei-Chin period, including Sui Wen-ti (r. 581–604).[49] In this context, the prophecy of the advent of a savior or buddha could easily be interpreted as a potential threat to social stability, for such a claim might attract a mass following and lead to the establishment of a cult that could become the breeding ground for a larger-scale uprising.[50] Considering the official sponsorship of this catalogue, we have strong grounds to suspect that its textual evaluations reflected not only ecclesiastical concerns for religious orthodoxy but also the political interests of the secular regime.

One final innovation introduced in the *Chung-ching mu-lu* involves condensed scriptures. Fa-ching and his colleagues criticized Seng-yu's evaluation of these types of texts as a prime source of confusion about canonicity, and moved to dissociate them from authentic translations.[51] They did this first by placing the *ch'ao-ching* that had appeared in the listings for anonymous translations in a new section entitled "separate compilations" *(pieh-sheng),* a designation intended to distinguish such texts from "scripture" *(ching),* and second by relisting with spurious scriptures those condensations that Seng-yu had designated as *ch'ao-ching.* This change, which was followed later by the T'ang cataloguers, was the result of more rigorous standards of textual criticism, which may have been partly a product of the collective scholarship of the twenty clerics who compiled the *Chung-ching mu-lu.*

There were other factors as well that contributed to the decline of *ch'ao-ching.* One is the fact that by this time efforts to bring structure and coherence to the whole of the Buddhist teachings had borne fruit and a number of *p'an-chiao* systems had been developed, the most important of which was authored by a contemporary in the T'ien-t'ai school, Chih-i (538–597).[52] The *Chung-ching mu-lu* reflects these scholarly advancements in the detailed and precise categories into which it organizes scriptures. If *ch'ao-ching* played a significant role in the early evolution of *p'an-chiao* schemata, as we argued earlier, then their usefulness would naturally diminish with continued advances in hermeneutical systems. Another factor may have been changing social conditions. Unlike the hostile environment within which Buddhism developed during Seng-yu's time, the religion found itself in a more supportive milieu during the Sui dynasty and gained wider acceptance within society. During this period, Buddhism enjoyed the munificent support of both Sui Wen-ti and the ruling aristocracy. Wen-ti even resolved to "protect and maintain the dharma" at the time of his ascension to the throne, and promulgated many measures to enact that resolve. His pro-Buddhist policies were extensive enough to enhance the political and social fortunes of the religion.[53] The decision to compile this catalogue was a product of these same policies, with his enthusiastic promotion of Buddhism as an ever-present backdrop. Thus Buddhists during Wen-ti's time were finally freed from their long-term concern about the viability of their religion on Chinese soil. This improvement in the fortunes of Buddhism seems to have played a role in the recategorization of certain *ch'ao-ching* as spurious, for Buddhists no longer felt Seng-yu's pronounced ambivalence about the status of such "quasi-authentic" scriptures.

Li-tai san-pao chi (Record of the Three Treasures throughout Successive Generations, by Fei Ch'ang-fang; 597)

The *Li-tai san-pao chi* is unique in the present survey in that it has no separate category for indigenous scriptures. Of the 197 suspicious and spurious scriptures listed in the contemporary *Chung-ching mu-lu,* which included most of apocryphal texts given in previous catalogues, Fei's catalogue ignores a little less than half (or approximately 42 percent). The rest are dispersed throughout its two major sections of chronological listings and topical listings for texts to be entered into the canon *(ju-tsang mu).* We will examine these texts to determine Fei's method of evaluation.

Fei judged only three scriptures to be Chinese forgeries. For two of these—the *T'i-wei Po-li ching* and the *Sa-p'o-jo-t'o chüan-shu chuang-yen ching*—Fei followed the earlier evaluation of Seng-yu, who had classified these texts as apocryphal in the *Ch'u-san-tsang chi-chi.*[54] For the *T'i-wei ching,* Fei apparently rejected the authenticity of the text because it includes the Chinese concepts of the five directions *(wu-fang)* and five phases *(wu-hsing).* For the *Sa-p'o-jo-t'o ching,* Fei noted, following Seng-yu, that its author, Miao-kuang, deceived the masses and was expelled from the Buddhist Order by the Liang court. The third text judged to be a forgery is the *Chan-ch'a ching* (Book of Divination), which is first recorded in the *Chung-ching mu-lu* under the title *Chan-ch'a shan-o yeh-pao ching* (Book of Divining the Requital of Good and Evil Actions). Fei's lengthy annotation to this scripture, which is translated in Whalen Lai's chapter in this volume, notes that the scripture had been identified as spurious by other cataloguers, such as Fa-ching, and had been banned by imperial order due to its association with the popular cultic practice of stūpa-confessionals *(t'a ch'an-fa).*[55] As was the case with Miao-kuang's creation, the categorization of the *Chan-ch'a ching* clearly illustrates the influence of the state in religious affairs. Fei's account also demonstrates the essential role of the cataloguers in the adjudication of a text.

The other group of scriptures for which Fei's treatment reflects past catalogue assessments is the texts originally classified as *ch'ao-ching* in the *Ch'u-san-tsang chi-chi* and as suspicious scriptures in the *Chung-ching mu-lu.* Fei's comments note the potential confusion that *ch'ao-ching* might cause the tradition, even though they had originally been written solely for the personal use of their compilers. Thus Fei shared Seng-yu's ambivalence toward these scriptures and declined to list them with either authentic translations or spurious forgeries.[56]

The eighty-eight other texts listed as apocryphal in the *Chung-ching mu-lu* Fei classified as authentic translations by either known or anonymous translators. Fei's ascriptions were already controversial during the T'ang period, as we know from other cataloguers' criticisms, and their validity continues to be debated in scholarly circles even today.[57] Some of Fei's new ascriptions are given without any indication of his sources, so there is obviously no way to verify their accuracy. Others are based on past catalogue data; but, oddly (or perhaps conveniently), the very sources upon which Fei said he drew were old catalogues that were unavailable and probably no longer extant in his time. We can only speculate, as has Tokiwa Daijō, that these listings of lost catalogues may have been incorporated into some of the catalogues that were still extant in Fei's time; but even these catalogues seem to have become lost after Fei's time, for we find no further references to them in catalogue literature.[58] Since all the sources Fei relied on (or claimed to have relied on) are either unspecified or lost, we have no means by which to confirm the validity of many of his ascriptions. Herein lies the chief reason for the controversies that have surrounded his ascriptions.

A few observations lead us to support the criticisms of later cataloguers and modern scholars in suggesting that some of the Fei's ascriptions were arbitrary ones for which he was personally responsible. First, Fei's ascriptions and the assessments of the *Chung-ching mu-lu* show discrepancies. Fei was an official of the translation bureau and was closely involved with translation activities sponsored by the state, and there is even speculation that he had participated in the compilation of the *Chung-ching mu-lu.*[59] Given this wholesale involvement with contemporary Buddhist activities, it is rather unrealistic to think that Fei possessed sources to which his fellow cataloguers lacked access, or that he never shared his findings with his colleagues—points that raise serious questions about the reality of the sources Fei claimed to have utilized.[60] Our suspicion deepens when we take into account Hayashiya Tomojirō's observation that scriptures previously listed as anonymous became works by known translators or were assigned to a specific dynastic period en masse in Fei's work, yet without evidential basis or corroboration in the sources that he cited in support.[61]

A second piece of evidence suggesting that some of Fei's attributions were arbitrary may be gleaned from his treatment of the scriptures recited by Ni-tzu (whom Fei calls by her clerical name, Seng-fa), which were first judged apocryphal in the *Ch'u-san-tsang chi-chi.* Fei refutes this adjudication by arguing that these scriptures had nothing to do with "divine revelations" *(shen-shou),* as Seng-yu had characterized them, but were instead "learned in a former life" *(su-hsi).* Fei also implies that Seng-fa was a saint who deserved special consideration when he notes that "those whose knowledge is congenital are saints while those whose knowledge is acquired by learning rank second." In support of his argument, Fei cites the life of T'an-ti (fl. third century), who at youth naturally attained realization without a teacher, and who recollected events of his past life as a renowned dharma master *(fa-shih),* all of which was corroborated by one of his disciples from that previous incarnation. Fei concludes that Seng-fa's scriptures were ones that she had recited in her former existence and were therefore authentic.[62] This case reveals Fei's propensity to legitimate scriptures regardless of their suspicious provenance, a propensity that may well have affected his evaluation of other scriptures previously considered to be of doubtful authenticity.

A third and corollary observation is the evidence of internal discrepancies in Fei's listings. Hayashiya has noted that Fei's catalogue as a whole shows inconsistencies between its chronological and topical sections, in that some texts appear only in one section or the other; if the listings were comprehensive and precise, the same sets of texts would have been included in both sections.[63] The scriptures presently under discussion reveal this same pattern: less than one fifth of the suspicious texts that Fei reclassified as authentic translations appear in both registers, the rest being only in one. In addition, we find at least five cases where the ascriptions in the two sections do not match: they appear as works by known translators in the chronological listings but as anonymous translations in the topical listings, or vice versa. These discrepancies point to the inconsistencies in, and arbitrariness of, Fei's ascriptions.

When all these indications are taken together, we may speculate that Fei's main objective in his catalogue was not "to make a clear distinction between the genuine and the spurious," as all his predecessors had attempted, but to minimize the number of scriptures of questionable pedigree, such as indigenous scriptures, anonymous translations, and condensed scriptures. In other words, Fei sought to enhance the credibility of the textual basis of Buddhism. Why would Fei have felt so strongly about such credibility, to the extent that it played the critical role in his evaluation of scriptures?

Hayashiya has suggested that polemical considerations may have been behind Fei's penchant for assigning arbitrary attributions.[64] Buddhist rivalries with Taoism, which had a long history going back as far as the fourth century, were still very much alive during the latter half of the sixth century, when Fei lived. We find contemporary references to existing tensions between Buddhism and the indigenous religions—tensions that were engendered by competition for imperial support.[65] This rivalry must have formed the backdrop to Fei's undertaking.

There is a particular aspect of the rivalry, however, that may be more directly relevant to Fei's work—namely, the rapid expansion of the Taoist corpus through its liberal appropriation of material taken from Buddhist texts. The biography of Fa-lin (572–640), one of Buddhism's most virulent polemicists, reports that Taoist scriptures were growing rapidly throughout this period by appropriating Buddhist materials, and that they were merely "patterned after Buddhist scriptures, with some alterations at the beginning and changes at the end."[66] Fa-lin even concludes, in his *Pien-cheng lun* (Treatise on the Defense of Orthodoxy), that all Taoist texts except Lao-tzu's *Tao-teh ching* had plagiarized Buddhist scriptures.[67] Although this startling conclusion can hardly be accepted at face value, direct borrowings and indirect influences from Buddhist scriptures can be confirmed in Taoist texts. As Erik Zürcher has noted, Taoist authors drew freely from Buddhist sources, and the specific examples he provides of such appropriations are quite similar to those given by Fa-lin.[68]

We cannot confirm incontrovertibly that the increase in Taoist texts led to Fei's lenient treatment of indigenous Buddhist scriptures, but we can at least infer that his catalogue was not compiled oblivious to the religious environment of his time. For some sixth-century Buddhists, scriptures that were not authentic translations or for which translators were unknown could have proved embarrassing, and would certainly have provided ammunition for critics of the authenticity of Buddhist scriptures and, more seriously, of Buddhism itself. There is one reason in particular that leads us to presume that Fei was especially sensitive to potential changes in the fortunes of the religion: his bitter personal experiences during the persecution of Buddhism by Emperor Wu of the Northern Chou dynasty (r. 560–578), during which he was forced to disrobe and return to lay life.[69] We may thus safely assume that one of the main functions of the *Li-tai san-pao chi* was to resolve any remaining issues of authenticity and thereby ensure the credibility of the Buddhist textual transmission. This aim demanded that Fei reduce to a minimum the number of suspicious and spurious scriptures by deleting them from his catalogue or relisting them as authentic translations.

Chung-ching mu-lu (Catalogue of Scriptures, by Yen-ts'ung, et al.; 602)

This *Chung-ching mu-lu* was the second catalogue compiled under Sui sponsorship, by a group of Buddhist experts led by Yen-ts'ung (557–610). Its primary objective was to correct a major defect in the first *Chung-ching mu-lu,* which had not differentiated extant and nonextant scriptures and hence had proved impractical in establishing the canon. Because of its careful notation of the status of each text it registered, this new *Chung-ching mu-lu* is regarded as a reliable and valuable source for investigating the currency of texts during the Sui.[70]

There are other differences between the two catalogues that are relevant to the treatment of indigenous scriptures. Unlike its predecessor, Yen-ts'ung's catalogue does not separate suspicious from explicitly spurious scriptures; instead, both are combined into a single category, termed "suspicious-spurious" *(i-wei),* which contains a total of 209 titles, including several *ch'ao-ching.*[71] Some of the suspicious or spurious texts of Fa-ching's catalogue are here reclassified as authentic translations, including such seminal texts as the *Fan-wang ching* (Book of Brahma's Net), *Jen-wang ching,* and *Ta-sheng ch'i-hsin lun.* Some of these listings correspond to those found in *Li-tai san-pao chi* and, lacking any other information as to why these reclassifications were made, we may hypothesize that Yen-ts'ung and his associates were influenced by Fei Ch'ang-fang's assessments, rather than arriving at their own conclusions based on independent investigation.

This *Chung-ching mu-lu* includes no comments that might allow us to ascertain its criteria of scriptural authenticity. But we can say, at the very least, that it is somewhat stricter than its predecessor in its attitude toward all texts—except translations. One way this rigorousness appears is in the catalogue's specific stricture against copying indigenous and condensed scriptures. Faithful observance of this restriction would virtually guarantee the loss of such texts, since xylographic printing had not yet been invented in the Sui period.[72] This, of course, was precisely what the catalogue intended. A second major effect of this strictness was to exclude from the canon all writings by Chinese Buddhist authors, including commentaries, treatises, and chronicles, which had formerly been accorded canonical status.[73] All in all, Yen-ts'ung's catalogue displayed much less tolerance toward indigenous Buddhist compositions than had any of its predecessors.

Ta T'ang nei-tien lu (The Great T'ang Record of Buddhist Scriptures, by Tao-hsüan; 664)

This catalogue by the renowned *Vinaya* master Tao-hsüan (596–667) includes 183 titles in a section entitled "Suspicious-Spurious Scriptures and Treatises" *(i-wei ching-lun).*[74] Of this total, which is fewer than both the 197 of the first *Chung-ching mu-lu* and the 209 of the second, twenty-seven titles are new additions and the remaining 156 derive from earlier catalogues. The principal reason for this reduction is that Tao-hsüan either omits or reclassifies as translations nearly half of the fifty-five texts that the first *Chung-ching mu-lu* had newly registered as of doubtful authenticity *(i-huo).* Hayashiya attributes this reduction to the pronounced influence of the *Li-tai san-pao chi:* Tao-hsüan not only followed the catalogue format initiated by Fei in combining topical and chronological listings, but also relied heavily on Fei's chronological listing.[75] Indeed, Tao-hsüan expressed confidence in the reliability of this part of Fei's catalogue, even though he was strongly critical of Fei's topical listing for indiscriminately mixing the spurious and genuine.[76]

Tao-hsüan's preface to his section on indigenous scriptures includes a few points that bear on his standards of scriptural authenticity and other aspects pertinent to our discussion:

> The end of those forgers is evil. As for those who revert to duplicity [by forging scriptures], from generation to generation we have not been free of their extravagances. Of that gang, some string together the bizarre and deceptive, while others meet with an evil fate because of adorning [authentic texts] with spurious [materials]. I must by all means ferret out among these [forged texts] those which have identical titles and which are therefore indistinguishable from the genuine, as is the case with the *T'i-wei* [*Po-li ching*] and the *Fa-chü* [*ching*].[77] If I do not personally pursue [this matter], then the ludicrousness of these deceptive titles and teachings will spread. Should they not be prohibited? Ever since the dharma was transmitted to the Middle Plain [viz., China], it has suffered three persecutions. Later when it reemerged into the open, mischief-makers [who forge texts] spread with abandon before the genuine scriptures could be ascertained. I have learned that they flourish right in front of my own residence. [The content of these texts consists of] popular customs and Taoism [lit., "old man of Meng," viz., Chuang-tzu]; it is certain that they derive from the gut feelings [of the people], and that they all

> pursue mundane experiences [lit., "affairs of the ears and eyes"]. Thus their ideas do not comply with [authentic] scripture. They will deceive and mislead later aspirants. They make my heart cold. Is it not sad?! The Final Age of the Dharma *(mo-fa)* has arrived here![78]

These comments convey, among other things, Tao-hsüan's personal exasperation over the continued production and widespread dissemination of forged materials and his aspiration to be personally responsible for bringing an end to their corrupting influences. In this regard, Tao-hsüan's attitude closely parallels those of Tao-an, Seng-yu, and others of his predecessors. Furthermore, Tao-hsüan's specific reference to the advent of *mo-fa* epitomizes the apprehension that all the cataloguers, beginning with Tao-an, had felt about the eventual fate of their religion. But with Tao-hsüan there is more emphasis on a sense of finality and acute urgency than on that general awareness of the dharma's decline expressed by Tao-an and Seng-yu. *Mo-fa,* the Final Age of the Dharma, follows the periods of the true dharma *(cheng-fa)* and semblance dharma *(hsiang-fa)* in the Chinese systematization of the different eschatological schemata presented in Indian texts. Based on this notion of the three stages of the dharma *(san-shih),* some Chinese Buddhists felt as early as the mid-sixth century that the final age had already set in. By the time of Tao-hsüan, therefore, these eschatological ideas were prevalent and any indication of the deterioration of the dharma could easily have been interpreted as signaling the arrival of *mo-fa.*[79] Given this contemporary context, Tao-hsüan may have felt even more pressure to eradicate undesirable textual elements than did cataloguers who preceded him.

Moreover, Tao-hsüan spells out the principal components that typify spurious scriptures: they include popular customs or "Taoist" elements, portray vulgar human emotion, or are concerned with worldly activities rather than spiritual advancement. When this characterization is taken together with the following statement, Tao-hsüan's perception of the function of *i-wei ching,* as well as his standards of scriptural authenticity, become clear: "The orthodox dharma is recondite; the ordinary and unsophisticated have yet to reach it. [These spurious scriptures] adapt to the vulgar in order to convert the inferior, altering the true teachings."[80] Tao-hsüan observes here that the purpose of indigenous scriptures is to convert the common people to Buddhism, and that these texts adapt their presentation of doctrine to the people's limited ability to understand. This observation has been sustained by several modern scholars, whose research has shown that many indigenous scriptures do indeed have an explicitly non-élite orientation.[81] Tao-hsüan thus typically presumed that a text's popular orientation or the presence of "vulgar" elements indicated its indigenous origins.

Tao-hsüan's statements also adumbrate the extent of contemporary scriptural forgery and prove that such texts did circulate. Scriptural forgery was not only a matter of catalogue statistics, but was also experientially confirmed: as Tao-hsüan said, "They flourish right in front of my own residence." Elsewhere he also makes concrete reference to the wide dissemination of these types of material, noting with reference to one group of indigenous texts that "all the above spurious scriptures and treatises are often found in the scriptural repositories *(ching-tsang)* of humanity; their copies are still numerous."[82] These accounts tell us that, despite the successive proscriptions of earlier cataloguers, the production and dissemination of indigenous scriptures were very much alive during Tao-hsüan's time. And some of these texts had successfully gained entry into the legitimate collection of scriptures, the Buddhist canon. Even the wholesale burning of spurious texts by the government, which Tao-hsüan himself reports, was insufficient to stem the tide.[83] His accounts illustrate well the dynamics underlying the composition of indigenous scriptures during this period in Chinese history.

Ta Chou k'an-ting chung-ching mu-lu (Catalogue of Scriptures, Authorized by the Great Chou, by Ming-ch'üan, et al.; 695)

The *Ta Chou lu* was an official catalogue compiled by a group of seventy monks, headed by Ming-ch'üan (d.u.), under the auspices of the dowager-empress Wu Chao (r. 684–704). Its general comment on indigenous scriptures adds nothing new to what we have already seen: apocryphal texts are those which claim to have been spoken by the Buddha *(fo-shuo),* but which reveal their true identity in either their style or content.[84] As was often the case with other cataloguers, we are provided with no specifics as to exactly what features would cause the style and content of a text to be called into question.

All indigenous scriptures in this catalogue are uniformly categorized as spurious, and there is no longer any listing for suspicious scriptures. Of the total of 231 titles registered in the section devoted to spurious scriptures *(wei-ching mu-lu),* 110, or 48 percent, are new, while the remaining 121 are relistings from earlier catalogues.[85] The latter figure is considerably smaller than those of the first or second *Chung-ching mu-lu,* or even the *Ta T'ang nei-tien lu.* This reduction may be partially attributed to the exclusion of all *ch'ao-ching,* but also occurred because the *Ta Chou lu* accepted without challenge many of Fei Ch'ang-fang's reclassifications of indigenous scriptures as authentic translations.[86] Fei's impact actually pervades the entire catalogue, and we have reason to suspect that this reliance on the *Li-tai san-pao chi* was motivated by polemical and political goals.

Perhaps the most prominent characteristic of the *Ta Chou lu* is its massive size: its 3,616 titles are some 60 percent more than any of the three Sui catalogues or the *Ta T'ang nei-tien lu,* each of which contained around 2,200 titles. Its exaggerated size was already controversial in contemporary Buddhist circles: Chih-sheng, who compiled the *K'ai-yüan shih-chiao lu* thirty-five years later, detected that the numbers of texts and *chüan* in the *Ta Chou lu* were vastly inflated and had no basis in reality.[87] Hayashiya has attributed the large increase to the *Ta Chou lu*'s indiscriminate inclusion of all titles that were recorded in previous catalogues. He also points out that the *Li-tai san-pao chi* served as its main source, for two reasons. First, Fei's entries included more ascribed translations than any other catalogue. Second, the prestige of Fei's catalogue had grown dramatically during the early T'ang, after it was selected in 648 to serve as the basis for a mural commemorating Chinese translation activities, which was painted by imperial order at the translation center at Ta-tz'u-en ssu.[88] The fact that the T'ang catalogues—and especially the *Ta Chou lu*—maintained the *Li-tai san-pao chi* attributions despite their obvious problems can be explained by the credibility that such official recognition lent to Fei's work.

We have already seen that earlier cataloguers were sensitive to Buddhist needs to compete effectively against rival religious groups. The compilers of the *Ta Chou lu* were prompted by similar motivations. In addition, they apparently sought to ingratiate themselves with Empress Wu, who was herself a pious Buddhist, and to overwhelm rival Taoists with the exhaustiveness of the Buddhist canon.[89] Buddhist attempts to gain political influence during this period have been ably demonstrated by Antonino Forte: Buddhists were responsible for the composition of a commentary on the *Ta-yün ching* (*Mahāmegha-sūtra;* Great Cloud Sūtra) and for an interpolation in the *Pao-yü ching* (*Ratnamegha-sūtra;* Rain of Jewels Sūtra), which provided the ideological justification for Wu Chao's usurpation of the throne.[90] The preface to the *Ta Chou lu* reflects the same general attitude: it addresses the dowager-empress as the Cakravartin of the Golden Wheel who, out of her great compassion, was born into this world to save suffering sentient beings.[91] And in fact we discover that five individuals involved in the compilation of the two aforementioned works were also among the team of seventy monks who compiled the *Ta Chou lu.*[92]

One conspicuous example of this catalogue's concern with political exigencies is found in its treatments of texts affiliated with the San-chieh chiao (Three Stages sect).[93] The earliest record of this sect's scriptures appears in the *Li-tai san-pao chi*'s section on Sui translations, where two titles are listed as being the works of its founder, Hsin-hsing (540–594). The *Ta T'ang nei-tien lu* added one title, listing a total of three texts in its section for works written by Chinese clerics and lay authors.[94] It is in the *Ta Chou lu* that a significant change takes place: there are now a total of twenty-two titles in twenty-nine *chüan,* and all are classified with indigenous scriptures. At the end of the listing, the cataloguers note:

> In the prime year of Cheng-sheng (695), we received an imperial order to classify [the above San-chieh chiao texts] as spurious scriptures. Together with miscellaneous prophetic documents *(fu-lu)* [of the Taoists], they were sent to the Office of Sacrifice. The doctrinal approach of the above texts has transgressed the intention of the Buddha and the schismatic establishment [of the San-chieh chiao] is heretical. These [texts], then, are subject to the same restrictions that were imposed upon these falsified, miscellaneous prophetic documents. An edict issued in the second year of Sheng-li (699) proclaimed that those training in the teachings of the San-chieh chiao are allowed [to practice] only alms-begging, long retreats *(ch'ang-chai),* abstinence from grain, observance of precepts, and sitting in meditation. Anything else would be illegal. Having been fortunate enough to receive this clear directive that removed past faults, we dare not register them in the wrong sections of the catalogue. We all comply with [the decision] to exclude [them from the canon], as a lesson for future [generations].[95]

This quotation shows that the decision to categorize the San-chieh chiao texts as spurious came as the result of an imperial decree, not of any critical investigation by the monk-cataloguers. The catalogue account reports only the sequence of events that led to the decision; and based on this account, it appears that the cataloguers had nothing to do with that decision. Such reclassification of indigenous Buddhist literature—meaning here doctrinal treatises and ritual tracts, not indigenous sūtras or condensed scriptures—was unprecedented, at least as far as catalogue records were concerned. Thus, for San-chieh chiao texts at the very least, reclassification was strictly nontextual: the adjudication of these texts by the cataloguers simply mirrors secular policy toward the group and its literature. But this policy could very well have been the result of pressure exerted by the Buddhists, including the cataloguers themselves. As we know from Forte's study, Buddhist monks who were close to the court were quite capable of manipulating secular authority in order to achieve their goals.[96]

K'ai-yüan shih-chiao lu
(Record of Śākyamuni's Teachings, Compiled during the K'ai-yüan Era, by Chih-sheng; 730)

The *K'ai-yüan shih-chiao lu* is generally regarded as the single most important bibliographical catalogue in terms of the role it played in the history of East Asian Buddhist canonical publications. Although it began as a private undertaking by a single individual, Chih-sheng (d.u.), it was adopted as an official catalogue soon after its completion, and its register of canonical texts *(ju-tsang lu)* served as the standard for the T'ang canon.[97] The content and organization of all successive canons from the late-T'ang period on were based on this catalogue, the only major difference being the addition of later translations and compositions. Especially significant is its influence on the printed editions of the canon, the earliest of which dates from 971–983, since these became the basis for later canons produced not only in China but also elsewhere in East Asia.[98]

The prominent status accorded to the *K'ai-yüan lu* is largely due to its impeccable organization, which eliminated all discrepancies between the two types of registers, topical and chronological, that had plagued earlier catalogues. In terms of its content, however, it was not without flaws. Close examination of its entries reveals that Chih-sheng did not completely succeed in his attempt to eliminate the arbitrary ascriptions that originated in the *Li-tai san-pao chi* and of which he was fully aware and critical.[99] Hayashiya has suggested that Chih-sheng was swayed by factors other than critical scholarship, including the undeniably pervasive influence of the *Li-tai san-pao chi* on other T'ang catalogues and on the content of existing canons.[100] Whatever the reason, the fact remains that traditional views that Chih-sheng "did not make the slightest mistake" in textual evaluation and that he "shut off the source of the perverse and spurious" are not borne out by a critical evaluation of the catalogue itself.[101] Moreover, this gap between traditional perceptions of the catalogue and its reality has crucial implications for the fate of the texts involved. Controversial texts that the *K'ai-yüan lu* treated as genuine entered the mainstream of the sinitic tradition, even though several of those texts had previously been judged spurious. By the same token, texts it listed as spurious were barred from the canon, and many of these were lost forever.[102]

The *K'ai-yüan lu* contains 406 titles in the section covering apocryphal scriptures, which is divided into those of doubtful authenticity and the explicitly spurious, restoring the bifurcation first made in Fa-ching's *Chung-ching mu-lu.*[103] The register of suspicious scriptures, which is entitled "Record of Doubtful [Scriptures] that Are to be Reexamined," lists fourteen titles. It is accompanied by the following comment, which defines the category:

> The Record of Doubtful Scriptures: It has been almost seven hundred years since Indian scriptures spread east. The teachings have flourished and waned, and the times, furthermore, have changed. From the beginning to the end [of this period], nearly ten thousand rolls [of scriptures] were transmitted in translation. These scriptures [lit., "sections and book wrappers"] have already been extensively investigated, but it is difficult to be thorough. Cataloguers include [certain texts] in [their listings of authentic scriptures] simply on the basis of what they hear, without inquiring in detail about their doctrinal purports and principles. Some [of the texts] included in those [listings] are dubious. Now I am afraid that the genuine and the spurious interlace and the authentic and unauthentic intertwine. For this reason, I have compiled this separate listing as a lesson for future [generations].[104]

According to this description, suspicious texts are those which have been considered authentic because their contents were not carefully scrutinized. Chih-sheng is well aware that the vicissitudes Buddhism experienced throughout its long history make it difficult to determine scriptural authenticity—a point duly noted by Tao-an nearly four centuries before. In practice, Chih-sheng relies on content analysis to ferret out spurious texts: he notes that suspicious scriptures hardly conform to the standard of authentic scriptures because their teachings are perverse and their discourses relate to ordinary human feelings. Included among these texts are such obvious examples as the *Ch'ing-ching fa-hsing ching* (Book of Pure Religious Practice), which "records and expounds on matters concerning Confucius, Lao-tzu, and Yen-hui," all names of indigenous Chinese sages.[105] Judging from Chih-sheng's comments, suspicious scriptures refer not so much to texts of indeterminate authenticity, as the term connotes—and as it had been used since the first *Chung-ching mu-lu*—as to those which include explicit evidence that they are not translations.

Chih-sheng's comments continue:

> Some say, "To disparage the sacred teaching is culpable; the sincere words of the Buddha should not be criticized." [But] the sūtra says, "As long as there is any doubt about what I [the Buddha] expound, you should not accept it." How much more so is this the case with these [suspicious scriptures]?! Acknowledging this principle, we must review whether they are authentic or unauthentic. [If no conclusion can be made,] then we will wait for all the learned ones to scrutinize together whether they are genuine or spurious.[106]

Chih-sheng's point here is that if a scripture is of indeterminate authenticity, it is best to be cautious and not accept it as a full-fledged translation. In this judgment he bases himself on a precedent established by the Buddha himself, who warned his disciples not to accept anything uncritically, even his own teachings—an admonition that has its locus classicus in the *Aṅguttara-nikāya*.[107] Thus Chih-sheng's comments show that he believed his approach to textual evaluation to be founded on a long-established principle that could be traced to the Buddha himself.

Chih-sheng's register of spurious texts, which is entitled "Record of the Falsified, which Confuse the Genuine," lists 392 titles. That total includes thirty-seven new additions, the rest being a cumulative listing from previous catalogues. He defines the category as follows:

> Spurious Scriptures: They are fabricated through perverted views, so as to confuse what is genuine scripture. During the almost two thousand years since the Great Master "hid his shadow," demonic teachings have arisen in competition with one another. Thus the true dharma declined and degenerated. Ever since those obstinate and foolish people spuriously fabricated all these scriptures with their wrong views and confused minds, [these falsified

> texts] beguiled prevalent customs, and their perverse language led the righteous astray. Is this not terribly pathetic? Now I am afraid that the true and the false would blend with one another, and authentic and unauthentic would become one. This would be comparable to [saying] that the precious jade from Mount K'un is of the same class as clay or stone and that genuine gold of the Bureau of Provisions is of equal value to lead or iron.[108] Now I will separate them so that the genuine and the spurious can be distinguished, just as the Ching and Wei rivers separate their flows and leave no taints behind.[109]

Here Chih-sheng outlines the activity of scriptural fabrication and its perilous consequences with a strong sense of indignation and exasperation, illustrating the point through Chinese similes—a technique that Tao-an had employed effectively in his own description of scriptural fabrication. Although Chih-sheng purports to give a definition of spurious scripture, he tells us little more than that they are written in perverse language, prompted by perverted views. More concrete criteria, however, can be inferred from his comments on individual scriptures. We will discuss these according to three discernible types of criteria.

The first major factor that would brand a work as spurious was known authorship. This is the case with the annotation to the *Kao-wang Kuan-shih-yin ching* (Book of Avalokiteśvara, from the Era of Prince Kao), which includes a detailed description of the circumstances under which the scripture came into existence. Chih-sheng notes that this text was transcribed from the oral recitation of a certain enlisted soldier named Sun Ching-teh. During the Northern Wei period, Sun was arrested for petty theft and sentenced to death. The night before his execution, a Buddhist monk appeared in a dream and taught him to recite the *Chiu-sheng Kuan-shih-yin ching* (Book of Avalokiteśvara, the Savior of Life), which, if recited a thousand times, would free him from his dire plight. The following day, at the execution site, he did as he had been instructed and was impervious to injury, despite repeated blows of the executioner's sword. Hearing that Sun had been protected through the efficacy of this scripture, the chief minister, Kao-huan (496–547), commuted his sentence, and the text came to circulate throughout the world.[110]

The second criterion was internal textual evidence. The first example displaying this standard is the *Yü-ch'ieh fa-ching ching* (Book of the Yoga Dharma Mirror), which is the subject of Forte's chapter in this volume. This scripture is purported to have been translated by Bodhiruci (572–727 [sic]), but Chih-sheng refutes this attribution by pointing out its composite nature and identifying its textual sources. He also identifies the author as being the monk Shih-li, an adherent of the San-chieh chiao, whose adherents revered the sūtra and regarded it as the foundation of their doctrine.[111]

A second text treated in this manner is the *Yao-hsing she-shen ching* (Book of the Essential Practice of Self-mortification), which is attributed to the famous T'ang translator Hsüan-tsang (602–664). Chih-sheng points out, however, that this ascription is clearly fallacious, because the text deviates from orthodox scripture in four ways. First, the transcription of "Vulture Peak in the Indian kingdom of Magadha" was the one used before Hsüan-tsang's reform of transcription equivalencies, and was no longer current. Second, the text mentions a charnel ground on Vulture Peak, which was impossible, since that mountain was situated inside the capital of Rājagṛha itself, and the presence of such a graveyard would have polluted the entire city. Third, the text says that the Buddha decided to "abandon his body" *(she-shen)*—that is, to commit ritual suicide—while he was still a disciple of Dīpaṃkara Buddha. This, however, goes against traditional accounts, which say that the Buddha received the prediction of his future buddhahood from Dīpaṃkara and subsequently went on to fulfill that prophecy. Fourth, the text claims that even the worst possible moral offense, such as murder, can be redeemed by the practice of *she-shen,* a claim that would invalidate the doctrine of moral retribution.[112]

A third such text is the *Fo-ming ching* (Book of Buddhas' Names), in sixteen *chüan.* Chih-sheng relates that this text expands upon a twelve-*chüan* translation by Bodhiruci (?–527), which bears the same title. He notes that this expanded *Fo-ming ching* is not only a haphazard mixture of lewd, vulgar language with sacred words; in addition, it also features such absurdities as referring to the travelogue of the pilgrim Fa-hsien (339?–420?) as a canonical sūtra (lit., "dharma-jewel," *fa-pao*) entitled the *Fa-hsien chuan ching* (Scripture of the Record of Fa-hsien). The text also wrongly divides one Sanskrit name or combines two separate names into one. These are, Chih-sheng states, but a few examples of the absurd errors in this text, which are too numerous to enumerate in detail.[113]

The third criterion followed by Chih-sheng combined internal textual evaluations with an external factor: socio-political considerations. The first example that exhibits this standard involves four scriptures that prophesy the advent of the Buddhist messiah Maitreya. Chih-sheng gives the following evaluation of these texts:

> The above four scriptures are all forgeries by deceitful lackeys. They expound such events as the imminent advent of Maitreya Buddha. Using such uncanny fallacies, they mislead and delude the ordinary and simple. Numerous people whose understanding is shallow believe and accept [these texts]. As a consequence, they end up becoming submerged [in the ocean of suffering]. Is this not injurious [to the religion]?[114]

According to traditional accounts, the advent of Maitreya is not to take place until incalculable years in the future, after the demise of the present Buddhist dispensation; consequently, to advise "the imminent advent of Maitreya Buddha" is contrary to the accepted doctrines of the religion.[115] Such a heresy could be easily manipulated to legitimate rebellions against secular authorities, and there are records between the end of Sui and the time of Chih-sheng of at least six such rebellions prompted by Maitreya messianism.[116] When these are taken into consideration, Chih-sheng's criticisms of these texts can be viewed as directed not simply against their heretical doctrines, but also against their political implications—the ill-effects their teachings could have on social stability—which so often became a reality.

Another example of this third criterion involves thirty-nine texts belonging to the San-chieh chiao. Following the *Ta Chou lu,* Chih-sheng lists all of them as spurious. His annotation repeats that of the *Ta Chou lu,* to which he adds the following comments:

> As for the compilations of Hsin-hsing, although they draw upon the scriptures, they are all fallaciously produced on the basis of the prejudiced view of his faction, and are contrary [to the orthodox teachings]. They not only go against the noble intent [of the Buddha], but also feign to be the true teachings. An edict issued in the twentieth year of K'ai-huang (600) banned all operations [of the sect].[117] But followers of this faction were already numerous and widespread. . . . Although Sui Wen-ti ended its operations, he could not extirpate its root and source. . . . In the thirteenth year of K'ai-yüan (725), an edict [was issued by Hsüan-tsung]: "The San-chieh chiao compounds in all the monasteries are hereby ordered to remove their partitions so as to make them mutually accessible to all monks living in other compounds, with whom they should share their residence. They cannot live separately. All San-chieh chiao compilations are banned and should be eliminated and destroyed. If these injunctions are not followed, their practices will influence and seduce others. Those who do not collaborate will be forced to disrobe."[118]

Chih-sheng notes that the persecution of the school goes back to the time of Sui Wen-ti and has continued through the reign of his own emperor, Hsüan-tsung. Chih-sheng classifies these texts as spurious for two reasons: their teachings do not conform to those of orthodox Buddhism, and their status within the contemporary socio-political context was controversial. Thus, San-chieh chiao scriptures represent still another instance in which the evaluation of texts was based not only on objective textual criteria but also on political considerations. The implication is that the cataloguers classified the San-chieh chiao texts as spurious in order to deny them any place in the textual basis of Buddhism —a measure made in compliance with the political agenda of secular authorities, who had proscribed the practices and texts of that lineage. Chih-sheng thus follows in the footsteps of Ming-ch'üan and others, as he indicates by incorporating their comments into his own annotation.

The section on spurious scriptures ends with fifty-four *ch'ao-ching* texts drawn from previous catalogue listings. The practice of classifying *ch'ao-ching* among spurious scriptures began with the first *Chung-ching mu-lu* but was ignored by the *Li-tai san-pao chi* and *Ta Chou lu*. Chih-sheng restores the prior practice, with the following comments:

> As for the above . . . fifty-four texts in 501 *chüan,* their titles are all appropriated from genuine scriptures, and their phraseology fluctuates; some blend a variety of doctrines and establish titles independent [of their original sources]. Even if [their contents do derive] from orthodox [scripture], I fear that they still involve an excessive mixture of jade and gravel. And even if there is a case in which a text judged spurious can be inferred to have a reliable textual basis, it is still difficult to decide whether to accept it as authentic or to reject it [lit., "to advance or to withdraw"]. Following the old catalogues, I now list them at the end of the spurious [register].[119]

These comments show that *ch'ao-ching* were of decidedly mixed quality. Some were outright fabrications that blended together miscellaneous doctrines, while others faithfully represented the scriptural orthodoxy of the time. Although Chih-sheng expresses some ambivalence toward the latter type, he nonetheless refrains from according them the status of authentic scripture. His attitude in reevaluating *ch'ao-ching* as spurious scriptures is one of prudence, an attitude that also characterizes his attempt to remedy discrepancies between topical and chronological listings and to reduce the number of arbitrary ascriptions found in past catalogues.

While most past cataloguers had stopped short of sketching out specific criteria for judging scriptures, Chih-sheng provided at least some precise textual criteria on which he based his evaluations, showing a marked improvement over the broad standards followed by previous cataloguers. Chih-sheng, after all, had the advantage of hindsight: the merits and mistakes of his predecessors helped him to improve the organization and content of his own catalogue.

Conclusion

The foregoing chronological survey of Chinese Buddhist catalogues has explored their views and attitudes toward indigenous scriptures and the criteria they used in evaluating those texts. Let us now summarize the major points of our discussion and briefly discuss their implications.

The Chinese cataloguers considered indigenous scriptures to be a threat to the purity and integrity of the textual tradition of Buddhism, which they presumed to have been pristinely transmitted from India and Central Asia. Most of them objected in the strongest possible terms to these native sūtras, holding themselves personally responsible for combatting their threat. Some of the cataloguers interpreted scriptural forgery as a direct product of the decline of the dharma, an integral feature of Indian, and later Chinese, Buddhist eschatology. Hence they understood the forgery of texts not as a historical accident, but rather as an inevitable fact with which Chinese Buddhists would have to cope. Given this backdrop, cataloguers considered their compilations to be crucial components in the task of protecting the dharma *(hu-fa),* one of their major functions being to expose those texts masquerading as authentic scripture.

The evaluation of suspect scriptures was based on both textual and nontextual criteria. Since, for the Chinese cataloguers, a scripture's authenticity was synonymous with its foreign provenance, one of the most obvious proofs that a text was legitimate was its non-Chinese (viz., Indian or Central Asian) origin. The effectiveness of this criterion was, however, limited, first due to the numerous scriptures that claimed to have been "translated anonymously," and second because of the unreliability of the translator colophons, which often included information at variance with data appearing in older catalogues. The repeated references to such discrepancies in the catalogues suggests that these colophons could be easily manipulated to assign a putative translator to an indigenous Chinese scripture—a plausible speculation, considering the large number of sūtras written in China during the manuscript period. Some cataloguers exercised prudence in dealing with these cases by placing such texts in a "suspicious" category; but that prudence did not always prevail, and many of these texts eventually entered the mainstream of the Chinese Buddhist textual transmission.

Analyses of style and content comprise another set of internal textual criteria. Some of the earlier cataloguers in particular asserted that the style and content of apocryphal texts were demonstrably inferior to authentic scripture and were thus easily detectable. Yet the accounts given by the cataloguers are rather vague and subjective, and their effectiveness in making credible decisions about the provenance of a text cannot easily be determined. Some of the T'ang cataloguers, to their credit, did try to introduce a semblance of scholarly objectivity to their analyses by pointing out specific internal evidences of forgery, such as the presence of native religious elements, heterodox doctrines and practices, and philological anomalies. The potential value to the cataloguers of these types of evidence can be verified by examining some of the extant indigenous scriptures, which do indeed display such features. When present, these features are admittedly conspicuous indications of Chinese origin, and hence the logical point to which the cataloguers would direct their attentions. The identification of such features does suggest that there was at least some progress made in the methodology of the cataloguers during the three-and-a-half centuries of catalogue compilation discussed in this chapter. There were, however, indigenous sūtras that evaded detection by the cataloguers. Many of these texts, which we might call "canonical apocrypha"—that is, indigenous scriptures that were able to insinuate themselves into the canon—acquired that envied status precisely because their style and/or content showed no apparent sign of Chinese provenance and they were thus able to pass themselves off as legitimate translations. Such problems bespeak the difficulties and complexities facing the scholar in evaluating the provenance and authorship of texts that the cataloguers, and thence the entire Chinese tradition, allowed to be entered in the listings of authentic scriptures.

Nontextual criteria that entered into the cataloguers' evaluation of texts included such things as socio-political considerations or polemical necessity. We have noted these concerns in Seng-yu's treatment of *ch'ao-ching* and in Fei Ch'ang-fang's arbitrary assignment of translator attributions and their uncritical acceptance by later cataloguers. But these pressures were also apparent in the cataloguers' treatments of texts that were perceived as leading to social and political upheaval, either by claiming the sanctity of their authors or the advent of messiahs, or through their advocacy of communal ritual practices. The proscription of the San-chieh chiao texts by the cataloguers stands out as part of a Buddhist strategy to influence secular rulers for polemical purposes. These examples show that the cataloguers, as proponents of Buddhism, were well aware that their religion did not, and could not, live in a vacuum; their evaluation of scriptures, therefore, sometimes mirrored the real and anticipated needs of the contemporary secular regime—ultimately serving, we must not forget, the Buddhists' own polemical purposes.

This survey of the Chinese Buddhist catalogues thus shows that, while there is substantial continuity in the style and approach of the catalogues, there is also some fluctuation in their standards of scriptural authenticity. These fluctuations are an inevitable corollary to the nature of the criteria already discussed. The internal criteria used were so subjective that divergent judgments about the legitimacy of scriptures were inevitable. And the very purpose of the nontextual criteria was for the cataloguers to accommodate and respond to the changing environment within which Buddhism operated. These fluctuations also illustrate the incompatible goals the cataloguers sometimes set for themselves: the rigorous promotion of Buddhist ideals and the protection of their religion's purity on the one hand, and the advancement of the Buddhist cause in China on the other. When the latter polemical concerns became the overriding goal in their evaluations, former arbitrary ascriptions were accepted uncritically by the cataloguers or the very standard of canonicity itself was manipulated in the perceived interests of their religion. Hence, while the ostensible purpose in compiling catalogues was to ensure that Chinese Buddhist scriptures conformed to the original Indian textual tradition, that task was neither clearcut nor facile. It may be said, then, that the ways in which indigenous scriptures were treated in the Buddhist catalogues portray in microcosm the range of pressures that Chinese Buddhism was under throughout its history.

NOTES

I would like to thank Professors David Johnson and Stephen Teiser for their valuable comments and suggestions on an earlier draft of this paper.

1. *Ching-lu* literally means "record of sūtras," but the actual content of the catalogues is more comprehensive than the term may suggest. It actually included all three divisions of the Hīnayāna and Mahāyāna texts, i.e., sūtras, *Vinaya* or preceptive texts, and śāstras, as well as Chinese treatises, Buddhist chronicles, biographies of monks, and so on. This general use of the word *ching* for all three divisions of Buddhist canonical literature reflects the fact that the distinctions among them were not yet known when the catalogue genre first evolved. The earliest catalogue to introduce these distinctions was the fifth-century *Chung-ching pieh-lu,* as recorded in the *Li-tai san-pao chi* (*T* 2034.49.125b24–c16). For the meaning of *ching-lu* and its historical background, see also Hayashiya Tomojirō's groundbreaking work, *Kyōroku kenkyū,* vol. 1 (Tokyo: Iwanami shoten, 1941), 3–6. Hayashiya intended to examine all major catalogues produced through the T'ang period in a total of three volumes, but unfortunately the project was never completed. The only finished volume treats primarily the *Tsung-li chung-ching mu-lu* of Tao-an, but it also includes a general discussion on the history of Buddhist catalogues. Throughout this article, I am much indebted to Hayashiya, as well as to Okabe Kazuo, whom I cite below, for further accounts of Buddhist catalogues.

2. For a comprehensive listing of Buddhist catalogues, see Yao Ming-ta, *Chung-kuo mu-lu-hsüeh shih* (Ch'ang-sha: Commercial Press, 1937), 231–237. Yao's listing does not include several catalogues reproduced in *Shōwa hōbō sōmokuroku,* vols. 2 and 3. Hayashiya suggests that some of the earliest catalogues had only "legendary" existence because they are recorded only in a single source (*Li-tai san-pao-chi* 15, *T* 2034.49.127b–c), with no other supporting evidence. He also speculates that the translators Chih Ch'en and Chih Ch'ien had each compiled catalogues that are not included among the extant listings. For discussion on these points, see Hayashiya, *Kyōroku kenkyū,* pp. 221–240.

3. Okabe Kazuo, "Kyōroku ni okeru kenjō shūden no chii," *Suzuki gakujutsu zaidan kenkyū nenpō* 11 (1974): 40, 53 n. 6.

4. The earliest Chinese bibliographical catalogues date from the end of the Former Han (206 B.C.E.–8 C.E.): the *Pieh-lu* by Liu Hsiang (78–6 B.C.E.), and the *Ch'i-lüeh* by his son Liu Hsin (?–23 C.E.). Although these catalogues no longer survive, they served as the model for the bibliographical section of the *I-wen chih* of the *Han-shu,* compiled by Pan-ku (32–92 C.E.). For the early history of the Chinese bibliographical tradition, see Yao Ming-ta, *Mu-lu-hsüeh shih,* pp.

23–60; Kuraishi Takeshirō, *Mokurokugaku,* Tōyōgaku bunken sentā series, vol. 20 (Tokyo: Tokyo daigaku Tōyō bunka kenkyūsho, 1973), 1–30. Note also that the compilation of catalogues was not the monopoly of Chinese Buddhists. The Tibetan Buddhist canon also contains scriptural catalogues—the *Denkar-Ma* catalogue, dating from the ninth century, being the earliest extant example. See Yoshimura Shūki, "Denkaruma mokuroku no kenkyū," in his *Indo daijō bukkyō shisō kenkyū: Kamarashīra no shisō* (Kyoto: Hyakkaen, 1974), 99–199; Marcelle Lalou, "Les textes bouddhiques au temps du roi Khri-sroṅ-lde-bcan," *Journal Asiatique* (1953): 313–353. For the dating of this catalogue, see David S. Ruegg, *The Life of Bu ston rin po che,* Serie Orientalie Roma, no. 34 (Rome: Istituto Italiano per il Medio ed Estremo Oriente, 1966), 19 n. 2. For a survey of Tibetan Buddhist catalogues, see A. I. Vostrikov, "Historico-Bibliographical Surveys of the Tibetan Buddhist Canon," in his *Tibetan Historical Literature,* trans. from the Russian by Harish Chandra Gupta, Soviet Indology Series, no. 4 (1970): 205–215.

5. For those aspects of Buddhist catalogues which are superior to secular catalogues, see Liang Ch'i-ch'ao, "Fo-chia ching-lu tsai chung-kuo mu-lu-hsüeh chih wei-chih," in *Fo-hsüeh yen-chiu shih-pa pien* (Shang-hai: Chung-hua shu-chü, 1936), 1; rpt. in *Fo-chiao mu-lu-hsüeh shu-yao* (Taipei: Ta-sheng wen-hua ch'u-pan she, 1978), 21–52; cited in Okabe Kazuo, "The Chinese Catalogues of Buddhist Scriptures," *Komazawa daigaku bukkyō gakubu kenkyū kiyō* 38 (1980): 8. For a comprehensive treatment of the history and development of Buddhist catalogues in China, see Hayashiya, *Kyōroku kenkyū,* pp. 3–209.

6. *K'ai-yüan shih-chiao lu* 1, *T* 2154.55.477a4–10.

7. What cataloguers term "suspect" or "spurious" scriptures we will call instead "indigenous scriptures" in this chapter, unless we are translating directly from original sources or the context demands the use of such pejorative terms. In the past, the majority of Japanese scholars, who opened this field of Buddhist Studies and who continue to be at its vanguard, have customarily employed the cataloguers' terms (J. *gikyō* or *gigi kyōten*). Only recently have terms less laden with such heavily pejorative connotations come to the fore. For example, Japanese translations of the *Yüan-chüeh ching* by Yanagida Seizan and of the *Liang-yeh ching* by Araki Kengo have been published under the title *Chūgoku senjutsu kyōten* (Scriptures Compiled in China). See Bukkyō kyōten sen series, vols. 13 & 14 (Tokyo: Chikuma shobō, 1986 & 1987, respectively). The English term "apocrypha" is decidedly more familiar to Western scholars than some of its counterparts; but its connotations in the Judeo-Christian tradition, as well as its pejorative implications, make it less than ideal in a Buddhist context. For the etymology and acquired meaning of the term "apocrypha," see Buswell's introduction to this volume; Edgar J. Goodspeed, *The Story of the Apocrypha* (Chicago: University of Chicago Press, 1939), 1–5; Bruce M. Metzger, *An Introduction to the Apocrypha* (New York: Oxford University Press, 1957), 179–180. See also Michel Strickmann's chapter in this volume for the suggestion of the term "original Chinese scriptures."

8. Several of these proscribed scriptures are reprinted in vol. 85 of the *Taishō* canon: a section titled "Doubtful and Spurious Scriptures" reproduces fifty-six texts (*T* 2865–*T* 2920) from the Stein, Pelliot, and Japanese collections of Tunhuang manuscripts, as well as from texts preserved in Japan. The Stein manu-

scripts reproduced there are based on the photographic reproductions of manuscripts made by Yabuki Keiki during his visit to the British Museum in 1922–1923. Yabuki's entire collection, including the above indigenous scriptures, is published in *Meisha yoin* (Tokyo: Iwanami shoten, 1930; rpt. Kyoto: Rinsen shoten, 1980), together with annotation to each of these texts in the companion volume, *Meisha yoin kaisetsu* (Tokyo: Iwanami shoten, 1933; rpt. Kyoto: Rinsen shoten, 1980). For a list of the Stein manuscripts not included in *Taishō* vol. 85, see Chen Miao-ju, "Ta-tsang-ching ku-i-pu pu-mu," *Tun-huang hsüeh* 6 (1983): 113–116. See also Huang Yung-wu, ed., *Tun-huang pao-tsang* (T'ai-pei: Hsin wen-feng ch'u-pan kung-ssu, 1981–), which reproduces major Tun-huang manuscript collections.

9. See Mochizuki Shinkō's *Jōdokyō no kigen oyobi hattatsu* (Tokyo: Kyōritsusha, 1930), 133–301, and his *Bukkyō kyōten seiritsushi ron* (Kyoto: Hōzōkan, 1946; rpt. 1978), 299–694. The latter work reproduces the former study, with some modifications.

10. There are a total of fifteen extant catalogues dating from the T'ang and earlier. The coverage in this chapter is limited to those most pertinent to our discussion. For the titles of the remaining catalogues, see Hayashiya, *Kyōroku kenkyū,* pp. 13–14.

11. The pioneering studies on indigenous scriptures made by Yabuki and Mochizuki, as well as more recently by Makita Tairyō, have shown that their doctrines and practices were the culmination of a process of adaptation and assimilation of Indian Buddhist theology to the indigenous Weltanschauung. See Yabuki, *Meisha yoin kaisetsu;* Mochizuki, *Seiritsushi ron;* and Makita, *Gikyō kenkyū* (Kyoto: Jimbun kagaku kenkyūsho, 1976).

12. Due to the extensive citation of this work, we have today most, if not all, of the material that comprised Tao-an's catalogue. There have been attempts to reconstruct this catalogue on the basis of the material preserved in the *Ch'u-san-tsang chi-chi.* See Tokiwa Daijō, *Kō Han yori Sō Sei ni itaru yakkyō sōroku* (1938; rpt. Tokyo: Kokusho kankōkai, 1973), 160–181; Hayashiya, *Kyōroku kenkyū,* pp. 383–426.

13. *Ch'u-san-tsang chi-chi* 5, *T* 2145.55.40a. Note that in our text the date of the catalogue is given as the second year of K'ang-ning. However, there was no such reign period during the lifetime of Tao-an. It has been concluded, based on the chronology of Tao-an's activities, that this was a scribal error for Ning-k'ang, which then gives the date of 374. For a detailed discussion on this problem, see Hayashiya, *Kyōroku kenkyū,* pp. 355–356. See also Ui Hakuju, *Shaku Dōan kenkyū* (Tokyo: Iwanami shoten, 1956; rpt. 1979), 19–21.

14. Hou Chi was a master of farming during the reign of Emperor Yao and became Minister of Agriculture under Emperor Shun. See *Shih-chi* 4, *Erh-shih-ssu shih,* Po-na pen ed., 1.71a. Pien Ho was a man of Ch'u who attempted to present a piece of jade to two successive kings; each time he was accused of lying and had his legs amputated as punishment. The legend first appeared in the *Han-fei tzu.* See W. K. Liao, trans., *The Complete Works of Han Fei Tzu,* vol. 1 (London: Probsthain, 1939; rpt. 1959), 13. See also *I-wen lei-chü* 83 (Peking: Chung-hua shu-chü, 1965), 1428.

15. The Ching and Wei rivers flow separately because their waters are murky and clear, respectively. See *Po-shih liu-t'ieh shih-lei chi,* vol. 2 (T'ai-pei: Hsin-

hsing shu-chü, 1969), 104. In a Buddhist context, dragons and snakes are similes for sages and ordinary men, respectively. See *Pi-yen lu* 7, *T* 2003.48.193a25–b1.

16. *Ch'u-san-tsang chi-chi* 5, *T* 2145.55.38b8–16.

17. For Tao-an's works, see Ui, *Shaku Dōan kenkyū,* pp. 52ff. Tao-an's expertise in matters of translation can be gleaned from his "Five Adaptations and Three Unchangeables" *(Wu-shih-pen san-pu-i),* certainly the most important translation theory in the history of Chinese Buddhism. See Ochō Enichi, *Chūgoku bukkyō no kenkyū,* vol. 1 (Kyoto: Hōzōkan, 1958), 236–255; Kenneth Ch'en, *Buddhism in China: A Historical Survey* (Princeton: Princeton University Press, 1964), 370–371.

18. Tao-an himself described the missing identity of scriptures before his time: "From the Han and the Wei up to the Chin, rather a lot of scriptures were introduced, but the names of the persons who transmitted these scriptures are missing. Later people sought out [such information], but there is no way to estimate their dates [of translation]" (*Kao-seng chuan* 5, *T* 2059.50.352a23–27).

19. Commenting on his predecessor's work, Seng-yu says that Tao-an made a comprehensive collection of scriptures and, upon scrutinizing it, both provided missing dates and translators' names and distinguished the genuine from the spurious; it is owing to his efforts that there was some basis for identifying numerous scriptures (*Ch'u-san-tsang chi-chi* 1, *T* 2145.55.1a–b; 15, 108a). Tao-hsüan, the compiler of the *Ta T'ang nei-tien lu,* says, "I have examined over thirty extant and nonextant [catalogues, and found that] all follow the record of An in assessing and determining translators and dates [of scriptures]" (*ch.* 10, *T* 2149.55.336a21–22). Chih-sheng, the compiler of the *K'ai-yüan shih-chaio lu,* repeats Seng-yu and adds, "Numerous records of later date [took Tao-an's record] as their source and expanded upon it. . . . [His catalogue] serves as a model for later generations" (*ch.* 10, *T* 2154.55.573a5–6). See also the *Chung-ching mu-lu* (*ch.* 7, *T* 2146.55.148c) by Fa-ching et al., for a similar appraisal.

20. Variant datings are given for the *Ch'u-san-tsang chi-chi.* Based on internal evidence, Naitō Ryūo suggests that the work was revised several times, the last version including material dating from the fourteenth year of the T'ien-chien era of the Liang dynasty (515 C.E.). See his "*Shutsu san-zō kishū* no senshū nenji ni tsuite," *Indogaku bukkyōgaku kenkyū* (hereafter *IBK*) 7.1 (1958): 162–163; idem, "Sōyū no chosaku katsudō," *IBK* 20.1 (1971): 284–285.

21. Naitō Ryūo identified conclusively that a Tun-huang manuscript, Pelliot 3747, is a portion of the *Chung-ching pieh-lu,* which predates the *Ch'u-san-tsang chi-chi.* See his "Tonkō zanketsubon *Shūkyō betsuroku* ni tsuite," *IBK* 15.2 (1967): 268–270. On this fragment, see also P'an Chung-kuei, "Tun-huang hsieh-pen *Chung-ching pieh-lu* chih fa-hsien," *Tun-huang-hsüeh* 4 (1979): 69–88; Okabe Kazuo, "Yakkyō to shakyō," *Tōyō gakujutsu kenkyū* 22:2 (1983): 16–18.

22. On the textual corruptions in this catalogue, see Okabe Kazuo, "Shitsuyaku zakkyōroku kenkyū no kaidai," *IBK* 21.2 (1973): 67–71. In later catalogues, these misplaced titles are reclassified in the section on indigenous scriptures.

23. *Ch'u-san-tsang chi-chi* 5, *T* 2145.55.38c. Seng-yu's synopses of the *Dīrghāgama* and *Nirvāṇa-sūtra* accounts derive from the following passages in those works: *Yu-hsing ching* (*Ch'ang A-han ching* no. 2), *T* 1.1.17c–18a; *Ta-pan-nieh-p'an ching* 9, *T* 374.12.421c–422a.

24. *Ch'u-san-tsang chi-chi* 5, *T* 2145.55.38c–39a.

25. On translation procedures, see Tsao Jen-p'ang, "Lun chung-kuo fo-chiao i-ch'ang chih i-ching fang-shih yü ch'eng-hsü," *Hsin-Ya hsüeh-pao* 5:2 (1963): 239–321; Ōchō Enichi, "Yakkyōshi kō," in his *Chūgoku bukkyō no kenkyū,* vol. 3 (Kyoto: Hōzōkan, 1979), 165–206.

26. For the canonical and indigenous sources for Yüeh-kuang t'ung-tzu, as well as the impact of this lore on religious uprisings, see Tsukamoto Zenryū, "Hokugi no bukkyōhi," *Tsukamoto Zenryū chosakushū,* vol. 2 (Tokyo: Daitō shuppan, 1974), 175–179; Sunayama Minoru, "Gekkō dōji Ryō Keiki no hanran to *Shurabikukyō,*" *Tōhō gaku* 51 (1976): 55–71; Erik Zürcher, "Prince Moonlight: Messianism and Eschatology in Early Medieval Chinese Buddhism," *T'oung-pao* 68 (1982): 1–59. For the identification of the *chia-shen* year as of Taoist origin, see ibid., pp. 21–22.

27. *Ch'u-san-tsang chi-chi* 5, *T* 2145.55.39a.

28. See note 18.

29. Hayashiya, *Kyōroku kenkyū,* p. 63.

30. The *Pi-ch'iu ying-kung fa-hsing ching* and *Chü-shih ch'ing-seng fu-t'ien ching,* for example, are attributed in the manuscripts to Kumārajīva and Dharmakṣema, respectively, but these attributions cannot be confirmed in other sources. Seng-yu consequently categorizes them as suspect scriptures. See *Ch'u-san-tsang chi-chi* 5, *T* 2145.55.39a.

31. Ibid., 39a–40c.

32. Ibid., 40b.

33. Ibid., 40b–c.

34. The other three *pārājikas* were homicide, grand theft, and sexual intercourse. These offenses were also included among the most serious transgressions proscribed in the T'ang "Regulations for the Clergy" *(Tao-seng ko),* some of which are presumed to go back as far as the Northern Wei period. Offenders were disrobed and subjected to appropriate punishments according to secular law. For reconstructed passages of this lost document, as well as discussion of its history and implementation, see Akizuki Kan'ei, "Dōsōkaku no fukkyū ni tsuite," *Rekishi* 4 (1952): 55–61; Moroto Tatsuo, "Hokugi no sōsei to dōsōkaku," *Akidai shigaku* 20 (1973): 1–17; idem, "Dōsōkaku to sono sekō ni tsuite," *Shūkan Tōyōgaku* 31 (1974): 68–94.

35. For the identification of Miao-kuang with Seng-kuang, one of the ten Buddhist rebels named by Fu I, see Sunayama Minoru, "Kōsa yōsō kō," *Tōhō shūkyō* 46 (1975): 45. See also Michel Strickmann's discussion on Miao-kuang in his chapter in this volume. For discussion of secular authorities' sensitivity toward demagoguery, see Moroto, "Hokugi no sōsei to Tō no dōsōkaku," pp. 12–16; idem, "Tō ōchō no sōgyō to toshin," in Akizuki Kan'ei, ed., *Dōkyō to shūkyō bunka* (Tokyo: Hirakawa shuppansha, 1987), 190–208. Demagoguery, or incitation of the masses through false claims, was not only one of the most hideous offenses listed in the "Regulations for the Clergy," but was also proscribed in the T'ang secular statutes.

36. *Ch'u-san-tsang chi-chi* 5, *T* 2145.55.37c.

37. Ibid., 37b–38b; ibid. 4, 21c–37b. For a list of over 450 *ch'ao-ching* found in the section of anonymous translations, see also Ono Genmyō, ed., *Bussho kaisetsu daijiten,* special vol., pp. 303–307.

38. Two of the five *ch'ao-ching* listed in the spurious section (viz., the *Ch'ao*

wei-fa she-shen ching and *Fa-yüan ching*) are also cross-listed among the forty-six *ch'ao-ching*. Their distinguishing feature was a topical organization of material gathered from multiple sources. In this feature, they might have served as the forerunners of Buddhist encyclopedias were it not for their neglect of citing the sources for their material. Although Okabe has attributed the double registration to the cataloguers' confusing of the two categories, it may also be due to changes introduced during different stages in the cataloguers' revisions. See Okabe Kazuo, "Sōyū no gigikyōkan to shōkyōkan," *Komazawa daigaku bukkyō gakubu ronshū* 2 (1971): 70. For discussion of the stages in the compilation of this catalogue, see Naitō Ryūo, "*Shutsu sanzō kishū* no senji nenji ni tsuite." For the affinities between *ch'ao-ching* and Buddhist encyclopedias, see Ōuchi Fumio, "Ryōdai bukkyō reijusho to *Kyōritsu isō*," *Tōhō shūkyō* 50 (1977): 55–82; Tachi Hiroyuki, "*Kyōritsu isō* o chūshin to shite mita Ryōdai bukkyō reisho no hensan jijō," *Bukkyōdaigaku daigakuin kenkyūkiyō* 10 (1982): 63–87, esp. 72–77.

39. For the background to early *p'an-chiao* systems, see Ōchō Enichi, *Chūgoku bukkyō no kenkyū,* vol. 2 (Kyoto: Hōzōkan, 1971; rpt. 1980), 145–161. Ōchō points out that the production of scriptural synopses throughout the fourth century reflects a heightened awareness of scriptural diversity. Systematic explanations of that diversity were not available, however, until Kumārajīva translated the *Ta chih-tu lun*. There is no reason to believe, however, that such need did not exist beyond the fourth century.

40. Okabe, "Shitsuyaku zakkyōroku no kenkyū," *IBK* 21.2 (1973): 69.

41. Okabe suggests that two works of Seng-yu, the *Shih-chia p'u* (*T* 2040) and the *Shih-chieh chi* (nonextant), both of which consisted solely of scriptural excerpts, were intended for Buddhist proselytization. They sought, however, to eliminate the abuses associated with *ch'ao-ching* by adding copious citations to sources. See Okabe's "Sōyū no gigikyōkan to shōkyōkan," pp. 71–72.

42. "It has been some five hundred years since the great dharma spread to the East. During this period, there were vicissitudes in the fate of the Buddhist teaching. Those with right view have praised [the dispensation], while the perverted and confused have criticized it. Vicious Confucians cling to style brand [Buddhism] as a heterodox doctrine; facile-tongued Taoists regard Buddhism as identical to their own teachings. . . . Thus, perverse arguments become more and more multifarious and false statements are thriving. . . . [Confucians and Taoists] dim the brilliance [of Buddhism] with the darkness [of their accusations], and falsely indict the greatness [of Buddhism] out of their pettiness. Although [such accusations] would not affect [the Buddhist dispensation] by even a hair's breadth, they tint the eyes and ears [of the people]; they would cause feeble-minded people to follow false words and be long deluded by them. . . . [I,] Yu, though of trivial learning, deeply aspire to disseminate and protect the calming words [of the Buddha]. These superfluous vulgarites exasperate my mind" (*Hung-ming chi* 1, *T* 2102.52.1a8–18).

43. Note that the number of indigenous scriptures in any given catalogue is cumulative, in that later cataloguers incorporate material from their predecessors. This is true not only of indigenous scriptures, but also of all other types of texts.

44. *Chung-ching mu-lu* 2, *T* 2146.55. 126b–127c; 138a–139a; 140a; 140c–141a; 142a;

143c–144a. For easier reference, see the special volume of the *Bussho kaisetsu daijiten,* pp. 451–453, in which all the entries are collected in one list.

45. *Ch'u-san-tsang chih-chi* 5, *T* 2145.55.38c & 40b.

46. *Chung-ching mu-lu* 2, *T* 2146.55.126c1–2; ibid. 4, 138b9–10.

47. Ibid. 2, 127c. The same comment is repeated elsewhere for another group of spurious scriptures; see ibid. *ch.* 4, 139a.

48. Ibid., 126c; 127a. The entries on the texts of Maitreya's advent actually make no reference to the immediacy of the event; we can infer this, however, from the annotations in *K'ai-yüan shih-chiao lu;* see *ch.* 18, *T* 2154.55.672c.

49. In the year preceding the compilation of this catalogue, people were forbidden to possess *ch'en-wei* material by Wen-ti's decree (*Pei-shih* 11, Po-na ed., p. 13038a–b). Yang-ti, the son of Wen-ti, even went so far as to dispatch envoys throughout the empire in search of books connected with *ch'en-wei* and had them all burned (*Sui-shu* 32, Po-na ed., p. 11594a). For the accounts of the dynastic persecution of these materials, see Yasui Kōzan and Nakamura Shōhachi, *Isho no kisoteki kenkyū* (Tokyo: Kangi bunka kenkyūsho, 1966), 260–264; Taira Hidemichi, "Sen'i shisō to bukkyō kyōten," *Ryūkoku daigaku ronshū* 347 (1954): 123–141.

50. See the references in note 34.

51. *Chung-ching mu-lu* 7, *T* 2146.55.148c–149c.

52. For discussion of Chih-i's *p'an-chiao* system, as well as those of his predecessors, see Leon Hurvitz, *Chih-I (538–597): An Introduction to the Life and Ideas of a Chinese Buddhist Monk* (Brussels: Institut Belge des Hautes Études Chinoises, 1962), 214–230.

53. In 590, shortly after the Sui unification of China, Wen-ti wrote in a letter to the renowned T'ien-t'ai master, Chih-i (538–597): "Formerly, when Emperor Wu of the Chou dynasty was destroying Buddhism, I, the Emperor, resolved to protect and maintain the Law. As soon as I received the Decree of Heaven, Buddhism was reestablished. As you, the Master, have freed yourself from worldly entanglements, disciplining yourself and saving others, I wish that you would lead and encourage the monks in order to expand the Great Religion" (*Fo-tsu t'ung-chi* 39, *T* 2035.49.360a15–17; Jan Yün-hua, trans., *A Chronicle of Buddhism in China: 581–960 A.D.* [Santiniketan: Visva-Bharati, 1966], 13). Wen-ti's pro-Buddhist policies included restoration and new construction of monasteries, temples, images, and stūpas, as well as the establishment of new institutions to edify monks: the Assembly of Twenty-five (Erh-shih-wu chung) and the Assembly of Five (Wu-chung). For more detailed discussion on Wen-ti's policy of protection and promotion of Buddhism, see Yamasaki Hiroshi, *Chūsei shina bukkyō no tenkai* (Tokyo: Shimizu shoten, 1942; rpt. 1947), 274–354.

54. See Fei's discussion in *Li-tai san-pao chi* 9, *T* 2034.49.85b and 97b–c.

55. Ibid. 12, 106c. For the *Chan-ch'a ching,* see Whalen Lai's chapter in this volume.

56. Ibid. 11, 96b–c. Note in this connection that those *ch'ao-ching* that were redesignated as *pieh-sheng* in the *Chung-ching mu-lu* are now dispersed throughout the catalogue without notation, thereby obscuring their distinction from the full translations. Note also that Fei included four of the six *ch'ao-ching* that were classified as spurious in the *Ch'u-san-tsang chi-chi* (but that were not registered in the

Chung-ching mu-lu), together with the critical comments of Seng-yu. See ibid., 96a, 98a.

57. Two T'ang cataloguers, Tao-hsüan and Chih-sheng, had explicit criticism of the ascriptions in the *ju-tsang mu* section. See *Ta T'ang nei-tien lu* 5, *T* 2149.55.279c; *K'ai-yüan shih-chiao lu* 10, *T* 2154.55.576c. Modern scholars have recognized that this catalogue serves as a precious repository of pre-Sui sources and have acknowledged its importance to the development of the catalogue genre through its new format of combining chronological and topical listings. At the same time, however, they have tried to address the problems surrounding the credibility of its scriptural attributions. For discussion of the merits and demerits of the *Li-tai san-pao chi,* see Hayashiya, "Zuidai kyōroku ni kansuru kenkyū," pp. 274–302; idem, *Kyōroku kenkyū,* pp. 83–85, 149–152; idem, *Iyakukyōrui no kenkyū,* Tōyō Bunko Publication Series A, vol. 30 (1945): 22–28, 43–46. See also Ui Hakuju, *Yakkyōshi kenkyū* (Tokyo: Iwanami shoten, 1971), 437–453. Ui examines thirty-four texts ascribed to An Shih-kao and concludes that they all are falsely ascribed; he believes that Fei Ch'ang-fang is responsible for thirty-two of those ascriptions. For a refutation of the criticisms, see Tokiwa, *Yakkyō sōroku,* pp. 41–73.

58. Fei's catalogue lists six extant and twenty-four nonextant catalogues (*Li-tai san-pao chi* 15, *T* 2034.49.125b–27c). Tokiwa asserts that Fei's numerous references to lost catalogues were drawn from then-extant works, most frequently from the *Liang-shih chung-ching mu-lu* by Pao-ch'ang (fl. fifth-sixth centuries). Except for the *Ch'u-san-tsang chi-chi* and the *Chung-ching mu-lu,* however, none of these catalogues are extant. See Tokiwa's *Yakkyō sōroku,* pp. 70–71.

59. Ōuchi Fumio, "*Rekidai sanbōki* no ichi kenkyū," *Bukkyō shigaku kenkyū* 25:2 (1983): 2–13. Fei served as the *pi-shou,* or "wielder of the brush," under two Indian masters, Narendrayaśas (490–589) and *Jñānagupta (523–600), during the K'ai-huang era (581–600). See *Li-tai san-pao chi* 12, *T* 2034.49.102c–104a.

60. Hayashiya speculates that both the *Chung-ching mu-lu* and *Li-tai san-pao chi* drew from the same set of five catalogues compiled during the Nan-pei ch'ao period (*Kyōroku kenkyū,* p. 83). We have no details on this point, however, for the volume in which Hayashiya was to present the full argument has never been published.

61. Hayashiya, "Zuidai kyōroku," pp. 82–84, 300–302.

62. *Li-tai san-pao chi* 11, *T* 2034.49.96c–97b.

63. Hayashiya, "Zuidai kyōroku," pp. 280–282. According to Hayashiya, the discrepancy stems from the fact that the topical section was based on the *Chung-ching mu-lu* and was not correlated to his own chronological section.

64. Hayashiya, *Kyōroku kenkyū,* pp. 38–39, 151.

65. *Hsü Kao-seng chuan* 23, *T* 2060.50.625a; 628b.

66. *T'ang hu-fa sha-men Fa-lin pieh-chuan* 2, *T* 2051.50.209c.

67. *Pien-cheng lun* 8, *T* 2110.52.544c.

68. Erik Zürcher, "Buddhist Influence on Early Taoism," *T'oung-pao* 66 (1980): 84–147. See also the chapter by Stephen R. Bokenkamp in this volume, and his "Sources of the *Ling-Pao* Scriptures," in Michel Strickmann, ed., *Tantric and Taoist Studies in Honour of R. A. Stein* (Brussels: Institut Belge des Hautes Études Chinoises, 1983), 434–486. The extent of Buddhist influence on Taoist texts can also be ascertained from a comprehensive collection of Taoist texts

influenced by Buddhist scriptures, compiled by Kamata Shigeo: *Dōzōnai bukkyō shisō shiryō shūsei* (Tokyo: Tokyo daigaku Tōyōbunka kenkyūsho, 1986).

69. *Hsü Kao-seng chuan* 3, *T* 2060.50.436b; *Li-tai san-pao chi* 15, *T* 2034.49.121a. See also Ōuchi Fumio, "*Rekidai sanbōki* no ichi kenkyū," pp. 2–4.

70. On the problems with the first catalogue, and the features of the second, see Hayashiya, *Kyōroku kenkyū,* pp. 77–82.

71. *Chung-ching mu-lu* 4, *T* 2147.55.172b–175a.

72. Ibid., preface, 150b. That copying scriptures was essential to their preservation and circulation is evident, for example, in the colophons of copied manuscripts, some of which specifically state that such activity was intended to ensure the circulation of the scripture. For examples, see Lionel Giles, *Descriptive Catalogue of the Chinese Manuscripts from Tunhuang in the British Museum* (London: British Museum, 1957).

73. Ibid. 6, *T* 2146.55.144a–148b; ibid. 2, *T* 2147.55.161b–c. Noted by Okabe, "Kyōroku ni okeru kenjō shūden no chii," p. 45. Okabe asserts (p. 42) that the initial *Chung-ching mu-lu* was the first catalogue to accord canonical status to the compositions of Chinese authors.

74. *Ta T'ang nei-tien lu* 10, *T* 2149.55.333c–336a.

75. For discussion of Tao-hsüan's use of the *Li-tai san-pao chi,* see Hayashiya, *Kyōroku kenkyū,* pp. 90–94.

76. *Ta T'ang nei-tien lu* 5, *T* 2149.55.279c.

77. The title *T'i-wei Po-li ching* bears the names of two merchants, Trapuṣa and Bhallika, who made an offering of nutriment to the Buddha after his enlightenment; the legend appears in *Jātaka* literature as well as in the *Vinaya.* This indigenous sūtra was first recorded in the *Ch'u-san-tsang chi-chi* (*T* 2145.55.39a); it is preserved in the Tun-huang manuscripts: Pelliot 3732, Stein 2051, and Peking *shuang* 15. *Fa-chü ching* is the title of a translation (*T* 210); its indigenous counterpart is not known to have existed before its reference in the *Nei-tien lu* (*T* 2149.55.335c). The Tun-huang manuscripts of this text and its commentary are reprinted in the *Taishō* canon, vol. 85, *T* 2901 and 2902.

78. *Ta T'ang nei-tien lu* 10, *T* 2149.55.333c18–26.

79. For discussion on the Chinese acceptance of, and attitudes toward, the concepts of *san-shih* and *mo-fa,* see Takao Giken, "Mappō shisō to shoka no taido," *Shina bukkyōshi gaku* 1:1 (1937): 1–20, and 1:3 (1937): 47–70; Yūki Reimon, "Shina bukkyō ni okeru mappō shisō no kōki," *Tōhō gakuhō* (Tokyo) 6 (1937): 205–215. For their Indian antecedents, see Étienne Lamotte, *Histoire du Bouddhisme indien des origines à l'ère Saka* (Louvain: Publications Universitaires, 1958), 210–222. It is ironic that some indigenous scriptures, including those advocating the advent of such saviors as Yüeh-kuang t'ung-tzu and Maitreya, are geared to these Chinese eschatological concerns. On this, see also Michel Strickmann's chapter in this volume.

80. *Ta T'ang nei-tien lu,* preface, *T* 2149.55.219b10.

81. The explicitly non-élite orientation of such texts is reflected in the designations "scriptures for the people" *(shomin kyōten)* or "scriptures for the masses" *(minshū kyōten),* which are used by Japanese scholars with reference to some indigenous scriptures. See Tsukamoto Zenryū, "Chūgoku no zaike bukkyō tokuni shomin bukkyō no ichikyōten," *Tsukamoto Zenryū chosakushū* 2:187–240; Makita Tairyō, "Hokugi no shomin kyōten," in *Gikyō kenkyū,* pp. 125–147;

Ishida Mizumaro, *Minshū kyōten,* Bukkyō kyōtensen series 12 (Tokyo: Chikuma shobō, 1986). For discussion of Taoist and popular beliefs in indigenous scriptures, see Mochizuki, *Daijō kyōten seiritsushi ron,* pp. 393–424.

82. *Ta T'ang nei-tien lu* 10, *T* 2149.55.336a16–17.

83. "Formerly, during the K'ai-huang era (581–600), the founder of the Sui compiled a scriptural catalogue that examined the spurious and the extravagant. [Such scriptures] amounted to five-hundred *chüan.* All of them have already been incinerated" (*Ta T'ang nei-tien lu* 10, *T* 2149.55.333c26–27). Tao-hsüan's commentary to the *Ssu-fen lü* also relates the same event (*Ssu-fen-lü shan-fan pu-ch'üeh hsing-shih ch'ao* 1, *T* 1804.40.3c). So far, I have not been able to confirm this incident in secular sources. However, such an incident may have been part of Wen-ti's proscription of *ch'en-wei* material, which we mentioned earlier (see note 49), because indigenous scriptures did contain elements of prophecy *(ch'en),* as was noted by the first *Chung-ching mu-lu* (*ch.* 4, *T* 2146.55.139a).

84. *Ta Chou k'an-ting chung-ching mu-lu* 15, *T* 2153.55.474c.

85. Ibid., 472a–475a.

86. According to Ono's comprehensive listing of indigenous scriptures, which traces the status of each text in all catalogues except the *Li-tai san-pao chi,* 119 scriptures that were assessed as doubtful or spurious in earlier catalogues were not registered as such in the *Ta Chou k'an-ting chung-ching mu-lu.* Of these 119, fifty-four texts were changed to translations (by known or anonymous translators), and fifty of those ascriptions were based on Fei's data. Especially revealing in terms of the influence of Fei's catalogue are eight texts that were unanimously listed as spurious in all previous catalogues, but that the *Li-tai san-pao chi* reclassifies as authentic.

87. *K'ai-yüan shih-chiao lu* 10, *T* 2154.55.579a.

88. This mural was designed to commemorate the achievements of the T'ang Trepiṭaka Hsüan-tsang (d. 664). It depicted the history of Buddhist translation activities in China from the Han period up through the T'ang by painting the famous translators, culminating in Hsüan-tsang. See Hayashiya, *Kyōroku kenkyū,* pp. 88–90. That the mural was based on the *Li-tai san-pao chi* is noted by Chih-sheng in his catalogue, *K'ai-yüan shih-chiao lu* 10, *T* 2154.55.578c. The construction of Ta-tz'u-en ssu and a translation-hall in its compound is recorded in Hsüan-tsang's biography, *Ta T'ang ku san-tsang Hsüan-tsang fa-shih hsing-chuang,* *T* 2052.50.218a–b.

89. Hayashiya, *Kyōroku kenkyū,* pp. 94–100.

90. Antonino Forte, *Political Propaganda and Ideology in China at the End of the Seventh Century* (Naples: Istituto Universitario Orientale, 1976), 125–145.

91. *Ta Chou k'an-ting chung-ching mu-lu* 1, *T* 2153.55.372c.

92. The five names are Teh-kan, Hui-yen, Chih-lien, Shen-ying, and Yüan-ts'e. See Forte, *Political Propaganda,* pp. 73, 172–174; *Ta Chou k'an-ting chung-ching mu-lu* 15, *T* 2153.55.475c–476a.

93. For a detailed discussion on the history and teaching of the San-chieh chiao, see Yabuki Keiki, *Sangaikyō no kenkyū* (Tokyo: Iwanami shoten, 1927; rpt. 1973). See also the chapters by Lewis and Forte in this volume.

94. *Ta T'ang nei-tien lu* 10, *T* 2149.55.332a.

95. *Ta Chou k'an-ting chung-ching mu-lu* 15, *T* 2153.55.475a9–15. Note that the comment cited mentions an edict issued in 699, which is four years later than

the date of the catalogue. The listing of San-chieh chiao texts was probably a later addition to the catalogue.

96. See the reference in note 90. For the effect of secular policy on the San-chieh chiao, see also the chapters by Forte and Lewis in this volume.

97. *Fo-tsu t'ung-chi,* in the entry for K'ai-yüan era, year 18 (730), reads: "The śramaṇa Chih-sheng of Sung-fu ssu in the Western Capital presented the *K'ai-yüan shih-chiao lu* in twenty *chüan,* which he compiled. The 5,048 *chüan* [that the catalogue contained] became the established number [for the canon]. By imperial order, it was entered into the canon" (*ch.* 40, *T* 2035.49.374c3–5). The *Hsü cheng-yüan shih-chiao lu,* a catalogue compiled in 945, reads: "*K'ai-yüan shih-chiao lu* circulated widely throughout the world, and continued to do so during the four courts of Hsüan-tsung, Su-tsung, Tai-tsung, and Teh-tsung" (*T* 2158.55.1048a23–26).

98. Scholars have identified three lineages among xylographic canons in East Asia: (1) the K'ai-pao (the earliest printed canon), Chin, Hsi-hsia, and two Korean editions; (2) southern editions; and (3) the Khitan edition. (The second Korean edition is actually based on both the K'ai-pao and Khitan editions.) According to a comparative study of the *Prajñāpāramitā* section of the canon by Chikusha Masaaki, the organization of these canons was based on either the *K'ai-yüan lu* or its derivative, the *K'ai-yüan shih-chiao lu lüeh-ch'u.* The wide dissemination of this catalogue can be also gleaned from the Tun-huang manuscripts, which include a copy of the catalogue itself as well as copies of scriptures the fascicle numbers of that conform to those found in the *K'ai-yüan lu.* On the three lineages of Buddhist canons and the role of the catalogue in creating a standard order for Buddhist canons, including the Khitan, see Chikusha, "Kittan daizōkyō shōkō," in *Uchida Ginpū hakushi sōju kinen Tōyōshi ronshū* (Kyoto: Dōbōsha, 1978), 311–329. For the different editions of the Buddhist canon, see also Paul Demiéville, "Sur les éditions imprimées du canon chinois," *Bulletin de l'École Française d'Extrême-Orient* 24 (1924): 181–218; Daizōkai ed., *Daizōkyō: seiritsu to hatten* (Kyoto: Hyakkaen, 1964).

99. For Chih-sheng's criticism of the *Li-tai san-pao chi,* see *K'ai-yüan shih-chiao lu* 10, *T* 2154.55.576c. Chih-sheng's attempts to eliminate Fei's ascriptions are apparent from the fact that twelve of the suspicious scriptures and nine of the spurious texts in his catalogue were formerly listed as authentic translations in the *Li-tai san-pao chi* and *Ta Chou lu.* However, there are several cases in which the arbitrary revisions of those catalogues are retained; these are usually noted by the statement, "translation [confirmed] by extant source," the "extant source" turning out to be none other than the *Li-tai san-pao chi;* there is no indication that Chih-sheng had any firsthand confirmation himself.

100. Hayashiya, *Kyōroku kenkyū,* pp. 100–110.

101. The *Sung kao-seng chuan* praises the *K'ai-yüan shih-chiao lu* as follows: "Chih-sheng . . . in the eighteenth year of K'ai-yüan, compiled the *K'ai-yüan shih-chiao lu* in twenty *chüan.* What is most significant [about this catalogue]? When dealing with texts that were variant translations of a single original or old items that bore new titles, other cataloguers [lit., "masters"] were confused by their style and mixed up the genuine and the false; [as a consequence,] some treated one scripture as two separate original texts, while others treated an abridged version *(chih-p'in)* as an independent translation. [But Chih-sheng]

evaluated each of them without making the slightest mistake. . . . It can be said that his excellent appraisal shut off the source of the perverse and spurious, and only here [in this catalogue is the true identity of texts] ascertained. . . . As far as the register of scriptural teachings *(ching-fa chih p'u)* is concerned, there is no one who surpasses Sheng" (*T* 2061.50.733c–734a).

102. In his study of indigenous scriptures, Mochizuki provides a composite listing of anomalous scriptures *(i-ching)* and indigenous scriptures taken from Chinese Buddhist catalogues, records of scriptures copied during the Nara period in Japan, and texts preserved in Japan or in the Tun-huang repository but never recorded. Of the total of 385 titles, eighty-four (22 percent) are listed as extant. See his *Bukkyō kyōten seritsushi ron,* pp. 315–339.

103. *K'ai-yüan shih-chiao lu* 18, *T* 2154.55.671b–680a.

104. Ibid., 671b17–21.

105. Ibid., 671c.

106. Ibid., 671c8–11.

107. "It is proper for you, Kālāmas, to doubt, to be uncertain. . . . Do not go upon what has been acquired by repeated hearing; nor upon tradition . . . nor upon what is in scriptures," *Aṅguttara-nikāya* I.189; translation from the *Kālāma Sutta: The Buddha's Charter of Free Inquiry,* Soma Thera, trans., The Wheel Publication series, no. 8 (Kandy: Buddhist Publication Society, 1963), 6. See also discussion in K. N. Jayatilleke, *Early Buddhist Theory of Knowledge* (London: George Allen & Unwin Ltd., 1963), chap. 4, "The Attitude to Authority," and chap. 8, "Authority and Reason within Buddhism."

108. Mt. K'un, better known as Mt. K'un-lun, was famous for its excellent jade as recorded in *Lü-shih ch'un-ch'iu, Huai-nan tzu,* and others; see *I-wen lei-chü* 83 (Peking: Chung-hua shu-chü, 1965), 1427–1428. The Shan-pu (Bureau of Provisions) as it appears in our citation cannot be found in the *Li-tai chih-kuan piao* (Tables of Official Posts from the Earliest Times to the Nineteenth Century); the rendering, therefore, is based on the homophonous graph. The office was one of the bureaus under the Minister of Rites during the T'ang. See Robert Des Rotours, *Traité des fonctionnaires et traité de l'armée* (Leiden: E. J. Brill, 1947), 91–92.

109. *K'ai-yüan shih-chiao lu* 18, *T* 2154.55.672a9–15. The simile of the Ching and Wei river also appeared in Tao-an's characterization of indigenous scriptures. See note 15.

110. Ibid., 674c–675a. For the origin and background of the legend of the scripture, see Makita, *Gikyō kenkyū,* pp. 272–289.

111. *K'ai-yüan shih-chiao lu* 18, *T* 2154.55.672b–c.

112. Ibid., 672b.

113. Ibid., 672a–b.

114. Ibid., 672c22–26.

115. For discussion of canonical scriptures on Maitreya and their doctrine, see Matsumoto Bunzaburō, *Miroku jōdoron* (1907; rpt. Tokyo: Heigo shuppansha, 1918).

116. Some of the religious uprisings that date from the Northern Wei period share the same ideological basis—the advent of a future buddha—and are thus considered to be the forerunners of later rebellions involving Maitreya. See Tsukamoto, "Hokugi no bukkyōhi." For discussion on religious uprisings dur-

ing the Sui period that were based on Maitreya cults, see Kegasawa Yasunori, "Zui matsu Mirokyō no ran o meguru ichi kōsatsu" *Bukkyō shigaku kenkyū* 23:1 (1981): 15–32. Similar movements during the T'ang and Sung periods are discussed in Shigematsu Shunshō, "Tō Sō jidai no Miroku kyōhi," *Shien* 3 (1931): 68–103.

117. This decree is first recorded in the *Li-tai san-pao chi,* in annotation to the discussion on San-chieh chiao texts (*T* 2034.49.105c). Since that catalogue is dated to 597, this note must be a later addition.

118. *K'ai-yüan shih-chiao lu* 18, *T* 2154.55.679a3–19.

119. Ibid., 680a17–20.

GLOSSARY

An Shih-kao 安世高
ch'ang-chai 長齋
ch'ao-ching 抄經
Ch'ao wei-fa she-shen ching 抄為法捨身經
ch'en-wei 讖緯
cheng-fa 正法
Ch'i-lüeh 七略
chia-shen 甲申
Chih Ch'en 支讖
Chih Ch'ien 支謙
chih-p'in 支品
Chih-sheng 智昇
ching 經
ching-fa chih p'u 經法之譜
ching-lu 經錄
ching-tsang 經藏
Chiu-sheng Kuan-shih-yin ching 救生觀世音經
Ch'u san-tsang chi-chi 出三藏集記
Chü-shih ch'ing-seng fu-t'ien ching 居士請僧福田經
chüan 卷
Chung-ching mu-lu 衆經目錄
Erh-shih-wu chung 二十五衆
Fa-ching 法經
Fa-chü ching 法句經
Fa-hsien 法顯
Fa-hsien chuan ching 法顯傳經
Fa-lin 法琳
fa-pao 法寶
fa-shih 法師
Fa-yüan ching 法苑經
fan-hsing 梵行
fei fo-ching 非佛經
Fo-ming ching 佛名經
Fo-po ching 佛鉢經
fo-shuo 佛說
Fu I 傅奕
fu-lu 符籙
gigi kyōten 疑偽經典
gikyō 偽經
Hou Chi 后稷
hsiang-fa 像法
Hsin-hsing 信行
Hsü cheng-yüan shih-chiao lu 續貞元釋教錄
Hsüan-tsang 玄奘
hu-fa 護法
i-ching 疑經
i-ching 異經
i-huo 疑惑
i-wei 疑偽
i-wei ching-lun 疑偽經論
I-wen chih 藝文志
ju-tsang lu 入藏錄
ju-tsang mu 入藏目
K'ai-yüan shih-chiao lu 開元釋教錄
Kao-huan 高歡
Kao-wang Kuan-shih-yin ching 高王觀世音經
Liang-shih chung-ching mu-lu 梁世衆經目錄
Li-tai san-pao chi 歷代三寶紀
Liu Hsiang 劉向
Liu Hsin 劉歆
Miao-kuang 妙光
Ming-ch'üan 明佺
minshū kyōten 民衆經典

mo-fa 末法
Ni-tzu 尼子
p'an-chiao 判教
Pan-ku 班固
Pao-ch'ang 寶唱
Pi-ch'iu ying-kung fa-hsing ching 比丘應供法行經
pi-shou 筆受
Pieh-lu 別錄
pieh-sheng 別生
Pien-cheng lun 辯正論
Pien Ho 卞和
Sa-p'o-jo-t'o chüan-shu chuang-yen ching 薩婆若陀眷屬莊嚴經
San-chieh chiao 三階教
san-shih 三時
Seng-fa 僧法
Seng-kuang 僧光
Seng-yu 僧祐
Shan-pu 膳部
shao-yü 少欲
she-shen 捨身
shen-shou 神授
Shih-chia p'u 釋迦譜
Shih-chieh chi 世界記
shih-i ching 失譯經
Shih-li 師利
shomin kyōten 庶民經典
su-hsi 宿習
Sun Ching-teh 孫敬德
t'a ch'an-fa 塔懺法
Ta Chou k'an-ting chung-ching mu-Lu 大周刊定衆經目錄
Ta T'ang nei-tien lu 大唐內典錄
Ta-tz'u-en ssu 大慈恩寺
T'an-ti 曇諦
Tao-an 道安
Tao-hsüan 道宣
T'i-wei Po-li ching 提謂波利經
Tsung-li chung-ching mu-lu 綜理衆經目錄
wei-ching 偽經
wei-ching mu-lu 偽經目錄
Wu Chao 武曌
Wu-chung 五衆
wu-fang 五方
wu-hsing 五行
wu-shih-pen san-pu-i 五失本三不易
yao-ch'en 謠讖
Yao-hsing she-shen ching 要行捨身經
Yen-ts'ung 彥悰
yin-yang 陰陽
Yüeh-kuang 月光

The *Consecration Sūtra*: A Buddhist Book of Spells

Michel Strickmann

Introduction

It might be thought perverse to claim that Chinese Buddhism remains a largely unknown subject. The number of books and articles in Western languages is steadily growing and is more than matched by the output of Japanese scholars. Nevertheless, most Western approaches to Chinese Buddhist Studies have been skewed and fragmentary. They have focused all but exclusively on traditional historiographical concerns. This fixed program of studies began to emerge in the thirteenth century with the appearance of universal chronicles of Buddhism written by Chinese sectarian historians. Such works have been used as summary checklists of the supposedly important topics in early Chinese Buddhist history. Yet their approach to the voluminous documentary evidence is no less selective and parochial than that of modern Japanese secular scholars. The T'ien-t'ai school was the dominant lineage of the time, and its authors' chief objective was to substantiate its claims to orthodoxy. Such chronicles, packed with personalities, fraught with anecdote, reveal only a portion of medieval Chinese religious history. This is the aspect on which all such compendia dwell: the great translators and the orderly transmission of orthodox teaching from one renowned master to the next. There remain a host of questions, of broader social significance and more profound interest, concerning the actual practice of religion. Of this enormous subject the standard historical sources give only oblique and tantalizing glimpses.[1]

Buddhism's influence on Chinese civilization was so complex and ornate, its textual and artistic remains so extensive, that we may suppose large areas to be still relatively unexplored. Certain autochthonous culture traits, too, are still understudied. Properly investigated, these might clarify many aspects of the adaptation and development of Buddhism in China. Taoism, China's own higher religion, has until recently been given particularly short shrift. Similarly neglected has been the diffuse and inorganic "popular religion" of the mass of the Chinese people—investigation of which must proceed in tandem with the still underdeveloped study of Chinese local history. The Six Dynasties period (the fourth through sixth centuries C.E.)—years that might well be termed China's gnostic centuries—was the time when China's enduring religious traditions were formed. We have firsthand materials for a convincing reconstruction of medieval Chinese religious life. Chinese spiritual literature flourished at this time, and much is preserved. Yet one of the strangest riddles of Sinology is how so little could have been done in proportion to the great quantity of original documents that survive.[2]

We may rejoice, however, that certain of the stereotyped attitudes that have for so long relegated religious studies to the badlands of Sinology are finally breaking down in the face of new and highly original research. Significant inroads have been made on hidebound notions of Buddhism. Ethnological observation and analysis have provided a point of departure. Outstanding work in this direction has recently been achieved in the study of South and Southeast Asia; indeed, no one interested in the history of Asian religions can afford to neglect the various ethnographical studies that have begun to appear in happy profusion.[3] The interest of such works is that they compare the still-living practices of "higher" religions with long written traditions, and in addition to being ethnographically sophisticated, their authors are familiar with a complex scriptural and exegetical literature.

Heartened by such examples, I believe that results as exciting as those derived from last-minute soundings in the field can be obtained through delving into the older religious literature. No literary tradition of Asian Buddhism promises greater riches than that of China, where the early development of printing preserved vast quantities of religious documents, and where the discoveries made at Tun-huang have given us a hoard of manuscript treasures. We may proceed in the assurance that much of what we discover will necessarily be new, and may indeed topple cherished notions. An open-minded investigation of Chinese scriptural literature promises to unearth new social and literary information in every period.

In no age is this more pronounced than in the literature of the fifth century, the middle of the Six Dynasties period. As one example, the study of religious syncretism has recently come into vogue among sinologists, with particular reference to the Ming dynasty.[4] I am inclined to question the validity of much of the research so far addressed to this topic, however. Most of the evidence adduced in illustration of fifteenth- and sixteenth-century syncretism can already be found together in scriptural texts written a thousand years earlier. Surely mixtures brewed of the same ingredients after such a lapse of time—and in traditions that, however altered they may have become, still remained essentially unbroken—can hardly have quite the same potency as when those elements first encountered each other so long before. Shall we then speak of "primary" and "secondary" syncretism? This is a problem that students of the later dynasties should at least come to perceive.[5] A particular interest attaches to Six Dynasties texts, for it is in that era that signs of the Great Fusion are first attested, in numerous documents of various communions. It could, in fact, be interesting and important to determine what elements of later syncretic thought were not already present in the bubbling spiritual alembic of fifth-century Chiang-nan. Our understanding of religious syncretism in China offers a striking instance of how insufficient knowledge of the formative age of Chinese religious traditions has promoted distortion and false emphases in discussion of later periods.

Here I propose to approach the realm of Chinese Buddhist apocrypha in fifth-century Chiang-nan through one of the Buddhist scriptures written during this period, the *Kuan-ting ching* (Book of Consecration; *T* 1331). Such works are for the most part either ignored or treated as second-class productions—as if native Chinese religious literature were somehow intrinsically less worthy of attention than Indian. I believe, on the contrary, that texts of this kind are not only supremely important in the long history of Chinese religions, but also deserve prominent consideration in the study of Buddhism as a whole.

The Value of Apocryphal Sūtras for Sinology

The history of Buddhism in China is far more than a simple chronicle of translation, and more than the record of a few eminent monks. For a full understanding of any scripture in the Chinese Buddhist canon, we need to understand its Chinese context as well. This may in part be studied in Chinese interpretive commentaries on translated Indian works, but even they do not tell the full story. Free creation and adaptation provide the most eloquent testimony to the sinification of the Indian religion, and this is most readily seen in that numerous class of Buddhist scriptures that were written in China—the texts referred to as Buddhist "apocrypha."[6] Recent concern with Chinese apocryphal sūtras has been closely linked with the study of manuscripts recovered from Tun-huang. Works produced by movements that were ultimately discredited, like the Three Stages sect (San-chieh chiao), and writings that were the object of systematic destructive criticism, like the *Book of Trapuṣa and Bhallika (T'i-wei Po-li ching),* were purged from the officially sponsored canonical collections; hence the excitement over their rediscovery at Tun-huang.[7] It should not be forgotten, however, that many original Chinese scriptures successfully defied critical vigilance and were included in every Chinese Buddhist canon; others were elevated or restored to canonical currency by the editors of the *Taishō* collection from manuscripts or xylographs preserved in Japan. Among these Chinese works are certain of the most authoritative books in the East Asian Buddhist tradition, including the *Jen-wang ching* (Book of Benevolent Kings), *Fan-wang ching* (Book of Brahmā's Net), and the *Ta-sheng ch'i-hsin lun* (Treatise on the Awakening of Faith According to the Mahāyāna). These three texts alone provided the foundations, respectively, for the Buddhist protection of the state, the internal legislation of the religious life, and an advanced philosophical analysis. Many other Chinese scriptures and treatises printed in the canon, like those that survive only in Tun-huang manuscripts, enjoyed enormous popularity, for greater or lesser periods of time, in particular regions or in certain strata of society. The Tun-huang discoveries have drawn attention to the importance for Chinese literary history of popular narratives on religious themes *(pien-wen).* Yet no less worthy of study is the relatively neglected subject of Chinese Buddhist literature as a whole, beginning with the Chinese scriptures. Even more than the Chinese commentatorial literature that occupies so large a part of the *Taishō* and "Supplementary" *(Zokuzōkyō)* canons, scriptures written in China are especially valuable for what they can tell us of a truly Chinese form of Buddhism. They form a corpus of considerable originality as well as syncretic power. They also embody the authoritative voice of another world. Like their Indian prototypes, these extended compositions presented themselves as authentic products of supramundane omniscience and dominion—but in this case, the machinery of authority was set in motion by Chinese clerics and was directed to an audience of their countrymen.

So much controversy has raged around the "authenticity" of certain celebrated Buddhist books now known only in Chinese versions that it has sometimes been forgotten that works written in Chinese are not necessarily to be despised. We have inherited an unfortunate legacy from traditional East Asian scholarship, with its emphasis on orthodox transmission; for an élite of medieval Chinese scholar-monks, the basic criterion of a sūtra's authenticity was its translation out of a foreign language. The modern Western emphasis on Indian Buddhist origins has tended to reinforce this view, though at least secular scholars need not believe that because a work's original language was Indian its phrases inevitably issued from Gautama's mouth. Yet it should also be clear that in terms of "authenticity" there is little to choose between a sūtra written in fourth-century Kashmir and one composed in fourth-century Ch'ang-an. With reference to the Buddha whose authority they claim, both are equally apocryphal; with regard to the religious conditions of their own time and place, they may both be of exceeding interest. Indeed, the importance of Chinese apocryphal sūtras may be proportionate to their distance from their nominal source. They offer a wide view of the acculturation and synthesis of Indian Buddhist elements on foreign soil. What is more, owing to the vast extent and particular historical nature of the Chinese literary tradition, it is generally possible to compare a given Chinese Buddhist text with abundant contemporary and co-local sources. Now that more is coming to be known of the contents of the Taoist canon, we may affirm that many Chinese Buddhist works can only be fully understood in the light of their Taoist analogues. Such is the case for the *Book of Consecration,* which not only exemplifies the development in Chinese of a genuine Indian scriptural genre, but also occupies a place of its own in Chinese ritual literature.

A reassessment of native Chinese scriptures is especially needful given the problems with attribution that plague the Chinese Buddhist canon. As a graphic example, in the standard *Taishō* edition, we find the translation of the *Book of Consecration* attributed to Śrīmitra (d. 343), who worked at the Eastern Chin capital, Chien-k'ang (modern Nanking). Were this attribution correct, the work would have a different type of interest, because apart from a short note on the disposition of a ritual area there are no other literary remains of this renowned Kuchean master, whose occult powers dazzled the aristocracy during the decades after the transfer of the Chin dynasty's seat of power to Chiang-nan.[8] The sūtra was not translated by Śrīmitra, however. It is one of the approximately four hundred Chinese Buddhist scriptures (out of some seventeen hundred extant works ostensibly rendered from Indian languages) that, in the opinion of Hayashiya Tomojirō, are wrongly dated and ascribed. Over forty years ago, Hayashiya published convincing evidence that nearly one-fourth of the translations in the *Taishō* canon were falsely attributed. Since that time, further critical work on certain groups of Chinese Buddhist texts has revealed new relationships among works that had long been incorrectly assigned.[9] Yet surprisingly little has so far been done to rectify the larger view of extant Chinese sources for the study of Buddhism. Students are not usually warned that many of the descriptive data attached to works in the *Taishō* canon are false or misleading, and there has as yet been no effort to integrate critical study of Chinese sources into a comprehensive manual of Buddhist bibliographic reference.[10] Those who use Chinese Buddhist texts exclusively to mirror Indian phenomena may question the urgency of such a project. But for scholars whose interest lies in Chinese Buddhism and the study of China generally, the importance of a critical reassessment of the available materials should be obvious. That such books were not translated from an Indian tongue makes them, in my opinion, all the more valuable.

Dhāraṇī-sūtras in Chinese Buddhism

For no period in Chinese history is such a reassessment of authorship and provenance more necessary than the early medieval period, the formative age of Chinese religious practice and institutions. At the same time, I would suggest that no Chinese Buddhist works are in greater need of study than the group to which the *Book of Consecration* belongs—namely, the dhāraṇī-sūtras, or books of spells or incantations. Such texts promise to be particularly rewarding, both because many examples date from the early medieval period and because they offer close analogies to contemporary Taoist writings. Dhāraṇī-sūtras were written in view of realization, not philosophical reflection. They were intended as the basis for rituals—efficient texts, we could call them—and we must envisage them as circulating among persons to whose needs they corresponded, lay persons as well as monks and nuns. In the perspective of Japanese sectarianism, such works come under the heading of "diffuse esoterism" *(zōmitsu),* and our text has consequently been classified by the *Taishō* editors among the Tantric, or "esoteric" scriptures *(mikkyō-bu).*[11]

Three great collections of dhāraṇī-sūtras were compiled in the Six Dynasties period. Besides the *Book of Consecration,* the others were the *Ch'i-fo pa-p'u-sa so-shuo ta t'o-lo-ni shen-chou ching* (Dhāraṇī-sūtra of the Seven Buddhas and Eight Bodhisattvas; *T* 1332) in four fascicles, which dates from the late fourth or early fifth century, and the *T'o-lo-ni tsa-chi* (Dhāraṇī Miscellany; *T* 1336) in ten fascicles, from the first half of the sixth century. Ōmura Seigai (1868–1927), whose work on the history of Tantric Buddhism in China is still unsurpassed, placed the *Book of Consecration* between these two collections. In fact, the *Book of Consecration*'s twelfth and final book is a version of the *Bhaiṣajyaguru-sūtra* made in 457, and Ōmura assigned the work as a whole to the second half of the fifth century.[12]

The dhāraṇī-sūtras have been almost entirely neglected in contemporary Buddhist studies. To be sure, Indologists have examined a number of well-attested Indian dhāraṇī-sūtras, most of them extant in more than one Chinese transcription. For modern Japanese sectarian scholarship, however, the dhāraṇī-sūtras as a group are too diffuse and heterogeneous, not to say too "magical," to have warranted serious and prolonged attention. As for the historiographical tradition, because of its main concern with outstanding personalities, it can find little room for discussion of a body of texts that is largely anonymous as well as unabashedly practical in orientation. Naturally, too, the question of "authenticity" still at times poses an insurmountable obstacle even for modern representatives of these two traditional schools.

The *Book of Consecration* is of particular interest among the dhāraṇī collections for the curious manner in which its spells have been constructed. It is well known that dhāraṇīs are supposed to have been unique to Buddhism. They were said to encapsulate vast quantities of doctrine in concentrated form, and their recitation is found described as a mnemonic device as well as a means of protection.[13] Mantras, in contrast, are shared by Buddhism with other Indian religions. They exhibit a remarkable linguistic or paralinguistic spectrum, ranging from directly intelligible phrases to seemingly meaningless single syllables; structurally they may resemble birdsong, music, baby talk, or the utterances of the insane.[14] Ōmura Seigai has already demonstrated from Chinese sources how mantras and dhāraṇīs were early confounded and intermingled in Buddhist practice, the term "spirit-spell" *(shen-chou)* being used for both.[15] Yet no examples of this very natural fusion are quite so striking as those discernable in our fifth-century scripture. Here we find genuine dhāraṇīs taken from other, earlier texts being entirely transformed into mantra-like lists of gods, with separate syllabic groupings personified and deified.

Structure and Contents of the Book

Several features confer on the *Book of Consecration* exceptional significance in the history of Buddhism:

1. It includes the earliest surviving Chinese version of the highly influential *Bhaiṣajyaguru-sūtra.*

2. It contains the first-known Buddhist versified oracle-text for divination, inaugurating a tradition now represented in every East Asian temple.

3. It gives the earliest description in surviving Buddhist literature of the abhiṣeka rite, "consecration," performed as an esoteric initiation for Buddhist believers and subsequently one of the hallmarks of Tantric Buddhism.

4. It is one of the first Buddhist texts to contain directives for acquiring merit on behalf of dead ancestors—a practice that was soon to become one of the most characteristic features of East Asian Buddhism.

5. It provides an early version of the legend that later became the tale of Mu-lien's (Maudgalyāyana's) descent to hell to rescue his mother: the origin-legend of the East Asian ghost-festival.[16]

6. Finally, the *Book of Consecration* is apparently the first Buddhist scripture to represent itself as a hidden "treasure-text," discovered in a cavern, a development very much akin to the Tibetan notion of *gter-ma,* which are briefly treated in Buswell's introduction to this volume.

The *Book of Consecration (Kuan-ting ching)* is a collection of twelve individual sūtras, each contained in a single fascicle *(chüan).*[17] The contents of an anthology are not easily summarized, but we may begin by giving a succinct table of the twelve sections into which our text is divided. Each book presents itself as an independent sūtra; each bears a title of its own, beginning with the words "Book of Consecration Spoken by the Buddha," and each opens with its own *nidāna,* or narrative of the circumstances in which the Buddha pronounced the text. The twelve books are as follows:[18]

	Title	Contents
1.	Spells of the 72,000 Spirit-kings that Protect Bhikṣus	protective rites
2.	Spells of the 120,000 Spirit-kings that Protect Bhikṣūnīs	protective rites
3.	Protective Spells of the Three Refuges and Five Precepts, to be Carried on One's Person	protective rites
4.	Protective Spells of the Hundred-knotted Spirit-kings	protective rites
5.	Incantations on Dwellings; the Spirit-kings that Guard One's Surroundings	rites of domestic protection
6.	The Circumstances of Tombs; Spells of the Four Quarters	sepulchral protective rites
7.	Devil-subduing Seals and Great Spells	exorcistic rites
8.	Great Spells of the Maṇiratna Book	therapeutic rites
9.	Summoning the Dragon-kings of the Five Directions and Treating Pestilent Infections	therapeutic rites
10.	The Oracle of Brahmā	divination
11.	Rebirth in the Ten Pure Lands of One's Desire	rites of salvation
12.	Eliminating Faults and Transcending Life-and-Death	rites of salvation

The twelfth chapter is of importance for understanding the nature of the work as a whole. It corresponds to the *Bhaiṣajyaguru-sūtra,* the scripture of the Buddha "Master of Pharmaka" (Bhaiṣajyaguru). The contents of this influential text are well known. In it, the Buddha informs Mañjuśrī about a bodhisattva named Bhaiṣajyaguru, who has vowed to be reborn as a buddha in a subsequent age of the dharma. His twelve vows are set forth in detail. The Buddha continues with an account of the merits accruing to those who have only so much as heard the name of that bodhisattva in some former existence; all such persons will be saved. The Buddha then asks his disciple Ānanda if he is able to believe all this. Ānanda responds in the affirmative, and adds fresh praises of the efficacy of belief in Bhaiṣajyaguru. A bodhisattva next comes forward and describes how when a person dies, the emissaries of Yama, king of the dead, lead off his inner spirits or "gods" *(shen)*. It seems that there are two "spirits born at the same time" *(t'ung-sheng shen)* who accompany every man throughout his life. It is of them that Yama will demand a full report concerning the newly dead person, whose destiny is to be decided by his tribunal. Let the faithful but do reverence to Bhaiṣajyaguru for seven days and seven nights, sculpting seven images of him before each of which they light seven great lamps, and reciting his scripture before this glorious array of light; Bhaiṣajyaguru will then restore consciousness even to one who stands on the threshold of death. Furthermore, by doing homage to Bhaiṣajyaguru a consecrated king can resolve all problems in his dominions: eclipses, drought, disease, demonic attacks, and the like. There follows a list of nine afflictions *(heng)* for which "the skillful means of spells and drugs" may be used. Finally, the *Bhaiṣajyaguru-sūtra* presents twelve great yakṣa-commanders, each the chief of a troupe of seven thousand yakṣas. They undertake to protect the reciter of Bhaiṣajyaguru's name and scripture from all harm.

Such at least is a summary of this sūtra as translated anew in 616. Apart from the twelfth book of the *Book of Consecration,* no other earlier rendering of this scripture has been preserved.[19] In addition to a Sanskrit manuscript recovered from Gilgit, we do have three seventh-century Chinese versions, as well as a Tibetan translation, and comparison suggests that the *Book of Consecration*'s compiler altered the text at a number of places. To him was probably due the precise information on characteristically Chinese demons and diseases contained in this version; we find, for example, reference to the various demons of a Southern Dipper and the North Star where the other texts speak of yakṣas and *rākṣasas,* and many other changes and additions are detectable.[20] The twelfth book was not the only part of the *Book of Consecration* to be derived from other independent texts, however. The title of the eighth book immediately alerts us to a parallel case. A *Maṇiratna-sūtra* (*T* 1393) had already been produced in Chiang-nan during the fourth century, by T'an Wu-lan. In that instance, where the original has survived, we can easily observe how Book Eight of our sūtra was modeled on the earlier work, with numerous modifications, additions, and deletions.[21] There are, in fact, many signs in the *Book of Consecration* of the compiler's indebtedness to earlier materials, though he has usually woven his sources together with considerable subtlety.

Although this work may belong with the composite dhāraṇī anthologies of its time, it is my belief—against modern Japanese scholarly opinion—that it is a unified whole, written with an intelligible purpose.

Despite the composite character of the text, there is no doubt that the *Book of Consecration* was constructed on a clear plan and had a unifying principle of order. References to "twelve sections" are found throughout, indicating that the twelvefold division was intentional and part of the author's original design.[22] It is also clear that earlier parts of the work anticipate themes that later chapters develop more fully.[23] The list of contents given above has also shown us that there was some system in the selection and organization of subject matter. Books One through Four contain instructions relative to personal protection, first of religious, then of laymen. The following two books are concerned with fortifying the environs, first of the living, then the dead, against spectral incursions. Books Seven through Nine treat of means to subdue and expel disease-demons, while the tenth book deals with divination, or diagnosis and prognosis. The final two books appropriately provide information on last things—rites of transcendence and rebirth in the paradises of the ten directions. We may tentatively suppose a rough numerological correlation of the work's internal divisions with the twelve vows of Bhaiṣajyaguru that open the crowning book of the series, the *Bhaiṣajyaguru-sūtra,* and with the pledges of faith given by the twelve yakṣa-commanders at its close. In fact, when we approach the collection head-on, we find that this duodecimal determination is no less characteristic of its content than of its form.

As even a casual perusal of the contents of the *Book of Consecration* will show, its individual books are principally concerned with bringing forward their own cohort of powerful spirits to assure the safety and felicity of the scripture's possessor. These spirit-names appear to be transcriptions from an Indian language, and several of them can be readily restored to an original Sanskrit form, such as Marīci and Caṇḍāla. Most, however, do not lend themselves so easily to reconstruction. The intended divisions between separate names are not always clear, and we might be tempted to surmise that certain of these uncouth compounds are simply free variations upon Sanskrit vocables, fashioned primarily for their sonorous power—a kind of pseudo-Sanskrit. Such is not the case, however. Most of these complex spirit-names prove to be wholesale adaptations of syllabic compounds appearing in dhāraṇī formulae found in translated works of Indian origin.[24] The ideological context within which these lists of names are presented is, of course, entirely in line with the pronouncements of canonical Buddhism on the assimilation of profane gods as well as demonic powers as guardians. The most redoubtable forces in the universe are subdued, converted, and bound by oath as protectors of the Buddha's dharma and of the faithful. All this is too familiar to require further comment. Our text is perhaps unique, however, in the extent to which this assimilation is performed: besides buddhas, bodhisattvas, and mighty gods of India, there are also divine forces of the five directions (in several variant enumerations), the powerful dragon-kings, and so on, down to the common or garden-variety demons that infested every corner of China. All were laid under contribution in the comprehensive work of protection. The specters are identified according to location (e.g., the earth) or the means by which they originally died (e.g., stabbed itself to death), their destructive action (e.g., eat men's intestines), form (e.g., forty-nine-headed mountain ogre), means of locomotion, cry, or other characteristic activities. This is a purely Chinese demonological repertory, and includes the demons of outlying countries and of such "tribal" peoples as the I, Man, and Ch'iang.

Japanese sectarian scholars have generally denied that the word "consecration" *(kuan-ting),* as found in our sūtra's title, is to be understood as designating a rite of empowerment by aspersion (abhiṣeka) of the sort that marks the stages of initiation into the mysteries of the later Sino-Japanese Tantric Buddhist system. Okada Keishō, for example, firmly states that the term "consecration" is not used in reference to the rite of transmission employed in Esoteric Buddhism in which water is sprinkled on the head of the aspirant; rather, it is a hyperbolic reference to the sūtra's meritorious efficacy.[25] This is an excellent example of the way that narrow sectarian concerns can obscure or distort plain fact. The Buddha expressly outlines the rite of consecration in the scripture's opening chapter. Despite its simplicity when compared with the refined system of seventh- and eighth-century Mantrayāna as still practiced in Japan, "consecration" here already clearly carries its full sense of a quasi-royal rite of empowerment.[26] The presence of this rite in a mid-fifth-century text is not surprising when we recall that abhiṣeka consecrates the tenth and final stage of the bodhisattva's career. In the translation of the *Avataṃsaka-sūtra* made in 419 not far from the place where our text was written, the royal analogy is fully spelled out.[27] Similar accounts appear also in the earliest translation of the *Laṅkāvatāra-sūtra,* made by Gunabhadra at Chien-k'ang in 443, in the *Suvarṇaprabhāsa* (translated in the northwest, at Liang-chou, ca. 414–426), and in the *Ch'an pi-yao ching* (Secrets of Dhyāna), allegedly translated by Kumārajīva at Ch'ang-an during the first quarter of the fifth century.[28] Thus abhiṣeka imagery was hardly lacking at the time when our sūtra's author worked. However, the description in our text is the earliest extant reference anywhere in surviving Buddhist literature to abhiṣeka as a concrete rite, performed in a Buddhist context by mortals rather than buddhas. The *Book of Consecration* should therefore be given full credit for the feature that it announces so prominently in its title, and it must henceforth be taken into account in studying the development of rituals that were to occupy a central position in later Tantric Buddhism.

Buddhist Apocalyptic and the Scripture's Origin and Destiny

The author of the *Book of Consecration* explicitly attempts to place his compilation within the historical development of Buddhism as a whole. Once the Buddha had pronounced the scripture, a young arhat in the assembly would undertake to disseminate it after the Buddha's death. In consequence, the work would soon become widely known, and during the first hundred years after the *parinirvāṇa* it would enjoy great popularity. By the second hundred years, however, most of the Buddha's disciples would already have obtained deliverance and so there would be less recourse to the scripture. During the third hundred years, the scripture together with the gods whose names it lists were to vanish into the earth, for there would be no further need of them at that time, when good would so greatly predominate over evil in the world.

In later ages, however, matters were unfortunately to be otherwise. Nine hundred years after the *parinirvāṇa,* the way of devils *(mo,* Skt. *māra)* will flourish. Heretics will arrogate matter from the Buddha's scriptures and claim it as their own. They will lead people to accept those adulterated writings and make them swear repeated oaths of secrecy, thus esoterizing their doctrines. The ruler of the Central State will be unable to understand the dharma completely and will impose restrictions on it. Because his mind is not concentrated, he will be led astray by heretics.[29]

In that ghastly epoch, there will appear in the world a bhikṣu named Universal Succor (P'u-chi). He will carry out ascetic practices in the mountains, wandering from cave to cave in search of a suitable spot for meditation. At last he will happen upon a grotto in which he will discover a jeweled casket. On opening it he will find the text of the *Book of Consecration* incised in letters of purple gold on tablets of sandalwood. He will do homage to the text and then begin to recite it and practice the rites prescribed therein. As the millennium approaches, in the final century of the dharma, the otherworldly host of saints will take pity on mankind in its time of greatest need. They will have that ascetic monk transmit the scripture to all classes of Buddhist disciples—monks and nuns, laymen and laywomen. Thanks to the protection of the potent spirits named in this text, the faithful will be enabled to win through the perils of the last years of the Law.[30]

Yet though intended for the benefit of all the Buddha's disciples, the text was nonetheless hidden and its transmission guarded by an esoteric rite. This secrecy appears to have been a function of futurity; the Buddha's predictions for later ages were an occult treasure to be carefully guarded by initiates against the envious curiosity of the profane. Our text contains numerous references to the final century of the dharma and the debased character of that time.[31] It is patent that the entire text was directed toward that troubled age, when the scripture was in fact "discovered"—a time that we can confidently identify with the mid-fifth century. It is clear that our author subscribed to the theory, current in China since the first complete translation of the *Lotus Sūtra* in 286, that the True Law *(Saddharma)* would be followed by its counterfeit *(Pratirūpakadharma)*. Although he does not specify the relative lengths of these two periods, the references just quoted indicate that he expected the total extinction of the dharma to occur following the thousandth year after the Buddha's *parinirvāṇa*. Thus he presumably sided with the majority of the sources available in mid-fifth-century China, which viewed the Counterfeit Law as beginning after the five-hundredth year.[32] At all events, for him the thousandth year was the critical moment, and a piercing eschatological note sounds from every book of our text.

Sources and analogues for our text's account of the last age can readily be found in the Buddhist literature of fifth-century Chiang-nan. The *Mahāparinirvāṇa-sūtra,* translated by Fa-hsien at Chien-k'ang in 417–418, describes the character of the times. In the last eighty years before the dharma's extinction, the *Nirvāṇa Sūtra* will be widely diffused throughout India, but evil monks, lax in their observances, will league with devils to destroy the True Dharma. They will compose their own scriptures and treatises, hymns and litanies, confounding the false with the true and distorting authentic writings. At that time the *Nirvāṇa Sūtra* will be subjected to much abuse and, finally, when the dharma is on the point of extinction, its text will disappear into the soil of Kashmir together with all the other *vaipulya-sūtras* of the Mahāyāna.[33]

An ultimate disappearance of scripture is also the climax of a dramatic apocalypse composed in fifth-century Chiang-nan, the *Fo-shuo fa mieh-chin ching* (Book on the Extinction of the Dharma; *T* 396). At a time after the *parinirvāṇa,* in a world corrupted by defilements, devils will flourish. They will join the Order to destroy the Law. They will break all the Buddha's precepts and slander and expel the bodhisattvas, pratyekabuddhas, and arhats of those days who still try to maintain the true practice. Among other misdeeds, these devil-monks will allow monasteries to fall into disrepair while they enter into trade on a large scale, in their lust for gain vending monastic slaves, fields, and agricultural produce and hoarding the profits, with no thought of charity. The time when the dharma is hovering on extinction will be marked by a great increase of pious works among women, whilst men display laxity, indifference, and contempt for monks.[34] The final years of the dharma will also be distinguished by more convulsively apocalyptic signs. Excesses of flood and drought will destroy the harvests, and rampant epidemics will leave corpses heaped across the land. The cycles of day and night will shorten and man's lifetime become briefer. Unbridled license will greatly reduce the human male's lifespan, and few will succeed in attaining sixty. As man's life shortens, however, woman's will lengthen until women regularly reach seventy, eighty, ninety, or even a hundred years of age. Then great floods will rise up suddenly; but in their obstinate refusal to credit the signs of the times, men will see nothing extraordinary in this and make no effort to reform. The bodhisattvas, pratyekabuddhas, and arhats of that time will not mingle with the doomed multitudes, who will be hunted down by devils. Rather, they will go into the mountains, the place of sanctuary, where they will survive, protected by devas. After some fifty-two years, first the *Śūraṅgama-sūtra* (*Shou-leng-yen ching; T* 945) and the *Pratyutpannasamādhi-sūtra* (*Pan-chou san-mei ching; T* 417) will disappear. Then the twelve divisions of scripture will all vanish, never to reappear. Their letters will be obliterated, and monks' robes will of themselves turn white.[35]

The *Book of Consecration* should therefore be restored to a much wider context of contemporary literature in which the imminent end of the dharma was described. Previous attempts of Japanese and Chinese scholars to relate such pessimistic views of the future of Buddhism to particular instances of governmental repression or restrictive official measures, such as the 446 proscription of Buddhism by the Northern Wei, need not detain us.[36] Special historical circumstances may have lent cogency and conviction to the narrative, but there is no need to search for contemporary incidents to explain the content of fifth-century Buddhist apocalyptic writings. The structure of Buddhist eschatology had been determined long before.[37] It is too often forgotten that according to the earliest scriptural prophecies, which announced a mere five hundred years as the duration of the True Law, Buddhism had already entered upon its era of final decline when it was introduced to China. There are numerous references to the imminent end of the religion in third-century Chinese translations, and it is clear that even at that time a substantial proportion of monks and laymen must have believed themselves to be living in the last days. Such is the ambiance in which our scripture was first revealed. Hidden in a cavern until the destined moment, it is thus apparently the earliest example of a "discovered" scripture, a class of Buddhist writings that has until now been better known from the Tibetan Tantric tradition.[38] Like all such long-concealed secret texts, it had been laid away against times very different from the days when the Buddha preached his Law in person.

Given its profound eschatological resonances, the *Book of Consecration* presents itself as a comprehensive manual of practice for the end of the dharma and clearly demonstrates that, in its author's view, the current age corresponded to the final years of the doctrine. This was confirmed by a wide spectrum of demonic manifestations: warfare, floods, disease.

Yet not only was the outside world thrown into confusion; within the Buddhist community itself the traditional guarantees provided by the precepts and their strict observance were at that time already greatly weakened. Official support for the Saṃgha was vacillating and insufficient. Worse, many of the official class put their faith and funds in other spiritual activities characteristic of that degenerate period—practices that the Buddha had foretold, and of which he had unmasked the true demonic nature. Although the *Book of Consecration* contained rites specially designed for the current age, they did not represent any innovation. Rather, they restored to currency material that had originally circulated to good effect in the time of striving and confusion immediately after the Buddha's *parinirvāṇa,* when the Master was no longer present in person to guide his disciples. Once some stability had been achieved in the Order, there was no longer any need for the sūtra's rites and so it vanished, together with all the protective gods whom it named. Gods and scripture had only reappeared now, at the dharma's end, when they were once more required. A discovered book implies a forgotten or neglected message, a pristine tradition that has not been deformed or distorted by long prior transmission among men. Thus the *Book of Consecration* was both close to the thought of the Founder and particularly suitable for contemporary conditions, which the Buddha in his omniscience had foreseen.

Such a uniquely endowed work might well arouse the hostility of elder monks, men with vested interests in the present decayed order of things, with comfortable positions in the hierarchy, and perhaps with a sound scholarly knowledge of authentic scripture. Such opposition is in fact anticipated in our text. After the ascetic monk discovers the sūtra in its mountain cavern, he will attempt to diffuse it as widely as possible. Yet few will be willing to receive it; many will deride it and refuse to accept it. When the monks of the last age learn that in various places a few masters are transmitting the scripture, they will claim (without ever having set eyes on the text) that those masters hold perverse views and are expounding heretical practices for their own profit. Detractors such as these will be punished for their calumnies in the form of ill fortune in this very lifetime.[39]

The calumnies put forward against this text by old and respected monks will themselves furnish confirmation of the scripture's prophecies. Their benighted rejection of the Buddha's own scripture will be the surest sign that the dharma has not much longer to last. If we may judge by these indications, it would seem that the man responsible for our sūtra was one of a group of younger monks, dissatisfied with existing clerical and social conditions, who drew inspiration from the eschatological message that echoed widely throughout fifth-century China.

The Authorship of the Scripture

The few modern critical evaluations of our text have all been based upon the analysis given by Seng-yu (445–518) in his *Ch'u-san-tsang chi-chi* (A Compilation of Notices on the Translation of the *Tripiṭaka*), the earliest surviving critical bibliography of Chinese Buddhist literature. Seng-yu classified the first eleven books together, in the category of translations of which the translator's name was unknown. He does not include the work among the translations attributed to Śrīmitra, and makes no mention of any such tradition.[40] According to Seng-yu, the original collection comprised the first nine books only; the final three books were a later addition.[41] The twelfth book, however, he separated from the others and placed in a class apart. It is found in his section on doubtful or fabricated scriptures, where he describes it as follows: "In the time of the Sung emperor Hsiao-wu ti, in the first year of the Ta-ming reign-period (457), the bhikṣu Hui-chien of the Lu-ye ssu in Mo-ling made up this work on the basis of the [authentic *Bhaiṣajyaguru-*]*sūtra.* It concludes with a rite for prolonging life, and this has caused it to circulate very widely in the world."[42]

Thus Seng-yu was of the opinion that the work in twelve *chüan* really represented three distinct entities: first, an older collection of nine books of spells; then, a subsequent addition of three other, independent works; and finally, though the first eleven *chüan* were, for Seng-yu, legitimate translations for which the translators were unknown, the twelfth and final *chüan* was in a class by itself. It was composed by a Chinese monk on the basis of an authentic scripture, and accordingly Seng-yu placed it in an entirely different category from the rest of the work, in the limbo of "fabricated" sūtras.

Seng-yu's classifications were the result of his own dominant concerns, which were, I suggest, different from our own. It is more to our purpose to note that the *Book of Consecration* already existed as an independent work in twelve *chüan* by the early sixth century, when Seng-yu listed the titles of its books in the same form in which they are found in the present text. In stating that Books Ten, Eleven, and Twelve were later additions, Seng-yu was, I believe, simply reacting to the difference between them and the preceding sections of the work. In assuming that the first eleven books represented genuine translations from an Indian language, he was allowing himself to be misled by their superficial similarity to a number of well-attested translations or transcriptions of dhāraṇī-sūtras, made in the fourth century, which had indeed served the work's compiler as models.

What is more, it seems probable that in noting the name of the monk Hui-chien, who is said to have composed the twelfth book of our sūtra in 457 at Lu-ye Monastery, Seng-yu has really named, dated, and localized the author-compiler of the entire work.

For Seng-yu, Hui-chien was simply the fabricator of the altered text of the *Bhaiṣajyaguru-sūtra* that comprises our sūtra's twelfth book. It is well known, however, that many hitherto anonymous works found authors or translators as time went on. Indeed, the further we advance from the formative period of Chinese Buddhism, the clearer becomes the picture of that period presented by successive Chinese sources—a situation that might cause any conscientious historian of the early middle ages to despair. Thus it is not surprising that whereas Seng-yu can only credit a single work to Hui-chien, the next major Buddhist catalogue, the *Li-tai san-pao chi* (Record of the Three Treasures throughout Successive Generations) of 597, is able to provide him with a substantial oeuvre—most of which had been simply listed by Seng-yu as anonymous translations. In the course of time a need was obviously felt to reduce the overwhelming mass of unanchored texts by safely assigning them to some earlier personage—for major works, a major figure; for minor texts, some lesser light. We can hardly feel much confidence in the historical accuracy of many attributions that still cling to the older translations as a result of such belated classificatory efforts. Yet we must also consider the criteria that led to these attributions. Were some founded on traditions that the critical Seng-yu had intentionally left aside? And even if the authors of later catalogues did not base their ascriptions on historical data, they must still have aimed at a certain verisimilitude. Through such attributions they were in fact introducing a number of significant sub-classifications into the extant corpus of Buddhist literature, and the works grouped together under a single name must therefore have had certain noteworthy features in common.

With this in mind, it is interesting to consider the list of works with which Hui-chien was credited a century and a half after he made his adaptation of the *Bhaiṣajyaguru*—mainly a series of tales from the *Āgamas*. A number of these short works bearing Hui-chien's name have been preserved in the canon. Though they are attributed to him as "translator," both of their main sources—the *Madhyamāgama* (*Chung A-han ching; T* 26) and the *Ekottarāgama* (*Tseng-i A-han ching; T* 125)—had been fully translated before the end of the fourth century. Thus Hui-chien, or whoever was responsible for these brief independent versions, was obviously rewriting and adapting on the basis of prior Chinese translations, exactly as the author of the *Book of Consecration* so frequently did. One of these adaptations from the *Ekottarāgama* includes a very curious appendix entitled "A Note on the Events Following the Buddha's *Parinirvāṇa*."[43] This clearly represents the *Book of the Bhikṣus After the Buddha's Parinirvāṇa,* included in the *Li-tai san-pao chi*'s listing of the putative works of Hui-chien. Its account of the evolving character of the Saṃgha in the successive centuries after the Buddha's departure from the world accords perfectly with the parallel information included in the *Book of Consecration.* Like that scripture, it describes the first three hundred years as an age apart that witnessed the progressive achievement of perfection by members of the Order. Three hundred years after the *parinirvāṇa,* the attainment of enlightenment will be almost simultaneous with the reception of monk's vows. Subsequently, as the distance from the Founder lengthens, we can see the emergence of all the characteristic derivative religious activities—meditation on and longing for the Buddha, worship of monks and teachers, ascetic practices in deserted places, scholarly endeavor, and pious construction projects. In the final century before the millennium, however, monks will be preoccupied with their own survival and personal profit, and as the last days draw nigh they will give themselves over to uncurbed violence and immorality. It seems then that there may be no inconsistency between the *Book of Consecration* and the various works attributed to Hui-chien at the end of the sixth century, which also include the famous *Ch'ing Pin-t'ou-lu fa* (Book on Inviting Piṇḍola; *T* 1689).[44]

Whether or not we are justified in retaining Hui-chien's name on any of these works, we must note that *Li-tai san-pao chi* has effectively brought together a body of cognate literature, and one that appears to represent an important current in fifth-century writing and practice. The contents of our sūtra offer many indications of the dominant interests and concerns of its author. There is repeated emphasis on reform of existing abuses and a return to stricter morality. The text several times notes the scorn of the worldly for ascetics: people mock monks who still adhere to the precepts and carry out the prescribed retreats in all their severity. The scripture itself was discovered by a *dhūta,* a wandering monk who had given himself up to austerities in the mountains and who, after finding the text, devoted himself to preaching its message in the towns. The work was patently directed to laymen as well as to monks, and its adaptation of tales from the *Āgamas* (like those in the independent little sūtras attributed to Hui-chien) seems to suggest the exigencies of popular preaching. Our sūtra's message was clearly meant to be taken directly to the people, and Seng-yu duly noted the wide diffusion that it had attained within fifty years of its composition. It would appear that our work came into being among a group that strongly advocated the practice of austerities, accompanied by the recitation of powerful spells. By these two ancient and complementary means they hoped to effect a reform of Buddhism, and to compel the vast otherworldly legions to do their bidding for the good of mankind in its hour of peril. To lay believers guarded by little more than the Three Refuges and five precepts, the sūtra bore a much-needed message of comfort.

Naming and numbering the gods with whom the faithful had been invested as soon as they accepted the Buddha's commandments, our text must have given its privileged lay recipients an enhanced sense of election and a certitude of salvation. Our author's synthesis provided them with a comprehensive view of human history together with a detailed program of salvation appropriate to the times in which they lived.

Taoism: The Demonic Religion of the Last Age

We have remarked that the *Book of Consecration* must be viewed as part of the great wave of Indian proto-Tantric practice that inundated Chiang-nan in the mid-fifth century. Through his various adaptations and rewritings of genuine translations from Sanskrit texts, our author contributed to the direct assimilation of many authentically Indian ritual elements. But several of the sūtra's dominant features can only be understood in relation to the practice of Taoism in fifth-century Chiang-nan. Taoism is several times noted with disapproval. For example, the epoch for which the *Book of Consecration* was destined would have its own particular religious character. The Buddha's original prophecy in the text notes that the final hundred years before the achievement of the millennium were to witness a great upsurge of demonic forces. At that time heretics would plagiarize Buddhist scriptures in order to fabricate sacred texts of their own. They would surround these writings with an aura of mystery, and before transmitting them would make their prospective recipients swear repeated oaths of secrecy and furnish numerous pledges of valuables and silk.[45] This is an unmistakable reference to Taoist scriptural transmission. Fourth- and fifth-century Taoist writings are quite specific about the pledges of gold and silk that are to accompany their own transmission, and they are eloquent concerning the infernal penalties that will be visited upon the offender and his ancestors in the event of unauthorized disclosure. At the same time, Taoist scriptures make it clear that these requirements establish between the aspirant and the hierarchy of the Tao a "pure" bond, intended as a definitive replacement of the blood offerings that formerly united the commonality of believers to the impure, carnivorous gods of popular religion.[46] From the beginning, Taoist priests had been at pains to reveal the true nature of those spirits of the dead whom the people benightedly worshiped as gods, and they had even set strict limits on the cult of ancestors. Such a reform of religious practice could be viewed as a remarkable autochthonous revolution in Chinese religion (as indeed it was, in my opinion), but the author of the *Book of Consecration* is anxious to unmask the pretensions of the Taoists themselves: their matter is derived from Buddhism, their inspiration is demonic, and their elaborate esoteric allurements are but another device of the Tempter, Māra.

During the fifth century Taoists, like Buddhists, had been enjoying unprecedented opportunities for patronage and institutional development. Early in the fourth century the religion founded by Chang Tao-ling in 142 had arrived south of the Yangtze; the second half of that century witnessed the creation of great new bodies of Taoist literature, in which the practices of the Way of the Celestial Master (T'ien-shih tao) were synthesized with the old occult tradition of Chiang-nan. First the Shang-ch'ing scriptures of the Mao Shan revelations (364–370) furnished a body of protocols for individual contemplative practice. Then the Ling-pao scriptures, written in the 390's, determined the definitive form of Taoist ritual as it evolved in the service of the state, the community, and the clan. In the course of the fifth century the basic texts of these two movements inspired innumerable new scriptures, and the first systematic classification of Taoist writings was made at that time. This Taoist literature furnished celestial authorization for the contemporary expansion of the religion, and such scriptural texts were effectively the objects of the oaths of secrecy and costly offerings that our sūtra's author has accurately described.[47]

That the idea of Taoism weighed heavily on our author's mind is shown by more than derogatory references to the rival system. The very substance of the *Book of Consecration* attests to Taoist influence. Its opening books comprise a catalogue of gods, and such inventories go back to the very beginnings of Taoism: they were an integral part of the religion's initiatory structure. Taoist "registers" *(lu)* contained lists of gods who were formally installed in members of the Taoist community, in progressively larger numbers as Taoists proceeded through a life cycle of initiations or investitures. Comparison with Taoist ritual texts of the period confirms that the author of the *Book of Consecration* found his inspiration in this genre of Taoist documents. The first several chapters of the *Book of Consecration* provided Chinese proto-Tantric devotees with comprehensive Buddhist "registers" of guardian deities who would accompany them through life's vicissitudes—battalions and regiments of a sort they would have known from Taoism.

A simple explanation for the many close parallels between such Buddhist writings as the *Book of Consecration* and Taoist texts is their virtual identity of function. Both were designed to guarantee the believer's physical security in a turbulent, apocalyptic age when demonic afflictions were particularly numerous and intense. To this extent their focus was essentially practical and worldly, and it is only natural that members of both communions should have had recourse to similar procedures in countering a threat that they envisaged in strikingly similar terms. We must remember, however, that these protective operations were always understood as being only preliminary to the ultimate work of transcendence. In our pardonable fascination with the demonic, we have said all too little about the rites of salvation with which our scripture concludes. Such material appears in Books Eleven and Twelve. The eleventh book describes ten paradises, one in each of the ten directions. Not only Amitābha's paradise in the West is available to the faithful at the moment of their death, we are told. They may be born in accordance with their desire in any of the pure lands of the ten directions. The twelfth and final book also contrasts Amitābha's region with the vision it presents of the Master of Pharmaka's Buddha-realm in the East. These descriptions document the popularity that Amitābha's cult had attained by the mid-fifth century, as well as our author's own contrasting orientation. Thus the ideals of ultimate transcendence that the *Book of Consecration* held out to the faithful were textually derived from Indian sources. Indian, too, was the esoteric ritual of empowerment from which the scripture took its title. Yet behind the panoply of foreign forms there was another, unheralded impulse, and it is clear that through his Indian rite of royal unction the sūtra's author was also consecrating many practices that were quintessentially Chinese.

This close familiarity with Taoism suggests that the *Book of Consecration* and other Chinese Buddhist scriptures must be studied in conjunction with contemporary and co-local Taoist texts. These writings freely adapt terminology, ideas, and practices from one another; indeed, the analogies between these two complementary forms of medieval Chinese scriptural creation speak for themselves. Only a large-scale comparative study of rites will enable us to determine the full extent of Buddho-Taoist textual and ritual interchangeability. Yet even now it should be easier to conceive of such a notion, given the extent to which the *Book of Consecration* draws upon contemporary Taoist matter and the variety of ways in which such "influence" is expressed.

Socio-Economic Background

Extending our comparison of the *Book of Consecration* with contemporary Taoist sources into the economic sphere may uncover clues to the possible motives of Buddhist scriptural creators. Having noted our author's derogatory comments on the costly pledge-offerings that accompanied Taoist scriptural transmission, we might not expect his text to yield direct economic data as succulent as that found in fifth-century Taoist scriptures, each of which effectively bears its own price-tag. Still, no religious book has ever come into being in a socio-economic void, and an adequate view of our author's opinions on this subject can be gained simply by collecting the references in his text to gift-giving and donations to the Saṃgha.

Such references abound in the eleventh book, which concerns the rites for rebirth in the paradises of the ten directions. Rapid rebirth under favorable circumstances depends on merit, such as may already be present and credited to one's account either as a heritage from one's forebears or as the product of one's own good actions. Should such merit prove to be lacking at the time of a person's death, it will need to be acquired speedily and in bulk by his descendants who remain in the world of the living. Indeed, whatever a person's stock of merit may be (and in time several means were developed for ascertaining this), pious descendants must always take care to assure an adequate supply for their progenitors' rebirth.[48] Hence prolonged funeral observances, characterized by abundant largess to the monkish officiants:

> The Bodhisattva P'u-kuang once more spoke to the Buddha: "There are still others who do not have faith in the Three Treasures and do not practice the precepts of the Law. Sometimes they revere the religion, sometimes revile it. Should their parents, brothers, or other clan members suddenly become ill and die, they will consequently fall among the Three Paths and Eight Difficult Conditions. If then their parents, brothers, or other family members cultivate felicity on their behalf, will they obtain those blessings or not?"
>
> The Buddha told P'u-kuang, "Of the felicity cultivated on those persons' behalf, they will receive one part in seven. Why is this so? Because during their lifetimes they did not have faith in the Tao and its merit. Therefore they are made to obtain only one seventh of the merit of those acts of felicity. If all the appurtenances with which the deceased enhanced his person—his halls, mansions, chambers, his gardens, groves, and ponds—are bestowed upon the Three Treasures, this will produce the very greatest felicity and the most powerful merit. By such means he can be drawn forth from the miseries of the hells, and will directly obtain deliverance from the afflictions of sorrow and suffering. He will attain lasting liberation, and will be reborn in one of the Pure Lands of the Buddhas of the ten directions."

Thus in the case of one whose Buddhist faith was less than perfect during his lifetime—and whose conscience can be entirely clear in matters of faith?—as much merit as his surviving descendants could acquire for him by ordinary ritual means could still be so heavily discounted that the sum might not be sufficient for his salvation. Only bestowal of all his property to the Buddhist establishment could unambiguously guarantee his posthumous happiness. How well these directives accord with what we know of the massive donations of property to the Saṃgha that became common practice in the course of the fifth century! Benefaction on such a scale makes even the most opulent offerings for Taoist textual transmission appear paltry in comparison. The very grandeur of this cosmic schema, in which only total bestowal assures full salvation, lends force to our author's contempt for the Taoists' niggling exactions. It is no accident that a religion that gave its adherents unlimited opportunity for the direct conversion of wealth into spiritual felicity was soon able to outstrip its native Chinese rival:

> The Buddha told the elder, "You should invite the assembly of sages at the end of the three months' recess, when their religious practices are about to be completed. You should return to your home and prepare all sorts of delicious food and drink, place them in pure vessels and present them to the monks. Also you should bestow on them fine vestments, every kind of flower and incense, gold, silver, and all manner of precious stones. This will cause you to obtain merit, and will allow your parents to be released from their difficulties and no longer to have the bodies of hungry ghosts."

It is not surprising that writings addressed by religious to their lay supporters should contain traces of enlightened self-interest. Moreover, our author is well ahead of any possible imputation of cupidity that might be leveled against him, with an advanced rationalization of almsgiving. As a result of the Buddha's explanations of the benefits of charity, as expounded in this scripture, living beings in times to come will no longer covet possessions. They will develop a disposition toward almsgiving and will make gifts to the needy until all have a sufficiency. Thus the state will prosper; an unprecedented flux of benefactions will have eliminated all disparity in possessions. By this means our author relates his program of ritualized Buddhist donations to the persistent Chinese ideal of equity, evoked for centuries under the sobriquet of T'ai-p'ing (lit., "Great Peace," that is, Grand Equality or Leveling).

Indigenous Religion in the *Book of Consecration*

The mutual influence between Buddhism and Taoism in fifth-century Chiang-nan is perhaps most clearly seen in the opposition of some of their texts to the religion of ordinary people outside the fold. Our scripture, for example, tells of the activities of other Chinese religious specialists, especially exorcistic operators who exhort the gullible, saying:

> "You have been injured by the god of a mountain, or of a tree, or again, of some asterism—is it not because you have offended the god of that star that you have become ill? You must offer a white ox or a white horse and various other kinds of living creatures and good things to eat and drink, and have singers perform in honor of those gods; then they will bring you good fortune and remove your sufferings. You will thereby obtain safety and felicity, and no longer have any fears or anxieties."[49]

Exorcists of this sort, outside the formal hierarchies of Buddhism and Taoism, represented the priesthood of what Taoists also termed "the gods of the profane" *(su-shen),* and fifth-century Taoist writings, too, contain repeated denunciations of their frenzied drumming and dancing and their ruinous and defiling rites of animal sacrifice.[50] In most

Taoist sources, the principal blame is set upon the unrestrained activity of the specters themselves, who lead the people astray by their demonic machinations.[51] Other Taoist texts explain that the ubiquitous specters have a necessary function in the present degenerate age. As the ultimate catastrophe approaches, in an accelerating rhythm of violence, the forces of evil are to purge the world of all evildoers and destroy themselves in the process. Thus the earth will be entirely purified and renewed, and all made ready for the destined imperium of the Tao and its elect.[52]

These demons pretending to be gods were unmasked and identified by Taoist priests as the unhallowed spirits of the dead. Whether such otherworldly agents were seen as gods, demons, or ancestors naturally depended on the individual's personal relation to them, and this classificatory ambiguity remains a constant in the study of Chinese religions.[53] The question of ancestor worship was later to pose insuperable difficulties for Christian missionaries in China. However, we do not always remember that Buddhist monks and Taoist priests were deeply concerned with similar problems throughout the formative period of Chinese religious life. Aspects of the Buddhist doctrinal approach to the question have indeed been studied.[54] But that the Taoists, too, were engaged on parallel lines of thought and action (being equally interested in restricting the hold of the diffuse Chinese religious tradition on the people at large) was until recently not generally recognized. Nor has the ritual aspect of the question been adequately investigated, for either religion. It was through ritual that a durable integration was effected between the all-pervasive elements of common Chinese tradition and the more exacting requirements of the organized hierarchized communions. The fundamental Buddhist and Taoist rites for the salvation of the dead were created during the late fourth and early fifth centuries, and thus our mid-fifth-century *Book of Consecration* is admirably situated to inform us on contemporary mortuary practice.[55]

Clearly the problems encountered by Buddhists in establishing their religion south of the Yangtze were not due only to the entrenched customs of the culturally and economically dominant Chinese population. The "lesser nations" within China's claimed frontiers, especially the numerous and widespread Yao and Miao peoples, were at that time still radically opposed to Chinese attempts at penetration—though in later centuries Buddhists and especially Taoists were to operate among them as powerful agents of sinification through religious conversion. Meanwhile, though, the "aboriginals" still belonged to the demonic fringes of Chinese civilization, and their system of therapy through bone-manipulation was hardly regarded as fitting human comportment.[56] In contrast, the Buddha's own prescriptions for the acquisition of merit and good fortune were said to be of extreme purity and simplicity. One must burn incense, scatter flowers, and do obeisance in the ten directions to the buddhas of the three ages. Then, on behalf of the departed, one should confess in a true spirit of repentance all one's transgressions. By this means one could obtain deliverance from sorrow.[57] These laconic directives in fact delineate the basic components of rites of salvation as they had been developing since the fourth century, though they hardly do justice to their complexity. The parallels between Buddhist and Taoist rituals for this purpose are many and striking, and testify to both the moral refinement and common legalistic foundations of the two religions. Their comparative study is a necessary prerequisite to understanding the way in which China's most enduring religious traditions came into being.[58]

Even this brief sketch suggests that the *Book of Consecration* gives a broad survey of the major types of religious phenomena to be observed in fifth-century Chiang-nan, and our author is careful to distinguish them all from one another. Despite his polemic bias, there is no casual confusion here between Taoist priests and practices and the exorcists and rites of ordinary Chinese religion (such as we still too often find in modern scholarly writings). The customs of the non-Chinese populations of the South are also clearly set off from Chinese practices. Nor is this surprising, given the obvious formal and sociological distinguishing features possessed by each of these complexes of officiants, rites, and believers—it would be well could sinologists try to emulate our text's descriptive precision in this matter. One feature, in our author's view, seems to be shared by all the "perverse" or "heretical" rites that he describes—namely, their use of the dead, in itself ill-omened: the manipulation of the formal administrative channels of the dead (Taoists), offering blood sacrifices to the spirits of the dead (the Chinese population at large), or the physical handling of the remains of the dead (non-Chinese peoples). According to our text, the aim of the Buddhists is, in distinct contrast to all of this, a transcendent one, concerned with the attainment of everlasting life in a celestial paradise. Such tendentious formulations must be examined with all due care. We find Taoist writers contemporary with our sūtra's author making precisely the same claims for their own rites in distinction to Buddhism and, once again, the much-abused religion of the people.[59] The dispassionate reader, conscious of some of these undercurrents, may relish our text's description of the marvelous efficacy of relics in the same Book Six that so takes the poor aboriginals to task for their bone-washing.[60] No religion can have a monopoly on extravagance, and our author was very much of his time and place. This was in a sense the whole point of his sūtra; he was at pains to repeat the Buddha's strictures on the special character of the age and locus, and on the text's particular appropriateness to them. Yet though he certainly must have known what he was about, our author may not always have felt at ease with some of the material he had chosen to present. This can be inferred from the evidence that he kept something of a chip on his exposed monkish shoulder.

The Legitimation of Apocryphal Texts: Eschatology and Political Dissidence

As we have remarked, the class of Buddhist texts to which the *Book of Consecration* belongs, along with its parallel Taoist scriptures, was intended for a period of cosmic and social crisis. They consequently share a common protective or therapeutic function, as in our sūtra, where healing techniques are joined by a procedure for divination. Such characteristic concerns invite speculation about the legal status of these writings and the masters who composed, practiced, and promoted them, for unauthorized healing and divination were constant objects of official displeasure and repression.[61] We may also be tempted to wonder about possible connections between such eschatologically obsessed productions and politically dissident movements. We know of a number of cases during the fifth and sixth centuries, both in Chiang-nan and in alien-ruled North China, in which monks were among the leaders of militant uprisings, and some of the numerous Candraprabhā-kumāra (Yüeh-kuang t'ung-tzu) and Maitreya apocrypha almost certainly had their origins in such milieux. In Chiang-nan under the Liang, a particularly famous incident involving the creation of a new scripture and its official condemnation is on record, though the work's connection with a subversive movement appears not to be established.

The *Sa-po-jo-t'o chüan-shu chuang-yen ching* (Book of the Adornments of the Family of Sarvajñatā [Omniscience]) was composed by the *dhūta*-religious *(t'ou-t'o tao-jen)* Miao-kuang. In 510, seven years after he had received the precepts, he claimed to possess auspicious signs or body-markings. He won over a number of nuns and laywomen in his native Ying-chou (Hunan), by whom he was acclaimed as a saint. The provincial Rector of the Saṃgha planned to have him expelled from the Order, but Miao-kuang covertly fled to the capital, where he lodged at the P'u-hung Monastery. It was there that he fabricated this scripture. He wrote it out on a screen that he covered with red gauze, and burnt incense and offered flowers before it. He attracted a great following of monks and nuns, laymen and laywomen, who made abundant offerings. But it came to be known how the movement had begun, and Miao-kuang was apprehended by the civil authorities. He was officially charged with having composed his holy book by making extracts from various authentic translated scriptures, to which he had added matter of his own creation. It was further averred that he had hired a calligrapher named Lu Yen to improve the work's literary style. Miao-kuang was condemned to death by decapitation, and Lu Yen was sentenced to ten years' banishment in the frontier guards. Soon afterward, an ecclesiastical commission of twenty distinguished monks was convened in Chien-k'ang, and the first item on their agenda was the case of Miao-kuang. They petitioned the throne and it was directed that they open an inquiry at the court; on that occasion, Miao-kuang fully confessed to all the charges laid against him. After discussion, the monks decided that he should be expelled from the Order in accordance with the *Vinaya* regulations. The emperor commuted his sentence of death, but since it was feared that were he banished to some remote region he might once more delude the people, he was committed to perpetual confinement. More than twenty copies of his scripture were recovered and burned at prefectural headquarters, together with the screen. But the eminent cataloguer, Seng-yu, the author of this narrative, who had been a member of the ecclesiastical commission, goes on to remark that copies of the work still survived here and there; he had set down this brief account of the affair lest they should lead some younger readers astray. Finally he notes that "Elder Sarvajñatā" was the name by which Miao-kuang's father had been known, that Miao-kuang's younger brother was called "Body of Adamantine Strength" (Chin-kang-te t'i), and that his disciples had been known as "Lions" (Shih-tzu)—or perhaps "children of the Master."[62]

The author of a new Buddhist scripture was clearly risking a good deal, at least in 510, when an imperial bodhisattva ruled in Chien-k'ang. Liang Wu-ti (r. 502–549) took his role as Buddhist monarch very seriously, and it is clear that his highly normative Buddhist dispensation imposed far closer controls on scriptural innovation than had hitherto been current. Our criterion of Buddho-Taoist literary parallelism would seem to bear this out, for we know that Taoists, too, came to labor under stern restrictions during Wu-ti's reign, and no new Taoist scriptures appeared under the Liang until an extensive series of revelations burst on the scene very shortly after the Buddhist emperor's death in 549.[63] Yet the description of Miao-kuang's activity closely parallels the actual practice of the *Book of Consecration*'s author as well. Of the latter, too, it might with justice be said that he composed his work of elements freely drawn from other Buddhist scriptures, to which he added matter of his own devising. He also imposed a sacred authority upon the resultant amalgam and, like Miao-kuang, certainly intended to attract a wide following among all four classes of disciples. We have seen how he anticipated strong criticism from his monastic seniors, conservative reaction of the sort that was to have such fatal consequences for Miao-kuang. Moreover, Miao-kuang is described as a *dhūta,* an ascetic, and we note a prominent strain of ascetic fervor running through the *Book of Consecration* as well. On the strength of these parallels, we can only assume that our sūtra's author was fortunate to be writing about 457 rather than in 510, for although an eager public may still have awaited new revelations, by then the winds of official doctrine were clearly set against scriptural novelties.

There could of course have been more to Miao-kuang's case than this, for other, later sources refer to his scriptural movement as an insurrection. "Rebellion" was ever a facile term for establishment chroniclers to apply to any form of activity that had not received the state's explicit blessing; I wonder if, in unquestioningly adopting the word, modern scholars may not be acceding a little too easily to the official party line. In civil eyes, Miao-kuang's having gathered a mixed group of monks, nuns, laymen, and laywomen seems to have been the prime transgression, or pretext for arrest, in a prosecution that clearly began and ended with the higher clergy. For the senior monks, as instruments of Wu-ti's Buddhist rule, the scriptural fabrication itself constituted Miao-kuang's most heinous crime. These represent the respective views of two complementary official orders, Saṃgha and secular, and both bear on complementary aspects of a single act, since perhaps more than any other form of literary activity, scriptural composition demands an immediate audience. The civil arm had always taken a dim view of unauthorized mixed gatherings. The significance of the proceedings against Miao-kuang, however, lies in what they reveal of the power granted senior members of the Saṃgha to act against authors of Buddhist scripture. It is thus no accident that strict Buddhist textual cataloguing, with sections opened for "suspect" *(i)* scriptures and "falsifications" *(wei),* really began during Wu-ti's reign.

Here I must divagate briefly on the subject of successful scriptural creation in relation to the civil authorities, so that the respective positions of our author, Hui-chien, and the luckless Miao-kuang may appear in sharper relief. Otherworldly texts had long counted among potential dynastic talismans; such had been the original function of the Han Confucian "apocrypha" *(ch'an-wei),* and by the fifth century, at least, Buddhist and Taoist masters, too, were encouraged to draw textual support for the reigning dynasty from their own resources of sacred literature. The Ling-pao scriptures appear to have been claimed as a dynastic treasure during the Liu-Sung (420–479). In 517, the Taoist T'ao Hung-ching (456–536) presented to the throne a corpus of visionary texts (though no scriptures were among them) recorded by a young disciple. He offered them as a token of the celestial powers' favor toward the Liang—and probably also as an attempt to forestall Wu-ti's new anti-Taoist measures of that year.[64]

Beyond their intrinsically auspicious, talismanic function, scriptures might be written to buttress imperial authority in other ways—inaugurating rites to protect the state, as in the case of the *Book of Benevo-*

lent Kings, or bringing welcome regulation into the religious life, like the *Book of Brahmā's Net.* Both these fifth-century apocrypha owe their remarkable success to their usefulness from the official point of view. Still other scriptural compositions achieved prominence as a result of their direct message; more than mute talismans, they were intended and employed as supramundane textual authority for imperial thrusts and parries in the play of court politics. As in the West, older, "authentic" scripture was scanned for clues, to discover new bases for royal prerogative—but in the absence of a fixed, immutable scriptural canon, interpolations and the composition of entire new scriptures were not excluded; indeed, such were among the principal means of mobilizing otherworldly resources in support of the monarch. Texts of this sort enhanced the emperor's traditional sacral role, and might be as effective in dominating the faction-ridden proceedings of the highest secular circles as in attracting popular support in less exalted milieux. In the same way that an imperial ideology infused eschatologically inspired risings in the provinces, a clever emperor and his advisers were always able to draw strategic weapons from the apocalyptic panoply that was kept in readiness in the foyers of certain Buddhist and Taoist masters.

Among outstanding examples of scriptural tampering in a monarch's best interests, we may mention one case concerning Sui Wen-ti (581–604) and another centering on Wu Chao (r. 690–704). A lengthy interpolation was made in the text of the *Śrīgupta-sūtra* as translated by Narendrayaśas (517–589). This work is one of a long series describing the destiny of Candraprabhā-kumāra, who will protect and promote the Buddha's Law when it is on the point of extinction. The interpolated passage states that Candraprabha will be born as ruler of the Sui, Tahsing by name; he will cause all the subjects of Sui to have faith in the Buddha's Law and himself will be fully devoted to the worship of the Buddha's alms-bowl, which will come eastward to the Sui at that time. After reigning half a century, he will become a monk and will be a great inspiration to his subjects.[65] Some one hundred years later, a significant interpolation was made in the text of the *Pao-yü ching (Ratnamegha-sūtra),* translated by Dharmaruci in 693, expanding that text's prophecy concerning a female monarch as a retrospective justification of Wu Chao's assumption of imperial power in 690.[66] These "respectable" Buddhist instances involved only tampering with duly translated canonical works and not the fabrication of an entire sūtra, although alterations in scriptural texts might be accompanied by a considerable array of supportive exegesis, as Wu Chao's case shows.

Greater exuberance in scriptural creation could naturally be manifested by officially sponsored Taoists, since documentary controls on the authenticity of their scriptures were necessarily less effective, although even Taoists felt obliged to claim that their sacred writings derived from originals in outlandish script, originals that they were sometimes rash enough to produce. Monarchs particularly renowned for their Taoist leanings, such as T'ang Hsüan-tsung (712–755) and the Northern Sung emperors Chen-tsung (997–1023) and Hui-tsung (1100–1126), were important foci of Taoist scriptural creation. Perhaps the most spectacular success of all must be credited to the Taoist who, in 1116, wrote and presented to Hui-tsung an enormous scripture, commonly known as the *Book of Salvation* (*Tu-jen ching;* HY 1), celebrating that ruler's theophany. The work was accepted with enthusiasm and set at the head of the first printed Taoist canon; it still opens the Taoist canon today.[67] Even in China, scriptural creation was not always a tale of obscure anonymity or a sorry end. There were moments when a well-made scripture was exactly what was indicated. The hapless Miao-kuang simply wrote at a bad time. In the case of the author of the *Book of Consecration,* however, the timing seems to have been most opportune.

Fortunes were made by scriptural authors during the fifth century. An account is on record of one Taoist writer who composed over fifty scriptures sometime in the 420's; by significantly upping the quantities of gold and silk that were to be furnished as pledges of secrecy by prospective recipients, he amassed wealth so great as to become almost proverbial in religious circles.[68] Within the Buddhist fold, the years when our sūtra's author worked also saw the production of texts such as the state-supporting *Benevolent Kings,* the Saṃgha-regulating *Brahmā's Net,* the *T'i-wei Po-li ching,* which harmonized Buddhist doctrine with traditional Chinese cosmology and morality, and many more. Interestingly, all this activity proceeded happily without interference from either secular or religious authorities; indeed, certain of these apocrypha must have been warmly welcomed in official circles.

During the fifth century the development and expansion of religious institutions was gathering extraordinary momentum in Chiang-nan. Scriptural proliferation was a natural concomitant of institutional growth, and all these fifth-century Buddhist apocrypha represented a legitimate mode of acculturation. Works in which Indian and Chinese elements were blended in accordance with contemporary requirements were an essential adjunct to direct translations in making Buddhist doctrine and practice accessible and intelligible to a wider Chinese audience. We could view them as a textual complement to popular preaching, an activity that also derived its material from an assortment of translated texts, on which it freely expatiated for the benefit of Chinese auditors.

The apocryphal sūtra's functions of appropriation, interpretation, and diffusion may have been all the more important at a time when the number of copies of translated texts was still relatively limited. Such scriptures surely reached many sectors of the population that neither heard nor would have cared to heed the discourse of learned monks. Moreover, the scholar-monks were far from infallible in textual analysis. It is instructive to recall the remarks on the *Book of Consecration* made by the cataloguer Seng-yu, whom we met once again as the narrator of Miao-kuang's dismal story. Seng-yu rightly saw that our sūtra's final book was not a direct translation but had been "fabricated" by Hui-chien on the basis of a translated text, just as Miao-kuang had "fabricated" his own seductive sūtra. Yet he was quite taken in by the bulk of the scripture, and classified its first eleven books as genuine, though anonymous, translations. Moreover, Seng-yu's reservations about Book Twelve clearly had no effect whatever on its popularity. Fifth-century scriptural authors obviously enjoyed many retrospective advantages, not the least of which was their distance of two or three generations from Liang Wu-ti's hypercritical bibliographers. Hence the persistence of many of these texts in successive Buddhist canons, and the undeniable imprint of fifth-century Chinese apocrypha on the Buddhism of China and Japan. Original Chinese scriptures are our most revealing sources on the practice of Chinese Buddhism. In them we find the sole record of rituals and beliefs that have long since vanished, as well as the earliest documentation of others that are still current throughout East Asia. Interpreted with sympathy and acumen, Buddhist apocrypha will stand revealed as a secret museum of Chinese ethnography.

NOTES

1. On the Chinese Buddhist universal histories, see Helwig Schmidt-Glintzer, *Die Identität der buddhistischen Schulen und die Kompilation buddhistischer Universalgeschichten in China; ein Beitrag zur Geistesgeschichte der Sung-Zeit,* Münchener Ostasiatische Studien, 26 (Wiesbaden, 1982), and Herbert Franke, "Some Aspects of Chinese Private Historiography," in W. G. Beasley and E. G. Pulleyblank, eds., *Historians of China and Japan* (London: Oxford University Press, 1961), 115–134, esp. 129–133. The present study of the *Book of Consecration* (hereafter *BC*) is drawn from a manuscript completed in December 1977, on the eve of leaving Kyoto for Berkeley. It forms part of a projected monograph on this scripture, to include fuller discussion of fifth-century Buddhism and the question of "apocrypha" generally, as well as translations and paraphrases of the entire *BC.* Since January 1978, photocopies of the complete 1977 typescript have been in circulation. One spectrum of diffusion has radiated from my Berkeley seminars, the other from my friend Anna Seidel, in Kyoto. Portions of the material have been developed and presented subsequently in my unpublished lectures and papers, "Buddhist Eschatology and Chinese Sovereignty" (University of British Columbia, March 1978), "Dhāraṇī-Sūtras in the Formation of Chinese Buddhism" (University of Southern California, May 1978), "Chinese

Views of the End of the World" (Harvard University, November 1980), and "Heralds of Maitreya" (Princeton University, May 1983). The tenth chapter of the *BC* was studied and translated in "Chinese Oracles in Buddhist Vestments" (Berkeley Workshop on Divination, July 1983). Chapter seven has been translated and placed in historical perspective in "The Seal of the Law: A Ritual Implement and the Origins of Printing," to be published in M. Strickmann, ed., *Classical Asian Rituals and the Theory of Ritual,* Religionsgeschichtliche Versuche und Vorarbeiten, 39 (Berlin: Walter de Gruyter, forthcoming 1990). The *BC* is also the subject of the first chapter, on spells and eschatology, of my book *Mantras et mandarins: le bouddhisme tantrique en Chine* (Paris: Gallimard, forthcoming 1991). Though the text offered in the present abridgement dates entirely from 1977, I have tried to update the annotation. I am most grateful to Robert Buswell for his aid and encouragement in exhuming this aging manuscript, and to Alison Bailey Kennedy for restoring color to its parchment cheeks.

2. The study of medieval Chinese Buddhism was given new impetus by the publication of Makita Tairyō's essays on original Chinese scriptures, *Gikyō kenkyū* (Kyoto: Jinbun kagaku kenkyūjo, 1976); there is now a collected edition of articles by this pioneer of the study of popular Buddhism: *Chūgoku Bukkyō-shi kenkyū* (2 vols., Tokyo: Daitō shuppansha, 1981–1984). Japanese scholars continue to publish copiously on Buddhist manuscripts from Tun-huang; one recent collection: Makita Tairyō and Fukui Fumimasa, eds., *Tonkō to Chūgoku Bukkyō,* Kōza Tonkō, 7 (Tokyo: Daitō shuppansha, 1984). A French research group under the direction of Michel Soymié has been fruitfully engaged in Tun-huang studies, and their publications offer much that is new: Soymié, ed., *Contributions aux études sur Touen-houang,* Hautes Études Orientales, 2 (Geneva/Paris: Droz, 1979); *Nouvelles contributions aux études de Touen-houang,* Hautes Études Orientales, 10 (Geneva: Droz, 1981); and *Contributions aux études de Touen-houang,* vol. 3, Publications de l'École Française d'Extrême-Orient, 135 (Paris, 1984). A new journal, *Cahiers d'Extrême-Asie,* published in English and French by the École Française d'Extrême-Orient in Kyoto, represents a fresh and provocative approach to East Asian traditions. The most substantial individual contributions in the West have been made by Anna Seidel and Erik Zürcher, both of whom intrepidly cross and re-cross the frontiers of Buddhism and Taoism. By Seidel: "Tokens of Immortality in Han Graves," *Numen* 29 (1982): 79–122; "Imperial Treasures and Taoist Sacraments: Taoist Roots in the Apocrypha," in M. Strickmann, ed., *Tantric and Taoist Studies in Honour of R. A. Stein,* vol. 2, Mélanges Chinois et Bouddhiques 21 (Brussels: Institut Belge des Hautes Études Chinoises, 1983), 291–371; "Le Sūtra merveilleux du Ling-pao suprême. . . . Contribution à l'étude du Bouddho-taoïsme des Six Dynasties," in M. Soymié, ed., *Contributions aux études de Touen-houang,* 3:305–352; "*Kokuhō;* note à propos du terme 'trésor national' en Chine et au Japon," *Mélanges à la mémoire de Monsieur Paul Demiéville, Bulletin de l'École Française d'Extrême-Orient* 69 (1981): 229–261; "Taoist Messianism," *Numen* 31 (1984): 161–173; "*Post-Mortem* Immortality or: the Taoist Resurrection of the Body," *Gilgul: Essays on Transformation, Revolution and Permanence in the History of Religions,* R. J. Zwi Werblowsky Festschrift, Studies in the History of Religions, Supplements to *Numen* 50 (Leiden: E. J. Brill, 1987), 223–237; and "Traces of Han Religion in Funeral Texts found in Tombs," in Akitsuki Kan'ei, ed., *Dōkyō to shūkyō bunka* (Tokyo:

Hirakawa shuppansha, 1987), 21–57. By Zürcher: "A New Look at the Earliest Chinese Buddhist Texts," (ms., 1975; partially published in the following article); "Late Han Vernacular Elements in the Earliest Buddhist Translations," *Journal of the Chinese Language Teachers Association* 12, 3 (1977): 177–203; "Buddhist Influence on Early Taoism: A Survey of Scriptural Evidence," *T'oung Pao* 66 (1980): 84–147; "Eschatology and Messianism in Early Chinese Buddhism," in W. L. Idema, ed., *Leiden Studies in Sinology,* Sinica Leidensia, 15 (Leiden: E. J. Brill, 1981), 34–56; "Prince Moonlight: Messianism and Eschatology in Early Medieval Chinese Buddhism," *T'oung Pao* 68 (1982): 1–75; and "Perspectives in the Study of Chinese Buddhism," *Journal of the Royal Asiatic Society,* 1982:161–176. See also Rolf A. Stein, "Avalokiteśvara/Kouan-yin, un exemple de transformation d'un dieu en déesse," *Cahiers d'Extrême-Asie* 2 (1986): 17–80; idem, *Grottes-matrices et lieux saints de la déesse en Asie Orientale,* Publications de l'École Française d'Extrême-Orient, 151 (Paris, 1988); Stephen F. Teiser, *The Ghost Festival in Medieval China* (Princeton: Princeton University Press, 1988); Paul Magnin, *La Vie et l'oeuvre de Huisi (515–577): Les origines de la secte bouddhique chinoise du Tiantai,* Publications de l'École Française d'Extrême-Orient, 116 (Paris, 1979); Kyoko Tokuno, "A Case Study of Chinese Buddhist Apocrypha: The *Hsiang-fa chüeh-i ching*" (M.A. thesis, University of California at Berkeley, 1983); and M. Strickmann, "India in the Chinese Looking-Glass," in D. Klimburg-Salter, ed., *The Silk Route and the Diamond Path: Esoteric Buddhist Art on the Trans-Himalayan Trade Routes* (Los Angeles: UCLA Art Council, 1982), 52–63; idem, *Chinesische Zaubermedizin; therapeutische Rituale* (Munich: Kindler Verlag, forthcoming 1990); and my forthcoming *Mantras et mandarins.* On the Tun-huang *pien-wen,* see Victor H. Mair, *Tun-huang Popular Narratives* (Cambridge: Cambridge University Press, 1983), *T'ang Transformation Texts* (Cambridge, Mass.: Harvard University Press, 1989), and his tour-de-force, *Painting and Performance: Chinese Picture Recitation and Its Indian Genesis* (Honolulu: University of Hawaii Press, 1988).

3. Note the work of such scholars as Richard Gombrich, *Precept and Practice: Traditional Buddhism in the Rural Highlands of Ceylon* (Oxford: Oxford University Press, 1971); S. J. Tambiah, *Buddhism and the Spirit Cults in North-East Thailand* (Cambridge: Cambridge University Press, 1970); idem, *World Conqueror and World Renouncer: A Study of Buddhism and Polity in Thailand against a Historical Background* (Cambridge: Cambridge University Press, 1976); idem, *The Buddhist Saints of the Forest and the Cult of Amulets: A Study in Charisma, Hagiography, Sectarianism and Millennial Buddhism* (Cambridge: Cambridge University Press, 1984); Gananath Obeyesekere, *Medusa's Hair: An Essay on Personal Symbols and Religious Experience* (Chicago: University of Chicago Press, 1981); idem, *The Goddess Pattini* (idem, 1984); Bruce Kapferer, *A Celebration of Demons: Exorcism and the Aesthetics of Healing in Sri Lanka* (Bloomington: Indiana University Press, 1983); Linda Conner, Patsy Asch, Timothy Asch, *Jero Tapakan: Balinese Healer; An Ethnographic Film Monograph* (Cambridge: Cambridge University Press, 1986); and Ruth-Inge Heinze, *Trance and Healing in Southeast Asia Today* (Bangkok: White Lotus, 1988). Among the material from mainland Southeast Asia, I would draw the Buddhist specialist's attention particularly to three works by François Bizot, published under the collective title "Recherches sur le bouddhisme khmer": *Le Figuier à cinq branches; recherches sur le bouddhisme khmer,* Publications de l'École Française d'Extrême-Orient, 107 (Paris, 1976); "La Grotte de la naissance,"

Bulletin de l'École Française d'Extrême-Orient 67 (1980): 221–273; and *Le Don de soi-même,* Publications de l'École Française d'Extrême-Orient, 130 (Paris, 1981). The information furnished by these studies is entirely new and central to the question of Buddhist acculturation; Bizot writes with rare intelligence and penetration. Cf. also his "Notes sur les *yantra* bouddhiques d'Indochine," in M. Strickmann, ed., *Tantric and Taoist Studies in Honour of R. A. Stein,* vol. 1, Mélanges Chinois et Bouddhiques 20 (Brussels: Institut Belge des Hautes Études Chinoises, 1981), 155–191. On the Himalayan front, the special issue of *L'Ethnographie* (vol. 83, nos. 100–101, 1987) on "Rituels himalayens," edited by Alexander W. Macdonald, now provides a superb conspectus of work in progress and may serve as an introduction to the entire field. For China, paradoxically, we are less abundantly supplied. The studies that may be recommended with confidence are those of Kristofer M. Schipper on Taiwan and the Taoist tradition, e.g., *Le Corps taoiste; corps physique, corps social* (Paris: Fayard, 1982); Brigitte Berthier, *La Dame-du-bord-de-l'eau* (Nanterre: Société d'Ethnologie, 1988), on Taiwan and Fukien; and Kenneth Dean, "Taoism and Popular Religion in Southeast China: History and Revival" (Ph.D. diss., Stanford University, 1988). But this is Taoism, and only in one region of China. At least anthropologists and historians have begun to collaborate in the study of traditional China; cf. David Johnson, Andrew J. Nathan, and Evelyn S. Rawski, eds., *Popular Culture in Late Imperial China* (Berkeley and Los Angeles: University of California Press, 1985); James L. Watson and Evelyn S. Rawski, eds., *Death Ritual in Late Imperial and Modern China* (Berkeley and Los Angeles: University of California Press, 1988). But where are the specialists in Buddhism? Even more troubling, where is the fieldwork on Japanese Buddhism? In this case, there is no excuse of long inaccessibility or political delicacy; Japanese Buddhism of all sorts is very much alive and visible. There is Carmen Blacker's *The Catalpa Bow: A Study of Shamanistic Practices in Japan* (London: Allen and Unwin, 1975; rev. ed., 1986). These so-called shamanistic practices all derive from Tantric Buddhism. Otherwise, the best work here is, as usual, in French: Laurence Berthier, *Syncrétisme au Japon; Omizutori: Le Rituel de l'Eau de Jouvence,* Cahiers d'Études et de documents sur les religions du Japon, 3 (Paris: Centre d'Études sur les religions et traditions populaires du Japon, 1981); Anne-Marie Bouchy, *Tokuhon ascète du nenbutsu,* Cahiers d'Études et de documents sur les religions du Japon, 5 (Paris: Centre d'Études sur les religions et traditions populaires du Japon, 1983); Laurence Berthier-Caillet, ed., *Fêtes et rites des 4 saisons au Japon* (Paris: Publications Orientalistes de France, 1981). Although many North American "Buddhologists" (as they barbarically term themselves) enjoy long periods of publicly subsidized residence in Japan, most seem to prefer the atmosphere of libraries and language schools to that of the society in which they temporarily dwell. Nor do American university programs in Buddhist Studies appear to encourage research and fieldwork in the living Buddhist tradition; their neo-scholasticism excludes the phenomenal world.

4. Cf. Sung-pen Hsu, *A Buddhist Leader in Ming China: The Life and Thought of Han-Shan Te-Ch'ing* (University Park: Pennsylvania State University Press, 1979); Judith A. Berling, *The Syncretic Religion of Lin Chao-en* (New York: Columbia University Press, 1980); Chün-fang Yü, *The Renewal of Buddhism in China: Chu-hung and the Late Ming Synthesis* (New York: Columbia University Press, 1981).

5. Students of Chinese religion might benefit from exposure to recent analy-

ses of syncretism in the Greco-Roman world; cf. P. Lévêque, ed., *Les Syncrétismes dans les religions grecque et romaine, Actes du Colloque de Strasbourg* (Paris: Presses Universitaires de France, 1973); F. Dunand and P. Lévêque, eds., *Les Syncrétismes dans les religions de l'antiquité* (Leiden: E. J. Brill, 1975). The latest and most comprehensive account of the "oriental" religions is Robert Turcan, *Les cultes orientaux dans le monde romain* (Paris: Les Belles Lettres, 1989).

6. The accuracy and appropriateness of using the term "apocrypha" in regard to the East Asian Buddhist tradition is broached in several chapters in this volume. "Unofficial" scriptures will not do for all our Chinese Buddhist "apocrypha," since many of them became quite as official as any of the others. "Original Chinese Buddhist scriptures" would be more accurate, but impossibly clumsy. We are obliged to assess the relation of the terms "apocrypha" and "pseudepigrapha" in an East Asian context. Although this latter word has been retained in the excellent work *La Bible: écrits intertestamentaires,* Bibliothèque de la Pléiade (Paris: Gallimard, 1987)—following the German precedent of E. Kautzsch and the English one of R. H. Charles—we find H. F. D. Sparks writing, "the term 'Pseudepigrapha' has been avoided altogether. Pseudepigrapha is, in any case, an ugly word. And when used in association with 'Apocrypha,' as it so frequently is, it can be very misleading. . . . The term therefore, though ancient, is best avoided" (Sparks, ed., *The Apocryphal Old Testament* [Oxford: Clarendon Press, 1984], xvii). It is nonetheless stimulating to juggle these categories in a Chinese context. We should recall the remarks of R. H. Charles, the great authority on inter-testamental literature, concerning the three distinct usages of the word "apocrypha" with reference to his field: laudatory, monitory, and as excluded from public access; see M. Strickmann, "India in the Chinese Looking-Glass," p. 57; "Heralds of Maitreya," p. 4; and the discussion in Buswell's chapter in this volume. Charles also noted an aspect of textual history that seems highly relevant to the study of Buddhist acculturation in China: "the Jewish apocrypha—especially the apocalyptic section—became the ordinary religious literature of the early Christians" ("Apocryphal Literature," *Encyclopaedia Britannica,* 11th ed. [Cambridge: Cambridge University Press, 1911], 2:177a–178a). It is provocative to maintain the Judeo-Christian analogy and envisage Indian Buddhism as the old dispensation and Chinese Buddhism as the new. In this New Dispensation, works deemed "apocryphal" in relation to Indian Buddhism became the "ordinary religious literature" of the Chinese, and it was in the form of this extended and disjointed Chinese New Testament that the Buddhist Law was given to East Asia. Regarding the parallel and closely associated terms "apocrypha" and "apocalyptic," I have tried to demonstrate their functional relationship in a social context in my Evans-Wentz lectures, "Apocalypse in China: Medieval Visions of the World and its Destiny" (Stanford University, 10–12 April 1989).

7. The San-chieh chiao is the focus of chapters in this volume by Antonino Forte and Mark Edward Lewis.

8. Erik Zürcher, *The Buddhist Conquest of China* (Leiden: E. J. Brill, 1959), 1:103–104.

9. Hayashiya Tomojirō, *Iyaku kyōrui no kenkyū* (Tokyo: Tōyō bunko, 1945), English summary, p. 3. Thorough revision of the *Vinaya* corpus has been carried out by Hirakawa Akira in his *Ritsuzō no kenkyū* (Tokyo: Sankibō busshorin, 1960).

10. The false ascriptions are enshrined in the standard index to the *Taishō* canon (*Taishō shinshū daizōkyō mokuroku,* rev. rpt., Tokyo: Taishō issaikyō kankōkai, 1969), the original edition of the *Tables analytiques du Taishō issaikyō, Hōbōgirin, Fascicule annexe* (Tokyo, 1931), and *The Korean Buddhist Canon: A Descriptive Catalogue* (Berkeley and Los Angeles: University of California Press, 1979). The revised edition of the Hōbōgirin index to the *Taishō* canon exhibits the first systematic progress on this front in centuries, since it simply omits the names of discredited or improbable translators. Sometimes the name of an unlikely translator is followed by a question mark, and occasionally a work is explicitly designated "apocryphal," as for example *T* 1484 and *T* 1485; Paul Demiéville, Hubert Durt, and Anna Seidel, eds., *Répertoire du canon bouddhique Sino-Japonais: édition de Taishō, Fascicule annexe du Hōbōgirin* (Tokyo: Hōbōgirin, 1978).

11. *Taishō shinshū daizōkyō,* vols. 18–21. "Diffuse" or "mixed" esoterism is traditionally distinguished from the mature seventh-century Mantrayāna, or "pure esoterism" *(junmitsu),* on which present-day Shingon and much of Tendai doctrine and practice claim to be based. Beyond *junmitsu*'s more systematic and complex character, the principal formal distinguishing feature between the two classes of literature is that the "diffuse" texts are spoken by the historical Buddha Gautama (the nirmāṇakāya), whereas the "pure" scriptures represent the word of Vairocana (the dharmakāya).

12. Ōmura Seigai, *Mikkyō hattatsu-shi* (1918; rpt., Tokyo: Kokusho kankōkai, 1972), 128–133.

13. The most recent and comprehensive descriptive analysis of dhāraṇīs is by Étienne Lamotte, *Le Traité de la grande vertu de sagesse,* vol. 4 (Louvain: Université de Louvain, Institut orientaliste, 1976), 1854–1869. The reader may also consult M. Winternitz, *History of Indian Literature,* vol. 2 (Calcutta: University of Calcutta, 1933), 380–387.

14. No simple contrast of putative meaning or meaninglessness provides an adequate definition of mantras, dhāraṇīs, or anything else. On mantras and their systematic study, see Harvey P. Alper, ed., *Mantra* (Albany: State University of New York Press, 1989), particularly the article by Frits Staal, "Vedic Mantras," pp. 48–95. Although several articles in the collection compare mantras in Vedic and Tantric ritual (Wade T. Wheelock, Sanjukta Gupta, André Padoux), there appears to be no direct confrontation of mantra and dhāraṇī in this stimulating but indexless book. See David Snellgrove, *Indo-Tibetan Buddhism* (Boston: Shambhala, 1987), vol. 1, pp. 141–144. On mantras in general, cf. also J. Gonda, "The Indian Mantra," *Oriens* 16 (1963): 244–297, rpt. in Gonda, *Selected Studies* (Leiden: E. J. Brill, 1975), 4:248–301; Agehananda Bharati, *The Tantric Tradition* (New York: Samuel Weiser, 1965), 101–163.

15. Ōmura, *Mikkyō hattatsu-shi,* p. 38ff.

16. Cf. Teiser, *The Ghost Festival in Medieval China,* p. 133.

17. *BC, T* 1331.21.495a–536b, hereafter cited only by page, register and line number (where relevant). The popularity of the work's three final books, at least, is attested by the number of manuscript copies recovered from Tunhuang. Transcripts of the twelfth book are particularly numerous, confirming the early-sixth-century observations of Seng-yu, to be discussed later. See Wang Chung-min, *Tun-huang i-shu tsung-mu so-yin* (Peking: Shang-wu yin-shu-kuan, 1962), 418. The first-published volume of the catalogue of the Pelliot Chi-

nese collection describes two incomplete copies of the twelfth book, one of them illustrated; see *Catalogue des manuscrits chinois de Touen-houang* 1 (Paris: Bibliothèque nationale, 1970), nos. 2014 and 2178 verso b. A Japanese manuscript copy of the sūtra made in 731 is preserved in a private collection: Tanaka Kaidō, *Nihon shakyō sōkan* (Osaka: Sanmeisha, 1953), 225; idem, *Nihon koshakyō genson mokuroku* (Kyoto: Shibunkaku, 1974), 32. There is a record of another Japanese copy, executed on 150 sheets of dark blue paper in 762: idem, *Nara shakyō* (Kyoto, 1947), 68. The *BC* is quoted in the *Ching-lü i-hsiang* of 516 (*T* 2121.53.17c8–29); the *Chu-ching yao-chi* of 659 (*T* 2123.54.37c2–18, 183a14–c3); the *Fa-yüan chu-lin* of 668 (*T* 2122.53.567a15–24, 754b15–c22, 924c18–925b22, 930c15–931b26, 952b6–c22); and the *Shih-shih yao-lan* of 1024 (*T* 2127.54.305a8–15, 310a6–14). The sūtra was also drawn upon by T'ang T'ien-t'ai authors such as Kuan-ting (561–632; *T* 1934.46.808c13) and Chan-jan (711–782; *T* 1912.46.308c4), as well as by noteworthy T'ang and Sung Pure Land masters, e.g. Shan-tao (d. 681; *T* 1957.47.25b25) and Yu-yen (1021–1101; *T* 1969.47.206a18). It was extensively employed by Tao-cho (562–645) in his *An-lo chi* (*T* 1958); see Satō Ken, "*Anrakushū* to gikyō," *Bukkyō daigaku kenkyū kiyo* 60 (1976): 79–134, esp. 95–101. It is cited eight times in the *San-chieh fo-fa* preserved in Japan: see Yabuki Keiki, *Sangaikyō no kenkyū* (Tokyo: Iwanami shoten, 1927), 598. The most detailed study of the sūtra is by Mochizuki Shinkō in the context of Pure Land doctrinal history: see his *Jōdokyō no kigen oyobi hattatsu* (1932; rpt. ed., Tokyo: Kyōritsusha, 1972), 209–222, reprinted in idem, *Bukkyō kyōten seiritsushi ron* (Tokyo: Hōzōkan, 1946), 409–424. See also the stimulating account by Alexander Soper, *Literary Evidence for Early Buddhist Art in China* (Ascona: Artibus Asiae, 1959; Supplementum 19), 170–178. Soper draws attention to a number of striking parallels between the *BC* and Near Eastern apocalyptic eschatology. Ono Gemmyō (*Bussho kaisetsu daijiten* [Tokyo: Daitō shuppansha, 1933], 2:113c–115a) records three lost commentaries on the *BC,* at least two of which were written toward the end of the seventh century. One of these, on the eleventh book of our sūtra, was the work of Hsing-kan (d.u.), who was among the nine eminent clerics responsible for devising the Buddhist justification of Wu Chao's assumption of imperial power in 690; see Antonino Forte, *Political Propaganda and Ideology in China at the End of the Seventh Century* (Naples: Istituto Universitario Orientale, 1976), 99. The *BC* is also found among the scriptures graven in stone at Fang-shan (Hopei). There is one complete version done during the T'ang in 831, and another accomplished under the Liao in 1088: *Fang-shan Yün-chu ssu shih-ching* (Peking: Wen-wu ch'u-pan she, 1978), 105; two stelae reproduced from the T'ang version, pls. 41–42; cf. p. 92. There is also an earlier independent engraving there of the twelfth chapter, the *Book of the Master of Pharmaka,* as remade by Hui-chien (ibid., p. 20 and p. 88). Begun early in the seventh century, the Fang-shan stone scriptures were intended to provide a permanent record of Buddhist teaching that would outlast the decline of the Law and the social pressures to which the Buddhist community was subject; cf. *Tsukamoto Zenryū chosakushū* 5 (Tokyo: Daitō shuppansha, 1975), 383–429. For a survey of other Chinese Buddhist scriptures in stone—often a startling feature of the landscape—cf. Michihata Ryōshū, *Chūgoku no sekibutsu sekkyō* (Kyoto: Hōzōkan, 1972).

18. In all printed canons except the Korean, the present Book Three came first. The true Book One was relegated to second place, and this appears to

have prevented certain scholars from perceiving the sequential structure of the text. In rearranging the order of Books One through Three, the *Taishō* editors followed the Korean edition and Seng-yu's early-sixth-century list of the sūtra's contents; their order is unquestionably the correct one.

19. Cf. Raoul Birnbaum, *The Healing Buddha* (Boulder: Shambhala, 1979).

20. *BC,* p. 533b23–24.

21. The *BC*'s version is about four times as long as T'an Wu-lan's original.

22. For example, *BC, ch.* 1, pp. 497b18, 497c6, 498b12, 498c20; *ch.* 6, p. 514c14; *ch.* 7, p. 517a10; *ch.* 8, p. 520c3. Needless to say, the usual application of this expression to the twelve divisions of canonical writings has no direct relevance here, though it may well have lent subliminal authority to our text's duodecimal structure.

23. The nine afflictions, for example, fully described in the final book, are already alluded to in Book One (*BC,* p. 497c27–28).

24. For example, cf. *BC,* p. 496a12–19 with the dhāraṇī at *T* 1352.21.865b25–c25 from the *Agrapradīpadhāraṇī-sūtra,* where the transcription employed in *BC* is very close to that used in T'an Wu-lan's translated text, with only slight variations.

25. *Bussho kaisetsu daijiten,* 2:113d.

26. For the text of the consecration rite, see *BC,* p. 497b12–24.

27. *Ta fang-kuang Fo Hua-yen ching, T* 278.9.527b.

28. *Leng-ch'ieh a-pa-to-lo pao-ching, T* 670.16.492c; *Chin-kuang-ming ching, T* 663.16.345b14; *Ch'an pi-yao fa ching, T* 613.15.256b, and 260b.

29. This is a reference to the success of Taoism; see the section below entitled "Taoism: The Demonic Religion of the Last Age."

30. *BC,* pp. 497b25–498a1.

31. Ibid., pp. 501a25–26, 511c8, 504c20, 512b15, 520c15, 523c19–21, 524a1–2, 529c2–3.

32. For a comprehensive presentation of the relevant scriptural sources, see Étienne Lamotte, "La disparition de la Bonne Loi," *Histoire du bouddhisme indien* (Louvain: Université de Louvain, Institut orientaliste, 1958), 210–222. The Counterfeit Law will begin after five hundred years according to chap. 88 of the *Mahāprajñāpāramitāsūtropadeśa* (*Ta-chih-tu lun, T* 1509.25.681b), as well as in Nāgārjuna's *Madhyamaka-śāstra* (*Chung-lun, T* 1564.30.1b). The *Bhadrakalpika-sūtra* (*Hsien-chieh ching, T* 425.14.21a) declares that the True Law and the Counterfeit Law will each last five hundred years, as does the *Karmāvaraṇapratiprasrabdhi-sūtra* (*Ta-sheng san-chü ts'an-hui ching, T* 1493.24.1094a), which was only translated under the Sui, however. Among the translations potentially available to our mid-fifth-century author, only the *Karuṇāpuṇḍarīka,* rendered once during the period 384–417 (*T* 158) and again in 419 (*T* 157), proposes a True Law of a thousand years and a sham one of five hundred (*T* 157.3.211b). Among later works, one chapter of the *Mahāsaṃnipāta-sūtra* also opts for a prolongation of the dharma until the fifteen-hundredth year, but allots only five hundred years to the True Law and a thousand to its counterfeit (*T* 397.12.379c5–9). In the *Mahāmāyā-sūtra,* too, the dharma is to become extinct after fifteen hundred years, and the characteristics of each of the fifteen successive centuries are described (*T* 383.12.1013b–c).

The still further prolonged schedules, as well as the tripartite schema in which a Final Law *(mo-fa,* Skt. *Paścimadharma)* is appended to the two prior stages of True and Counterfeit Laws, are not attested before the sixth century. The sole translated scripture in which the three terms are found together appears to be the *Mahāyānābhisamaya-sūtra* (*Ta-sheng t'ung-hsing ching, T* 673.16. 651c13), rendered in 570. The elaborate development of this notion is particularly Chinese, and reveals a characteristic obsession both with threefold classificatory systems and with chronology. Takao Giken has studied views concerning the Final Law expressed in the writings of sixth- and seventh-century Chinese authors: "Mappō shisō to shoka no taido," *Shina bukkyō shigaku* 1-1 (1937): 1–20; 1-3 (1937): 47–70. It is well known that Hui-ssu (515–577), the teacher of Chih-i (538–597), confidently dated the beginning of a ten-thousand-year Final Law to 434; it had been preceded, in his reckoning, by five hundred years of True Law and a thousand of Counterfeit Law (*Nan-yüeh Ssu ta-ch'an-shih li-shih yüan-wen, T* 1933.46.786b–c; cf. Magnin, *La Vie et l'oeuvre de Huisi,* pp. 104–116.). Ching-yüan (d. 639), the monk responsible for the *Tripiṭaka* engraved in stone at Fang-shan (ca. 40 kilometers southwest of Peking), dated the start of the Final Law from 554, also after a millennium and a half of True and Counterfeit Law; *Tsukamoto Zenryū chosakushū* (Tokyo: Daitō shuppansha, 1975), 5:343–344. The considerable extension of the dharma's lifespan, albeit in debased form, that we note from the sixth century on may be explained by various causes: attempts to account for time passed without the definitive end, prophesied since the third century, having occurred; efforts to push back the Buddha's dates, to give him a more respectable antiquity in relation to the development of ancient Chinese culture; and perhaps most cogently, as a means of accounting for some of the many years still to elapse between the present time and the destined advent of Maitreya, whose coming, at least for the canonically conventional, was still immensely distant. There is now another survey of the various chronological schemata in David Wellington Chappell, "Early Forebodings of the Death of Buddhism," *Numen* 17 (1980): 122–154. I must note, though, that the "succinct and helpful overview" by Kumoi Shōzen of which Chappell makes conspicuous use is simply an unacknowledged paraphrase in Japanese of Lamotte's 1958 chapter, "Prophéties relatives à la disparition de la Bonne Loi": "Hōmetsu shisō no genryū," in Ōchō Enichi, ed., *Hokubi Bukkyō no kenkyū* (Kyoto: Heirakuji shoten, 1970), 287–297.

33. *Fo-shou ta-pan-ni-huan ching, T* 376.12.894c8–16; ibid., p. 895a16–18. On the eschatological references in this portion of the *Nirvāṇa Sūtra,* see Takasaki Jikidō, *Nyōraizō shisō no keisei* (Tokyo: Shunjūsha, 1974), 163ff. During his travels and studies abroad (399–414), Fa-hsien heard an Indian monk preach a sermon, in Ceylon, about the Buddha's almsbowl. The bowl was destined to travel in successive centuries to Tocharia, Khotan, Qarashahr, China, and eventually back to Ceylon and India, before mounting up to Maitreya's heaven. After the bowl has gone, the Buddha's Law will gradually disappear; the human lifespan will be reduced to five years, all foodstuffs will vanish, wickedness will flourish, and violence will break out. Those destined for salvation will escape into the mountains. When the evildoers have all exterminated one another, the Elect will return to the world and practice good deeds. Longevity will then increase, until people are living lives of 80,000 years. Maitreya will descend, and Buddhism will spread throughout the world. The Indian monk provided an exact

timetable for all this, but Fa-hsien admits that he neglected to record it at the time. He did ask to make a copy of the scripture on which the discourse was based, but the monk told him, "There is no scripture; I was simply reciting the tradition"; cf. James Legge, *A Record of Buddhistic Kingdoms* (Oxford, 1886), 109–110. Though there was no scripture in India or Ceylon describing the almsbowl's fateful journey to the east, before the fifth century was out one had appeared—in China. *The Book of the Laying-out and Funeral after the Buddha's Extinction* (*Fo mieh-tu hou kuan-lien tsang-sung ching, T* 392) tells the whole story. This Chinese apocryphon belongs to the genre of Buddhist testaments: predictions made by the Buddha on his deathbed. The major work in this group is of course the *Mahāparinirvāṇa-sūtra,* of which Fa-hsien had brought back the most complete version. It seems significant that Fa-hsien, scarcely an apocalyptic personality, should be responsible for bringing to China some of Buddhism's most influential apocalyptic material. He went to India, he tells us, chiefly to obtain texts on monastic regulations.

34. *Fa mieh-chin ching, T* 396.12.1118c17–1119a19.

35. Ibid., 1119a19–b4. The whitening of religious robes connotes their wearers' automatic laicization. Curiously enough, this literary topos became a concrete trait of later Maitreyan movements, whose members clothed themselves in white. In *Samantabhadra's Book of Verification,* a Chinese apocalyptic text of the late sixth century, for example, we find repeated reference to "the white-robed religious and laymen"—presumably members of the group for whom this scripture constituted a primary revelation; *P'u-hsien p'u-sa shuo chen-ming ching, T* 2879.85.1362c–1368b. For more on this sūtra see Forte, *Political Propaganda,* pp. 271–280.

36. Mochizuki, *Jōdokyō no kigen oyobi hattatsu,* pp. 213–214; T'ang Yung-t'ung, *Han Wei liang-Chin Nan-pei ch'ao fo-chiao shih* (1938; rpt. ed., Taipei: Ting-wen shu-chü, 1976), 598–599. Tsukamoto Zenryū shares the complex of associations that automatically links Buddhist eschatological apocrypha with government repression and rebel movements under the northern dynasties; see his *Shina bukkyōshi kenkyū, Hokugi hen* (Kyoto: Kōbundō shoten, 1942), reprinted as vol. 2 of *Tsukamoto Zenryū chosaku shū* (Tokyo: Daitō shuppansha, 1974), 141–185.

Comparable data concerning Buddhist-inspired insurrections under the southern dynasties have now been gathered by Sunayama Minoru in his article "Kōsayōsō kō," *Tōhō shūkyō* 36 (1975): 29–62. Quite apart from the evidence we have presented for the translation and composition of Buddhist eschatological narratives in fifth-century Chiang-nan, fourth- and fifth-century Taoist literature written south of the Yangtze teems with analogous apocalyptic references; cf. Christine Mollier, "Messianisme taoïste de la Chine médiévale: Étude du *Dongyuan shenzhou jing* (Ph.D. diss., Université de Paris VII, 1986). Regarding Taoism, at least, a strong case can be made for the northward movement of texts and ideas throughout the fifth and sixth centuries. Alexander Soper has gathered data on similar trends in art: "South Chinese Influence on the Buddhist Art of the Six Dynasties Period," *Bulletin of the Museum of Far Eastern Antiquities* 32 (1960): 47–112.

37. Apart from the chronological considerations set forth in n. 31 above, there was a series of legends regarding the foreign kings who would put an end to Buddhism. Lamotte has shown that these tales crystallized about events in

Indian history that occurred in the second century B.C.E., forming a nucleus of lore which could be reactivated and brought up to date as occasion warranted; see his *Histoire du bouddhisme indien,* pp. 217–222.

38. The comparison has already been suggested by Mochizuki, *Jōdokyō no kigen oyobi hattatsu,* p. 214. Kaneko Eiichi has appropriately contributed a chapter on the hidden scriptures of the rNying-ma-pas to Makita Tairyō's book on Chinese Buddhist apocrypha, *Gikyō kenkyū* (Kyoto: Jinbun kagaku kenkyūjo, 1976), 369–386. Now see Michael Aris, *Hidden Treasures and Secret Lives* (London: Kegan Paul, 1989).

39. *BC,* p. 498a17–18, 498b1–15; for comparable passages, see pp. 407b3–11, 511c8–19.

40. The attribution to Śrīmitra is first found in the *Li-tai san-pao chi* of 597 (*T* 2034.49.69a12–26), one of the many false ascriptions made by that catalogue.

41. *Ch'u-san-tsang chi-chi, T* 2145.55.31a25–29.

42. Ibid., 39a22–24.

43. *Fo p'an-ni-huan hou-pien chi, T* 145.2.870b28–c14.

44. On Piṇḍola's legend and subsequent role in monastic life, see Sylvain Lévi and Edouard Chavannes, "Les seize arhat protecteurs de la Loi," *Journal Asiatique* ser. 2, vol. 8 (July–August 1916):5–50, and vol. 9 (September–October 1916):189–304; Mujaku Dōchu (1653–1745), *Zenrin zōki-sen* (Tokyo, 1964), 117–119; Mochizuki, *Bukkyō daijiten,* 5:4333c–4335a, *Hōbōgirin* (Binzuru s.v.), and John Strong, "The Legend of the Lion-Roarer," *Numen* 26 (1979): 50–88.

45. *BC,* p. 497c12–15.

46. Cf. Michel Strickmann, "The Mao Shan Revelations: Taoism and the Aristocracy," *T'oung Pao* 63 (1977): 22–30.

47. On the origins and diffusion of the Shang-ch'ing literature of Mao Shan (Kiangsu), see Strickmann, "The Mao Shan Revelations," passim, and *Le Taoïsme du Mao Chan; chronique d'une révélation,* Mémoires de l'Institut des Hautes Études Chinoises, vol. 17 (Paris: Collège de France, 1981); Isabelle Robinet, *La Révélation du Shangqing dans l'histoire du taoïsme,* Publications de l'École Française d'Extrême-Orient 137, 2 vols. (Paris, 1984). For the Ling-pao scriptures, cf. Stephen R. Bokenkamp, "Sources of the *Ling-pao* Scriptures," in M. Strickmann, ed., *Tantric and Taoist Studies,* 2:434–486.

48. For a famous example of such a merit-divining technique, see Whalen Lai's chapter in this volume; also, M. Strickmann, "Chinese Poetry and Prophecy: The Written Oracle in East Asia," to appear in A.-M. Blondeau and K. Schipper, eds., *Essais sur le rituel,* vol. 3, Bibliothèque de l'École des Hautes Études, Section des Sciences Religieuses 94 (Louvain/Paris: Peeters, forthcoming 1990).

49. *BC,* p. 499a13–17.

50. *Ming-chen k'o* (Statutes of the Numinous Perfected), HY 1400, pp. 9b8–10a4; late-fourth century, no. 11 in Bokenkamp's list of the Ling-pao scriptures ("Sources of the *Ling-pao* Scriptures," p. 481).

51. *Lu hsien-sheng tao-men k'o lüeh* (Master Lu's Statutes for the Taoist Community, Abridged), HY 1119, p. 1a4–9; by Lu Hsiu-ching (406–477), an outstanding Taoist master of mid-fifth century Chiang-nan.

52. See, for example, the statements in the basic prophetic text of the Mao Shan revelations of 364–370, *Shang-ch'ing hou-sheng tao-chün lieh-chi* (Annals of the

Lord of the Tao, Sage of Latter Time, of Shang-ch'ing): "In the *chia-shen* year, earlier and thereafter and at that very time, the Good shall be selected and wrongdoers destroyed. Above shall mingle pestilence and flood, whilst war and fire join everywhere below. All wrongdoers will be annihilated and the workers of evil shall perish utterly. Those who love the Tao will hide in the earth, whilst the Good will ascend up into the mountains. The noisome host of the afflictors will everywhere run riot and will be cast into the gaping abyss. So shall the final judgment be effected. Then in the year *jen-ch'en,* on the sixth day of the third month, the Sage will descend and shine forth in the presence of the multitude" (HY 442; Strickmann, *Le Taoïsme du Mao Chan,* pp. 214–215).

53. For comparable questions of interpretation in present-day Taiwan, see David K. Jordan, *Gods, Ghosts, and Ancestors* (Berkeley and Los Angeles: University of California Press, 1972) and—in Arthur P. Wolf, ed., *Religion and Ritual in Chinese Society* (Stanford: Stanford University Press, 1974)—A. P. Wolf, "Gods, Ghosts, and Ancestors," pp. 131–182 and C. Stevan Harrell, "When a Ghost becomes a God," pp. 193–206.

54. The question has been studied notably by Michihata Ryōshū in his *Tōdai bukkyō-shi no kenkyū* (Kyoto: Hōzōkan, 1957; rpt. 1967), and especially in his *Bukkyō to Jukyō rinri* (Tokyo: Heirakuji shoten, 1976) and *Chūgoku bukkyō to shakai fukushi jigyō* (Kyoto: Hōzōkan, 1967). Michihata's *Bukkyō to Jukyō* (Tokyo: Regulus Library, 1976) studies the mutual influence of Buddhist and Confucian mortuary rites, and is thus a useful demonstration of the functional aspect of a phenomenon that has more usually been dealt with on its rather bland and banal theoretical side.

55. See especially the entire sixth book of the *BC.*

56. These customs are described in *BC,* p. 512b13–29, where it is said that when a person dies they encoffin his body and put it in a cliffside cave. When someone becomes ill, the coffin is opened and the bones are examined, then washed, in order to obtain good fortune and a cure for the sickness. On these typically Yao practices, see Wolfram Eberhard, *The Local Cultures of South and East China* (Leiden: E. J. Brill, 1968), 103–107.

57. *BC,* p. 512c2–4.

58. The development of Buddhist penitential rites has been studied by Shioiri Ryōdō, "Shihai dōjō sanhō no seiritsu," in *Dōkyō kenkyū ronshū,* Yoshioka Yoshitoyo Festschrift (Tokyo: Kokusho kankōkai, 1977), 501–521. Their codification by Hsiao Tzu-liang (460–494) is described by Willy Vande Walle in his study and translation of Hsiao's *Ching chu-tzu ching-hsing fa-men* (in the *Kuang Hung-ming chi, T* 2103.52.306b–321b): *Methode van rein gedrag voor de volgeling van het reine vertoeven: Een boeddhistisch compendium over de penitentie door Hsiao Tzu-liang* (Gent, 1976).

59. Cf. *San-t'ien nei-chieh ching* (Inner Explanation of the Three Heavens), where it is said that "Lao-tzu has charge of transformation through life, Śākya through death" (HY 1196, 1.9b5–10a7). For similar passages in other Taoist texts see Zürcher, *Buddhist Conquest,* 1:306. For a comparable association of Taoism with life, Buddhism with death, in modern Taiwan, see Philip Chesley Baity, *Religion in a Chinese Town* (Taipei: Chinese Association for Folklore, 1975), 136–188.

60. *BC,* p. 513a3–12.

61. Unauthorized healing and divination were also forbidden by the internal regulations of both Buddhism and Taoism. On the Buddhist and Taoist adaptation of induced spirit-possession for diagnosis and exorcism, cf. Strickmann, *Mantras et mandarins,* chap. 4: "Exorcisme et spectacle"; on the genesis of *I-ching*-derived divination in Buddhist and Taoist contexts, see idem, "Chinese Poetry and Prophecy: The Written Oracle in East Asia."

62. *Ch'u-san-tsang chi-chi, T* 2145.55.40b–c. This case has now also been adduced by E. Zürcher, "Perspectives on the Study of Chinese Buddhism," p. 167; cf. Kyoko Tokuno's chapter in this volume.

63. The revelations of "Ch'in-ming ch'i-chen"; cf. HY 164, 674, 1117, 1377. For a study of the major text in this corpus, HY 1117, cf. Yoshioka Yoshitoyo, *Dōkyō to Bukkyō,* vol. 3 (Tokyo: Kokusho kankōkai, 1976), 75–219.

64. Michel Strickmann, "A Taoist Confirmation of Liang Wu Ti's Suppression of Taoism," *Journal of the American Oriental Society* 98 (1978): 467–474.

65. *Fo-shuo Te-hu ch'ang-che ching, T* 545.14.849b–c; now cf. Zürcher, "Eschatology and Messianism in Early Chinese Buddhism," pp. 47–48. For the legend of the Buddha's almsbowl, see note 33, above.

66. Forte, *Political Propaganda.* Forte has now substantially expanded his illumination of Wu Chao's reign in a new book, *Mingtang and Buddhist Utopias in the History of the Astronomical Clock; The Tower, Statue and Armillary Sphere Constructed by Empress Wu,* Serie Orientale Roma 59, Publications de l'École Française d'Extrême-Orient, 145 (Rome/Paris, 1988).

67. Michel Strickmann, "The Longest Taoist Scripture," *History of Religions* (1978):331–351. In an exemplary monograph, *Taoist Books in the Libraries of the Sung Period: A Critical Study and Index,* Oxford Oriental Institute Monographs 7 (London: Ithaca Press, 1984), Piet van der Loon finds that "there is hardly any evidence that new movements or cults were represented" in the first printing of the Taoist canon (p. 44). My own view was inferred from the anomalous position of the new 61-*chüan Book of Salvation* and its various commentaries in the first section of the canon. But van der Loon has established that at least 56 percent of the twelfth-century canon's contents were missing by 1445, when the Ming dynasty sponsored the last Taoist canon to be compiled, the only one that has survived. Thus van der Loon would doubtless attribute these anomalies to the fifteenth-century compilers (ibid., pp. 61–62).

68. Strickmann, "The Mao Shan Revelations," pp. 19–22, 45–48.

GLOSSARY

Chan-jan 湛然
Chang Tao-ling 張道陵
Chen-tsung 眞宗
Ch'iang 羌
Chien-k'ang 建康
Chih-i 智顗
Chin-kang te-t'i 金剛德體
Ching-yüan 靜琬
Ch'u san-tsang chi-chi 出三藏集記
chüan 卷
Fang-shan 房山
Hsing-kan 行感
Hsüan-tsung 玄宗
Hui-chien 慧簡
Hui-ssu 慧思
Hui-tsung 徽宗
i 疑
I 夷

junmitsu 純密
kuan-ting 灌頂
Kuan-ting ching 灌頂經
Ling-pao 靈寶
lu 籙
Lu Hsiu-ching 陸修靜
Lu-yeh ssu 鹿野寺
Lu Yen 路琰
Man 蠻
Mao Shan 茅山
Miao 苗
Miao-kuang 妙光
mikkyō-bu 密教部
mo 魔
mo-fa 末法
Mo-ling 秣陵
Pao-yü ching 寶雨經
pien-wen 變文
P'u-chi 普濟
P'u-hung ssu 普弘寺
P'u-kuang 普光
Sa-po-jo-t'o chüan-shu chuang-yen ching 薩婆若陀眷屬莊嚴經
San-chieh chiao 三階教
Seng-yu 僧祐
Shan-tao 善導
Shang-ch'ing 上清
shen 神
shen-chou 神呪
shih-tzu 師子
su-shen 俗神
Sui Wen-ti 隋文帝
Ta-hsing 大行
T'ai-ping 太平
Tao-cho 道綽
T'ao Hung-ching 陶弘景
T'i-wei Po-li ching 提謂波利經
T'ien-shih tao 天師道
t'ou-t'o tao-jen 頭陀道人
Tu-jen ching 度人經
t'ung-sheng shen 同生神
wei 偽
Wei-shu 緯書
Wu Chao 武曌
Yao 傜
Yao-shih 藥師
Ying-chou 郢州
Yu-yen 有嚴
Yüeh-kuang t'ung-tzu 月光童子
zōmitsu 雜密

Stages of Transcendence: The *Bhūmi* Concept in Taoist Scripture

Stephen R. Bokenkamp

Methodological Issues: The Buddho-Taoist Interplay

The Taoist appropriation of Buddhist ideas goes beyond simple influence or passive borrowing.[1] To a greater or lesser extent, the goal of Taoists in adapting Buddhist elements conformed with the early theory that Buddhism originated when Lao-tzu went west to convert the barbarians.[2] That is, Taoist scripture sought to show the derivative nature of Buddhism and the greater conformity of its own version of Buddhist teachings to the special conditions of China.[3]

While certain Taoist authors labored to portray Buddhism as the less acceptable of the two religions, the authors of Chinese Buddhist apocrypha, we might imagine, sought to prove the reverse. Still, whether furnishing the authoritative resolution to a doctrinal dispute or attempting to augment the appeal of their faith to a Chinese audience, these Buddhists responded primarily to Chinese issues. Paradoxically, both they and their Taoist counterparts were embarked upon the same enterprise —the remolding of Buddhism to Chinese specifications.

Many of the texts that were the most extreme—and the most successful—in this joint venture were eventually judged "apocryphal" in their respective camps. Buddhist scriptures were determined to be "fabricated" or of "doubtful" provenance, while comparable Taoist scriptures were not only expunged from the canon but, as we shall see, emended.[4] Often such attempts at rectification came too late, at least from the perspective of the doctrinal purist, so that the modern Chinese strains of these two religions owe at least as much to creative apocryphal fermentation as to the produce of the original vineyards.

Here I will focus on only one aspect of this complex process: the Taoist appropriation of the Mahāyānist doctrine of specific stages in the bodhisattva's advance to buddhahood and the concomitant articulation of the bodhisattva path in Buddhist apocryphal scripture. This dialectic involves not "pure" Taoism and "pure" Buddhism, for such creatures never existed—nor even "apocryphal" Buddhism and "apocryphal"

Taoism—but the creative interplay between basic Buddhist tenets and ingrained Chinese worldviews as reiterated in Taoist scripture.[5] Finally, Buddhist accounts of the bodhisattva path were to play a role in the formulation of the "sudden-gradual" debate in Chinese Buddhism. The oft-noted fact that this controversy in some sense "responded" to native Chinese concerns requires that we also explore the ways in which Taoism may have participated in setting the terms of this dispute.[6]

We must proceed with caution. First, as a matter of course, our inquiries must be textually based. Often it is possible to do no more than cite the earliest textual reference to a certain idea, despite the fact that the idea itself may have gained currency earlier, say in a Chinese interpretation (or misinterpretation) of a Buddhist translation. A second and related factor that must be kept constantly in mind is that the majority of educated Chinese understood Buddhism only in translation. It is unlikely that more than a small fraction of the Chinese Buddhist priesthood of any period was able to understand the nuances of Sanskrit terminology.[7] As self-evident as this may seem, it is a factor that has a constant bearing on our study. Too often Taoist texts, as well as Buddhist scriptures composed in China, are seen as "distorting" the true message of Buddhism when in fact they are faithful to the nuances of the sinitic garb in which (again in good faith) Indic notions have been clothed. How much patiently ground ink was spilled, for example, in the effort to explicate the concept of śūnyatā (nullity, nothingness, emptiness), hidden as it was behind the Chinese word *k'ung* (empty, hollow, circumscribed space), the connotations of which extended to nothing more insubstantial than the contents of an overturned bowl?

Finally, our study is hampered by the fact that at several times during the sixth and seventh centuries, concerted efforts were made by Taoists to expunge or emend passages in Taoist scripture too overtly drawn from Buddhist texts. This move was almost certainly launched as a result of a growing recognition among Buddhist polemicists of the derivative nature of many Taoist scriptures. In fact, evidence for certain Taoist borrowings often survives only in Buddhist polemical treatises. A brief review of the textual impact of Buddho-Taoist controversies will help to bring this factor into focus and provide a backdrop against which to examine Buddhist contributions to the styles of transcendence.

The earliest recorded controversy over Taoist scriptural appropriations of Buddhist doctrines centered on Ku Huan's (420–483) *I-hsia lun* (Discourse on the Chinese and the Barbarians), a treatise defending the Taoist canonical view that Buddhism was but a version of Taoism that had been watered down for foreign tastes.[8] Among the angry responses from defenders of the Buddhist faith were two letters from Hsieh Chen-chih (fl. ca. 470).[9] In one of these, Hsieh states: "The *Ling-pao* [Scriptures] *of Wondrous Perfection* excerpt passages from the *Lotus Sūtra* and are particularly clumsy in their use of this material."[10] The *Ling-pao* (Numinous Treasure) scriptures are those which Erik Zürcher found to contain "the lion's share of Buddhist loans of all types and levels."[11] The earliest corpus of *Ling-pao* texts, those to which Hsieh refers, were composed in the Chiang-nan region (near modern Nanjing) by Ko Ch'ao-fu (fl. ca. 400), a grandnephew of the well-known Ko Hung (282–343).[12]

Ko Ch'ao-fu's goal in composing his scriptures was to fashion a compelling fusion of the most sublime religious knowledge of his day—the T'ai-ch'ing tradition of meditative alchemy, the Shang-ch'ing tradition of personal apotheosis centering on the visionary texts of Yang Hsi (330–?), and the strains of Mahāyāna Buddhism currently popular in Chiang-nan. It is this latter component of the scriptures that most concerns us here.

Fully half of Ko Ch'ao-fu's scriptures are structured in a manner strikingly similar to Buddhist scripture. They are pronounced in heavenly parks and villas bearing pseudo-Sanskrit names by the supreme deity of the *Ling-pao* dispensation, the Heavenly Worthy of Prime Origin *(Yüan-shih t'ien-tsun).*[13] The name of this deity is clearly modeled on one of the epithets applied to the Buddha, "Heaven-honored One" *(t'ien-tsun).*[14] The Heavenly Worthy's primary interlocutor, who might in this role be compared to Mañjuśrī, is the Most High Lord of the Tao *(T'ai-shang tao-chün),* an avatar of Lao-tzu.[15] Even the contents of the Heavenly Worthy's sermons literally bristle with Buddhist elements—pseudo-Sanskrit mantras spoken for the salvation of mankind, gāthās, versions of the *pañcaśīla,* and a cosmology that includes the Buddhist ten heavens and thirty-three heavens.

Ko Ch'ao-fu had anticipated objections such as those of Hsieh Chen-chih concerning his appropriation of materials from the most popular scriptures of his day. He did not claim to have received the powerful *Ling-pao* revelations himself; instead, he situated them earlier in time, claiming that they had been revealed to his ancestor Ko Hsüan (fl. ca. 240), who is known in the texts as the Transcendent Duke Ko *(Ko hsien-kung).* Further, he portrayed the nature of the *Ling-pao* scriptures themselves in such a way that they might be immune to charges of plagiarism: they originated as "heavenly script" *(t'ien-wen)* formed of primal plasmas in the void at creation. All later scriptures, Buddhist and Taoist alike, are merely imperfect copies of this original, transformative revelation.

Ku Huan's answer to Hsieh Chen-chih's allegations is in line with this latter claim: "The heavenly script of the *Wondrous Scriptures of Ling-pao* issued from the void. Their source is not the *Lotus Sūtra;* rather, Kumārajīva and Seng-chao rewrote our Taoist scriptures as the *Lotus Sūtra.*"[16]

The *Ling-pao* scriptures continued to figure prominently among those scriptures criticized for their inclusion of Buddhist elements. The *Hsiao-tao lun* (Treatise Deriding the Taoists), written by Chen Luan in 570 after his attendance at three Buddho-Taoist debates sponsored by Emperor Wu of the Chou, cites a number of suspect passages.[17] Chen goes so far as to allege that Taoist authors did not even understand the passages they copied. Another way of putting this, more compatible with our own investigative role, is that Taoists tended to understand such passages differently than would the educated Buddhist clergy.

Fa-lin, in his *Pien-cheng lun* (Treatise on the Argument for Orthodoxy) of 626, a response to Fu I's (554–639) memorial to the throne attacking Buddhism, repeats many of the passages plagiarized in Taoist scriptures and already cited in the *Hsiao-tao lun*.[18] By this time, the polemical fervour of Buddhist apologists seems to have prompted a significant reaction in the Taoist ranks. Ch'en Tzu-liang's (d. 632) commentary to the *Pien-cheng lun* records the fact that Taoist authors had begun to replace the more offensive Buddhist terms in their scriptures with terminology more explicitly Chinese in origin.[19] Some forty years later, Tao-shih, in his *Fa-yüan chu-lin* (Forest of Gems in the Garden of the Law) of 668, cites such newly altered passages as well as scriptural alterations dating from 570 (in response to Chen Luan's *Hsiao-tao lun*) to 664.[20]

Although the dating of manuscripts is perhaps not so precise as the direct testimony of Buddhist authors, evidence from Tun-huang supports the assertion that there was a widespread movement to rectify early Taoist scripture. Ōfuchi Ninji has noted the presence of Buddhist terminology in Sui period *Ling-pao* manuscripts, which was subsequently changed to more properly Taoist terms in manuscripts of the same scriptures dating from the end of the seventh or eighth centuries.[21]

This purgation of Buddhist elements extended even to Taoist encyclopedias, which we might otherwise expect to provide us with citations from proscribed or altered scriptures. The *Wu-shang pi-yao* (Secret Essentials of the Most High), begun under imperial auspices during the Buddhist persecutions of 574 and completed soon thereafter, now lacks thirty-seven and a half of its original one hundred chapters.[22] The missing chapters contained much that would be of interest to us here, including sections *(p'in)* on the ten heavens, saṃsāra, *bodhicitta,* and retribution. The *Tao-chiao I-shu* (The Pivot of Meaning of Taoism), composed early in the T'ang period by Meng An-p'ai (fl. ca. 700), although still containing useful information on Buddhist borrowings that will be discussed below, has lost a chapter and a half of its original ten chapters.[23] The missing portions included Taoist discussions of the *triyāna* and the six pāramitās.

The above evidence points to nothing less than a reorientation of the Taoist religion, beginning in the latter part of the sixth century and continuing into the T'ang, brought about in response to Buddhist polemics. Thus the task of exploring the interplay between Buddhism and Taoism during their formative period in China is rendered at once more difficult and more necessary, for the primary evidence occurs in texts that were emended and sometimes even suppressed. We are fortunate that so much of the indigenous Buddhist and Taoist literature survived, despite the fact that scholars of later ages judged it "apocryphal."

The Buddhist *Bhūmi* Scheme

The concept of ten discrete stages in the spiritual development of a bodhisattva toward buddhahood (Skt. *daśabhūmi,* Ch. *shih-ti* or *shih-chu*) is by no means a static one in Buddhist literature. Before looking at the Taoist versions of this concept, it might be well first to trace, in broad outline, its development in Chinese Buddhist scripture. We will not attempt to elaborate all the permutations of the bodhisattva stages in Buddhist literature, but rather to trace a conceptual matrix into which we might fit apocryphal variations on the theme.

The earliest Mahāyāna formulation of the bodhisattva career seems to have been one of four stages, found in the *Mahāprajñāpāramitā-sūtra.* The *Bodhisattvabhūmi-sūtra,* also of respectable antiquity, outlined a seven-stage path that was to be highly influential. When later sūtras fixed the number of *bhūmis* at ten, the eighth stage was generally described as one from which the bodhisattva could no longer regress but would only advance. Still, there was no agreement in the Sanskrit literature as to the exact nature of all ten stages.[24] A ten-stage system is set forth in the *Mahāvastu-,* the *Gaṇḍavyūha-,* and the *Daśabhūmika-sutrās.* These differ from one another and there is scholarly disagreement on which deserves priority.[25]

The apparent contradictions were by no means resolved in China, nor were they allowed to stand unaltered. Translated Chinese sūtras record the introduction into China of two discrete versions of the ten *bhūmis.* The earliest to appear was the *P'u-sa pen-yeh ching* (Basic Endeavors of the Bodhisattva; hereafter *Pen-yeh ching*) of Chih Ch'ien (fl. ca. 220–252). This scripture follows primarily the *daśavihāra* of the *Gaṇḍavyūha,* but also shows evidence of *Mahāvastu* influence: for example, the second stage, *chih-ti* (controlling the stage), seems to translate the *Mahāvastu*'s *baddhamānā* (fastening), and the ninth stage, *liao-sheng* (understanding birth), follows the *Mahāvastu*'s stage eight, *janmanirdeśa* (ascertainment of birth).[26]

In a letter composed sometime around 377, the Buddhist scholar Tao-an (312–385) states that he has just received a translation of the *Daśabhūmika-sūtra* with an account of the ten stages both more extensive than and quite different from the one found in Chih Ch'ien's translation.[27] This newer work, the *Chien-pei i-ch'ieh chih-te ching* (Scripture of the Gradual Completion of All Knowledge and Virtue), was reported to have been translated by Dharmarakṣa but to have remained hidden in Liang-chou (modern Kan-su) together with his translation of the *Mahāprajñāpāramitā.* Tao-an was quite skeptical about this, since he had talked with masters from that area who had mentioned nothing about these exciting works. Although we, too, may have grounds for disbelieving the attribution of this translation to Dharmarakṣa, there is no doubt that it is an accurate translation of the *Daśabhūmika-sūtra.*[28]

The really curious thing, though, is that this newer and admittedly more accurate version of the ten *bhūmis* never eclipsed the other. Instead, both versions were joined to become twenty of the expanded forty-two stages of the bodhisattva path of the *Avataṃsaka-sūtra.* The first version, which appeared initially in Chih Ch'ien's *Chien-pei ching* and was later modified in the *Shih-chu tuan-chieh ching* (*T* 309), became the "ten abodes" *(shih-chu)* of the *Avataṃsaka.* Both the Indic source and the Chinese development of this version are highly problematical, but as we have seen, the ten abodes appear to be based on the *daśavihāra* of the *Gaṇḍavyūha,* with modifications drawn from the *Mahāvastu.* The second version of the ten stages, introduced into China with the mysteriously rediscovered *Chien-pei ching,* is based on the *Daśabhūmika-sūtra* and became the ten *bhūmis (shih-ti)* of the *Avataṃsaka.* These twenty stages, supplemented by the ten practices *(shih hsing),* the ten goals *(shih hui-hsiang),* and the final two stages, pervasive enlightenment *(teng-chüeh)* and sublime enlightenment *(miao-chüeh),* were more or less fixed after the translation of the *Avataṃsaka.*

The *Avataṃsaka* was a highly influential scripture in China and later in Japan, the centerpiece of the Hua-yen school *(Kegonshū),* for which there is no counterpart in Indian Buddhism. The first translation of the *Avataṃsaka* was done by Buddhabhadra in 420 (in 60 *chüan*), and another was completed by Śikṣānanda in 695–699 (in 80 *chüan*) at the request of Empress Wu. The central action of the scripture is the progress of Mahāvairocana Buddha to full enlightenment, a process that carried him along a new and more complex forty-two-stage path.

The importance of the *Kegonshū* in Japan has ensured that the origin of the *Avataṃsaka* from a single Sanskrit or Prākrit text has never been seriously questioned. Even Nakamura Hajime, who finally comes to the conclusion that the text must have been translated in Central Asia, since it mentions China and Kashgar, avers that the original must have been a much lengthier version of the *Gaṇḍavyuhā* than is represented by the "fragments" that have come down to us.[29] We need not come to any conclusion on this complex problem here, except to note that the articulation of an expanded bodhisattva path as represented in this scripture seems to follow the same principles of systematization that we will find continued in sūtras unambiguously written within the Chinese cultural sphere, for the development from forty-two to fifty-two stages was accomplished in scriptures now generally recognized as apocryphal.

For the purposes of this chapter, we will concentrate on the fifth-century *P'u-sa ying-lo pen-yeh ching* (Book of the Original Acts that Serve as Necklaces for the Bodhisattvas; hereafter *Ying-lo ching*), for it is the first scripture to unambiguously tie an additional ten stages, the "ten stages of belief" *(shih-hsin),* to the forty-two-stage path of the *Avataṃsaka.*[30] In addition, this text had a demonstrable influence on the Taoist stages of transcendence. We need to note in passing, however, two other roughly contemporary apocryphal scriptures that treat of the ten stages of belief. The *Jen-wang ching* (Book of Benevolent Kings), falsely ascribed to Kumārajīva, presents the ten stages of belief for the consideration of the bodhisattva, particularly the benevolent king of the title, who is facing the chaos attending the extinction of the dharma. The *Fan-wang ching* (Book of Brahmā's Net), likewise attributed to Kumārajīva, focuses on the rectification of the Saṃgha, a process involving a unique forty-stage path of advancement.[31] Obviously, then, the systematization of the bodhisattva path was a major concern for Chinese Buddhism during this period.

The above outline has shown us something of the filiation of texts that contributed to the elaboration of the *bhūmi* concept in China, but we still have not come very close to the heart of the matter—the attraction such dry, bureaucratic formulae might have had for the medieval Chinese. Before speculating on why the author of the *Ying-lo ching* found it necessary to add yet another ten stages to the forty-two of the *Avataṃsaka,* we need to examine the comparable formulae of China's own religion.

The *"Bhūmi"* Scheme of the Original *Ling-pao* Scriptures

The bureaucratic and hierarchical nature of the unseen realms in Chinese religion is by now well known. From earliest times, the Chinese visualized the celestial imperium as a simulacrum of the worldly monarchy, with its presiding thearch *(Ti)* and descending grades of officials. As a result of this native ideology, Taoism had from the beginning outlined a path of spiritual advancement roughly analogous to the *bodhisattva-bhūmi.* This vision is still prominent in the *Ling-pao* scriptures composed by Ko Ch'ao-fu in the waning years of the fourth century. The supreme deity of the *Ling-pao* dispensation is, as already noted, the Heavenly Worthy, who resides in the highest of heavens, the Grand Veil Heaven *(Ta-lo t'ien).* Under his sway come a multiplicity of governors and functionaries, including the buddhas and bodhisattvas of the ten *kṣetras,* transcendent dukes, transcendent ministers, and the stellar perfected beings.

The *Ling-pao* scriptures hold out to the initiate the hope of entering this celestial bureacracy at one of the lower grades. From this point one might, through unremitting practice, ascend through the ranks to one of the higher positions, which brought with them the perquisites of deathlessness and physical incorruptibility. That is, one might advance through the stages of transcendent beings *(hsien-jen)* to become a perfected being *(chen-jen)*. The scriptures explain this in terms of paronomastic glosses:

> Transcendent *(*si̯än)* means "transit" *(*ts'i̯än)*, the gradual advance from the status of commoner to that of a sage. Perfected *(*ti̯ĕn)* means "durable" *(*k'i̯ĕn)*, that is, never again suffering decay or destruction. From the status of transcendent; one refines oneself to become a perfected being. Thus there are ascending grades of transcendents and ranks of precedence among the perfected.[32]

This ordering of the unseen realms betrays no traces of Buddhist influence and in fact goes back to the earliest Taoist scriptures. The number of ranks usually given is nine since, in Chinese numerology, nine corresponds to the apex of yang.[33] Sometimes the number of ranks is given as seven, another yang number. Such groupings of functionaries correspond to the number of classes of officials in such traditional texts as the *Li-chi*.

Early in the development of the Taoist religion, the rankings of divinities were divided into three categories of nine—the nine transcendents, the nine perfected, and the nine sages *(chiu-sheng)*.[34] These three sets of inhabitants of the macrocosm corresponded in the microcosm to the spirits residing in the three divisions of the human body. The gradual perfection of the individual through the refinement of his corporeal deities exactly mirrored the ascent in rank of the celestial deities, for in point of fact, all these various divinities were no more than emanations of the all-inclusive body of the Tao.[35]

This complex of ideas was largely in place by the time the Buddhist *bhūmi* concept was introduced. Consequently, we find little Buddhist influence on such accounts as are found in scriptures of the Shang-ch'ing and T'ai-ch'ing traditions. The *Ling-pao* scriptures, too, found room for the nine transcendents and company, but their plan for individual apotheosis owed something more to Buddhist *bhūmi* descriptions.

The *Ling-pao* scriptures were particularly influenced by the translations of Chih Ch'ien, which were highly popular among gentry circles in fourth-century Chiang-nan. As I have shown elsewhere, the first two sections of Chih Ch'ien's *Pen-yeh ching,* those dealing with the buddhas and bodhisattvas of the ten directions and the bodhisattva vows, were copied almost verbatim into the *Ling-pao* scriptures.[36] It is not surprising to find, then, that the third section of this scripture, that outlining the ten *bhūmis,* also has its counterpart in the *Ling-pao* scriptures.

One of the *Ling-pao* texts, the *Chih-hui shang-p'in ta-chieh* (Major Precepts of the Upper Chapter of Wisdom), describes the precepts and practices appropriate to two kinds of disciple, the disciple of unsullied faith *(ch'ing-hsin ti-tzu)* and the disciple of ten cycles *(shih-chuan ti-tzu).*[37] The term "disciple of unsullied faith" is an adaptation of the early Buddhist rendering of *upāsaka (ch'ing-hsin shih)* and *upāsikā (ch'ing-hsin-nü),* standard terms for the Buddhist laity found in such texts as Dharmarakṣa's translation of the *Lotus Sūtra.* Meaning literally "men and women who serve," these terms denote those lay Buddhists who not only believe, but who also provide the four items necessary for the existence of the priesthood: clothing, shelter, food, and medicine. Although support of the priesthood is enjoined on the disciple of unsullied faith, the *Ling-pao* concept places more emphasis on the benefit to be obtained by the disciple:

> The disciple of unsullied faith appears in this world. He can obtain surcease of vexation and deliverance from all suffering. His body enters into the luminescence and, within his form, all is pure and correct. He may summon ghosts and command spirits. He may quell demonic essences. In ten cycles he may obtain ascent as an airborne spirit *(fei-t'ien,* Skt. *deva).*[38]

Thus the disciple of unsullied faith has entered into the first of ten "cycles" *(chuan)* that will lead him into the highest of heavens. That this is indeed a Taoist version of the *bhūmi* concept is clear from a further description of the disciple of unsullied faith. He is one who "arouses the thought of the self-generating Tao" *(fa tzu-jan tao-i),* a phrase that echoes Chih Ch'ien's description of the *prathamacittopādi-bodhisattva* as one who "arouses the thought of the Tao" *(fa tao-i).*[39] Further indication of the possible influence of Chih Ch'ien's translation is to be found in the *Ling-pao* assertion that one who arrives at the end of the ten cycles will achieve the rank of transcendent king *(hsien-wang).* Although the name Chih Ch'ien provides for the tenth *bhūmi* is *pu-ch'u,* which we might translate "filling the position," rather than the more suggestive translation *kuan-ting* (consecration) of the *Avataṃsaka,* his brief descriptions make it clear that the position to be filled is that of dharma king.[40] The *Ling-pao* "transcendent king," then, is an analogue of the dharma king.

Another *Ling-pao* scripture, the *Ming-chen k'o* (Ordinances of the Luminous Perfected), contains a passage even more closely analogous to Chih Ch'ien's descriptions of the ten *bhūmis.*[41] In ten paragraphs, the *Ordinances* lay out the meritorious activities appropriate to each cycle, as well as the position in heaven to which one will return at death and the increased terrestrial rank awaiting one in the next life. This progression of life, death, ascent to heaven, and rebirth is what is meant by a single "cycle" *(chuan).* The description of the second cycle, for example, reads:

> One who in this life studies diligently, practicing the scriptures and teachings, who swallows celestial essences and pneumas tirelessly and without slacking, who practices the retreats in the appropriate dress, exhaling and inhaling to refine his body, and who thereby garners merit and spreads the virtue of responsibleness, will have his name inscribed in the heaven of Shang-ch'ing. He will achieve death through liberation of the corpse and will travel the five holy mountains as a lower transcendent. In the next life, he will be born among men to receive anew the Law and the scriptures, and will be honored as a master. If in this cycle his Tao is complete, he may ascend to transcendence, flying up in broad daylight. His rank would then reach that of higher perfected.[42]

This passage helps to clarify several important points. First, the term "cycles" retains here its full Taoist significance. Even in the highly moralistic *Ling-pao* scriptures, the ultimate goal for the Taoist was to refine his physical substance so as to merge his luminous internal deities with the stellar stuff of the heavens. Such corporeal refinement, analogous to the metallurgical smelting process, is accomplished in earlier Taoist traditions through arduous meditation practices or the ingestion of elixirs. In fact, the term "ten cycles" recalls the "nine-times recycled elixir" *(chiu-chuan tan)* that, through nine stages of firing, became more and more subtle until it shared in the nature of the stars, the purest crystallizations of the primordial Tao, and was capable of working this same feat within the corruptible human body.[43] But in the *Ling-pao* scriptures, the process is achieved entirely through ritual means.

To be sure, the disciple begins with meditation practices, the "inhaling and exhaling" of the above passage, during this life, but the transmutation of the physical frame is finally carried out in a most striking manner after death, through the agency of a mortuary text ritually bestowed upon the departed. In the *Ling-pao* burial ritual contained in the *Mieh-tu wu-lien sheng-shih ching* (Transit Through Extinction by the Refinement of the Five for the Revivification of the Corpse), we find a document to be buried with the disciple of unsullied faith commanding the spirits to attend to this process.[44] We learn here that the body of the departed is to be conducted to a "palace of supreme darkness" where it is to be transformed with purifying celestial essences "augmenting and refining its form, so that its bones are fragrant and its flesh perfumed, unperishing for a hundred million kalpas." Meanwhile, the *hun*-soul is to be conducted to the "southern palace" where "it will be provided with raiment and nourishment to remain in the realms of brightness."[45] These two purified elements will then be reunited for rebirth after a specified number of years.[46]

Significantly, we find this process designated in the *Ling-pao* texts by the Buddhist term *mieh-tu* (Skt. nirvāṇa), which literally meant something like "destruction [of the cycle of rebirth] and crossing [the sea of suffering into nonexistence]" in Buddhist texts. Here, though, the term seems to have been read as an adverb-verb construction ("oblivion-crossing" or "transit through extinction") rather than as a compound verb. In this fashion, the troubling Buddhist notion of nonexistence as a spiritual goal is redefined in terms of the post-mortem refinement of the physical body known in earlier Taoist texts as "liberation of the corpse."[47]

Equally important for our inquiries is the fact that each of these cycles is made to correspond not only to a stage of transcendence but also to a celestial rank. From each stage one may ascend into the heavens to assume whatever title one's efforts have won, without returning to earth for further rebirths. In fact, by the eighth cycle, one's celestial rank already equals that of a ten-cycle "disciple of the Most High [Lord Lao]," the deified Lao-tzu.[48] While adopting this more laborious system of spiritual advancement, the *Ling-pao* scriptures kept open the possibility that those of superior attainments might, in the words borrowed from old Taoist texts, "fly up in broad daylight," bypassing the whole process.

Perhaps even more shocking for the orthodox Buddhist is the fact that the *Ling-pao* scriptures seek to perceive transcendent ranking in earthly social status. Each rebirth finds the disciple with a higher position in the social order, first promising only that he will be born among men *(jen)* and finally that he will be born in the "palace of an emperor or king." The *Fa-lun tsui-fu* (Blame and Blessings of the Wheel of the Law) continues the Taoist practice of using the status terms "upper nobility," "middle nobility," and "lower nobility" to designate levels of spiritual advancement. The upper nobility must undergo one further death and rebirth as a believer to reach the highest levels of transcendence, the middle nobility three, and the lower nobility nine.[49]

All of this is exemplified in the Transcendent Duke Ko Hsüan's own account of his previous lives.[50] As the first human recipient of the *Ling-pao* scriptures, his story was of particular interest to the thirty-three earthbound transcendents, both Buddhist and Taoist, who gathered to hear him. At first he describes a discouraging cycle of rebirths during which he descended even to rebirth as a pig and a sheep. Once he was reborn as a minor functionary and, vowing to improve his lot through rebirth into a rich family, provided Taoists with incense and oil and aided the poor. He is indeed reborn as a rich man, but one who hunts and fishes, injuring the myriad beings; so he again falls into the hells at death.

When he finally vows to "follow the Tao in all things," he enters the first stage of transcendence. Even when he is reborn to a rich family as a military man (one who "destroys the myriad forms of life" but still practices the Tao), the Most High intervenes before he can suffer the torments of hell, transporting him straight to heaven. Beginning with his vow to follow the Tao, Ko Hsüan recounts a total of nine lives of increasing prosperity and material blessings. Interestingly, in each of the final six of these lives he vows to become something specific in the succeeding life so that he might advance his practice of the Tao, and each time he is able to achieve his desires.

Anyone acquainted with the Buddhist doctrine of saṃsāra must regard all this as a highly mechanized interpretation, if not as one altered almost beyond recognition. Zürcher has pointed out how the *Ling-pao* scriptures managed to resolve the conflict between Buddhist karma and collective guilt *(ch'eng-fu).*[51] Here the frightening notions of saṃsāra and nirvāṇa have been tamed through bringing them into line with traditional Chinese notions concerning the fate of the body at death. Paradoxically, this has been accomplished through recourse to another Buddhist concept, the stages of bodhisattvahood, which has been fashioned into a consciously applied device by which all might eventually merge with the Tao. Ko Ch'ao-fu must have been aware that he was making the *Ling-pao* control of the cycles of birth and death almost too rigid when he added the cautionary tale of Ko Hsüan coming to grief when he practiced the Tao only that he might be reborn as a rich man.

In a more skeptical vein, we might also remark with Michel Strickmann that all too many of the scriptures produced in China bore their own price tag.[52] Certainly the wealthy and powerful would have been more favorably inclined toward a religion that regarded them, solely by virtue of their station, as already well along the road to salvation.

The early-fifth century *Ling-pao* scriptures, then, were the first Taoist texts to make use of the *bhūmi* concept. If they ever contained a more unified description of the stages of transcendence or provided names for them in imitation of the *bhūmi* names, nothing survives in the scriptures as we now have them. Subsequent Taoist scriptures were to develop one aspect of this complex—the *Ling-pao* claim that one could ascend directly to the celestial bureaucracy from any stage—while expanding the number of stages in direct imitation of the Buddhist developments we have already outlined. This was not to escape the notice of Buddhist polemicists.

The Stages of Transcendence in Later Taoist Scriptures

An intriguing passage drawn from Taoist scripture is cited, by chapter name only, first in the *Hsiao-tao lun* and again in the *Pien-cheng lun.*[53] In the fuller form presented in the latter work, the passage reads as follows:

> The "Chapter on Saving the Kings" of a Taoist scripture states: "The Heavenly Worthy announced to the King of Ch'un-t'o: 'All the sages who have

achieved the Tao, even to the tathāgatas as innumerable as the sands of the Ganges, have begun from the status of commoner and accumulated good actions to achieve it. Of the immeasurable masses along the ten stages of transcendence, there are those who were lifted up at once to their stage and also those who [gradually] attained their *bhūmi* from the position of commoner. Why is this? If one's merit is great, then it is a single ascent; if one's merit is lesser, then it takes ten ascents. Ten ascents means to rise up through the ten abodes, from the *pramuditā* to the *dharmamegha* stage. When one's external signs are complete, one appears in the diamond body.' "

We would be at a loss to place the chapter cited here had the *Pien-cheng lun* not elsewhere recorded information on this scripture:

> The *Pen-hsiang ching* [Scripture of Original Forms] has also changed [the Buddhist] ten stages of practice, ten goals, and ten *bhūmi* to the ten stages of transcendence, the ten conquering stages, and the ten abodes . . . from *pramuditā* to *dharmamegha*. When all the characteristics [of buddhahood] are complete, they call it the diamond body.[54]

Unfortunately, though predictably, not much of the mid-sixth century *Pen-hsiang ching* remains to us. Scattered citations in Taoist collectanea, as well as fragments recovered from Tun-huang, indicate that it was once a lengthy and influential scripture heavily influenced by Buddhism.[55] The "Chapter on Saving the Kings" is not among the fragments. Two separate works survive in the Taoist canon that were once part of this scripture.[56] While neither mentions our chapter heading, one of them, now entitled the *Pen-hsiang yün-tu chieh-ch'i ching* (Scripture on the Rotation of Kalpa-periods from the Original Forms), does contain the following discussion between the Heavenly Worthy and a Taoist by the name of Yen Ming, which parallels the above citation:

> Yen Ming asked: "Can the ten stages of transcendence be achieved all at once or must one cycle through them one by one?" The Heavenly Worthy answered: "From the first stage of transcendence to the tenth stage, there is a progression. One cannot make them all equal in a single cycle. Why is this? There are commoners who move to the tenth stage of transcendence, and there are also those who have heard but are unenlightened and are unable even to move to the first stage of transcendence. This is because in practice there are the adept and the clumsy; in understanding there are the near and the far."[57]

Although the setting and interlocutor are different, this passage discusses the same subject as that cited in the *Hsiao-tao lun* and *Pien-cheng lun*. Both passages employ the same Taoist terminology and develop the argument along the same lines, but arrive at opposite conclusions. Given what we have learned of the Taoist expurgation of Buddhist elements from their texts, it is not farfetched to give priority to the Buddhist citations of the passage.[58] The very fact that this scripture became the subject of controversy was enough to lead to its virtual disappearance. There is certainly sufficient cause for Taoists to have wanted to revise the name of the kingdom as well, for Ch'un-t'o is one of the transliterations used for Cunda, the name of the man who provided Śākyamuni with his final meal. The *Pen-hsiang yün-tu chieh-ch'i ching* passage is highly likely to be a revised version of an original passage cited in our Buddhist sources.

Significantly, the chief disagreement between this passage as cited in the *Hsiao-tao lun* and the *Pien-cheng lun,* and as it appears in the received scripture, is identical to one of the significant debates within Buddhism itself—that between sudden and gradual approaches to enlightenment. The *Pen-hsiang ching,* if our evidence is to be believed, once contained an account of a thirty-one-stage path similar to the bodhisattva path of the *Avataṃsaka.* In addition, it reiterated the *Ling-pao* scripture's old claim to the secret of "one ascent" *(i-chü).*

The final Taoist scripture that we will examine presents an even more puzzling case textually than those we have already discussed. In 679, the Master of the Law P'an Shih-cheng (585–682) held a series of audiences with the T'ang Kao-tsung Emperor at a Taoist observatory on Mt. Sung for the purpose of initiating him to the Taoist faith. A transcript of these discussions, a sort of overview of Taoism, is to be found in the Taoist canon.[59]

At the end of this three-chapter work is a rather long (six-page) citation from an unnamed scripture.[60] This citation contains a discussion between a perfected being by the name of Hai-k'ung Chih-tsang (Skt. **Sāgaraśūnya-jñānagarbha*), whose name, constructed to sound like a transcription of Sanskrit, means "sea-like emptiness, storehouse of wisdom," and the Heavenly Worthy. The Heavenly Worthy expounds to his questioner a forty-one-stage path composed of ten faiths, ten practices, ten goals, and ten cycles, along with a final stage, the Heavenly Worthy *bhūmi (ti),* which is clearly modeled on the two final types of buddha-enlightenment. No discussion of the initial thirty stages is included, but the ten cycles are discussed briefly. Since this passage represents the only surviving explicit Taoist account of the ten cycles, I have translated this section in the appendix to this chapter.

The scripture from which this passage seems to have been drawn, the *Hai-k'ung chih-tsang ching* (hereafter *Hai-k'ung ching*), survives in the Taoist canon with all ten chapters attributed to it in various sources seemingly intact.[61] The passage in question, however, is, oddly, not to be found. Even stranger, the same work that cites the long passage we have been discussing also contains another citation from this scripture listing yet another version of the ten cycles.[62] These names for the ten cycles do appear in the extant scripture, but they appear as a simple list, just as they do in the source that cites them.[63] Further, this same variant version of the ten cycles, one which does not parallel any of the Buddhist *bhūmi* formulations, is cited in the *Tao-chiao i-shu.* After discussing *in extenso* various versions of the ten stages, Meng An-p'ai provides the received *Hai-k'ung ching* list, adding only "in this case, the meaning of cycle is again different."[64]

Again we seem to have run head-on into Taoist revisionism. In this case, however, all the citations originate in Taoist sources. Numerically, the odds are against the *Hai-k'ung ching* ever having contained a forty-one-stage path of transcendence, for we have not only the testimony of the received scripture itself but of two collectanea as well—despite the fact that one of these contradicts itself! I think that we have seen enough by now, though, to suspect strongly that the obviously Buddhist-influenced list mysteriously appended to P'an Shih-cheng's text is the original one. An analysis of the Buddhist sources of the *Hai-k'ung ching* only serves to confirm this hypothesis.

According to an apologetic treatise written in 696, the *Chen-cheng lun* (Treatise on Discerning the Orthodox) of Hsüan-i, the *Hai-k'ung ching* was fabricated by the two Taoists Li Hsing and Fang-chang sometime shortly after the founding of the T'ang.[65] Kamata Shigeo has written an excellent study of the Buddhist sources of the *Hai-k'ung ching* and has identified passages drawn nearly verbatim from a number of Buddhist scriptures.[66] Kamata's analysis has not led him to the apocryphal *Ying-lo ching,* but there are indications in the extant version of the Taoist scripture that the *Ying-lo ching* is to be numbered among its models.

According to the version of the scripture that appears in the Taoist canon, Hai-k'ung chih-tsang was a two-thousand-year-old perfected being who sat beneath an isolated tree answering the questions of passersby with such spiritual perspicacity that he gathered a large number of disciples. The scripture itself is composed of the Heavenly Worthy's responses to questions posed by this pseudo-Śākyamuni and his disciples. At one point, the disciple Ta-hui removes a pearl necklace he is wearing and presents it to the Heavenly Worthy, who, when pressed to accept it, magically transforms it into thirty-six thousand necklaces of white jade, gold, berylline, carnelian, and amber. This multitude of gems, he explains, is as nothing compared to the countless souls he has come to save.[67] A similar event occurs in the *Lotus Sūtra,* but the specific image of necklaces of various precious metals and stones can be traced to the apocryphal *Ying-lo ching,* which mentions necklaces of bronze, silver, gold, berylline, *maṇi*-gem, and diamond, representing the stages of the ten abodes, the ten practices, the ten goals, the ten *bhūmis,* and pervasive enlightenment and sublime enlightenment, respectively.[68]

As it now stands, the miracle of the necklaces leads to no specific doctrinal point in the *Hai-k'ung ching,* but the five sorts of necklaces must once have corresponded to the five parts of the transcendent path that we find only in our mysterious fragment: the ten faiths, ten practices, ten goals, ten cycles, and the Heavenly Worthy *bhūmi*. Further, the fragment of the *Hai-k'ung ching* constitutes the only Taoist reference I have found to the ten stages of faith, a concept that appears exclusively in apocryphal Buddhist scriptures. When the *Hai-k'ung ching* list is compared to that of the three Buddhist apocrypha that mention these stages, no two are identical. The *Hai-k'ung ching* list does, however, match exactly with the first half of the *Jen-wang ching* list and the latter half of the *Ying-lo ching* list. This fact reinforces Kamata's characterization of the *Hai-k'ung ching* as a rather ingenious cut-and-paste job and furthers our conviction that the *Ying-lo ching* was one of its sources.

Conclusion

The scattered fragments of text we have so painstakingly reconstructed show clearly that one current in Taoism, the original *Ling-pao* scriptures and later works descended from them, followed closely the development of the bodhisattva path in Chinese Buddhism. The "ten cycles" of Ko Ch'ao-fu's *Ling-pao* scriptures are based on the earliest Buddhist translation dealing with the *daśabhūmi;* the mid-sixth-century *Pen-hsiang ching,* as Buddhist polemicists lost no time in pointing out, follows the *Avataṃsaka;* and the mid-seventh-century *Hai-k'ung ching* incorporates the ten beliefs of such apocryphal sūtras as the *Ying-lo ching.*

From the beginning, Taoist scriptures modified these ideas in accord with Chinese expectations and beliefs. Viewed from the standpoint of the prospective Chinese adherent, such refinements were attractive indeed. From our survey, three such compromises have emerged with particular clarity. The same sorts of concession can, I think, be traced in the Buddhist scriptures written in China.

First, despite their constant espousal of Mahāyānist universalism, the *Ling-pao* scriptures present their ten cycles as a method, comparable to other Taoist methods but superior to them, of personal, corporeal transcendence. The scriptures stress a mechanistic sort of post-mortem transmutation of the body and its souls, and further hold out the hope that one can control one's fate in future lives through vows. The disciple is even allowed to choose his rate of advancement along the path. Through strict adherence to the precepts and practices, one may "transcend" intermediate stages. One may also advance stage by stage, unable or unwilling to keep all the precepts.[69] The *Pen-hsiang ching* offers the same options.

The same sorts of compromise for the benefit of the Chinese laity are evident in Chinese apocryphal scriptures. The *Ying-lo ching,* for instance, allows the initiate to spend one, two, or even three kalpas laboring through the initial ten stages of belief. Such a person, beginning as one totally unaware of the Three Treasures—Buddha, dharma, and

Saṃgha—might spend many lifetimes mastering the ten precepts and the initial vows before the emergence of *bodhicitta,* that point where earlier outlines of the bodhisattva path began. During this preparatory period, one is still accorded the title "bodhisattva"; such a one is a "bodhisattva in name only" or "bodhisattva in intention."[70]

Then again, there are those people with good intentions who just cannot seem to keep promises. These, too, are provided for:

> To have received the precepts and yet break them is better than not to have received the precepts and yet keep them. There is such a thing as a bodhisattva who has transgressed, but no such thing as one outside the path who has not transgressed. Thus one who receives [and keeps even] one of the precepts is called a "one-part bodhisattva."[71]

Although other descriptions of the path do not easily countenance retrograde movement, the *Ying-lo ching* stipulates that an adept can ascend as high as the seventh abode *(ch'i-chu)* and still backslide without losing the possibility of later advancement.[72] Like one who has failed his official exam, the aspirant is allowed another try. This concession bothered later scholars such as Fa-tsang (643–712), systematizer of the Hua-yen school, who tried to explain away the passage:

> These are but words of exhortation. There is no real regression. [The Buddha] merely feared for those on the initial [stages of the path] and wanted to urge them not to be negligent.[73]

Second, like the *Ling-pao* scriptures, there is a tendency in apocryphal Buddhist scriptures to perceive spiritual status in earthly rank and wealth. Since this is a point already well illustrated in this volume, a single example from the *Ying-lo ching* will suffice:

> From [the eighth *bhūmi*] on up, one manifests the signs of a buddha, is born in the palace of a king, and leaves home to achieve the way.[74]

Such statements appeal to prospective believers, particularly those of rank and status, in the same ways and for the same motives that we have traced in our Taoist examples.

Finally, we need to broach a subject that we have caught glimpses of all along, although it is too vast and complex to be handled in a work of this length. The "sudden-gradual" controversy within Chinese Buddhism, a debate of great significance that eventually led to the founding of the Ch'an school, is consistently discussed in terms of a vague sort of "Chinese context" in which it grew. The *Chuang-tzu* text and "Neo-Taoist" *hsüan-hsüeh* are generally cited as contributing to, if not constituting in themselves, this indefinite atmosphere that led to such profound changes in the Buddhist religion. I believe that our knowledge has now advanced to the point where we can consider the possible contribution to this debate of Buddhism's major rival for the hearts and minds of the Chinese people—the Taoist religion.

The earliest Taoist texts to take notice of Buddhism generally do so in ways critical of the plodding and "gradual" approach of that religion to transcendence. Yang Hsi, in one of the earliest Taoist passages to deal specifically with rebirth, speaks of a lower class of "earthbound transcendents" who, through merit, are able to "leave their clans" to be reborn. All these must leave a foot-bone with the lords of the underworld as surety, and their rate of spiritual advancement is painfully slow, even when compared to other sorts of "earthbound transcendents."[75] Although Buddhism is not mentioned by name here, it is not difficult to see what Yang Hsi is talking about.

More specific is the following characterization drawn from a text roughly contemporary with the *Ling-pao* scriptures:

> Lao-tzu is the lord of living transformation; Śākyamuni is the lord of transformation by death. This is why Lao-tzu was born from his mother's left armpit and is lord of the left. The left is the side of yang breaths and rules the Azure Palace and the registers of life. Śākyamuni was born from his mother's right armpit and is lord of the right. The right is the side of yin breaths and the black records of the registers of death . . . *Even though the transformation of the right* [*Buddhism*] *is not so quick and easy as that of the palace of the left* [*Taoism*], the fact that they return to perfection through cycles of life and death is also good.[76]

The *Ling-pao* scriptures, while adopting the Buddhist *bhūmi* concept and wholeheartedly endorsing rebirth as a path to transcendence, cherished as well this notion of the "quick and easy" *(su-i)* superiority of the Taoist way. Certainly, the prospect of a superior adept's making a single ascent to the realms of transcendence far outstripped contemporary Buddhist insistence that all must sluggishly advance one stage at a time. As the Master of Law Sung Wen-ming (fl. ca. 550) wrote of the *Ling-pao* ten cycles: "There are those who rise up through surpassing enlightenment and those who must ascend through the ranks."[77] The expression "surpassing enlightenment" *(ch'ao-wu),* based on the *Ling-pao* assertion that one might "leap over" *(ch'ao-ling)* intermediate stages, already parallels the Buddhist term for sudden enlightenment or "simultaneous comprehension" *(tun-wu).*[78]

We have seen that the *Pen-hsiang ching*'s claim that there were those who could rise in "one ascent" *(i-chü)* over intervening stages of transcendence was deleted from the text after it was featured prominently in Buddhist polemical treatises. The very ubiquity of this sort of assertion in even the tattered remnants of texts on the Taoist stages of transcendence is enough to alert us to the fact that here might be a matter of some importance.

At the same time, apocryphal scriptures must also have played a role in developing ways to bypass these burgeoning lists of stages, precepts, and vows that would daunt even the most ardent seeker of the Way. The *Ying-lo ching,* though concerned primarily with those on the initial stages of the path and itself guilty of helping to lengthen the bodhisattva path with its ten stages of belief, dares to raise the notion of "sudden enlightenment" *(tun-chüeh)* and "gradual enlightenment" *(chien-chüeh),* concluding that "there are no gradually enlightened world-honored ones, but only suddenly enlightened tathāgatas."[79]

Our own arduous ascent through the Taoist stages of transcendence brings with it no promise of sudden enlightenment, but rather a daunting awareness of the distance yet to be traversed. We have learned that scriptures in the *Ling-pao* tradition cannot be studied without reference to Buddhist apocrypha. At the same time, examples such as those given above show clearly that the concerns of such Taoist scriptures, highlighting as they do Chinese approaches to the Buddhist faith, might best guide our study of Buddhist apocrypha—and the history of Chinese Buddhism as a whole.

Appendix

The following is a translation of a major portion of the *Hai-k'ung chih-tsang ching* fragment which provides the only names for the "ten cycles" to have come down to us.[80] Although this account differs markedly from that of the early *Ling-pao* scriptures—for one thing, the comprehension of Buddhist concepts is much firmer—it clearly owes a debt to that earlier Taoist formulation as well as to the Buddhist texts it copied.

At that time, the Heavenly Worthy was in the Seven Treasure Palace of Purple Tenuity in the *Chia-i* Heaven discoursing on the Wondrous Way to an audience of seven trillion.[81] Among those masses was a perfected [being] named Hai-k'ung chih-tsang who, kowtowing, asked the names of the ten cycles and various ranks by which the myriad forms of life at the mystic portal might, through the arousal of faith, enter the Tao, ascending and descending through the Three Clear Regions.[82]

At this time, the Heavenly Worthy announced to Hai-k'ung chih-tsang: "You should be aware of the order of the stages—the three ranks and the ten cycles—by which the great sages of the ten directions first entered into the Tao. Listen attentively to me now: before entering the ten cycles, one advances along the three ranks. What are the three ranks? . . . The first is the [ten stages of] belief, the second is the [ten stages of] practice, and the third is the [ten stages of] goals. . . .

[Following this, the Heavenly Worthy lists the names of the ten beliefs, the ten stages of practice, the ten goals, and the "ten obstructions blocking the perfected who have entered the Way." No explanations are given of these.]

What is the significance of the ten cycles?

1. One verifies one's Tao-nature, its truths and wondrous principles. As a result, this cycle is named the "cycle of ascertained verities" *(cheng-shih chuan).*

2. One achieves the completion of the wondrous precepts of purity and the wondrous precepts of unsullied purity, thus fully departing from the obstructions of vexation and selfishness.[83] Thus this is named the "cycle of departing from obstructions" *(li-chang chuan).*

3. After hearing the passionless *(wu-lou,* Skt. *anāsrava)* good Law, one contemplates and practices it so that it shines forth and is clearly revealed. Thus this is the "cycle of luminescent antidotes *(tui-chih,* Skt. *pratipakṣa)*" *(kuang-ming tui-chih chuan).*

4. Vexations become as tinder, burnt to cinders by the fire of wisdom. This is called the "cycle of blazing wisdom fires" *(chih-huo hsiao-jan chuan).*

5. One is able to appear in the world with a passionless, sagely wisdom. One does good deeds as expedient means *(fang-pien,* Skt. *upāya),* free from the various vexations and having discarded the passionate mind. One thereby brings to submission the numerous demons. Thus this is called the "cycle of power over demons" *(ch'üan-mo chuan).*

6. One enters the deepest wisdom and arrives on the opposite shore. Benefitting both oneself and others, one's wisdom and virtue are made manifest. Thus this is called the "cycle of virtue manifest before one's eyes" *(hsien-ch'ien hsien-te chuan).*

7. One refines oneself through the principle of signlessness *(wu-hsiang fa,* Skt. *alakṣaṇatva),* thereby completing one's powers, like a man gradually walking ever farther away.[84] Thus this is called the "cycle of the radiant wisdom of distant traveling" *(yüan-hsing kuang-hui chuan).*

8. One's virtue finds full fruition in signlessness. In one's practice there is no flaw. Thus this is called the "cycle of motionlessness" *(pu-tung chuan).*

9. With unobstructed wisdom, one expounds the Law to all beings. Through one's own accomplishments, others are benefited. Thus this is called the "cycle of the mutual response of concentration (Skt. samādhi, dhyāna) and wisdom" *(ting-hui hsiang-ying chuan).*

10. One's body of the Law (Skt. *dharmakāya*) is complete in all particulars. One's virtues are whole. One arrives at completely independent mastery *(tzu-tsai,* Skt. *aiśvarya).* As a result, this is called the "cycle of the completion of the dharma stages" *(fa-ti chiu-ching chuan).*

At this point the grand gentleman receives the position of king of the Law. Or again, he is like a prince among kings who has achieved independent mastery. Still, at this position in the ten cycles, there is a minute obstruction that he has not yet escaped or controlled. Because of this slight obstruction, one has still not entered the Heavenly Worthy *bhūmi*. In the Heavenly Worthy stage, all affairs are completed, all virtues are whole, and one's Tao-nature and wisdom-nature are equal and undifferentiated. . . . One's three bodies (Skt. *trikāya*)—the dharma body, reward body, and response body—one's vows, one's benefits, all are complete.

NOTES

I would like to thank Robert Buswell for his invaluable support and criticism at all stages in the preparation of this work, which began as a seminar paper under Lewis R. Lancaster at the University of California in the spring of 1982. I also gratefully acknowledge the suggestions of Lewis R. Lancaster, Kyoko Tokuno, and Ron Davidson. Responsibility for all views and conclusions expressed herein is, of course, mine. A good part of the rewriting of this paper was done under a grant from the Japan Foundation.

1. On Taoist appropriation of Buddhist ideas, see Erik Zürcher, "Buddhist Influence on Early Taoism: A Survey of Scriptural Evidence," *T'oung-pao* 66 (1980): 84–147. See also Fukui Fumimasa, "Dōkyō to Bukkyō," in Fukui Kōjun et al., eds., *Dōkyō,* vol. 2 (Tokyo: Hirakawa shuppansha, 1983), 95–134, and Yoshioka Yoshitoyo, *Dōkyō to Bukkyō,* vol. 1 (Tokyo: Nihon gakujutsu shinkyōkai, 1958); vol. 2 (Tokyo: Nihon gakujutsu shinkyōkai, 1959); vol. 3 (Tokyo: Toshō kangyōkai, 1976).

2. On this, the *hua-hu* theory, consult first Erik Zürcher, *The Buddhist Conquest of China,* Sinica Leidensa vol. 11 (Leiden: E. J. Brill, 1959), 1:288–320.

3. On at least three notable occasions during the period under consideration here, Taoists seriously proposed to the throne that their view of things be accepted as state orthodoxy and that Buddhists be either driven from the Saṃgha or forced to accept the role of subsidiary servants of the Tao. These Taoist practitioners were Ku Huan (420–483), Wei Yüan-sung (fl. ca. 570), and Fu I (555–639). On Wei Yüan-sung, see John Lagerwey, *Wu-shang pi-yao: somme taoïste du VIe siècle* (Paris: Publications de l'École Française d'Extrême-Orient, 1981), 124:1–33, and Tsukamoto Zenryu, "Hokushū no haibutsu ni tsuite," *Tōhō gakuhō* 16 (1984): 29–101; 18 (1950): 78–111. On Fu I, see Sun K'o-k'uan, *Han-yüan tao-lun* (Taipei: Lien-ching ch'u-pan shih-ye kung-ssu, 1977), 34–95.

4. On the Buddhist bibliographic classifications mentioned here, see Kyoko Tokuno's chapter in this volume.

5. For a clear statement of the scholarly misapprehensions that have grown up concerning the supposed purity of orthodox Buddhism as against the reputed inauthenticity of apocryphal sūtras, see the introduction to Michel Strickmann's chapter in this volume.

6. See, *inter alios,* Peter N. Gregory, "Introduction," in Peter N. Gregory, ed., *Sudden and Gradual: Approaches to Enlightenment in Chinese Thought,* Studies in East Asian Buddhism, no. 5 (Honolulu: University of Hawaii Press, 1987), 1–3.

7. I have recently demonstrated this fact with regard to one item of Chinese Buddhist terminology, *pi-yü,* which rendered the Sanskrit *avadāna* (parable), *upamā* (simile), and *dṛṣṭānta* (analogy). Despite this potentially confusing state of affairs, Buddhist scholars of the caliber of Chi-tsang (549–623) and Chih-i (538–597) regularly explain the term *pi-yü* not by reference to the Sanskrit word it might translate in any particular case, but to the constituent graphs of the Chinese term itself, in the manner of traditional exegesis. See my forthcoming "Chinese Metaphor, Again: Reading—and Understanding—Imagery in the Chinese Poetic Tradition," *Journal of the American Oriental Society* 109, no. 2 (Summer 1989).

8. The *I-hsia lun* is cited, with textual variants, in (1) Ming Seng-shao's (first half of the sixth century) *Cheng erh-chiao lun,* found in the *Hung-ming chi* (hereafter *HMC*), *T* 2102.52.37b15–38a16; (2) the *Nan-ch'i shu* (Peking, *Chung-hua shu-chü,* 1972), 54:931–932; and (3) the *Nan-shih,* (Peking, *Chung-hua shu-chü,* 1976), 75:1875–1877.

9. These letters are collected in the *HMC, T* 2102.52.41b28–42c26.

10. Ibid., 42c14–15.

11. Zürcher, "Buddhist Influence," p. 143.

12. On the *Ling-pao* scriptures, see Stephen R. Bokenkamp, "Sources of the *Ling-pao* Scriptures," in Michel Strickmann, ed., *Tantric and Taoist Studies in Honour of R. A. Stein, Mélanges chinois et bouddhiques* 21 (Brussels: Institut Belge des Hautes Études Chinoises, 1983), 2:434–486, and idem, "Ko Ch'ao-fu," in William H. Nienhauser, Jr., ed., *The Indiana Companion to Traditional Chinese Literature* (Bloomington: Indiana University Press, 1986), 479–481. A list of the original *Ling-pao* scriptures, determined by a Tun-huang catalogue studied by Ōfuchi Ninji in his "On *Ku Ling-pao ching,*" *Acta Asiatica* 27 (1974): 34–56, appears on pp. 479–486 of the former work. I have compared and sometimes accepted textual variants drawn from the Tun-huang manuscript versions of these texts. A different view of the origins of this scriptural corpus has been presented by Kobayashi Masayoshi in a series of articles: "Ryū-sō ni okeru reihō-gyō no keisei," *Tōyō Bunka* 62 (1982): 99–137; "Reihō sekishō gohen shinbun no shisō to seiritsu," *Tōhō Shūkyō* 60 (1983): 23–47; "Taijō reihō gofujo no seisho katei no bunseki," pt. 1, ibid. 71 (1988): 20–43; pt. 2, ibid. 72 (1988): 20–44. Kobayashi proposes that, although the *Ch'ih-shu chen-wen* (HY 22) may have been written by Ko Ch'ao-fu, the rest of the corpus was most likely the work of a group of Taoists surrounding Lu Hsiu-ching (406–477). One of his primary pieces of evidence for this is the level of the Buddhist borrowings in various *Ling-pao* scriptures. His work does help to determine various strata in the text, but it does not, in my view, constitute definitive proof that the original *Ling-pao* corpus was not the work of Ko Ch'ao-fu, the traditional "recipient" of the texts. I address this question in detail in a forthcoming article. The fifty- to sixty-year discrepancy between our respective datings of the corpus is not important to the argument of the present chapter.

13. By "pseudo-Sanskrit" I mean to designate names incomprehensible in normal literary Chinese, written largely with Buddhist transcription characters, in which recognizable Buddhist terminology sometimes appears. See Zürcher, "Buddhist Influence," pp. 109–112, and Bokenkamp, "Sources of the *Ling-pao* Scriptures," pp. 462–465.

14. This epithet is, in turn, an abbreviated form of the words spoken by the Buddha immediately after his birth: "Above the heavens and below the heavens, only I am honored" *(t'ien-shang t'ien-hsia wei wo wei tsun),* as recorded in the second-century translation *Hsiu-hsing pen-ch'i ching* (Scripture of the Origins of Our Practice; *T* 184.3.463b14). See also Chih Ch'ien's translation of the same sūtra, *T* 185.3.473c2–3.

15. See the *Wu-ch'eng-fu shang-ching* (Upper Scripture of the Talismans of the Five Correspondences), HY 671, 1:1b on this name for Lao-tzu.

16. This reply is quoted by Chen Luan in his *Hsiao-tao lun, Kuang hung-ming chi* (hereafter *KHMC*), *T* 2103.52.150c25–28.

17. *KHMC, T* 2103.52.143c–152c.

18. *Pien-cheng lun, T* 2110.52.489c–550b.

19. See, for instance, ibid., 544b20–22.

20. *Fa-yüan chu-lin, T* 2122.53.703a14–703c17. See also such comments as that at 706a12–13: "The Taoists' newly altered text says. . . ."

21. Ōfuchi Ninji, *Tonkō dōkyō mokurokuhen* (Tokyo: Fukubu shoten, 1978), 52.

22. *Wu-shang pi-yao,* HY 1130. The greater part of this damage seems to have been done during the T'ang, for the bibliographical sections of the two standard T'ang histories list the *Wu-shang pi-yao* as a work of only seventy-two chapters. See Liu Hsü (887–946) et al., *Chiu T'ang shu* (Old Standard History of the T'ang) (Beijing: Chung-hua shu-chü, 1975), 47:2030, and Ou-yang Hsiu (1007–1072) et al., *Hsin T'ang-shu* (New Standard History of the T'ang) (Beijing: Chung-hua shu-chü, 1975), 59:1520. For a translation of the complete table of contents for the *Wu-shang pi-yao* that was recovered from Tun-huang, see Lagerwey, *Somme taoïste,* pp. 49–71.

23. *Tao-chiao i-shu,* HY 1121. The complete table of contents is given following the preface.

24. Har Dayal, *The Bodhisattva Doctrine in Buddhist Sanskrit Literature* (London: Routledge & Kegan Paul, 1932), 270–291.

25. For much more detail on the controversies surrounding this question, see Kanbayashi Ryūjō, *Bosatsu shisō no kenkyū* (Tokyo: Nihon tosho sentā, 1961); Akira Hirakawa, "The Rise of Mahāyāna Buddhism and Its Relationship to the Worship of Stūpas," *Tōyō Bunkō Memoires,* ser. B, 22 (1963): 65–69; and Hajime Nakamura, *Indian Buddhism: A Survey with Bibliographic Notes* (Ogura: Kansai University of Foreign Studies, 1980), 195–200.

26. Kanbayashi, while arguing against the thesis I will present below that all these versions of the *daśabhūmi* are somehow fused in the *Avataṃsaka,* concurs that Chih Chien's list owes something to the *Mahāvastu.* See his *Bosatsu shisō,* pp. 147–151.

27. The letter is recorded in the *Ch'u-san-tsang chi-chi, T* 2145.55.62a4–62c21. Zürcher has identified the author and discussed the contents of this letter in his *Buddhist Conquest,* 1:196–197.

28. It is possible, too, that this text was attributed to the famous translator because of his involvement with a quite different *bhūmi* sūtra, the *Yogācārabhūmi* (*T* 606). See Nakamura, *Indian Buddhism,* p. 171.

29. Nakamura, *Indian Buddhism,* pp. 94–197, citing his *Kegon shisō kenkyū.*

30. *P'u-sa ying-lo pen-yeh ching* (hereafter *Ying-lo ching*), *T* 1485.24.1010b–1023a. Notice of this scripture first appears in Seng Yu's *Ch'u- san-tsang chi-chi* (A Com-

pilation of Notices on the Translation of the *Tripiṭaka,* composed 494–497?; *T* 2145.55.62a4–62c21), where it is listed among the miscellaneous scriptures for which the name of the translator has been lost. The *Chung-ching mu-lu* (Catalogue of Scriptures, composed 594; *T* 2146.55.55.115b) lists it as a sūtra with only one translation, by Chu Fo-nien (fl. ca. 390), while the *Li-tai san-pao chi* (Record of the Three Treasures throughout Successive Generations, composed 597; *T* 2034.54.44.89c3) states that it was translated in the fourth year of the Liu-Sung *yüan-chia* reign period (427) by the dhyāna master Shih Chih-yen. Mochizuki Shinkō has discussed the spurious nature of these attributions in his *Bukkyō kyōten seiritsu shiron* (Tokyo: Hōzōkan, 1946), 147–151. Particularly interesting here is the reappearance of the name Chu Fo-nien in connection with this scripture. Mochizuki has suggested that the attribution of the *Ying-lo ching* to Chu Fo-nien may be the result of a confusion with the twelve- or fourteen- chapter *P'u-sa ying-lo ching* (*T* 656) that Chu Fo-nien did translate. Our brief survey of the *bhūmi* concept's development in China has, however, shown the pivotal nature of another work attributed to Chu Fo-nien, the *Shih-chu tuan-chieh ching.* It is possible that the attribution of the *Ying-lo ching* to the same man is an attempt to associate it with the version of the bodhisattva path regularized by the scholarly monk Tao-an. Mochizuki has further pointed out that the *P'u-sa ying-lo ching* uses old translation terms, while the *Ying-lo ching* does not. I have found the same old translation terms in the *Shih-chu tuan-chieh ching.* This further underscores the fact that while the *Shih-chu tuan-chieh ching* may well be correctly attributed, the *Ying-lo ching* decidedly was not.

31. I do not mean to address here the problem of which scripture was the first to introduce the concept of "ten faiths." Fa-tsang (643–712), the Hua-yen patriarch, traced the ten faiths to the *She ta-sheng lun (Mahāyānasaṃgraha).* Kuan-ting (561–632) and other T'ien-t'ai exegetes held that the concept first appeared in the *P'u-sa ying-lo pen-yeh ching* itself. See Robert E. Buswell, Jr., *The Korean Approach to Zen: The Collected Works of Chinul* (Honolulu: University of Hawaii Press, 1983), 92 n. 203.

32. *Pen-hsing yin-yüan ching* (Scripture of the Basic Activities and Causations [of the Sages]), HY 1106, 12b10–13a2. The phonetic reconstructions used here are the Ancient Chinese of Bernhard Karlgren's *Grammata Serica Recensa* (Stockholm: Museum of Far Eastern Antiquities, 1972).

33. The *T'ai-p'ing ching* (Scripture of Great Peace), for instance, lists nine ranks of beings from slaves to the "formless divine men who are endowed with pneuma." See Max Kaltenmark, "The Ideology of the *T'ai-p'ing ching,*" in Holmes Welch and Anna Seidel, eds., *Facets of Taoism: Essays in Chinese Religion* (New Haven: Yale University Press, 1979), 31–32. On the controversy over the dating of this text, parts of which are undoubtedly of Han authorship, see B. J. Mansvelt-Beck, "The Date of the *T'ai-p'ing ching,*" *T'oung-Pao* 66:4–5 (1980): 150–182.

34. See, for instance, the record of P'an Shih-cheng's (585–682) initiation of Li Chih (T'ang Kao-tsung, r. 649–683) into the principles of the Taoist faith recorded in the *Tao-men ching-fa* (Initiatory Scriptures and Doctrine), HY 1120, 1:3a5–8, where these classes of divine beings are discussed.

35. For more on this important concept, barely outlined here, see Kristofer Schipper, "The Taoist Body," *History of Religions* 17 (1978): 355–386, and, for more detail, his *Le corps taoïste* (Paris: Fayard, 1982).

36. Bokenkamp, "Sources of the *Ling-pao* Scriptures," pp. 468–471.

37. *Chih-hui shang-p'in ta-chieh,* HY 457. Kusuyama Haruki, in his "Seishin deshi kō," *Chūgoku no shūkyō, shisō to kagaku,* Festschrift in honor of Makio Ryōkai (Tokyo: Kokusho kankōkai, 1984), 139–155, has studied the meaning of the term "disciple of unsullied faith" as it relates to the transmission of precepts and the ranking of Taoist adepts.

38. *Chih-hui shang-p'in ta-chieh,* HY 177, 5a5–7. My use of the masculine pronoun in translating texts from the *Ling-pao* tradition is not unconsidered; these texts are decidedly misogynistic, even for the Chinese tradition. For entrance into the heavens, the female adept was required to take on a male form. See Bokenkamp, "Sources of the *Ling-pao* Scriptures," pp. 473–475.

39. *Chih-hui shang-p'in ta-chieh,* HY 177, 5a1. Cf. *Pen-yeh ching, T* 281.10.449c22.

40. The bodhisattva of stage nine, for example, is occupied with studying the duties of a dharma king, and the bodhisattva of stage ten with "establishing the dharma in the innumerable kingdoms" (*Pen-yeh ching, T* 281.10.450b29–450c12).

41. *Ming-chen k'o,* HY 1400, 4a3–7a5.

42. Ibid., 4a8–4b2.

43. On the elixir of nine cycles and Taoist concepts of physical transcendence, see Michel Strickmann, "On the Alchemy of T'ao Hung-ching," in Welch and Seidel, eds., *Facets of Taoism,* 169–178.

44. For a translation and discussion of this passage, see Stephen R. Bokenkamp, "Death and Ascent in *Ling-pao* Taoism," *Taoist Resources* 1.2 (1989): 1–20.

45. *Mieh-tu wu-lien sheng-shih miao-ching,* HY 369, 7b–8a.

46. The number of years given is usually thirty-two. The scriptures promise this result not only for the disciple, but also for his or her ancestors to the ninth generation. This doctrine is singled out for criticism by Chen Luan in his *Hsiao-tao lun* (*KHMC, T* 2103.52.146a–147b), with the simple and perhaps tongue-in-cheek observation that, since the time of the sage kings of antiquity, no one has ever observed Taoists or their nine generations of ancestors emerging from the tomb.

47. Meng An-p'ai defines *mieh-tu* as follows: "The corpse and skeletal frame do not decay; such spirits as Grand Unity protect the corpse so that, in some cases, it returns to be reborn in human form after a certain number of years" (*Tao-chiao i-shu,* HY 1121, 2:23a3 ff.). Among recent studies on the practices and beliefs surrounding the concept of "liberation of the corpse," the following should be consulted: Joseph Needham, *Science and Civilization in China* (Cambridge: Cambridge University Press, 1972) 2:301–304; Isabelle Robinet, "Metamorphosis and Deliverance from the Corpse in Taoism," *History of Religions* 19.1 (1979): 57–70; and Anna Seidel, "Post-Mortem Immortality, or: The Taoist Resurrection of the Body," in S. Shaked, D. Shulman, and G. G. Stroumsa, eds., *GILGUL: Essays on Transformation, Revolution and Permanence in the History of Religions* (Leiden: E. J. Brill, 1987), 223–237.

48. The stress on the eighth stage also seems to reflect the notion of a critical stage in the bodhisattva's career, during which he attains "equanimity toward the nonorigination of dharmas" and is released from the material body. This is a vestige of the earlier seven-*bhūmi* scheme with enlightenment coming at the eighth stage. See Zürcher, *Buddhist Conquest,* 1:382 n. 157. We note as well that Chih Ch'ien's translation for the eighth *bhūmi* is "youthful perfected [being]"

(t'ung-chen), which, for the Taoist, could only mean one who has already been translated to celestial realms to continue his advancement.

49. These status terms are first used to gauge levels of spiritual insight in *Lao-tzu* 41, without, of course, any notion of rebirth.

50. This account is to be found in the *Pen-hsing yin-yüan ching,* HY 1107, 3a6–5b8.

51. Zürcher, "Buddhist Influence," pp. 135–141.

52. See Michel Strickmann's comments in his chapter of the present volume.

53. *Hsiao-tao lun, KHMC, T* 2103.52.151a9–14. *Pien-cheng lun, T* 2110.52.545a2–8.

54. *Pien-cheng lun, T* 2110.52.543b28–543c1.

55. Since the *Pen-hsiang ching* is cited in the *Hsiao-tao lun,* we may date it to the mid-sixth century and, although we would expect to find citations in the *Wu-shang pi-yao,* nothing survives. The earliest extant Taoist citations occur in the *Shang-ch'ing tao-lei shih-hsiang* (HY 1124, composed ca. 650). Ōfuchi Ninji's study of Tun-huang fragments of this scripture reveal that it boasted at least twenty-three chapters *(p'in).* See his *Mokurokuhen,* pp. 295–304.

56. The other is simply titled the *Pen-hsiang ching,* HY 319. This scripture does mention the ten stages of transcendence *(shih hsien),* but does not elaborate and makes no mention of the other stages listed in Buddhist citations.

57. *Pen-hsiang yün-tu chieh-ch'i ching,* HY 319, 7b7–10.

58. In all my research into this question, I have yet to discover a single falsified citation of a Taoist scripture, though there are occasions when Buddhist polemicists have abbreviated citations.

59. *Tao-men ching-fa,* HY 1120.

60. Ibid., 3.17a8–20a7.

61. *Hai-k'ung chih-tsang ching* (hereafter *Hai'k-ung ching*), HY 9.

62. *Tao-men ching-fa,* HY 1120, 1.12a6–8.

63. *Hai-k'ung ching,* HY 9, 1.19b10–20a1. In fact, the ten cycles listed here appear to be simply a gloss on the term "ten cycles" as it appears in the text. Tun-huang fragments of this text are unhelpful in resolving this problem since, though in some cases fairly lengthy, they do not contain the passage in question. See Ōfuchi, *Mokurokuhen,* pp. 310–315.

64. *Tao-chiao i-shu,* HY 1121, 1:16b3–6.

65. *Chen-cheng lun, T* 2112.52.569c12–13.

66. Kamata Shigeo, *Chūgoku bukkyō shisōshi kenkyū* (Tokyo: Shunjusha, 1968), 82–101. Kimura Kiyotaka, in his "Zōhō ketsugikyō no shisōteki sekaku," *Nanto bukkyō* 33 (1974): 10–12, has also shown the debt of chapter ten of the *Hai-k'ung ching* to the apocryphal *Hsiang-fa chüeh-i ching.*

67. *Hai-k'ung ching,* HY 9, 1.13a10–14b5.

68. *Ying-lo ching, T* 1485.24.1012c6–1013a14.

69. For an interesting illustration of this, see Bokenkamp, "Sources of the *Ling-pao* Scriptures," pp. 471–472.

70. *Ying-lo ching, T* 1485.24.1017a14–16.

71. Ibid., 1021b15–16.

72. Ibid., 1014b27–1014c5.

73. *Ta-sheng ch'i-hsin lun i-chi, T* 1846.44.280a2–8.

74. *Ying-lo ching, T* 1485.24.1016c18–19.

75. *Chen-kao,* HY 1010, 16.12a1–7.

76. *San-t'ien nei-chieh ching* (Scripture of the Inner Explanations of the Three Heavens), HY 1196, 1.9b5–10a4. This text was written at some time during the Liu-Sung Dynasty (422–479).

77. Cited in the *Tao-chiao i-shu,* HY 1121, 1.16a10–16b1.

78. We need to take quite seriously R. A. Stein's remarks on the meaning of the term *tun-wu.* See his "Sudden Illumination or Simultaneous Comprehension: Remarks on Chinese and Tibetan Terminology," Neal Donner, trans., in Peter N. Gregory, ed., *Sudden and Gradual: Approaches to Enlightenment in Chinese Thought,* Studies in East Asian Buddhism, no. 5 (Honolulu: University of Hawaii Press, 1987), 41–65. Certainly the terms that Taoists use to describe similar ideas connote not so much suddenness as simultaneity, in that they describe a leap over intervening stages of development.

79. *Ying-lo ching, T* 1485.24.1018c8–21.

80. *Tao-men ching-fa,* HY 1120, 3:17a8–20a7.

81. On the "Palace of Purple Tenuity," the celestial residence of the Heavenly Worthy, emperor of heaven, located visibly in constellations surrounding the pole star, see Edward H. Schafer, *Pacing the Void: T'ang Approaches to the Stars* (Berkeley: University of California Press, 1977), 47–53. The *Chia-i* Heaven is the eighth heaven of the north in the *Ling-pao* version of the thirty-three heavens *(trayastriṃśās)* that, for the Buddhists, encircled Mt. Sumeru. See Bokenkamp, "Sources of the *Ling-pao* Scriptures," pp. 463–465.

82. The "Three Clear Regions" is a collective term for the three heavens directly beneath the Grand Veil Heaven: the Heaven of Jade Clarity, the Heaven of Upper Clarity, and the Heaven of Grand Clarity.

83. Several levels of precepts are found in the *Hai-k'ung ching.* The lowest level is the ten "prohibitive precepts" *(chin-chieh),* based on the ten Mahāyāna precepts (see HY 9, 1.29b6–8). The more advanced precepts of purity *(ching-chieh)* are positive injunctions based on a version of the bodhisattva vow in which one vows not to achieve enlightenment until all sentient beings have done so, while the precepts of unsullied purity *(ch'ing-ching chieh)* constitute various meditations on such things as the fact that the body is not the true self (see HY 9, 2.7a6–7b1 and 6.1a3–9a6).

84. Signlessness is one of the three gates to liberation in Buddhism, entered when one realizes the emptiness of the characteristics of phenomenal objects. This growing awareness is here expressed in the image of a person "gradually walking ever farther away." The principle of signlessness is discussed in the *Hai-k'ung ching,* HY 9, 1:9b4–12a3.

GLOSSARY

ch'an 禪
ch'ao-ling 超陵
ch'ao-wu 超悟
Chen-cheng lun 甄正論
chen-jen 真人
Chen Luan 甄鸞
Ch'en Tzu-liang 陳子良
Cheng erh-chiao lun 正二教論
ch'eng-fu 承負
cheng-shih chuan 證實轉
ch'i-chu 七住
Chia-i (heaven) 賈奕
Chiang-nan 江南
chien-chüeh 漸覺

Chien-pei i-ch'ieh chih-te ching 漸備一切智德經
Chih Ch'ien 支謙
Chih-hui shang-p'in ta-chieh 智慧上品大戒
chih-huo hsiao-jan chuan 智火燒然轉
chih-ti 治地
Chin 晉
chin-chieh 禁戒
ching-chieh 淨戒
ch'ing-ching chieh 淸淨戒
ch'ing-hsin-nü 淸信女
ch'ing-hsin shih 淸信士
ch'ing-hsin ti-tzu 淸信弟子
chiu-chuan tan 九轉丹
chiu-sheng 九聖
Chiu T'ang shu 舊唐書
Chou Wu-ti 周武帝
Chu Fa-hu 竺法護
Chu Fo-nien 竺佛念
Ch'u san-tsang chi-chi 出三藏記集
chuan 轉
ch'üan-mo chuan 權魔轉
Chuang-tzu 莊子
Ch'un-t'o 純陀
Chung-ching mu-lu 衆經目錄
Chung-sheng nan 衆聖難
Fa-lin 法琳
Fa-lun tsui-fu 法輪罪福
fa p'u-t'i hsin 發菩提心
fa tao-i 發道意
fa-ti chiu-ching chuan 法地究竟轉
Fa-tsang 法藏
fa tzu-jan tao-i 發自然道意
Fa-yüan chu-lin 法苑珠林
Fan-wang ching 梵王經
Fang-chang 方長
fang-pien 方便
fei-t'ien 飛天
Fu I 傅奕
Hai-k'ung Chih-tsang 海空智藏
Hai-k'ung chih-tsang ching 海空智藏經
Hsiang-fa chüeh-i ching 像法決疑經
Hsiao-tao lun 笑道論
Hsieh Chen-chih 謝鎮之
hsien-ch'ien hsien-te chuan 現前顯德轉
hsien-jen 仙人
hsien-wang 仙王
Hsin T'ang-shu 新唐書
Hsiu-hsing pen-ch'i ching 修行本起經
hsüan-hsüeh 玄學
Hsüan-i 玄嶷
hua-hu 化胡
Hua-yen 華嚴
hun 魂
Hung-ming chi 弘明集
i-chü 一舉
I-hsia lun 夷夏論
jen 人
Jen-wang ching 仁王經
Kao-tsung 高宗
**k'i̯ĕn* 堅
Ko Ch'ao-fu 葛巢甫
Ko Hsüan (*hsien-kung*) 葛玄(仙公)
Ko Hung 葛洪
Ku Huan 顧歡
Kuan-ting 灌頂
kuan-ting 灌頂
Kuang hung-ming chi 廣弘明集
kuang-ming tui-chih chuan 光明對治轉
k'ung 空
Lao-tzu 老子
li-chang chuan 離障轉
Li-chi 禮記
Li Chih 李治
Li Hsing 黎興
Li-tai san-pao chi 歷代三寶紀
Liang-chou 涼州
liao-sheng 了生
Ling-pao 靈寶
Ling-pao ching 靈寶經
Liu Hsü 劉煦
Liu-sung 劉宋
Lu Hsiu-ching 陸修靜
Lung-an 隆安
Meng An-p'ai 孟安排
miao-chüeh 妙覺
mieh-tu 滅度
Mieh-tu wu-lien sheng-shih ching 滅度五煉生尸經
Ming-chen k'o 明真科
Ming Seng-shao 明僧紹
Nan-ch'i shu 南齊書
Nan-shih 南史
Ou-yang Hsiu 歐陽修
P'an Shih-cheng 潘師正

Pen-hsiang ching 本相經
Pen-hsiang yün-tu chieh-ch'i ching 本相運度劫期經
Pen-hsing yin-yüan ching 本行因緣經
Pen-yeh ching 本業經
pi-yü 比喻
Pien-cheng lun 辨正論
p'in 品
pu-ch'u 補處
P'u-sa pen-yeh ching 菩薩本業經
P'u-sa ying-lo ching 菩薩瓔珞經
P'u-sa ying-lo pen-yeh ching 菩薩瓔珞本業經
pu-tung chuan 不動轉
San-t'ien nei-chieh ching 三天內解經
Seng-chao 僧肇
Seng-yu 僧祐
Shang-ch'ing 上淸
Shang-ch'ing tao-lei shih-hsiang 上淸道類事項
She ta-sheng lun 攝大乘論
Shih Chih-yen 釋智嚴
shih-chu 十住
Shih-chu tuan-chieh ching 十住斷結經
shih-chuan ti-tzu 十轉弟子
shih-hsien 十仙
shih-hsin 十信
shih hsing 十行
shih hui-hsiang 十廻向
shih-ti 十地
**si̯än* 仙
su-i 速易
Sui 隋
Sung Wen-ming 宋文明
Ta-hui 大慧
Ta-lo t'ien 大羅天
Ta-sheng ch'i-hsin lun i-chi 大乘起心論義記
T'ai-ch'ing 太淸
T'ai-p'ing ching 太平經
T'ai-shang tao-chün 太上道君
T'ang Kao-tsung 唐高宗
Tao-an 道安
Tao-chiao I-shu 道教義樞
Tao-men ching-fa 道門經法
Tao-shih 道世
teng-chüeh 等覺
ti 地
Ti 帝
**ṭi̯ĕn* 真
t'ien-shang t'ien-hsia wei wo wei tsun 天上天下唯我為尊
T'ien-t'ai 天臺
t'ien-tsun 天尊
t'ien-wen 天文
ting-hui hsiang-ying chuan 定慧相應轉
**ts'i̯än* 遷
tui-chih 對治
tun-chüeh 頓覺
Tun-huang 敦煌
tun-wu 頓悟
t'ung-chen 童真
tzu-tsai 自在
Wei Yüan-sung 衞元嵩
Wu-ch'eng-fu shang-ching 五稱符上經
wu-hsiang fa 無相法
wu-lou 無漏
Wu-shang pi-yao 无上祕要
yang 陽
Yang Hsi 楊羲
Yen Ming 炎明
yin 陰
yüan-chia 元嘉
yüan-hsing kuang-hui chuan 遠行光慧轉
Yüan-shih t'ien-tsun 元始天尊

The Textual Origins of the *Kuan Wu-liang-shou ching*: A Canonical Scripture of Pure Land Buddhism

Kōtatsu Fujita

Translated by Kenneth K. Tanaka

Translator's Introduction

In China, the *Kuan Wu-liang-shou ching* (Book on the Contemplation of the Buddha of Immeasurable Life) played a more vital role in the early phase of Pure Land Buddhist development than any other Pure Land sūtra.[1] From the Sui to the Sung period, at least forty commentaries were written, most of which were compiled prior to the year 800.[2] That the preeminent Chinese Pure Land proponent, Shan-tao (613–681), wrote as his magnum opus a commentary on the *Kuan Wu-liang-shou ching* (hereafter *KWC*) underscores its centrality.[3] Further, the other major commentaries on this sūtra, by Ching-ying Hui-yüan (523–592) and T'ien-t'ai Chih-i (538–597), left a profound impact beyond the traditional boundaries of the Pure Land school in China, Korea and Japan.[4]

Three factors account for the importance of the *KWC* in the early development of Pure Land Buddhism in East Asia. First, it served as a canonical scripture that advocated two of the leading forms of practice for rebirth: contemplation *(kuan)* and oral recitation of the name *(ch'eng-ming)* of Amitābha. As will be discussed below, contemplation generated much interest among the Chinese Buddhists of the early fifth century, as seen in the translation of several "contemplation sūtras" during that period. Oral recitation, too, received focused attention and made the teaching more accessible to a large number of lay people than did the more inhibiting and demanding ethical and contemplative practices. Recitation allowed even those who had committed transgressions to realize rebirth.[5] Second, some modern scholars have argued that the pathos experienced by Lady Vaidehī in the preface section of the *KWC* (see below) reinforced the growing sense of human spiritual deprivation and societal pessimism in China of the second half of the sixth century. The story confirmed for the Buddhists of the period the arrival of the Final Age of the Dharma *(mo-fa)* in light of the natural disasters and continual warfare that culminated in the persecution of Buddhism from 577 to 580 by Emperor Wu of the Northern Chou.[6] Third, as evidenced by the numerous commentaries written on the *KWC,* this sūtra was instrumental in generating considerable scholarly discussion of Mahāyāna doctrinal issues. One such issue dealt with the ranking of the nine grades of rebirth within the framework of the general Mahāyāna path system (mārga).[7] In this process, the *KWC* helped to bring the Pure Land teaching to center stage for many scholar-monk exegetes, beginning in the sixth century.[8]

The *KWC* begins with a prologue devoted to the story of King Ajātaśatru and his parents, the former King Bimbisāra and Lady Vaidehī. Upon learning from Devadatta about his father's failed attempt to kill him at birth, Ajātaśatru imprisons Bimbisāra with the intention of starving him to death.[9] However, Lady Vaidehī succeeds in keeping Bimbisāra alive by secretly feeding him during her visits. When Ajātaśatru discovers his mother's clandestine activity, in great anger he also imprisons her. Deeply saddened by her son's action, Vaidehī seeks Śākyamuni Buddha's counsel and requests rebirth in a realm devoid of suffering. The Buddha then illuminates and displays for her the countless realms in the ten quarters of the universe, from which Vaidehī selects Buddha Amitābha's Sukhāvatī.

The Buddha proceeds to expound the required practices for aspirants to Amitābha's Pure Land. These practices include the "three purified acts," comprised of faithfully caring for one's parents and teachers, adhering to precepts, and reciting the Mahāyāna sutras. Through his supernormal powers, the Buddha then leads Vaidehī and others to see Amitābha's realm and thereby to acquire insight into the nonproduction of dharmas.

Out of concern for future beings who will be without the benefit of the Buddha's "revelation," Vaidehī inquires about the way for their rebirth. In response, the Buddha instructs her in the sixteen kinds of contemplations, beginning with contemplation of the setting sun in this Sahā world and moving on to the physical dimensions of Sukhāvatī, such as the ground, trees, and lakes, and to the features of Buddha Amitābha and his attendant bodhisattvas Avalokiteśvara and Mahāsthāmaprāpta. The last three contemplations have as their object the nine grades of rebirth that detail people of varying ability and attainment. The instruction on the contemplation constitutes the primary subject of the main body of the sutra. The *KWC* concludes by assuring Lady Vaidehī of her imminent rebirth and admonishing the reader to expound the espoused teaching of the sutra.

Background of the "Translation"

The *Kuan Wu-liang-shou ching* has long been counted among the "three Pure Land sūtras," along with the *Wu-liang-shou ching* (Larger Sukhāvatīvyūha-sūtra) and the *A-mi-t'o ching* (Smaller Sukhāvatīvyūha-sūtra). Traditionally, it has been referred to as the *Kuan Wu-liang-shou-fo ching* or *Wu-liang-shou kuan ching*[10] and is considered to have been translated by Kālayaśas (Chiang-liang-yeh-she; 383?–442?) during the Liu-Sung period.

The earliest catalogue to record this sūtra translated by Kālayaśas was the *Fa-ching lu* (Catalogue of Scriptures Compiled by Fa-ching; compiled in 593) from the Sui period. It notes, "*Wu-liang-shou kuan ching* in one fascicle: during the Yüan-chia Era (424–453) of Liu-Sung, śramaṇa Kālayaśas translated this [text] at Yang-chou."[11] It is this entry that was adopted by all later catalogues.[12] However, Seng-yu's *Ch'u-san-tsang chi-chi* (A Compilation of Notices on the Translation of the *Tripiṭaka;* compiled ca. 502–515)—the earliest extant catalogue, which was composed prior to the *Fa-ching lu*—included the *KWC* in its fourth section on "records of miscellaneous sūtras by anonymous translators."[13] But the *Kao-seng chuan* (Biographies of Eminent Monks; compiled in 519) by Hui-chiao records—as did the *Fa-ching lu*—that Kālayaśas translated the *KWC.*[14] Also, according to two catalogues from the T'ang period, the *Nei-tien lu*[15] (Catalogue of Inner Scriptures, Compiled During the Great T'ang Period; 644) and the *K'ai-yüan lu*[16] (Catalogue of Śākyamuni's Teachings, Compiled During the K'ai-yüan Era; 730), Tao-hui's (d.u.) *Sung-ch'i lu* (Catalogue of Scriptures, Compiled During the Sung-ch'i Period; n.d.) listed Kālayaśas' translation of the *KWC.* Since the *Sung-ch'i lu* was already lost when Fei Ch'ang-fang (d.u.) of the Sui period compiled his *Li-tai san-pao chi* (Record of the Three Treasures Throughout Successive Generations)[17] in 597, the reference to the *KWC* in the *Biographies of Eminent Monks* constitutes the oldest scriptural evidence for its existence among extant texts.

The *Ch'u-san-tsang chi-chi* most likely included the *KWC* among sūtras whose translators were unknown either because Seng-yu was unaware of the assumption that Kālayaśas was its translator or because he disagreed with that ascription. Although this does cast a certain degree of doubt on the authenticity of the reported translator, it does not constitute sufficient reason for rejecting Kālayaśas' authorship entirely. In fact, in compiling the section on "records of miscellaneous sūtras by anonymous translators" (in which the *KWC* was included), Seng-yu personally noted, "Due to the low level of scholarship and a need for still more research, many places [in this catalogue] have not been fully understood. May the great erudite scholars rectify these deficiencies!"[18] As these words indicate, Seng-yu felt a need to leave room for future clarification. It was precisely in this context that Hui-chiao, writing so soon after Seng-yu, must have found sufficient evidence to emend the latter's position and ascribe the translation to Kālayaśas. Though Hui-chiao (497–554) is chronologically later than Seng-yu (445–518), Hui-chiao's opinion should still be considered reliable since he was not that far removed from Kālayaśas.

According to the *Biographies of Eminent Monks,*[19] Kālayaśas was originally from the Western Region and was well versed in the *Tripiṭaka* of the *Sūtra, Vinaya,* and *Abhidharma;* however, he was most of all a meditator who concentrated on meditative practices and "ceaselessly transmitted samādhi to various countries." He arrived in the Sung capital of Chien-k'ang in the first year of Yüan-chia (424) and, while residing at Tao-lin Monastery on Chung Mountain, orally transmitted—at the request of a certain śramaṇa Seng-han (d.u.)—two sūtras, the *Yao-wang Yao-shang kuan* (Contemplation on Bhaiṣajyarāja and Bhaiṣajyasamudgata; hereafter Bhaiṣajyarāja Contemplation Sūtra)[20] and *KWC.* It is also reported that "[Seng]-han immediately transcribed [the texts]." The *Biographies of Eminent Monks* comments further, "As a secret technique for turning back obstacles and a great cause [leading to rebirth in] the Pure Land, the two sūtras were widely chanted and circulated throughout the Sung Empire." Kālayaśas later moved to Chiang-ling (Hu-pei) and in the nineteenth year of Yüan-chia (442) traveled through the Western Region of Min-shu (Kan-su, Szu-ch'uan) propagating meditative training. He later returned to Chiang-ling, where he died at the age of sixty.

The exact year of his death is unclear according to this account, but as far as the date of the translation of the *KWC* is concerned, it is believed to be between the first and the nineteenth years of Yüan-chia (424–442). The *KWC* would thus have been translated shortly after 421, which is believed to be the year of the translation of the *Wu-liang-shou ching* (Sūtra on the Buddha of Immeasurable Life)—that is, the so-called Saṃghavarman or K'ang Seng-k'ai (d. 276 or 280) translation of the *Larger Sukhāvatīvyūha-sūtra,* which is now presumed to have been co-translated by Buddhabhadra (359–429) and Pao-yün (376–449).[21] For this and other reasons (discussed below), this dating is considered historically accurate.

There are, however, some catalogues that instead list Dharmamitra (356–442) of the Liu-Sung period as the translator of the "*Kuan Wu-liang-shou-fo ching* in one fascicle." One of these is the *Ta-Chou lu* (Catalogue of the Great Chou Period; compiled in 695),[22] based on which the *K'ai-yüan lu* lists the *KWC* as a "lost text."[23] Both note that this listing originally appeared in the *Pao-ch'ang lu* (Catalogue by Pao-ch'ang; compiled in 518) of the Liang period. However, this cannot be readily trusted since neither Fei Ch'ang-fang, who relied heavily on the *Pao-ch'ang lu,* nor any of the catalogues prior to the *Ta-chou lu*—beginning with the *Ch'u-san-tsang chi-chi*—makes any such reference.

Dharmamitra's biographies appear in the *Ch'u-san-tsang chi-chi,*[24] *Biographies of Eminent Monks,*[25] and Pao-ch'ang's *Ming-seng chuan ch'ao* (Notes to Biographies of Distinguished Monks).[26] According to these sources, he was originally from Chi-pin (either Gandhāra or Kashmir) and was an adept of meditation. In the first year of Yüan-chia (424), he came to Shu and later went to Chien-k'ang via Ching-chou; at Ch'i-huan Temple in the capital, he translated such meditation sūtras as the "[*Ch'an ching* (Meditation Sūtra),] *Ch'an-fa yao* (Essentials of Meditation Method), *P'u-hsien kuan* (Samantabhadra Contemplation), and *Hsü-k'ung-tsang kuan* (Ākāśagarbha Contemplation)."[27] He later moved to the small monastery of Ting-lin on Chung Mountain where he died in the nineteenth year of Yüan-chia (442) at the age of eighty-seven (eighty, according to the *Ming-seng chuan ch'ao*).

In these biographies there is no reference connecting Dharmamitra with the translation of the *Kuan Wu-liang-shou-fo ching.* Hence the incorrect attribution recorded in the *Ta-Chou lu* and *K'ai-yüan lu* could be due to a possible confusion of the two teachers due to the similarities in their biographies; both Dharmamitra and Kālayaśas were meditation specialists who arrived in the Sung capital of Chien-k'ang at virtually the same time, and both translated several meditation sūtras.[28] Whatever the reason for the confusion, there is today virtually no basis on which to accept Dharmamitra as the translator of the *Kuan Wu-liang-shou-fo ching.*

The *Li-tai san-pao chi* by Fei Ch'ang-fang includes a reference to a "*Kuan Wu-liang-shou-fo ching* in one fascicle" that appeared in the Latter Han and Eastern Chin records of sūtras by anonymous translators, as if to suggest that two other earlier translations different from that of Kālayaśas existed.[29] It claims to quote from the section on "records of miscellaneous sūtras by anonymous translators" found in the *Ch'u-san-tsang chi-chi,* but this statement is without any basis in fact. As noted earlier, the *Ch'u-san-tsang chi-chi* lists only one translation of the *KWC* and shows no evidence of having consulted the Latter Han and the Eastern Chin records of sūtras by anonymous translators. Thus this entry ought to be seen as nothing more than an interpolation by Fei Ch'ang-fang, especially in light of the fact that Chih-sheng, the compiler of the *K'ai-yüan lu,* also rejected the view that two such translations ever existed.[30] A modern scholar has consequently gone so far as to castigate the *Li-tai san-pao chi* entry as "an outrageous fabrication."[31]

In this connection, the *Ching-t'u wang-sheng chuan*[32] (Biographies on Rebirth in the Pure Land) by Chieh-chu (986–1077) and the *Lo-pang i-*

kao[33] (Accounts of Rebirths in the Country of Bliss) by Tsung-hsiao (1151–1214) in the Sung period both refer to a certain Seng-hsien who arrived in Chiang-nan at the beginning of the Eastern Chin, during the T'ai-hsing era (318–321). He is depicted in these texts as if he were already aware of a *"Shih-liu kuan ching"* (Sixteen Contemplations Sūtra) —in other words, the extant *KWC* or another sūtra with the same content—that discusses "the three matters and the causal vows [leading to rebirth in] the Pure Land, and the graded rebirth of the nine classes." This, of course, is a later attribution that cannot be trusted; though the *Biographies of Eminent Monks* tells us that Seng-hsien was a devotee of Amitābha Buddha, there is nothing else that suggests his connection with the *KWC.*[34]

We have looked at the various records pertaining to the Chinese translations of this sūtra. There are also, however, Uigur translations of the *KWC.* One of them is the one-page manuscript discovered in the Turfan area that was brought back by the Ōtani expedition. A photocopied manuscript, with an edited text and translation by Tachibana Zuichō, is found in the *Niraku sōsho.*[35] Haneda Tōru has published a revision of Tachibana's reading,[36] but despite differences of opinion on the reading of the text, there is no doubt that the Uigur fragment corresponds to a section from the tenth contemplation on Avalokiteśvara.[37] Although the text does not correspond exactly to the Chinese translation, it is generally believed to be a retranslation from the Chinese, based on such evidence as the occurrences of transliterated Chinese terms.[38] This view is supported by the fact that the majority of the extant Uigur Buddhist literature was retranslated from Chinese translations.[39]

A theory was once put forth asserting that a text similar to the *KWC* was found among Sogdian manuscripts. This view was expressed by Hans Reichelt, who, in editing and translating into German a Sogdian fragment of a "Meditation Sūtra" *(Der Dhyāna-Text),* pointed out its similarity to the *KWC.*[40] Although this theory has in recent years been introduced to Japan,[41] based on thorough analysis of this meditation text Friedrich Weller has demonstrated that it corresponds to the *Kuan fo san-mei hai ching* (Sūtra on the Sea of Samādhi Attained through Contemplation on the Buddha; hereafter Samādhi Sea Sūtra).[42] Therefore, we must conclude for now that no Sogdian translation of the *KWC* exists.

Problems Pertaining to Compilation

As already alluded to, it is a well-known fact that no Sanskrit original of the *KWC* presently exists, nor is there any Tibetan translation that would lend support to the earlier existence of a Sanskrit text. Even the Uigur translation is undoubtedly a retranslation from the Chinese, thus giving the extant Chinese *KWC* the status of an original scripture. However, as already discussed, there has never existed more than one translation of the text by Kālayaśas, and even this translation was beset with questions regarding its authenticity.

Kālayaśas is also credited with the translation of a sūtra from a similar textual background, the *Bhaiṣajyarāja-sūtra,* which also lacks both Sanskrit and Tibetan counterparts as well as any other Chinese version. The same circumstances apply to the other contemplation sutras translated around the same time: the *Samādhi Sea Sūtra*[43] by Buddhabhadra; the *Kuan p'u-hsien p'u-sa hsing-fa ching* (Sūtra on the Contemplation of the Cultivation Methods of the Bodhisattva Samantabhadra; hereafter Samantabhadra Contemplation Sūtra)[44] and the *Kuan Hsü-k'ung-tsang p'u-sa ching* (Sūtra on the Contemplation of the Bodhisattva Ākāśagarbha; hereafter Ākāśagarbha Contemplation Sūtra)[45] by Dharmamitra; and the *Kuan Mi-le p'u-sa shang-sheng tou-shuai-t'ien ching* (Sūtra on the Contemplation on Maitreya Bodhisattva's Ascent to Rebirth in the Tuṣita Heaven; hereafter Maitreya Contemplation Sūtra)[46] by Chü-ch'ü Ching-sheng (d.u.). Although a Tibetan translation of the *Maitreya Contemplation Sūtra* is found in the sDe-dge and Lhasa editions[47] (but not in the Peking, sNar-thaṅ, or Co-ne editions of the Tibetan Buddhist canon), this is a retranslation from the Chinese, suggesting that in Tibet as well no Sanskrit originals to these sūtras were known. Given such circumstances surrounding these contemplation sūtras, we cannot treat the nonexistence of a Sanskrit original for the *KWC* as an isolated case.

It cannot be determined categorically what the Sanskrit title of the *KWC* might have been.[48] We are especially unclear as to what the Sanskrit term was for *kuan* (contemplation). Although *kuan* commonly translates the Sanskrit term *vipaśyanā,* the context in which the word is used in the sūtra corresponds instead to dhyāna.[49] There is, of course, no guarantee that the present Chinese title is a literal translation of the original Sanskrit title. At any rate, uncertainties abound even concerning the title of this text.

If we were to accept that Kālayaśas translated a Sanskrit text of the *KWC,* that Sanskrit original would have to have been compiled at least by the early fifth century. There is, however, no evidence to substantiate its existence in India by that time. Although one scholar has suggested that this sūtra is alluded to in Vasubandhu's *Wu-liang-shou ching yu-p'o-t'i-she yüan-sheng-chieh,* commonly called the *Ching-t'u lun* (Treatise on the Pure Land), there has been no general scholarly acceptance of this proposal and it is highly unlikely that there ever will be.[50]

The nonexistence of an original text casts serious doubts on any assumption that the present extant version of the *KWC* was compiled in India. Based on the evidence just given, several hypotheses rejecting the Indian compilation theory have been proposed recently in Japan. These views can be roughly divided into two: the Central Asian compilation theory and the Chinese compilation theory. I will therefore analyze the grounds on which these two positions are based and then attempt to determine which constitutes the correct position.

The Central Asian Compilation Theory

Kasugai Shinya[51] was probably the first to propose this view. According to his theory, the *KWC* and the other contemplation sūtras were compiled as essentials or abridged texts of Indian Mahāyāna to meet the demand for specialized religious practices, which in turn were stimulated by the liberal tendencies that prevailed at the time in Gandhāra. Based on evidence such as the places of origin of the translators of these contemplation sūtras, the compilation of this sūtra took place in the Western Region, Hsi-yü. In discussing the compilation of the "three Pure Land sūtras," Nakamura Hajime has stated:

> The *KWC* is believed to have been compiled much later [than the other two sūtras], somewhere in Central Asia. Even if it were compiled in India, it has intimate ties with various areas of Central Asia.[52]

In other words, while leaving open the possibility of its compilation in India, Nakamura basically accepts the Central Asian compilation theory.

What, then, constitute the bases for this position? Although the sources that would convincingly support this theory are not sufficiently adequate in my opinion, one can nevertheless point out the following pieces of evidence.

The first piece of evidence is the fact that Kālayaśas and the other translators of the contemplation sūtras had close ties with Central Asia. While the veracity of the claim that Kālayaśas actually translated the sūtra has been called into question, there is as yet no compelling reason to reject this claim; the same basic doubt can be raised concerning the translators of the other contemplation sūtras as well. Although Kālayaśas is said to have been from the Western Region, we have no detailed information on his activities prior to his arrival in the Sung capital, other than that he continuously taught the meditation technique of samādhi throughout the various countries.

Much more is known about the activities of the other contemplation-sūtra translators before coming to China. Dharmamitra, a monk who specialized in meditation, was born in Chi-pin (either Kashmir or Gandhāra) and arrived in the Liu-Sung capital of Chien-k'ang by way of the northern trade route, along which are found such places as Kucha, Tun-huang, and Liang-chou.[53] Chü-ch'ü Ching-sheng, a cousin of King Chü-ch'ü Meng-sun of the Northern Liang Dynasty, was a meditator who studied in Khotan, Turfan, and Kara-khoja, and later escaped to Chien-k'ang after the invasion of the Northern Liang in 439 by Emperor T'ai-wu (r. 424–452) of the Northern Wei.[54] It is noteworthy that Chü-ch'ü Ching-sheng is said to have "obtained in the Turfan area two contemplation sūtras, one on Avalokiteśvara and the other on Maitreya, of one fascicle each." The former has been lost, but it is well documented that the compilation of the latter *Maitreya Contemplation Sūtra* took place in the Turfan vicinity. The Turfan area had close ties at this time with Buddhism in Northern Liang where both Mahāyāna and Hīnayāna Buddhism were actively practiced and numerous adepts of meditation and supernatural powers were produced.[55] These factors suggest that the other contemplation sūtras, including the *KWC,* were probably compiled in this general vicinity.

Among the translators of the contemplation sūtras, only Buddhabhadra, who translated the *Samādhi Sea Sūtra,* had no direct ties with Central Asia, for he was born in Kapilavastu in North India and came to China via the southern sea route. However, he studied for several years in either Kashmir or Gandhāra, and upon arriving in Ch'ang-an he enjoyed close association with Kumārajīva and was attended by Pao-yün, a recent returnee from the Western Region and India. Together with Pao-yün, Buddhabhadra co-translated the *Larger Sukhāvatīvyūha-sūtra,* which was based in all likelihood on a newly obtained manuscript from India. Buddhabhadra also translated the *Avataṃsaka-sūtra,* based on a Sanskrit manuscript obtained from Khotan.[56] For all these reasons, Buddhabhadra is believed to have been highly knowledgeable about Central Asia. It is therefore possible to hypothesize that the original manuscript of the *Samādhi Sea Sūtra* also came from the Central Asian region along with the other contemplation sūtras.

Another argument in support of the Central Asian compilation of the *KWC* pertains to the contemplation of the Buddha *(kuan-fo)* and the contemplation of the image *(kuan-hsiang).* In its eighth and thirteenth contemplations, this sūtra advocates contemplation practices using buddha and bodhisattva images as objects; it subsequently discusses contemplation on the form-body and the primary and secondary marks of Amitābha Buddha, Avalokiteśvara Bodhisattva, and Mahāsthāmaprāpta Bodhisattva in the ninth, tenth, and eleventh contemplations, respectively.[57] This kind of Buddha-contemplation and image-contemplation, while common in the other contemplation sūtras, is discussed in greatest detail in the *Samādhi Sea Sūtra.*

According to Buddhist art historians,[58] the general state of Gandhāran Buddhism and its art can be largely discerned in the descriptions of contemplations on images and their auspicious marks found in the *Samādhi Sea Sūtra.* For example, this sūtra describes a Buddha image with a mustache,[59] which is one of the unique characteristics of Gandhāran Buddhas; it even records the size of the famous cave in Nagarahāra, the area near modern Jalalābād in northern Afghanistan, where the shadow of the Buddha's figure remains.[60] Both of these descriptions, it is believed, would not have been possible without knowledge of Buddhist conditions in the Gandhāra region; hence it is assumed that they coincide with what Buddhabhadra had observed previously in northwest India during his stay there.[61] At any rate, if we accept the view that Gandhāran Buddhism and its art are indeed clearly reflected in the *Samādhi Sea Sūtra,* this would provide a key for assessing the other contemplation sūtras, including the *KWC.*

In examining the *KWC* in this light, we find a tendency to enlarge enormously its descriptions of the auspicious primary and secondary marks of buddhas and bodhisattvas. For example, in the ninth contemplation, the bodily marks of Amitābha Buddha are described, including the comment that "the height of the Buddha is six hundred thousand *niyutas* of *koṭis* of *yojanas,* innumerable as the sands of the Ganges River." It is not unreasonable to assume that this description recalls the colossal buddha images of Bāmiyan.[62] In describing the crown halo of Avalokiteśvara Bodhisattva in the tenth contemplation, the sūtra also states, "There are five hundred miraculously transformed buddhas just like Śākyamuni Buddha in this crown halo." One theory has proposed that the Śākyamuni Buddha described here refers to the thirty-five- (or thirty-eight-) meter-high buddha image located in the eastern part of Bāmiyan.[63]

However, in the thirteenth contemplation, Amitābha Buddha is said to fill the whole sky when revealing his great body but to become a statue of only *chang-lu* (about 288 cm) or *pa-ch'ih* (about 124 cm) when revealing his small body. We may therefore be hard put to prove any associations between the descriptions found in the sūtra and such giant buddha images as those found at Bāmiyan.[64]

Nevertheless, it cannot be denied that the *KWC* primarily describes the huge bodies of buddhas and bodhisattvas. It is not unnatural to infer from this that the translators of this sūtra had in mind large buddha images, probably much larger than human size. Furthermore, in describing the appearance of Amitābha Buddha in the nineteenth contemplation, the sūtra states, "The crown halo of that buddha is like hundreds of millions of trichiliocosms; in that halo there are millions of *niyutas* of transformation buddhas, as innumerable as the sands of the

Ganges River."[65] According to one art historian, buddha images of similar style—a number of transformation buddhas standing at an angle, lined up in a radiating pattern within the halo—have been found among artifacts from Gandhāra as well as from Khotan.[66] Moreover, in this sūtra Amitābha Buddha together with his two attendant bodhisattvas (seventh and eighth contemplations),[67] a common Central Asian art motif, are already found in their highly developed forms. The *KWC* also describes in detail the iconographic details unique to the bodhisattvas Avalokiteśvara and Mahāsthāmaprāpta. In fact, it states with regard to the thirteenth contemplation, "All beings can recognize Avalokiteśvara and Mahāsthāmaprāpta merely by looking at the head features."[68] Such references suggest that this text could not have been written by anyone not in close contact with images of these bodhisattvas.

In the history of Buddhist images in China, although the Gandhāran influence was felt quite early in China, stone buddha images did not become widespread prior to about 400. The gilt bronze images that have survived are small, all 30 to 40 centimeters in height. It is reported that the appearance of images human-sized and larger does not begin until the carving of the great stone caves at Yün-kang from the second half of the fifth century.[69] Admittedly, there are textual allusions from the fourth century to various methods of image-making, such as the report of Tao-an (312–385) casting a gilt bronze image that was *chang-lu* (about 288 cm) in height,[70] but not a single such artifact survives today. In Central Asia, in contrast, the Gandhāran buddhas were generally adopted in near-original form, and it appears that such colossal buddha images were already being made in Central Asia around 400.[71] Thus, outside India, Central Asia becomes the most likely candidate for having provided the background for the image-contemplation discussed in the *KWC*.

This evidence provides the foundation for the Central Asian compilation theory of this text, though we must realize that the argument is not totally convincing. Yet on the basis of historical and geographical considerations, the choice of a Central Asian origin theory seems quite appropriate. This is particularly true when one is not completely convinced by the Indian compilation theory but is unable to accept that the *KWC* might have been written in China.

The Chinese Compilation Theory

Let us now consider the second theory. The possibility of a Chinese origin for the *KWC* is not inconceivable, since a careful analysis of the sūtra reveals obvious Chinese elements. Tsukinowa Kenryū, I believe, was the first person to advocate the Chinese compilation theory.[72]

According to him the *KWC,* like the other contemplation sūtras, was compiled by some eminent monk during the Yüan-chia Era (424–453) of Liu-Sung, in consultation with meditation adepts who were then converging on China. The sūtra was compiled in response to a growing interest within the Buddhist community concerning the practice of meditation, as well as to combat the competition posed by Taoism. However, since Tsukinowa's report appeared in the form of a résumé, the details of his argument are unclear.[73] Soon afterward, Suzuki Munetada also put forth the Chinese compilation theory,[74] calling into question the likelihood of India as the place of compilation and then tracing the possible route by which this sūtra was transmitted. For this theory to hold up, one would need to answer the question of when and by whom the sūtra was compiled. Although Suzuki attempted to answer these questions, his study did not lead to any decisive conclusion.

Thus the arguments for Chinese compilation are also not totally convincing; but in analyzing the *KWC,* the following evidence can be offered in support of this position.

First, the sūtras to which the *KWC* are most indebted are the Chinese translations of the *Larger* and *Smaller Sukhāvatīvyūha.* For example, the *KWC* idea of Amitābha Buddha and his attendant bodhisattvas coming to escort the practitioner to the Pure Land at his deathbed is believed to have been borrowed from these two sūtras and greatly elaborated into the new form of the "nine grades of rebirths." The version of the *Larger Sukhāvatīvyūha-sūtra* that the *KWC* drew upon was the *Wu-liang-shou ching,* translated by Saṃghavarman or K'ang Seng-k'ai (though in my opinion actually translated by Buddhabhadra and Pao-yün). We know this because some of the terms adopted (as italicized below) are found only in that version: "that which the power of the vows of *Fa-tsang pi-ch'iu* [i.e., Bhikṣu Dharmakāra] accomplishes"[75] (seventh contemplation); "*Fa-tsang pi-ch'iu's* forty-eight vows"[76] (section on the middle-lower grade); "endowed with *shih-nien* [ten thoughts]"[77] (section on the lower-lower grade). Due to its adoption of such terms, the *KWC* could not be a direct translation of an original Sanskrit rescension but must instead have utilized sūtras that had already been translated into Chinese.

In comparing the *KWC* with the other contemplation sūtras, parallelisms in doctrine, terminology, and translation style are undeniably apparent. Some of the more obvious examples are shown in the Table (only the *Ākāśagarbha Contemplation Sūtra* is omitted, since its earliest version is too brief for proper comparison).[78] In assessing the parallels in the Table, it is patently clear that, if the *KWC* had been redacted in China, it must have been composed with close attention to the style and terminology of other contemplation sūtras. Moreover, one should note the Chinese-tinged terms that can be detected in these passages—for example, "reciting the name" *(ch'eng-ming)* of the buddha or bodhisattva. Since the same term also appears in the *Ākāśagarbha Contemplation Sūtra*[79] (not listed in the Table), the idea of reciting such a name is common to all the contemplation sūtras under discussion. However, as most of the occurrences of name-recitation cannot be traced back to Sanskrit texts, the idea is considered to have originated primarily within the religious milieu of Chinese translations of Buddhist scriptures.[80] From this point of view also, Chinese elements are clearly detectable in the *KWC*.

Among the contemplation sūtras, the *Samādhi Sea Sūtra* is undoubtedly the only one that was translated prior to the *KWC*,[81] and it has been suggested that the redaction of the *KWC* was strongly influenced by it.[82] There is also reason to believe that the *KWC* was influenced by the *Maitreya Contemplation Sūtra*. For example, the *KWC* states with regard to the sixth contemplation, "Furthermore, there is a musical instrument hanging stationary in the sky that makes sounds on its own without being played, like [that produced by] the deity Jeweled Streamer [T'ien pao-chung]."[83] This "deity Jeweled Streamer" has a highly specialized meaning, and Jeweled Streamer—the first of the five great deities of Tuṣita Heaven—appears in the *Maitreya Contemplation Sūtra*.[84] In other words, the redactor of the *KWC* is believed to have consulted passages in this sūtra in compiling his own text.[85]

In this connection, it can be shown that contemplation sūtras other than the *KWC* also utilized existing Chinese translations of sūtras and commentaries in their redactions. For example, the *Samādhi Sea Sūtra* quotes from numerous sūtras, and among them are three references to the names of the ten buddhas of the ten directions[86] clearly taken from the *Pao-yüeh t'ung-tzu suo-wen ching* (Sūtra on the Questions of Prince of Jeweled-Moon) quoted in the "I-hsing p'in" (Chapter on Easy Practice) of Kumārajīva's translation of the *Daśabhūmika-vibhāṣā*.[87] Elsewhere, the *Samādhi Sea Sūtra* refers to a "samādhi of nonexistence-only" *(wei-wu san-mei)*;[88] this is believed to be based on the *Wei-wu san-mei ching* (Book of the Samādhi of Nonexistence-Only), a sūtra that Tao-an had earlier determined to be apocryphal.[89] The term "samādhi of nonexistence-only" is also found in another sūtra reported to have been translated by Kālayaśas, the *Bhaiṣajyarāja Contemplation Sūtra*.[90] If we accept Kālayaśas as the translator of this sūtra, the employment of this technical term provides us with some sense of Kālayaśas' attitude toward and manner of translation. Also found in the *Bhaiṣajyarāja Contemplation Sūtra* are phrases that are believed to be based on the *Samādhi Sea Sūtra*.[91] Next, it is well known that the *Samantabhadra Contemplation Sūtra* is heavily indebted to Kumārajīva's translation of the *Saddharmapuṇḍarīka-sūtra* —so much so that it is often referred to as "a concluding sūtra of the

Lotus Sūtra."[92] The *Ākāśagarbha Contemplation Sūtra* acknowledges in the text itself its debt to the *Chüeh ting pi-ni ching (Vinayaviniścaya-sūtra),*[93] translated anonymously during the Eastern Chin.[94] The idea of reciting the name of the thirty-five buddhas, as found in the *Ākāśagarbha Contemplation Sūtra,* is also discussed in the *Bhaiṣajyarāja Contemplation Sūtra.*[95]

Although we have looked at some examples from the other contemplation sūtras, there are even more traces of ideas adopted from Chinese translations of Buddhist scriptures in the *KWC.* One of the more glaring examples is the division of the sūtra into sixteen contemplations. Such divisions did not begin with the *KWC;* in the *Ch'an pi yao-fa ching*[96] (Sūtra on the Mystical Essential Methods of Meditation), categories like "meditation on the impurities" and "buddha-contemplation and image-contemplation" are divided into about thirty contemplations. This meditation sūtra is thought to have been translated by either Kumārajīva or Dharmamitra,[97] but whoever the translator may have been, it circulated just prior to or contemporaneously with the *KWC.* Hence it is thought that it probably had an impact on the latter's categorization of contemplation techniques.

Also, as already pointed out by Mochizuki,[98] the well-known *KWC* doctrine of the "three minds" *(san-hsin)*—"sincere mind" *(chih-ch'eng hsin),* "deep mind" *(shen-hsin),* and "mind of raising a vow to transfer one's merits" *(hui-hsiang fa-yüan hsin)*—may be connected to the "direct mind" *(chih-hsin),* "deep mind" *(shen-hsin),* and "mind of transference" *(hui-hsiang hsin)* that appear in the "Chapter on the Buddha Land" of Kumārajīva's translation of the *Vimālakīrtinirdeśa-sūtra.*[99] Also, such concepts in the *KWC* as the "samādhi attained through buddha- contemplation"[100] (*nien-fo san-mei;* in the eighth and ninth contemplations) and "samādhi wherein the buddhas appear in front of oneself"[101] *(chu-fo hsien-ch'ien san-mei;* in the section on the benefits) are obviously influenced by the *Pan-chou san-mei ching (Pratyutpanna*[*buddhasaṃmukhāvasthita*] *samādhi-sūtra).* Moreover, such phrases as "This mind becomes a buddha; this mind is a buddha"[102] (*shih-hsin tso-fo, shih-hsin shih-fo;* eighth contemplation) have direct parallels in the *Pan-chou san-mei ching.*[103] Also, the idea of acquiring "the approach to knowledge of the hundred dharmas"[104] *(po-fa ming-men)* and thereby entering the Stage of Rejoicing *(Pramuditā-bhūmi)*—as discussed in the sections on the upper-lower and lower-upper grades—is probably adopted from similar passages either in Kumārajīva's translation of the *Daśabhūmika-sūtra*[105] or in the "Chapter on the Ten Stages" in Buddhabhadra's translation of the *Avataṃsaka-sūtra.*[106] Although these parallels do not constitute irrefutable evidence, they do lend greater credibility to the hypothesis that the *KWC* made much use of various sūtras translated previously into Chinese.

Strong Chinese elements can also be seen in the literary style and narration of the sūtra. For example, there is a passage, "We praise the names of the opening titles of the twelve divisions of Mahāyāna sūtras,"[107] in the section on the lower-upper grade. Since sūtra titles in a Sanskrit text do not ordinarily appear at the beginning but at the end of the sūtra, we are inclined to believe that this section drew upon a translated Chinese text.

Based on these findings, it is highly unlikely that the *KWC* is a direct, literal translation of a Sanskrit (or Prākrit) original. We must, therefore, accept that there is sufficient evidence to support the opinion that this sūtra was compiled in China.[108]

Preliminary Conclusion

How does this evidence compare to that which supports the theory of a Central Asian compilation? If the Indian composition of the text is rejected, then which of the two opposing theories is to be accepted? I believe that both theories have points worthy of our attention but that neither is able to offer decisive evidence for choosing it over the other. For now I will thus take a compromise position, by partially accepting both theories. That is to say, merely because Chinese elements can be detected in the sūtra does not mean that it was composed in China. At the very minimum, I believe that the core of the *KWC* transmitted a form of meditation that was then practiced somewhere in Central Asia, possibly in the Turfan area. When translating the sūtra, Kālayaśas probably did so orally, since it is reported, as already noted, that the śramaṇa Seng-han served as his scribe.[109] In this process, the sūtra's concepts and expressions assumed a Chinese coloring, since numerous Chinese-translated scriptures were consulted and utilized, beginning with the *Wu-liang-shou ching*. It is these factors that support the Chinese compilation theory. An eclectic position such as this is apt to lack clarity, but it is the most appropriate position to take without more convincing evidence.

I have already delineated my views on the problems surrounding the compilation of the *KWC*. Through this outline it is clear that, while Pure Land doctrines that appear in the text might be Indian in origin, they exhibit extensive development that could only have taken place outside India, in Central Asia or China. Therefore, although the *KWC* is undoubtedly a valuable source for the study of early Pure Land Buddhism, it must be treated as a source of quite a different pedigree from that of the *Larger* and *Smaller Sukhāvatīvyūha-sūtras*.

Parallel Passages in the *KWC* and Other Contemplation Sūtras

KWC	*Bhaiṣajyarāja*	*Samādhi Sea*	*Samantabhadra*	*Maitreya*
T 365.12	*T* 1161.20	*T* 642.15	*T* 277.9	*T* 452.14
Recite the name of Buddha; "nan-wu A-mi-t'o-fo." pp. 345c15; 346a19	663c8; 665a28	661a12–13	391c17; 392b3	420a13; 420b26
Eliminates transgressions accumulated during eight million or countless kalpas of births and deaths. 342a27–28; 343b12, etc.	662a11–12, 14	655b4–5, 7	393b24–25	420b28–29
Transformation buddhas; transformation bodhisattvas; incarnate Avalokiteśvaras and Mahāsthāmaprāptas. 343b22–23; 344b5–6ff.	661a1; 662c5, 11, 19	649b14ff.	389c20ff.	418b24ff.
To perform this contemplation is called the correct contemplation; if one performs other contemplations, it constitutes a heretical contemplation. 342a4–5	663a27–28	649b16–17ff.	393c1–2	419c10
Maṇi jewels fastened on Śakra's head; Kiṃsuka jewels; Brahmā-maṇi jewels. 342b10; 343a1–2	663b14	648b26; 683a10	390a11–12	419a14, c24–25
Jambunāda gold. 342b16; 343a25, etc.	663b10	648c6		419c22–23
When one's life is about to end, Amitābha Buddha and Avalokiteśvara and Mahāsthāmaprāpta, along with a great assembly of countless [attendants] . . . will appear in front of the practitioner. 345a24–b24	661b27–28, c18–19	693c1–2		420b11–13
World-honored One, what should we call this sūtra? How should we receive and keep in mind the essentials of this teaching? 356b5–6	666b4–5	696b20–21		420c14

KWC	*Bhaiṣajyarāja*	*Samādhi Sea*	*Samantabhadra*	*Maitreya*
T 365.12	*T* 1161.20	*T* 642.15	*T* 277.9	*T* 452.14
You should keep in mind the Buddha's words. You should carefully keep in mind these words. 342a26; 346b15	666a22	666b11; 696b29		420c15
Preached suffering, emptiness, impermanence, nonsubstantiality and the pāramitās. 342c1	662c12	681a16 684c16		419a6–7, b12–13
Countless hundreds of thousands of dhāraṇī formulas. 345a4	663a7		391b22	418b28–29, c1–2
Be filial and support one's parents, serve one's teachers and elders, be of compassionate mind and do not kill. 341c9–10	661a26–27	690c9	394a29	
Amitābha Buddha dwelt amidst the sky. 342c16–17		683a23; 689c27; 690b1–2	393b21	
Whether you close or open your eyes, all is clear; the mental eye will open and become clear and distinct, and [see] clearly. . . . 324a3–4; 343a25–26		649a10; 650a24; 665b21	390c3–4, 8–9, 24	
Samādhi in which buddhas appear in front [of the practitioner]. 346b3		693c7–8; 695b10	390c29	
Tathāgata, Arhat, Samyaksaṃbuddha. 343a23–24		688a15–16 692c1–2		420b19–20
Just as in the short time that a strong man takes to bend and stretch his arm. 345c4–5		647a19–20; 669a9; 682a26		420a15

NOTES

Author's note: For an update reflecting my most recent views on this subject, I refer readers to my book *Kanmuryōjukyō kōkyū* (Kyoto: Shinshū Ōtaniha shūmushu shuppanbu, 1985).

Translator's note: This paper is a translation of a section from Kōtatsu Fujita's *Genshi Jōdo-shisō no kenkyū* (A Study of Early Pure Land Buddhism) (Tokyo: Iwanami shoten, 1970), 116–136, with a few additions and emendations made by Professor Fujita. Due to time constraints, the Translator's Introduction was not submitted to Professor Fujita for his review. The translator is solely responsible for its content.

1. *KWC, T* 365.12.
2. Ono Gemmyō, ed., *Bussho kaisetsu daijiten,* vol. 2 (1932; reprint, Tokyo: Tokyo shoseki, 1975), p. 199c–d.
3. *Kuan Wu-liang-shou fo ching shu, T* 1753.37.
4. *Kuan Wu-liang-shou ching i-shu, T* 1749.37, and *Kuan Wu-liang-shou fo ching shu, T* 1750.37. Scholars are in general agreement that the latter work attributed to Chih-i is of much later compilation, between the second half of the seventh and the first half of the eighth centuries. In Satō's view, the followers of the T'ien-t'ai tradition felt a need for a commentary on this sūtra, due to its popularity and the fact that the eminent exegetes of the other traditions had their commentaries. See Satō Tetsuei, *Tendai daishi no kenkyū* (Kyoto: Hyakken, 1961), 567–568, 594–597. For details on Hui-yüan's influence on Korean Buddhism, see Etani Ryūkai, *Jōdokyō no shin kenkyū* (Tokyo: Sankibō busshorin, 1976), 55–61.
5. The recitation is advocated for those of the low grades of rebirth at their "deathbeds" (*KWC, T* 365.12, pp. 345c15, 346a19).
6. See, for example, Nogami Shunjo, *Chūgoku Jōdokyo-shi* (Kyoto: Hōzōkan, 1971), 74–77; Tsukamoto Zenryū, Shibayama Zenkei, and Nishitani Keiji, "Dialogue: Chinese Zen," *The Eastern Buddhist,* n. s. 8, no. 2 (October 1975):78; Kenneth Ch'en, *Buddhism in China* (Princeton: Princeton University Press, 1972), 345–346.
7. For example, the rankings are found in the commentaries by Hui-yüan (*T* 1749.37.182a12–c22), Chi-tsang (*T* 1753.37.244c13–245a15), Shan-tao (*T* 1753.37.248b7–250a8), and the one falsely attributed to Chih-i (*T* 1750.37.193b28–c1).
8. In this regard, Hui-yüan's commentary mentioned above played an important seminal role. See Kenneth Tanaka, *The Dawn of Chinese Pure Land Buddhist Doctrine: Ching-ying Hui-yüan's Commentary on the Visualization Sutra* (Albany: State University of New York Press, 1990).
9. The background leading to this is a well-known story. King Bimbisāra, worried because he was without an heir, went to a soothsayer who predicted that a certain holy man would die and be reborn as the crown prince. Bimbisāra, however, could not wait for this holy man to die; he had the holy man killed, and soon afterward Queen Vaidehī became pregnant. But since the soothsayer also warned that the crown prince would harbor a hatred for his parents and be an enemy to his father, the royal parents decided to drop the newborn baby from a high tower. See Ryūkoku University Translation Center,

trans., *The Sutra of Contemplation of the Buddha of Immeasurable Life* (Kyoto: Ryūkoku University, 1984), 119. This work contains a full, lucid translation of the *KWC.*

10. For example, see *K'ai-yüan lu* 5, *T* 2154.55.523c.

11. *Fa-ching lu, T* 2146.55.116c.

12. See *Li-tai san-pao chi* 10, *T* 2034.49.92c; *Jen-shou lu* 1, *T* 2147.55.152b; *Nei-tien lu* 4 & 5, *T* 2149.55.260a, 291b; *Ching-tai lu* 1, *T* 2148.55.184b; *Ku-chin shih-ching t'u-chi* 3, *T* 2151.55.361c; *Ta-chou lu* 3, *T* 2153.55.39c; *K'ai-yüan lu* 5 & 12, *T* 2154.55.523c, 595b; *Chen-yüan lu* 7, *T* 2156.55.820c.

13. *Ch'u-san-tsang chi-chi, T* 2145.55.22a.

14. *Kao-seng chuan, T* 2059.50.343c.

15. *Nei-tien lu, T* 2149.55.260a.

16. Ibid., 523c.

17. *Li-tai san-pao chi* 15, *T* 2034.49.127c.

18. *Ch'u-san-tsang chi-chi, T* 2145.55.21c.

19. *Kao-seng chuan, T* 2059.50.343c. See Robert Shih, trans., *Biographies des moines éminents (Kao seng tchouan) de Houei-kiao* (Louvain: Institut Orientaliste, 1968), 147–148.

20. *Yao-wang Yao-shang kuan, T* 1161.20.

21. See Fujita, *Genshi Jōdo-shisō no kenkyū,* pp. 62–96.

22. *Tao-chou lu, T* 2153.55.389c.

23. *K'ai-yüan lu, T* 2154.55.524b, 629c.

24. *Ch'u-san-tsang chi-chi, T* 2145.55.115a–b.

25. *Kao-seng chuan, T* 2059.50.342c–343a.

26. *Ming-seng chuan ch'ao, ZZ* 1.2B.7.1.10.

27. No reference can be located for the *Ch'an-ching. Ch'an-fa yao (= Ch'an-pi yao-fa ching), T* 613.15; *P'u-hsien kuan (= Kuan P'u-hsien hsing-fa ching), T* 277.9; *Hsü-k'ung-tsang kuan (= Kuan Hsü-k'ung-tsang p'u-sa ching), T* 409.13.

28. See Tsuboi Shun'ei, *Jōdo sanbukyō gaisetsu* (Tokyo: Ryūbunkan, 1956; rev. ed., 1981), 332.

29. *Li-tai san-pao chi, T* 2034.49.54b & 74a.

30. *Kai-yüan lu, T* 2154.55.484c & 509b.

31. Mochizuki Shinkō, *Jōdokyō no kigen oyobi hattatsu* (Tokyo: Kyōritusུsha, 1930; rpt. ed., Tokyo: Sankibō, 1977), 326; idem, *Bukkyō kyōten seiritsushi-ron* (Kyoto: Hōzōkan, 1946; rpt. ed. 1978), 226.

32. *Ching-t'u wang sheng chuan, T* 2071.51.109b.

33. *Lo-pang i-kao, T* 1969B.47.235b.

34. *Kao-seng chuan, T* 2059.50.395b–c.

35. Tachibana Zuichō, "Uiguru-yaku no *Kanmuryōjukyō,*" *Niraku sōsho* 1 (1912): 22–41.

36. Haneda Tōru, "Niraku sōsho dai-ichigō o yomu," *Gei-bun* 3-10 (1912): 82–90; also found in *Haneda hakushi shigaku ronbunshū,* vol. 2 (Kyoto: Tōyōshi-kenkyū-kai, Kyōto-daigaku, 1958), 546–553.

37. Kudara has recently carried out a more thorough revision of the fragment. See Kudara Kōgi, "*Kanmuryōjukyō*—uiguru-yaku danpen shutei," *Bukkyō-gaku kenkyū* 35 (1979): 33–56.

38. Ibid. As an example of transliteration of Chinese sound, it is shown that "bilingamani" in Uigur is a transliteration of the Chinese "p'i-leng-chia-mo-

ni" (*Mathews* nos. 5158, 3845, 590, 4541, 4654, respectively) and "quansi im" of "kuan-shih-yin" (*Mathews* nos. 3575, 5790, 7418, respectively).

39. A Uigur fragment of the *KWC* was also found recently among the Turfan Collection of the Academy of Sciences of the German Democratic Republic. See Peter Zieme, "A New Fragment of the Uigur *Guanwuliangshoujing,*" *Ryūkoku daigaku bukkyō bunka kenkyūsho kiyō* 20 (1982): 20–29.

40. Hans Reichelt, *Die soghdischen Handschriftenreste des Britischen Museums,* I. Teil (Heidelberg: Carl Winters Universitatsbuchhandlung, 1928), S. 33–56 (Der Dhyāna-Text). This constitutes an edition (and its German translation) of a sūtra found among the Sogdian manuscripts in the Stein collection (O.R. 8212(85)). Cf. A. Stein, *Serindia,* vol. 2 (Oxford: Clarendon, 1921; rpt. ed., Delhi: Motilal Banarsidass, 1980), 924.

41. Ishihama Juntarō, "Sai'iki Kodaigo no butten," in Sai'iki bunka kenkyū-kai, ed., *Sai'iki bunka kenkyū,* vol. 4 (Kyoto: Hōzōkan, 1961), 36.

42. Friedrich Weller, "Bemerkungen zum soghdischen Dhyāna-Texte," *Monumenta Serica* (Journal of Oriental Studies of the Catholic University of Peking) 2 (1936–1937): 341–404; 3 (1938): 78–129.

43. *Kuan fo san-mei hai ching, T* 642.15.

44. *Kuan p'u-hsien p'u-sa hsing-fa ching, T* 277.9.

45. *Kuan Hsü-k'ung-tsang p'u-sa ching, T* 409.13.

46. *Mi-le p'u-sa shang-sheng tou-shuai-t'ien ching, T* 452.14.

47. Ui Hakuju et al., eds., *Chibetto daizōkyō somokuroku,* (Sendai: Tōhoku-daigaku, 1934), no. 199; Takasaki Jikidō, ed., *Tōkyō-daigaku shozō rasaban Chibetto daizōkyō mokuroku* (Tokyo: Tōkyō-daigaku, Indo-tetsugaku Kenkyū-shitsu, 1965), no. 200.

48. Chi-tsang, in his *Kuan Wu-liang-shou ching i-shu,* suggests a Sanskrit title for the *KWC,* "If we preserve the foreign sound, it would be 'Fo-t'o p'an-che a-li-yeh a-mi-t'o fo-t'o hsiu-to-lo' *(Buddhabhāṣitāryāmitabuddha-sūtra?).*" However, this cannot be supported. See Chi-tsang's commentary, *T* 1752.37.233c. In *Nanjio* 198, the title is listed as *"Buddhabhāshitāmitayurbuddha-dhyāna(?)-sūtra,"* but this title was rejected later, as it no longer appears in Tokiwa Daijō et al., eds., *Daizōkyō Nanjō mokuroku hoseisakuin* (Japanese Alphabetical Index of Nanjiō's Catalogue of the Buddhist *Tripiṭaka*) (Tokyo: Nanjō hakushi kinen kankōkai, 1930), 17.

49. The Tibetan translation of the title of the *Maitreya Contemplation Sūtra* is *Ḥphags pa byaṅ chub sems dpaḥ byams pa dgaḥ ldan gnam du skye ba blaṅs paḥi mdo* (The Sacred Sūtra on Bodhisattva Maitreya's Rebirth in the Tuṣita Heaven; see n. 47); since the title does not translate *kuan,* it does not help us in inferring its Sanskrit original.

50. Ōhara Shōjitsu, "*Kanmuryōjukyō* to *jōdoron:* kangyō chūgoku senjutsu ni taisuru ichi-gimon," *Ryūkoku daigaku ronshū* 359 (1958): 1–14. Vasubandhu's *Treatise on the Pure Land* is found in *T* 1524.26.

51. Kasugai Shinya, "*Kanmuryōjukyō* ni okeru shomondai," *Bukkyō bunka kenkyū* 3 (1953): 41–42; Kasugai Shinya and Tōdō Kyōshun, "Jōdo kyōten no keisei," in Miyamoto Shōson, ed., *Bukkyō no konponshinri* (Tokyo: Sanseidō, 1956), 523–530.

52. Nakamura Hajime, "Jōdo sanbukyō no kaisetsu," *Jōdo sanbukyō,* vol. 2, Iwanami Bunko (Tokyo: Iwanami shoten, 1964), 207.

53. *Ch'u-san-tsang chi-chi* 14, *T* 2145.55.105a–b; *Kao-seng chuan* 3, *T* 2059.50.342c.

54. *Ch'u-san-tsang chi-chi* 14, 106b–c; *Kao-seng chuan* 2, 337a.

55. Ogasawara Senshū, "Kōshōkoku no bukkyō kyōgaku," in *Bukkyō shigaku ronshū: Tsukamoto hakushi shōju kinen* (Kyoto: Tsukamoto hakushi shōju kinen kai, 1961), 136–147.

56. *Ch'u-san-tsang chi-chi* 14, *T* 2145.55.103b–104a; *Kao-seng chuan* 2, *T* 2059.50.334b–335c. See Shih, *Biographies des moines éminents,* pp. 90–98.

57. *KWC, T* 365.12.340c–346b. Henceforth, specific references to passages in the *KWC* will be not be given.

58. Ono Genmyō, *Kendara no bukkyō bijutsu* (Tokyo: Heigo Shuppansha, 1923), 77–114; Takata Osamu, *Butsuzō no kigen* (Tokyo: Iwanami shoten, 1967; rpt. ed. 1983), 241, 432.

59. *Kuan fo san-mei hai ching, T* 642.15.648a–657a.

60. Ibid., 679b–681b.

61. Takata, *Butsuzō no kigen,* p. 432. Takata states with regard to *Samādhi Sea Sūtra,* "It would be safe to view this sūtra as having been compiled in northwest India at a rather late period." He has, in other words, accepted the Indian compilation theory. Since strong Chinese elements can nevertheless be detected in the sūtra, there is a need to investigate the problems surrounding its compilation.

62. See Nakamura, "Jōdo sanbukyō no kaisetsu," p. 206.

63. Ono Genmyō, *Daijō bukkyō geijutsu shi no kenkyū* (Tokyo: Kanao-bun'endō, 1927), 33–34; idem, *Bukkyō no bijutsu to rekishi* (Tokyo: Kanao-bun'endo, 1937), 98–99.

64. Watanabe has expressed the view that the *KWC* is unrelated to the Buddhist cultural milieu that produced the colossal buddha images at Bāmiyan. See Watanabe Shōkō, *Okyō no hanashi,* Iwanami Shinsho (Tokyo: Iwanami shoten, 1968), 203.

65. *KWC, T* 365.12.343b.21–22.

66. Higuchi Takayasu, "Amida sanzonbutsu no genryū," Bukkyō geijutsu 7 (1950): 112.

67. *KWC, T* 365.12.342c.11–343b.14.

68. Ibid., 344c.5–6.

69. Mizuno Seiichi, *Chūgoku no bukkyō bijutsu* (Tokyo: Heibonsha, 1968), 7ff., esp. 30, 43–60, 66–67, 122–124.

70. *Kao-seng chuan* 5, *T* 2059.50.352b. See Ui Hakuju, *Shaku Dōan kenkyū* (Tokyo: Iwanami shoten, 1956; rpt. ed., 1979), 30–33.

71. See Kumagai Norio, "Sai'iki no bijutsu," in Sai'iki bunka kenkyū-kai, ed., *Sai'iki bunka kenkyū,* vol. 5 (Kyoto: Hōzōkan, 1962) 30off, esp. 63; Ueno Teruo, "Sai'iki no chōso," ibid., 213–238.

72. Tsukinowa Kenryū, "Butten no shijū," in Bungaku tetsugaku shigaku kai rengō, ed., *Kenkyū ronbunshū IV, kenkyū ronbun shōroku-shi* vol. 3 (Tokyo: Nihon gakujutsu kaigi jimukyoku, 1953), 90–91.

73. The entire text of Tsukinowa's "Butten no shijū" is included in a posthumously published volume, Tsukinowa Kenryū, *Butten no hihan-teki kenkyū* (Kyoto: Hyakkaen, 1971), 3–173. In it, Tsukinowa strongly asserts the Chinese compilation theory by pointing out numerous inconsistencies and occurrences of non-Buddhist, indigenous Chinese expressions within the *KWC.*

74. Suzuki Munetada, *Kihon daijō: Jōdo bukkyō* (Tokyo: Meiji Shoin, 1959; rpt. ed., Tokyo: Gannandō, 1978), 103–109.

75. *KWC, T* 365.12.343a11–12.

76. Ibid., 345c4–5.

77. Ibid., 346a19.

78. Translator's note: While all of the *KWC* passages have been translated in the table, only textual references are provided for the passages from the other sūtras because such parallels become less apparent when rendered into English. Interested readers are encouraged to consult the texts themselves. Line numbers have been added to the column information for ease of reference.

79. *Kuan Hsü-k'ung'tsang p'u-sa ching, T* 409.13.677bff.

80. Kagawa Takao, "Shōmyō shisō no keisei," *Indogaku bukkyōgaku kenkyū* (hereafter *IBK*) 11.1 (1963): 38–49. Also, see Fujita, *Genshi jōdo-shisō no kenkyū,* 547.

81. If we accept Buddhabhadra as the translator of the *Samādhi Sea Sūtra,* the translation can then be assumed to have taken place on Lu-shan ca. 411 or at Chien-k'ang ca. 420–422. See *Ch'u-san-tsang chi-chi* 14, *T* 2145.55.104a; *Kao-seng chuan* 2, *T* 2059.50.335c.

82. There are numerous passages in the *Samādhi Sea Sūtra* that are similar to those of the *KWC* besides those already listed in the table; but the comparisons of each of these parallel passages will not be given here. Shikii Shūjō, *"Kanbu-tsuzanmaikaikyō* to *Kanmuryōjukyō," IBK* 13.1 (1965): 227–230.

83. *KWC, T* 365.12.342c8–9.

84. *Mi-le p'u-sa shang-sheng tou-shuai-t'ien ching, T* 452.14.419b: "At that time in the heavenly palace of Tuṣita Heaven, there were five great deities. The first was named Jeweled Streamer. From his body he rains down the seven jewels that scatter within the palace walls. Each of the jewels transforms into countless musical instruments that hang stationary in the sky and make sound without being played."

85. In this instance, the translation of the *Maitreya Contemplation Sūtra* is considered to have preceded that of the *KWC,* though this view is not necessarily conclusive. Nevertheless, this opinion succeeds in avoiding any dating conflicts, since it is probable that the former sūtra was translated in the vicinity of Turfan ca. 435 (though in Chien-k'ang it is said to be ca. 453)—several years before Emperor T'ai-wu's invasion of the Northern Liang in 439—while the *KWC* is assumed (as discussed above) to have been translated between 424–442. However, if the *Maitreya Contemplation Sūtra* was translated in 453, new doubt will probably be cast upon the view that Kālayaśas was its translator.

86. *Kuan fo san-mei hai ching, T* 643.15.678a, 688b–c, 694a–b.

87. *Shih-chu p'i-p'o-sha lun, T* 1521.26.41b–42c.

88. *Kuan fo san-mei hai ching, T* 643.15.666a (footnote), 690a.

89. *Ch'u-san-tsang chi-chi* 5, *T* 2145.55.38c.

90. *Kuan Yao-wang Yao-shang erh-p'u-sa ching, T* 1161.20.664b–c, 666a.

91. Ibid., 662c, 663a, 664b–c.

92. *Kuan Pu-hsien p'u-sa hsing-fa ching, T* 277.9.389cff. In the text, *"Fa-hua ching"* and *"Miao fa-hua ching"* can be detected more than once.

93. *Chüeh ting pi-ni ching, T* 325.12.38c.

94. *Kuan Hsü-k'ung-tsang p'u-sa ching, T* 409.13.677b.

95. *Kuan Yao-wang Yao-shang erh-p'u-sa ching,* *T* 1161.20.664b. For sūtras that refer to the names of the thirty-five buddhas as well as other buddha names, see Shioiri Ryōdō, "Chūgoku bukkyō ni okeru butsumyōkyō no seikaku to sono genryū," *Tōyōbunka kenkyūsho kiyō* 42 (1966): 221ff.

96. *Ch'an pi yao-fa ching,* *T* 613.15.242bff.

97. Sakaino has advocated the Dharmamitra position, while Satō has chosen Kumārajīva. Mizuno has recently come out in support of Satō's position. See Sakaino Kōyō, *Shina bukkyō seishi* (Tokyo: Bukkyō Nenkansha, 1935; rpt. ed., Tokyo: Kokusho Kankōkai, 1972), 862; Satō Taishun, *Kokuyaku issaikyō: kyōshū-bu,* pt. 4 (Tokyo: Daitō Shuppansha, 1928; rpt. ed., 1980), 177; Mizuno Kōgen, "Zenshū seiritsu izen no zenjō shisōshi josetsu," *Komazawa daigaku kenkyū kiyō* 15 (1957): 22.

98. Mochizuki, *Bukkyō-kyōten seiritsushi-ron,* p. 227.

99. *T* 475.14.538b. The "direct mind" is similar in meaning to the "sincere mind" *(chih-ch'eng hsin)* of the *KWC,* for Seng-chao's commentary on the *Vimalakīrtinirdeśa-sūtra* explains, "Kumārajīva said, 'Direct mind means truthful mind *(ch'eng-shih hsin).'* " See *Chu wei-mo-chieh ching* 1, *T* 1775.38.335c. One also sees in the *Wu-liang-shou ching* the terms "sincere mind" and "deep mind" but not "mind of raising a vow to transfer one's merits."

100. *KWC,* *T* 365.12.343b13, 29.

101. Ibid., 346c3.

102. Ibid., 343a21.

103. *Pan-chou san-mei ching,* *T* 417.13.899b, *T* 418.13.906a: "This mind becomes a buddha . . . this mind is a Buddha." This passage in the corresponding Tibetan version is, "sems kyis sans rgyas byed pa ste . . . sems ñid ṅa yi saṅs rgyas te." See Paul M. Harrison, ed., *The Tibetan Text of the Pratyutpanna-buddha-saṃmukhāvasthita-samādhi-sūtra* (Tokyo: The Reiyukai Library, 1978), 37.

104. *KWC,* *T* 365.12.345b4–5.

105. *Shih-chu ching,* *T* 286.10.503a.

106. *Ta-fa-kuang fo hua-yen ching,* *T* 278.9.547b.

107. *KWC,* *T* 365.12.345c13.

108. Recent findings have greatly strengthened the position of the Chinese-compilation theory. Nogami, for example, has suggested that the category of the "nine grades" *(chiu-p'in)* of rebirth in the *KWC* may have had as its model the practice of dividing the people into nine classes as discussed in "Ku-chin-jen-piao" of the *Han-shu,* or the practice of "laws regarding the nine grades of officials" *(chiu-p'in-kuan-jen-chih-fa)* that was established in the Ts'ao-wei period (220–265) for the purpose of appointing and promoting its officials. From a different angle, Yamada has analyzed the occurrences of the term "Wu-liang-shou-fo" (a translation of Amita Buddha or Amida Buddha). Based on this analysis, Yamada suggests that the *KWC* is the result of having amalgamated three previously unrelated parts: (1) the Ajātaśatru story, (2) the first thirteen contemplations, and (3) the last three contemplations on the nine grades of rebirth. The conclusion was then added to adhere to the sūtra format. Yamada's assertion that the three parts were previously unrelated is based largely on his finding that the term "A-mi-t'o-fo" is confined almost exclusively to the first and the third parts, while occurrences of "Wu-liang-shou-fo" are virtually all found in part two, the first thirteen contemplations. Even the exceptions—two

occurrences of "A-mi-t'o-fo" in part two and one occurrence of "Wu-liang-shou-fo" in part three—pose no problem for Yamada's theory, for they are explained as an attempt on the part of the compiler to "smooth out" the transition from one part to the next. At any rate, Yamada's findings have definitely lent strong support to the Chinese-compilation theory. See Nogami Shunjō, *Chūgoku Jōdokyō-shiron* (Kyoto: Hōzōkan, 1981), 178–183; Yamada Meiji, "Kangyō kō—Muryōju-butsu to Amida-butsu," *Ryūkoku daigaku ronshū* 408 (1976): 76–95.

109. It should be noted that while Seng-han's biography appears in the *Kao-seng chuan* 7, *T* 2059.50.370b, there is no reference to his role as a scribe relative to the *KWC*.

GLOSSARY

A-mi-t'o ching 阿彌陀經
A-mi-t'o-fo 阿彌陀佛
Ch'an-pi yao-fa ching 禪秘要法經
chang-liu 丈六
ch'eng-ming 稱名
ch'eng-shih hsin 誠實心
Chiang-liang-yeh-she 畺良耶舍
chih-ch'eng hsin 至誠心
chih-hsin 直心
Ching-t'u wang-sheng chuan 淨土往生傳
chiu-p'in 九品
chiu-p'in kuan-jen chih fa 九品官人之法
chu-fo hsien-ch'ien san-mei 諸佛現前三昧
Ch'u san-tsang chi-chi 出三藏記集
Chüeh-ting pi-ni ching 決定毘尼經
Fa-hua ching 法華經
Fa-tsang *pi-ch'iu* 法藏比丘
Fo-t'o p'an-che a-li-yeh a-mi-t'o fo hsiu-to-lo 佛陀槃遮阿利耶阿彌陀佛修多羅
hui-hsiang fa-yüan hsin 廻向發願心
hui-hsiang hsin 廻向心
K'ai-yüan lu 開元錄
Kao-seng chuan 高僧傳
ku-chin jen-piao 古今人表
kuan 觀
Kuan-fo san-mei-hai ching 觀佛三昧海經
Kuan Hsü-k'ung-tsang p'u-sa ching 觀虛空藏菩薩經
Kuan Mi-le p'u-sa shang-sheng tou-shuai-t'ien ching 觀彌勒菩薩上生兜率天經
Kuan P'u-hsien p'u-sa hsing-fa ching 觀普賢菩薩行法經
Kuan-shih-yin 觀世音
Kuan Wu-liang-shou-fo ching 觀無量壽佛經
Li-tai san-pao chi 歷代三寶紀
Lo-pang i-kao 樂邦遺稿
Ming-seng chuan ch'ao 名僧傳抄
nan-wu A-mi-t'o-fo 南無阿彌陀佛
Nei-tien lu 內典錄
nien-fo san-mei 念佛三昧
pa-ch'ih 八尺
Pan-chou san-mei ching 般舟三昧經
p'i-leng-chia-mo-ni 毘楞伽摩尼
po-fa ming-men 百法明門
san-hsin 三心
shen-hsin 深心
Shih-chu ching 十住經
Shih-chu ching p'i-p'o-sha lun 十住經毘婆沙論
shih-hsin tso-fo, shih-hsin shih-fo 是心作佛是心是佛
shih-nien 十念
Ta-chou lu 大周錄
Ta-fang kuang-fo hua-yen ching 大方廣佛華嚴經

Wei-mo-chieh suo-shou ching 維摩詰所說經
wei-wu san-mei 惟無三昧
Wu-liang-shou ching 無量壽經
Wu-liang-shou ching yu-po-t'i-she yüan-shen chi 無量壽經優波提舍願生偈
Wu-liang-shou fo 無量壽佛
Wu-liang-shou kuan ching 無量壽觀經
Yao-wang Yao-shang kuan ching 藥王藥上觀經

The *Chan-ch'a ching:* Religion and Magic in Medieval China

WHALEN LAI

There is a tendency to regard philosophy as élite reflection while relegating magic to the base level of folk superstition, conveniently dividing thereby the intellectual few from the vulgar many. However, this two-tiered model of society, first employed by David Hume in his essay *Natural History of Religion*[1] and followed by many modern scholars of religion, more often distorts reality than clarifies it. It is not uncommon that we find both aspects together in one text, revered by social élites and common folk alike. The *I ching* (Book of Changes), for example, combines both aspects: its philosophical appendix is an integral part of its core handbook of fortune-telling. Though of a later date, the appendix serves to draw out certain implicit *theoria* about the universe assumed by the core praxis itself.

A Chinese Buddhist text sharing many of the same characteristics, which enjoyed a remarkably similar career, is the *Chan-ch'a shan-o yeh-pao ching* (Book of Divining the Requital of Good and Evil Actions, henceforth *CCC*). This is a sūtra compiled in China during the late sixth century C.E.[2] As its title implies, it is a scripture giving instructions for a process by which the karmic retribution due from past good and evil deeds could be divined. As a karmic fortune-telling text, it is the Buddhist answer to the *I ching.* Like the *I ching,* it contains a sophisticated philosophical appendix, which was so profound that at one point the *CCC* was suspected of having inspired the *Treatise on the Awakening of Faith According to the Mahāyāna* (*Ta-sheng ch'i-hsin-lun,* henceforth *AFM; T* 1666), easily the *summa buddhologica* of Far Eastern Buddhism.

The interesting admixture of ideas found in this text raises some intriguing questions. What is the exact relationship between "magic" and "religion" in general, and in medieval Chinese Buddhism in particular? And what could have linked the *CCC,* known primarily for its praxis, to the *AFM,* principally renowned for its *theoria?* In addition, the *CCC* provides us with an interesting case study of what it meant to be a Chinese Buddhist apocryphon and how such texts were evaluated by the tradition.

The Origin and Background of the *CCC*

Since its earliest appearance, the *CCC* has been controversial.[3] A Sui catalogue of sūtras, the *Li-tai san-pao chi* (Record of the Three Treasures throughout Successive Generations), compiled in 597 C.E. by Fei Ch'ang-fang (d.u.), notes in fascicle twelve:

> The *CCC:* In two fascicles; no listing in the various catalogues. The colophon says that it was translated by P'u-t'i-teng [Bodhidīpa?; d.u.][4] outside China, but it seems to be a spurious work of recent origin. It now appears in several canonical collections, and is being copied and circulated.
>
> There was a monk in Canton who sponsored a confessional [performed] before a stūpa [representing the Buddha-jewel]. He made use of two strips of leather, and on one he had written "good" and on the other "evil." The practitioners were told to throw these [like lots]. Those who came up with "good" were told that they would be blessed with good fortunes. Those who came up with "evil" were told that misfortune awaited them.
>
> The monk also urged the people to smite themselves *(tzu-p'u)* so as to offset punishment otherwise due *(mieh-tsui).* He succeeded in gathering around him a following of males and females who mingled together [too freely]. In Ch'ing-chou [Shan-tung], a layman also sponsored a similar confessional.
>
> In the thirteenth year of the K'ai-huang era (593), someone reported [the cult] to the Canton magistrate, charging that it was bewitching the people. Upon being investigated, [defenders said] that the stūpa-confessional was based on the *CCC* and that the method of *tzu-p'u* was based on common canonical instructions on [how to do penance by throwing oneself on the ground] "as if Mt. T'ai were crumbling."
>
> The Canton Prefect *(Ssu-ma)* Kuo I [d.u.] went to the capital and personally reported the affair in some detail to the Chih-chou Office. The throne doubted this defense [of the cult as based on] the *CCC,* and ordered the Vice President of Religious Records *(Nei-shih shih-lang),* Li Yüan-ts'ao [d.u.], to accompany Kuo I to the Pao-ch'ang Temple so as to consult [the sūtra-cataloguer] Fa-ching and the other learned monks. They submitted that the *CCC* was not found listed in prior catalogues, and pointed out that no specific site where the translation took place had been given. Furthermore, they noted that the manner in which the stūpa-confessional was practiced was unlike any [other such formula] found in the various sūtras. They advised that the cult not be followed. A memorial was then issued banning these practices. Later, however, a Brāhmaṇa came and said that such rites were in fact found in India.[5]

The judgment against the *CCC* had already been made three years earlier (574) by Fa-ching in his sūtra catalogue.[6] But it is significant that, by 597, Fei would have appended the reference in which an Indian vindicates the practice and would have accepted the apology that since the *CCC* was translated "outside China," the translation site could consequently not be verified. This support reflects popular sympathy for the *CCC,* but leaves us with little reason to believe either of these rationalizations.

The *CCC* is structured as follows. The first of its two fascicles deals with the confessional rites and the divination method; it is this praxis that the Canton cult supposedly modified. The second fascicle is devoted to a *theoria* of the one mind; it is this section that provides a philosophical base for the practice of the cult. The philosophical idealism there is so similar to that found in the *AFM* that direct borrowing between the texts is all but certain. Assuming for the moment that the *CCC* was written after the *AFM* but before the rise of the Canton cult, this would place the *CCC* sometime between 550 and 590. The *CCC* is most likely an early Sui (581–589) text; Japanese scholars have placed it in the decade between 580 and 590.[7]

Although the first reference to cultic uses of the *CCC* comes from South China, and Fei's report gives the impression that it thence spread north to Shan-tung, it would appear more likely that the geographical origin of the text is in the North.

The North is the source of many other fabricated sūtras during this period.[8] The reason for this geographical distribution is that northern China did not nurse the "recipient mentality" toward the words of the Buddha that was prevalent in the South. Being in many ways an extension of the Central Asian Saṃgha, the northern Saṃgha instead developed a "progeny mentality." This distinction means that whereas monks in the South would more often compile sūtra-catalogues to keep track of what had been received from outside China, the northern Saṃgha would instead generate its own sūtras, just as Buddhists had done previously in Central Asia.

The northern Saṃgha was larger than its southern counterpart, and had a broader socio-economic base. It also demonstrated greater expediency when it came to populist concerns. Thus, for example, after the first persecution of Buddhism in the North (446–452), the architects of the Buddhist revival did not follow the usual course of collecting books and compiling catalogues in order to salvage their tradition. Instead, it appears that these leaders were more actively involved in translating new sūtras, writing new texts, including such indigenous scriptures as the *T'i-wei Po-li ching* (Book of Trapuṣa and Bhallika), and actively proselytizing among the masses. The *CCC* therefore reflects to me more of this northern agenda.

In this same context, the *CCC* shows plausible ties with the stūpa-confessional appearing in the *Yu-p'o-sai chieh ching* (*Upāsakaśīla-sūtra; T* 1488), a major bodhisattva preceptory text directed at the laity, which Dharmakṣema introduced to Liang-chou. As we will see, the *CCC* also has close affinities with the *AFM,* an apocryphal treatise suspected to be of northern provenance. In addition, the *CCC* is affiliated with a Kṣitigarbha corpus, the major texts of which are the *Ti-tsang p'u-sa ching* (Book of Kṣitigarbha Bodhisattva; *T* 2909), the *Ti-tsang p'u-sa pen-yüan ching* (Book of the Original Vows of Kṣitigarbha Bodhisattva; *T* 412), and the *Ta-fang-kuang shih-lun ching* (Expanded Book of the Ten Wheels; *T* 410). Kṣitigarbha Bodhisattva was highly honored by Hsin-hsing (540–594), a northern monk and founder of the Three Stages sect (San-chieh chiao),[9] which is covered in the chapters in this volume by Mark Lewis and Antonino Forte.

While the cult of Kṣitigarbha may have had Indian or Central Asian antecedents, this corpus, in the opinion of some, seems to have been compiled in China.[10] The *Shih-lun ching* in this corpus is an eschatological text focusing on the this-worldly teachings that precede Maitreya's termination of mundane history. This apocryphon supplies the scenario for the teaching of the *CCC,* and its "ten wheels" are presumed to have inspired the *CCC*'s use of the ten divination "wheels," or tops. The reliance on divination as a means to counter the uncertainties of the Final Age of the Dharma *(mo-fa)* parallels the prominent use of dhāraṇīs in other eschatological apocrypha produced in China. Since the Liang-chou monks under Dharmakṣema did not have the same sense of eschatological urgency—they usually presumed they were in the less severe age of the semblance dharma—the *CCC* should thus be regarded as a text deriving from a later development in the sixth century.

In addition, the *CCC* draws upon the so-called tathāgatagarbha tradition and refers explicitly to a *Liu ken-chü ching* (Sūtra of the Six Faculty-Aggregates)[11] that is also cited in the *Ratnagotravibhāga* (*Chiu ching i-sheng pao-hsing lun; T* 1161), translated in 508 by Ratnamati in Loyang.[12] All these factors make it more probable that the *CCC* was compiled in the North, and that it only made its way south later, eventually finding an enthusiastic following in Canton. The suggestion that the *CCC* borrowed from a text translated by Paramārtha (Chen-ti) in Canton itself may now be discounted.[13] Neither Paramārtha nor his circle would have approved of the *CCC*'s advocacy of "suchness permeated by ignorance (avidyā)," a doctrine that is contrary to the *Mahāyānasaṃgraha* as translated by Paramārtha. The Canton cult's confessional ritual is also excessive and very unlike the kind of penance commonly practiced by the southern élite.[14]

The two fascicles of the *CCC* have each stirred up modern scholarly controversies. The praxis of the first fascicle raises the question of whether the self-inflicted punishment practiced by the Canton cult is Buddhist or Taoist in origin. Related to the *theoria* of the second fascicle is the question of whether the text borrowed from the *AFM,* or vice versa. We will deal with these two questions in our analysis of the two fascicles below.

The First Fascicle: Penance and Karmic Divination

The *CCC* is an eschatological text that recognizes in the present the telltale signs of the degeneration of the dharma *(mo-fa).* During this last age, it is not easy for men to arouse even the most fundamental of Buddhist virtues, or faith *(śraddhā)*. Appropriately, therefore, the *CCC* is taught at the request of a bodhisattva named Chien-ching-hsin (Firm and Pure Faith):

> Bodhisattva Firm and Pure Faith then said, "As the Buddha previously taught, 'Once I have passed away, after the demise of the true dharma and the end of the semblance dharma age, [the world] would enter the age of the degenerate dharma. At such time, the merit of sentient beings will be paltry and there will be a multitude of sorrows and troubles. The kingdom will suffer repeated chaos; harm and calamity will occur. . . .' "[15]

We find a similar echo of the need to secure faith in the *AFM,* a work that aimed to effect the "awakening of faith" in Mahāyāna.[16]

The *CCC* offers thereby a merciful expediency for the weak at heart, so that they too might arouse the requisite faith. However, rather than teaching that method himself, the Buddha deferred instead to Bodhisattva Kṣitigarbha (Earth Womb). First, he related Kṣitigarbha's bodhisattva career, vows, and powers, to show that he is more than qualified to teach the sūtra.[17] In this, the *CCC* clearly draws on the Kṣitigarbha corpus mentioned earlier, and openly establishes Kṣitigarbha as teacher and savior of the hour.[18] The expediency proffered involves a Buddhist form of divining destinies.

Spinning the Wheel of Fortune

To men of little faith, Kṣitigarbha first offers a means by which perplexed persons might come to know their karmic standings:

> [The person] should use the wooden-wheel divination method, by which he may then divine and observe the good and evil karmic deeds accruing from the past, and with it the joy or sorrow, fortune or calamity, that will appear in the present.[19]

The wooden "wheel" turns out to be a spinning top; "turning the wheel of dharma" is thus "spinning the top." For that reason, we will translate "wheel" in those contexts henceforth as "top":

> First, the person should carve a piece of wood the length of the little finger. Across its middle, an inch from both ends, he should carve out four flat surfaces; the two ends should be tapered. This is so that when he raises his hand and throws it sideways, it will spin with ease. For that reason, it is called a "top." By using this form, a person may destroy wrong views and the web of doubts, and "turn" thereby toward the noble path that leads to the abode of peace (nirvāṇa); for this reason, it is called "turn."[20]

Three sets of four-sided tops are then designed, each set serving a specific purpose:

> There are to be three sets of divinations using these tops. What are the three? The first is a set of ten divinatory tops that can reveal the various good and evil deeds committed in the past. The second is a set of three tops measuring the actual strength of these karmic forces, that is, whether they are near [i.e., imminent] or distant [weak, i.e., yet to surface]. The third is a set of six tops that can verify the various modes in which retribution is received in the three times [past, present, and future].[21]

The first set employs ten tops. On each four-sided top, one should inscribe on two opposite sides one of the ten wholesome actions *(daśakuśalakarmapatha)* and its opposite unwholesome action, leaving two unmarked sides (denoting "neither"):[22]

> Taking up the wooden top, [the person performing the divination] should throw it sideways on a sanctified area . . . trusting that the messages divined would indeed be truthful in every respect. The result may be all good in all ten cases, or all evil, or a combination, or neither.[23]

This can be done for oneself or on someone else's behalf. It is this use of the ten tops that the Canton monk simplified into the casting of two leather lots.

Turning up some of the ten wholesome actions holds out the promise of salutary rewards; turning up the unwholesome actions forecasts later retributions. By drawing all ten blanks—symbolizing here the transcendence of karmic good and evil—the person is deemed to be without any further defiled outflows *(anāsrava)*. A mix of good and evil indicates either that karmic forces are weak or that contrary forces are canceling each other out. Of course, the fortunate one should not simply rejoice but continue to persevere; the unfortunate one should not despair but should work to mend his ways.

The next set involves three tops that measure the strength of the karmic forces. One of the three is marked as representing bodily actions, the second as speech, and the last as mental activities. Traditionally, the first three of the ten wholesome and unwholesome actions are considered to be performed via the body, the next four through speech, and the last three through mind. The degree of the karmic impact of these actions is indicated by markings made on the four sides of each of the three tops. One mark is long and thick; the second is short and thin; the third is thick and deep; the fourth thin and shallow. The first two denote the quality of the good. The second two denote the weightiness of the evil. A throw resulting in a strong fortune would be taken to mean that the blessing would be imminent; a weak misfortune would mean the punishment would take some time to manifest itself. Discrepancies between the first and second sets of forecasts were to be handled with prudence, as we will see later.[24]

The third set involves six tops. These go into the specific destinies:

> To divine the specific fortunes within the three times, a set of six tops should be carved out of wood. On these tops, the numbers 1, 2, 3, 4, 5, 6, 7, 8, 9, 10,

> 11, 12, 13, 14, 15, 16, 17, 18 should be inscribed, one number to each of the three sides [leaving one blank surface in each of the six wheels]. . . . The person should then throw [each wheel in] this set thrice [i.e., a total of eighteen times]. The numerical total [of the outcomes] is then added up, and the good or evil fortune incurred can then be checked against the list.[25]

What follows then is a table of 189 possible fates:[26]

Nos. 1 to 160 = the present
161 to 171 = the past
172 to 189 = the future

By drawing sixteen "blanks," one achieves what in fact is a 190th fate: gaining the "gainless" *(wu-so-teh,* Skt. *anupalabdhi)* here and now. This is the lowest possible number. Equally difficult to come by is the highest possible number, 189; this means getting the top numbers (3, 6, 9, 12, 15, 18) thrice each and means that "forsaking the body, one attains the Mahāyāna" in the future. "Past" fortunes mean learning one's previous rebirth. Thus, no. 161 is the encouraging news that one has come into this human life from a previous life in hell, whereas no. 171 is having had the good fortune of hearing the profound dharma—one of the best prebirth conditionings one can have had.

A simple statistical analysis of the 190 fortunes shows many overlaps, several symmetries, and about a two-to-one ratio of good fortunes to bad:

(1) The first forty-five (nos. 1–45) are devoted to matters of spiritual advancement. Nos. 1, 3, and 4, for example, go with the attainment of the nonbacksliding status in the Great, the Middle, and the Lesser Vehicles (i.e., as buddha, bodhisattva, arhat).
(2) The last twenty-nine (nos. 161–181) deal symmetrically with the standard paths in prebirths and rebirths.
(3) Nos. 116 to 122 deal almost symmetrically with the state, including bold indictments of evil kings.[27]
(4) About fifteen items (nos. 144–160), just before the last twenty, are concerned with physical sickness and suffering.

The majority of fates—especially those given by the middle numbers, which are statistically the ones most likely to come up—deal with this-worldly benefits. The classic examples would be no. 49, promising wealth; 50, offering official positions; 51, longevity; and 52, immortality.

Makita Tairyō sees in all these the perennial Chinese love for fortune-telling and the Chinese assumption that any and all such requests for signs, if sincerely made with singleness of mind, would be answered.[28] The *CCC* is, to him, another example of a "plebeian scripture" *(shomin kyōten)* in search of "this-worldly benefits" *(gense rieki).*

Such blanket categories, however, often do more to obscure than to reveal; they are not always that helpful in understanding medieval faiths, where "sublime" wisdom (what we see in fascicle two) and "crude" magic (what we see in fascicle one) seem perfectly at home with each other. After all, it is still customary at Japanese temples in our time for one and all to have their fortunes told.

That the middle numbers in the fortunes describe mundane benefits cannot be denied. But it would be misleading to assume that the *CCC* is predominantly concerned with such worldly concerns. The apparent lopsidedness may be due to the simple fact that present fates tend to be more specifiable than future and past ones. Even there, moreover, the standard concerns for money and fame are minimal; more of the fortunes deal with the perennial human anxieties over interpersonal relationships.

Far more important than the divination itself, however, is the cult of penance that is its presupposition. Thus, the overall structure of the *CCC* is soteriologically oriented, with due attention to the *yānas* and the pāramitās; it is not just another worldly divination text. In fact, it warns against "various worldly fortune-telling arts that are greedy after, and obsessed with, mere happiness."[29]

Not fatalism, not magical manipulation, but, ultimately, confession and purgation are what ensure the success of the divination, which is only the beginning of a long spiritual journey. This penance, however, brings up a controversy over possible Taoist input in the scripture.

The Tzu-P'u Controversy

In reviewing the Canton cult, Harvard sinologist Lien-sheng Yang discovered a possible Taoist precedent from the later Han. The religious T'ai-p'ing Tao movement had practiced a similar rite of penance involving slapping oneself on the cheeks and knocking one's forehead on the ground. Other acts of penance included beating oneself on the chest, smearing ashes on face and body, and rolling in the mud.[30]

Yang noted how the Buddhists of the Six Dynasties period first criticized the Taoists for such immoderation, as a consequence of which the practice seems to have disappeared during the T'ang-Sung era. Indeed, by classical Buddhist standards, such emotional demonstrations would have been judged aimless and counterproductive. The irony is that such Taoist expressions were apparently adopted by the Buddhists of the Sui period. By the T'ang, the Buddhists outdid the Taoists in this regard.

Yang noted that the *T'ai-p'ing ching* (Book of the Great Peace) specifies that "knocking the head on the ground and *tzu-p'u*" are only effective for removing "light offensives."[31] The T'ien-shih Tao tradition was known to have flourished in the coastal areas. Canton and Shan-tung, where the *CCC* cult was found, were also located in that general area.

Because of that fact, and considering that the *CCC* itself did not endorse blatantly masochistic acts, I think Yang is right in positing Taoist legacies in the Canton cult.

To this, Yoshioka Yoshitoyo and Hu Shih have offered their own analyses.[32] Within the complex exchange, the most relevant item in our context is this: for the word *tzu-p'u* (to smite oneself on the cheek), Hu Shih suggests instead reading *tzu-p'u* (to fall down). Moot points of philology aside, since the action reported is accompanied by the analogy to "Mt. T'ai crumbling,"[33] it should be describing the dejection of throwing oneself headlong to the ground in an urgent plea for forgiveness. If so, Hu Shih is correct in so emending the compound. But this brings up another problem: the two different postures assumed in India and China during such supplication. The Indian custom is less emotional; one kneels before the Buddha with the "five *cakras* (wheels) touching the ground."[34] The five wheels, or points, are what mark the knees, the elbows, and the forehead. This is homage done in a kneeling position, but with the palms turned upward and the forearms lifted. The traditional Chinese expression is "throwing the four *t'i* on the ground," with palms turned downward and the forearm touching the ground. Physiologically, it is harder to "crumble like Mt. T'ai" using the Indian posture.

However, by the Six Dynasties period, the native metaphor of "like T'ai-shan crumbling" had found its way even into translations of Sanskrit scriptures, as the ample citations from both Taoist and Buddhist materials given by all three scholars show. Though this trio of scholars hesitated to suggest a single Buddhist text's contribution to the Buddho-Taoist syncretism of the Canton cult, I would propose as a possible consideration the *Upāsakaśīla-sūtra,* a popular lay-bodhisattva preceptory text, introduced by Dharmakṣema, that had gained currency in the Northern Wei.[35] Besides employing the metaphor of Mt. T'ai, this scripture also specified that the confession of wrongs should be done before the Three Jewels, but especially before the Buddha. This adumbrates the importance of the stūpa in the Canton cult.

The mode of penance aside, is divination of karmic futures a "Taoist" corruption or has it a legitimate Buddhist base? At first glance, it would seem that the historical Buddha would have rejected divination as another useless magical ritual; indeed, divination and fortune-telling are prohibited in the *Vinaya* and in Chinese apocryphal preceptory texts, including the *CCC* itself.[36] The karma doctrine should not normally predispose itself toward such fortune-telling, even though theoretically the Buddha has knowledge of the destinies of all men and is free to reveal it. The casting of lots in Canton is too similar to known folk practices and to the use of the *I ching* for us to deny that there was input from Chinese religion.[37] The use of a top only adapted a Buddhist symbol for casting the lots.[38] The *CCC* might have found implicit canonical support for its tops in Kṣitigarbha's legendary ten wheels, but this is a very tenuous link.[39]

The most specific archetype of the *CCC* divinatory act, traced by Morita Ryūsen, is a legend involving Ānanda related in the *Fu-fa-tsang yin-yüan chuan* (Record of the Events in the Transmission of the Dharma-Receptacle).[40] This legend tells of the verification of current good and bad mental intent by the use of white and black stones, a method much simpler than the *CCC*'s and employed for a somewhat different purpose, but still quite suggestive.[41]

In the end, we must conclude that the divinatory portions in the first fascicle of the *CCC* belie native proclivities for fortune-telling more than any known Buddhist practice to date. Having said that, we should return to the fundamental presupposition for a successful divination: sincerity in penance.

Penance and Confession

Before each spinning of the top, a rite of purification is required. For example, prior to beginning with the first set, the practitioner has to seek out a quiet place where he sets up a buddha statue and the *CCC* on an altar that is properly decked with a canopy, flowers, and incense. Then he bathes and puts on clean clothes, harboring all the while a sincere mind. He pays homage to the Three Jewels and makes the bodhisattva vow to aspire to wisdom and compassion, promising to fulfill the six perfections (pāramitās), the four infinite states of mind *(apramāṇya),* and the knowledge of nonproduction *(anutpādajñāna)* and the selfsame *(samatā).* The penitent then pays homage to Kṣitigarbha a figurative one-thousand times, for guidance, protection, and deliverance from all hindrances and in hopes of attaining unwavering faith. Only after fulfilling these preliminary qualifications does he pray for the blessings needed to make the divination effective.

The karmic standing that the wheels foretell is only the most preliminary stage in the full program of *śīla,* samādhi, and prajñā (precepts, meditation, and wisdom). Thus, prior to using the next set of six tops, the text says:

> Sons of Good Families! In the future, there will be various sentient beings who will want to be free from birth, old age, sickness and death, who are ready to arouse the thought [of enlightenment, i.e., *bodhicitta*] and cultivate samādhi and formless wisdom. They should first examine the good and evil actions that were performed during their past lives [using the first set of ten tops] and measure their quality and quantity [using the second set of three tops]. If it turns out that the evil actions are many and weighty, the person should not so quickly practice samādhi or prajñā. Rather, he should first cultivate confessional rites.[42]

The purgation for those with weighty sins is even more demanding:

> First, retiring to a quiet place, the person sincerely repents past wrongs. He chants the names of the buddhas and vows henceforth to pursue the Good. To stay alert throughout, he might circumambulate the buddha-statue. The confessional is repeated six times morning and night, and may continue for days on end: 7 and multiples of 7—14, 21, up to 49 (7 × 7), or 100, even 1,000 days.[43]

After seven days of such penance, the sinner should consult the set of three tops each morning at dawn. If body, speech, and mind are indeed shown to be pure, this is taken as an indication that the confessionals have removed the evil karma. Some people might then see light, smell fantastic aromas, or even receive dream visits from buddhas and bodhisattvas, although any such sightings prior to the achievement of true purity are illusory and false.[44] It is only after the completion of this *śīla* step that one may go on to practice samādhi. However, since not everyone can pursue meditation, a person can appeal to Kṣitigarbha instead. The text then continues with a fairly long excursion into the administration and observance of various preceptory rules within the Order.[45] Because of its attention to the rules of discipline, the *CCC* should be seen, as suggested earlier, as a part of the northern bodhisattva preceptory tradition rooted in Dharmakṣema.[46]

For the whole divinatory system to work, the person must have the sincere quality of mind known as "ultimate mind" *(chih-hsin).*[47] By a double entendre, this ultimate mind is what enables the truthful predictions of the divination to "reach" *(chih)* the "mind" *(hsin)*:

> Sons of Good Families, the ultimate mind of which I speak has briefly two aspects: (1) the ultimate mind of one first learning and aspiring to bodhisattvahood, and (2) the ultimate mind of one who is completely absorbed in concentration of mind and comes into complete correspondence with spiritual courageousness. It is only when you have this type of ultimate mind that you will attain the Good. This second type of ultimate mind has three degrees: superior, average, inferior. The first is the one mind wherein thoughts are no longer disturbed and the mind abides in the absolute of absolutes. The second is the courageous mind, which forges ahead single-mindedly, without lassitude and with no concern [should he even lose] his life. The third is the profound mind that is in accord with the dharma and will never backslide.[48]

Repentant men can consult the first set of ten tops; those yet to attain the preliminary type of ultimate mind may consult the second set of three tops; only those with proven purity of body, speech, and mind may consult the third set of six tops.

Sincerity of mind is not just a prerequisite for prognostication; it involves the structure of reality itself. The one mind, the superior form of the second type of ultimate mind, validates the construction of the six tops thus:

> Know that all these numbers [used in the third set of divinations] derive from the number one. They have the one as their basis. These numerical forms

> reveal that the aggregates of the six faculties all derive from the innately pure mind of the tathāgatagarbha, that is, the one real realm. That they have the one real realm as their basis is what is meant by the statement that they rely on the one real realm. Because of the presence of ignorance (avidyā), which does not realize this one real realm, deluded thoughts and speculations manifest the deluded [six] spheres of objects, producing discrimination, attachment, the accumulation of karma, and the process of causation. Thus arise the eyes, the ears, the nose, the tongue, the body, and the mind, making up the six faculties. Dependent on these six faculties, the six consciousnesses arise in respect to the corresponding external sense objects of form, sound, smell, taste, tangibles, and ideas (dharmas). Based on these six consciousnesses, perceptions arise that are unfavorable toward or favorable toward, and neither unfavorable nor favorable toward, these six sense objects. Thus are born the eighteen types of feelings.[49]

From the one came the many, and the one rules the many. As the one mind subsumes the six consciousnesses, so the one controls the six tops. The premise here is philosophical monism, and the natural emanation of the one into the many. We are reminded here of Wang Pi's (226–249) eulogy of the one (principle) as the basis of the many (manifestations) in his exegesis of another divinatory text, the *I ching*.[50]

However, mind and reality may not always be in correspondence. When the mind is insincere, or not ultimate, then the expected results of the divination would "not reach the mind" *(pu-chih-hsin)*. This doctrine of "noncorrespondence" *(pu-hsiang-ying)* allows the *CCC* to dismiss any mistaken predictions:

> If joy and sorrow, fortune and calamity, as well as defilements and karmic habituations [revealed through the tops] indeed fit [the experience of the person divining], this is deemed "correspondence." If they do not fit, this is *pu-chih-hsin* ["not reaching the mind," i.e., not of the ultimate mind]. That [prediction] is then deemed to be false.[51]

Other nonalignments can occur and would be taken care of similarly. Thus the system has some safeguards against mistold fortunes.[52] As a whole, the *CCC* method of divination, in the hands of the pious, should work quite satisfactorily.

The Second Fascicle: Beyond Karma and Toward Prajñā

It is to explain further this relationship between mind and reality that the second fascicle speculates on the symmetry between the one mind and the one ultimate reality in ways very similar to the *AFM*.

The AFM Controversy

Early on, the *CCC* was drawn into the debate over another spurious work, the *AFM*. This is not the place to go into all the details of this controversy, so only the relevant essentials will be included. Originally thought to have been the work of Aśvaghoṣa, as translated by Paramārtha in Canton around 550, the *AFM* is now recognized by most scholars to be a Chinese apocryphal composition. Kashiwagi Hiroo has recently reviewed this whole controversy.[53]

Although Kashiwagi still has doubts as to whether any Chinese Buddhist in the sixth century could produce, in seeming isolation and anonymity, this highly integrated, doctrinally comprehensive work, I shall proceed under the assumption that it was compiled in China. A detailed refutation of Kashiwagi's position and demonstration of the sinitic elements in this text is not possible here.[54] At one time this issue divided the scholarly world into two opposing camps. The major Japanese protagonists were Mochizuki Shinkō, arguing for Chinese authorship, and Tokiwa Daijō, defending its Indian provenance. That early debate still provides the best introduction to the controversy.[55]

The facts are these: The first known reference to the *AFM* is in the biography of the monk T'an-ch'ien (542–607), an adherent of the southern branch of the Ratnamati lineage of Ti-lun *(Daśabhūmikasūtropadesa)* specialists in the northern capital of Loyang. T'an-ch'ien must have been a pivotal figure in the origin of the *AFM,* because all the early commentaries on that text derive from his lineage. Here is a simplified lineage chart, the asterisks marking those who had taught and/or commented on the *AFM:*

The southern branch of the Ti-lun school
based in Loyang

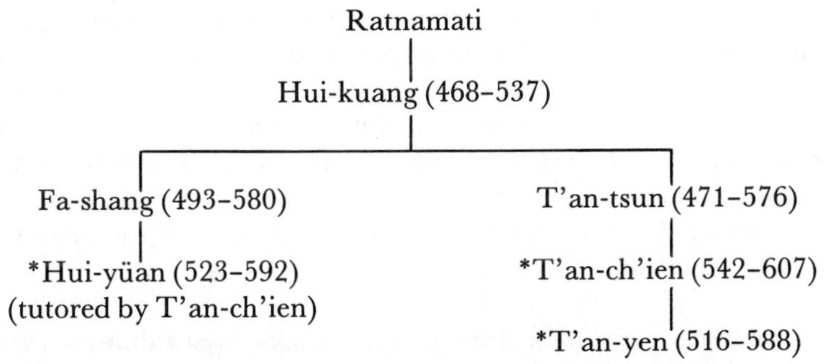

During the anti-Buddhist persecution of 574–576,[56] T'an-ch'ien and other eminent northern monks fled south. Renowned for his learning, T'an-ch'ien was apparently already well versed in the *AFM* before coming south in 577. If so, the *AFM* would appear to have turned up in the North sometime in the middle of the sixth century. However, on his trip south, T'an-ch'ien discovered the *She-ta-sheng lun (Mahāyānasaṃgraha),*

translated in 563 in Canton by Paramārtha.[57] Paramārtha is alleged to be the translator of the *AFM,* but confirmation of that is lacking. Furthermore, none of Paramārtha's students in Canton listed the *AFM* in their areas of expertise.

Instead, the first scholars of the *AFM* came from the circle of T'an-ch'ien. It is T'an-ch'ien who instructed Hui-yüan and T'an-yen. T'an-yen was his disciple, but Hui-yüan was of the same dharma generation, being, like T'an-ch'ien, a disciple of Fa-shang. In age Hui-yüan was T'an-ch'ien's elder, but he humbly studied under T'an-ch'ien. Both Hui-yüan and T'an-yen then commented on the *AFM.* Assuming that the *AFM* is of Chinese origin, when looking for a potential author[58] one would naturally have to look back beyond these commentators. Since Hui-yüan was of the same generation as T'an-ch'ien, both would probably have accepted the attribution of *AFM* to Aśvaghoṣa on authority from someone more senior in their lineage. Since there is no evidence that Fa-shang had any knowledge of the *AFM,* the most plausible choice then falls on T'an-tsun, the teacher of T'an-ch'ien. This reasoning would place the *AFM* in the North around 550, circulating among adherents of the southern branch of the Ti-lun school. I think this scenario is the most sensible way of positioning the *AFM* within the complex sectarian environment of medieval Chinese Buddhism.

Mochizuki, however, had a more complicated theory. He held that the *AFM* was authored by T'an-tsun and then redacted by T'an-ch'ien after the latter's trip south. The redaction was necessary to reconcile the different interpretations of the *ālayavijñāna* and the trikāya then held by the two Ti-lun branches in the North and by the She-lun school in the South.[59]

Though ingenious, this theory is open to criticism. It assumes, first, that both the authorship and the redaction of the treatise occurred within a very limited period of time and, second, that there was already an acute awareness of sectarian differences at that relatively early date. But since these two problems are not immediately relevant to our present concern with the *CCC,* I will defer their discussion for now.[60]

The particulars of sectarian debates in sixth-century China aside, the *AFM* contains elements that defy any easy assignation of Indian or Central Asian provenance. To list just a few:

- an analysis of evolution through a three-six (three subtle, six gross) devolution of mind, which does not fit the standard eight consciousnesses;
- a theory of a mutual permeation between suchness and ignorance, as if these were polar entities, a view that violates basic dicta in Yogācāra epistemology;
- a numerical progression from one to five that seems at first to be sim-

ilar to Abhidharmic lists, until one realizes that it involves a monistic One being present in all the subsequent numbers;

- in short, the *AFM* has a unique understanding of:

  One Mind
  Two Aspects
  Three Greats (Mahā)
  Four Faiths
  Five Practices

  Moreover, to satisfy this sequence from one to five, a refuge in suchness was added to the traditional three refuges of the Buddha, Dharma, and Saṃgha in order to create a fourfold faith; and finally, *prajñāpāramitā* was removed from the traditional six perfections in order to yield the necessary five practices.

The *AFM*'s structure can therefore best be explained by recognizing in it the influence of the Chinese cosmology of the One, yin-yang theory, three-six numerology, and the progression into the five processes.

It was during the long controversy over the authenticity of the *AFM* that the *CCC* too became involved. Mochizuki discovered that a Silla monk, Ch'ongu Chinsung (d.u.), had already charged the *AFM* with being a forgery. Chinsung had noticed the similarity between the *AFM* and the philosophical sections of the *CCC*. Since the *AFM* was a śāstra, a treatise attributed to a Buddhist exegete, it naturally had to have been derived from the *CCC,* a sūtra that was the authentic word of the Buddha.[61] But since the *CCC* had been judged conclusively to be a forgery, the *AFM,* Chinsung claimed, would have to be forgery upon a forgery. Agreeing with Chinsung, Mochizuki took the generally inferior quality of the *CCC,* both philosophically and stylistically, as indicating that it was written before the *AFM.*[62]

Tokiwa disagreed. To him, the imprecision of the *CCC* showed instead that it was a bad copy of the more refined and comprehensive *AFM.* On this particular point, Tokiwa was right, as Mochizuki seems later to have conceded.[63] The only other possibility is that the second fascicle of the *CCC,* which is so obviously related to the teachings of the *AFM,* may have been appended to what was originally a single-fascicle text on divination. To discount this scenario, we have to appreciate the integrity of the two parts of the text.

The Doctrine of the One Mind

Fascicle two of the *CCC,* though seemingly independent, is an appropriate sequel to fascicle one. After the *śīla* of penance and the samādhi of the ultimate mind, the *CCC* here goes on to describe the prajñā of mind-only idealism. The passage often cited as paralleling the *AFM*'s core message is this:

> The mind that is thus described has two characteristics. What are the two characteristics? The first is the mind's inner characteristic; the second is the mind's outer characteristic. The mind's inner characteristic also has two aspects. The first is the true aspect; the second is the deluded aspect. The true aspect pertains to the essential form of the mind's substance. It is suchness *(tathatā)* without variance, pure and complete, without hindrance or obstructions, so fine that it is hard to perceive. This is because it pervades everywhere and is permanent and indestructible, and therefore establishes, produces, and nurtures all dharmas.[64]

Judging from the less technical language used here, this passage seems most likely to be a liberal paraphrase of the *AFM* doctrine of the one mind qua *dharmadhātu* having the two aspects of suchness and birth-and-death.[65] It could not have been the other way around, because the qualifiers the *CCC* uses—namely, "inner" *(nei)* and "outer" *(wai),* "true" *(chen)* and "deluded" *(wang)*—are less technical and exacting than the vocabulary of the *AFM.* For example, although the adjective "deluded" is employed by the *AFM* to describe consciousness and its functions, it is never used to designate the negative aspect of the one mind; the term the *AFM* uses there is "the mind of birth and death." Likewise, the adjective "true" *(chen)* is never used in *AFM* to describe "the mind of suchness." In the *AFM, chen* appears only as a part of the compound *chen-ju* (suchness); nowhere does the text use *chen* by itself or in opposition to *wang* (deluded).[66] It was, rather, Ching-ying Hui-yüan, one of the earliest commentators to the *AFM,* who categorized the core consciousness as *chen* (true) and *wang* (deluded) in the section on the "eight consciousnesses" *(pa-shih lun)* in his *Ta-sheng i chang* (Treatise on the Doctrines of Mahāyāna).[67] The *CCC* should be taken as an early commentatorial text on the *AFM,* as indeed Kashiwagi has done in his book on the *AFM.*[68]

Furthermore, in the first fascicle of the *CCC,* the author favored certain expressions that he used quite freely, for example, *wu-sheng wu-mieh* (no birth, no death). However, in the second fascicle, where he was constrained to comply with the standardized expressions of the *AFM* itself, we find him shifting back to *pu-sheng pu-mieh* (not birth, not death) instead.[69] The mixture of independent and borrowed expressions in the two fascicles accounts for some of the rough edges of the *CCC.*

It is conceivable that the *CCC* was originally in one fascicle, consisting of the present first fascicle, with its concern for fortune-telling, plus some limited philosophical justification of the three sets of tops using the ten wheels of Kṣitigarbha and the scheme of the six faculty-aggregates (times three to yield the eighteen *dhātus*). If so, the reference to the *Sūtra of the Six Faculty-Aggregates* is then sufficient as a scriptural justification of the use of the tops, and the more elaborate psychic scheme that draws from the *AFM* might then be considered to have been appended later. The problems with this hypothesis are that the *CCC* is always known to the sūtra cataloguers as having been in two fascicles, and that the stylistic differences between the two parts seem due more to literary refinement than to obvious changes of authorship. Structurally speaking, the speculations on the one mind, on *chih-hsin* (ultimate mind), and on the "correspondence" between mind and reality in the first fascicle anticipate so well the mind-only philosophy of the second fascicle that a single-author theory would seem to be preferred.

For reasons stated earlier, the *CCC* is probably copied from the *AFM,* rather than vice versa. As in the *AFM,* the goal is "Mahāyāna," meaning not the school, but the Absolute. To attain this, Kṣitigarbha stresses faith:

> The initial practice that is also the basic deed is the so-called reliance on the one real realm so as to cultivate faith and understanding *(hsin-chieh,* Skt. *adhimukti).* This is because, as the power of faith and understanding increases, a person may quickly gain entrance to the lineage of bodhisattvas.[70]

Faith and understanding mean recognizing the embryonic buddha that is innate within oneself:

> The one real realm is the substance of the mind of sentient beings. From the very beginning, it has never been born or destroyed; it is innately pure and free from all hindrances and obstructions. It is similar to empty space, because it entertains no differentiation. It is equipoised, all-pervasive, permeating everywhere. It fills the ten directions, and is the ultimate, monistic characteristic. It is nondual, undifferentiated, unchanged, unaltered, and is subject neither to increase nor decrease.[71]

The minds of sentient beings, the minds of adherents of the three vehicles, and the minds of the buddhas are the same suchness.

As in the *AFM,* all differentiations are seen as ultimately unreal, being similarly reduced to ignorance (*wu-ming,* Skt. *avidyā*) or its accomplice, deluded thought *(wang-nien, wang-hsin,* Skt. *vikalpa):*

> All the myriads of dharmas are produced by deluded thought and have the deluded mind as their basis. However, this deluded mind has no form of its own; it too exists in dependence on the [external] sense realms. That is to say, conditioned by thought *(nien),* the person senses and knows the sense realm before him; therefore, [this subjective knower] is called the mind. Furthermore, although this deluded mind and the corrupting sense realms arise symbiotically and simultaneously, this deluded mind can serve as the master of all these sense realms. Why is this? This is because the deluded mind does not realize the monistic characteristic of the *dharmadhātu.* Thus, it is said that

> the mind is subject to ignorance and, conditioned by the power of that ignorance, the deluded sense realms appear. [In the same manner,] if ignorance ceases, so would the sense realms.[72]

The *CCC*'s discussion on the mind is less complete than the *AFM*'s. For example, it does not know of the "water and wave" analogy or the "three subtle and six coarse" mentation formula.[73] Nor does it coopt the terms "original enlightenment" *(pen-chüeh)* and "incipient enlightenment" *(shih-chüeh)* from the *AFM*. The omission of both these and the "three greatnesses"—the three aspects of the *mahā* of Mahāyāna or the trikāya (three bodies) theory[74]—was cited by Mochizuki as proof that the *CCC* predated the *AFM*. The simpler explanation is that the *CCC* needed from the *AFM* only what would help support its divinatory praxis: namely, the theory of mind.

For the *CCC*, the omnipresence of the tathāgatagarbha is what is important:

> Again, this mind is called the tathāgatagarbha. It is replete with immeasurable, infinite, incomprehensible, and pure meritorious karma, which is free from defiled outflows. . . . Nothing can lie outside this [mind that is the] dharmakāya's fruition. Realize that the dharmakāya of the various buddhas that is now found within the bodies of all sentient beings is likewise indestructible. When the defilements are destroyed, one would revert back to this dharmakāya.[75]

Following the *Śrīmālādevīsiṃhanāda-sūtra*'s contention concerning the incomprehensible paradox of a "pure yet impure" tathāgatagarbha,[76] the *CCC* explains the "mutual permeation" of suchness and ignorance:

> Because of the power of permeation *(vāsanā)* due to the causes and conditions of ignorance, the deluded sense realms are made manifest. And because of the causes and conditions due to permeation by these deluded sense realms, there arises a mind that accords with these deluded perceptions and that assumes there is "I" and "mine." This produces the accumulation of all types of karma [that result in the person] receiving the pain of birth and death (saṃsāra). It is said that the dharmakāya is [nonetheless] called a sentient being. If thus the permeation of the dharmakāya that is a sentient being exerts a positive counterinfluence, then the defilements [of such a person] would gradually weaken, and he would learn to abhor the world and seek the way to nirvāṇa. Placing faith in the one reality, he would cultivate the six perfections *(ṣaṭ pāramitāḥ)* and all the limbs of bodhi *(bodhyaṅga)*. [Such a person] is called a bodhisattva . . . [and, ascending the stages of practice,] comes to be called a buddha.[77]

This idea of a mutual permeation of suchness and ignorance is unique to the *AFM*. It is not something endorsed by the *Mahāyānasaṃgraha* or later by Hsüan-tsang's Chinese Wei-shih school. Its presence in the *CCC* rules the text out as a "southern" work from Paramārtha's coterie.[78] The presence of this ideology also clinches the view that the *CCC* is an early commentary on the *AFM*.

The CCC as an Apocryphon that Anticipates a New Orthodoxy

The *CCC* may not be as sophisticated philosophically as the *AFM,* but its teachings contain intimations of future Chinese Buddhist understandings of the dharma: shades of Ch'an (Zen), Hua-yen, and the distinction between Mind Only and Consciousness Only. In that, this apocryphon was a harbinger of later sinitic orthodoxy.

To begin with, the *CCC* is more than just a bad copy of the *AFM.* At several key points, it advances its own reading of the tradition. The *AFM* conjoins the emptiness philosophy of Mādhyamika with the mind-only doctrine of Yogācāra without explicitly ranking the two systems hierarchically. The *CCC* comes out with a strong statement on behalf of the superiority of emptiness:

> Those who want to cultivate faith and understanding by relying on the one real realm should practice two forms of contemplation *(vipaśyanā):* first, the contemplation on "mind and consciousness only" *(wei-hsin-shih);* second, the contemplation on "suchness as real". . . . There are two types of people [seeking faith and understanding]. What are the two types? The first is the type with keen faculties; the second is the type with dull faculties. The keen one already knows that all external sense realms are only the creation of the mind and are, therefore, false and unreal, like a dream or a conjurer's trick. . . . He need practice [only] the *vipaśyanā* of "suchness as real." The dull one, however, should first learn the *vipaśyanā* of "mind and consciousness only."[79]

The *AFM* accepts the devolution of the one mind as emptiness into the duality of the subject-object consciousness,[80] but the *CCC* openly deprecates Yogācāra as being a philosophy that knows that reality is of "mind and consciousness only" without truly comprehending "the emptiness that is suchness." This position is comparable to that taken by T'ien-t'ai. And the use of the expression "mind and consciousness only" *(wei-hsin-shih)* adumbrates the later Hua-yen claim of the superiority of Wei-hsin (Mind Only) over the Wei-shih (Consciousness Only) ideology of Hsüan-tsang's Yogācāra school.[81]

The *AFM* encourages the meditation on the uniformity of all forms *(i-hsing san-mei,* Skt. *ekacaryā samādhi),* but generally it gives few actual instructions as to how to proceed with that practice. The *CCC* is more thorough in its praxis, outlining in considerable detail its process of spiritual development and even calling it *chien-wu* (gradual enlightenment):

> The gradual achievement of buddhahood is generally of four types. What are the four types? The first is achieving buddhahood by virtue of the completion

of faith: that is, relying on the stage *(bhūmi)* of one's spiritual lineage *(chung-hsing-ti,* Skt. *gotra),*[82] one acquires the definitive faith that the myriad of dharmas are neither produced nor destroyed but are, rather, always pure and selfsame, and are something not to be sought after.

The second is achieving buddhahood by virtue of the completion of understanding: that is, relying on the stage of understanding and actual practice *(chieh-hsing-ti),* one deeply understands the *dharmatā* and realizes that the deeds of the tathāgatas are inactive and inoperative. One arouses here no dualistic thought concerning saṃsāra and nirvāṇa, and harbors no fear.

The third is achieving buddhahood by virtue of the completion of attainment: that is, relying on the stage of the purified mind *(ching-hsin ti),* one attains the undifferentiated, quiescent dharma-wisdom and incomprehensibly spontaneous action, because one has no more thoughts of seeking after anything.

The fourth is achieving buddhahood by virtue of the completion of all the meritorious qualities of [the bodhisattva stages]: that is, relying on the ultimate stage of the bodhisattva *(chiu-ching p'u-sa ti),* one is able to remove all hindrances, because the dream of ignorance has ended.[83]

Even if Morita is right in regarding these four types of practice as an expansion of the *AFM* doctrine of the three types of arousal of *bodhicitta (san fa-hsin)*—namely, of faith, practice, and attainment[84]—the expanded thesis here is noteworthy. This is so because, although the *CCC* terms these four steps of enlightenment "gradual," the first formula of "achieving buddhahood through the completion of faith" would later appear in the writings of Hua-yen exegetes as representing sudden enlightenment. Just as the *CCC*'s idea of "mind and consciousness only" would later be radicalized into Mind Only versus Consciousness Only, so its seminal understanding of the phases of enlightenment would later be polarized into sudden versus gradual enlightenment.

The *CCC* goes on to analyze the stages involved in that meditative ascent. The following is only a synopsis, the original being too long to translate in full:

Furthermore, one should know that there are three kinds of mundane dhyānas [meditations] associated with characteristics that are to be learned. What are the three? (1) Faith and understanding that do not involve expedients that result in backsliding into the world . . . ; (2) faith and understanding that do not involve expedients that result in backsliding into the two vehicles . . . ; and (3) faith and understanding that do involve expedients. That is to say, relying on the one real realm, one cultivates the two contemplative methods of *śamatha* and *vipaśyanā;* one can have faith and understanding in the fact that all dharmas are born only of mind and perceptions, like dreams and conjurers' tricks. . . . The cultivator of all samādhis and dhyānas should [also] know that there are ten graded approaches that include all the activities of the dhyānas: . . . (1) the expediency of absorbing one's thoughts [that give rise to objects in the sense realms]; (2) attempting to remain on

> one's meditation topic *(ching-chieh,* Skt. *gotra);* (3) the initial abiding on the object, clearly understanding it, knowing what comes in and out [of the mind]; (4) skillful abiding on the object, attaining rectitude of mind; until (5) as one's contemplation becomes skillful and courageous, one turns toward further advancement; (6) gradually gaining harmony [of mind], ease, and joy, one eliminates doubts and gains faith and understanding, thereby comforting oneself; further (7) triumphantly, one advances with resolute will, attaining limited psychic correspondence, enough to know the benefits that are in store for oneself; (8) one progresses steadfastly, attaining superior attributes that will perfect the counteractive techniques *(pratipakṣa);* (9) one is now able to generate external virtues at will, and come into correspondence [with reality] at will, without any mistakes or failings; finally, (10) if one goes on to cultivate further practices, what one has attained so far may again be aroused skillfully and successfully, in the proper sequence; one can now come and go at will, having transcended all natural limits.[85]

These ten stages are aligned methodically with the progress from the lowly "mind and consciousness only" through the three dhyānas, the stages of the common person, to the two vehicles, until the adept finally arrives at the one vehicle. The knowledge of emptiness finally brings an end to all discrimination, and the pilgrim realizes that "saṃsāra is nirvāṇa and nirvāṇa is saṃsāra."[86] Such attempts at correlating mental states and the stages of praxis were typical of the Ti-lun school and are also at the heart of the schematization that gave the *AFM* its seemingly integral structure. Although the correlations made in the *CCC* are hardly flawless, they did help to popularize such connections drawn in Chinese Buddhism between mind and practice.

At the end of the text, after stressing once more the promise of help from Kṣitigarbha, the *CCC* sums itself up by giving a list of its variant titles:

> At the time, the Bodhisattva-Mahasattva Firm and Pure Faith addressed the Buddha: "Oh World-honored One, what is this teaching that you have so expounded in the *Sūtra of the Six Faculty-Aggregates?*"
>
> The Buddha answered, "This is called the *CCC,* also called *Dispelling the Various Hindrances to Aid the Growth of Pure Faith,* alias *Revealing to Mahāyāna Aspirants the Skillful Means to Advancement that Manifest the Ultimate Meaning of the Real,* also called *Comfortingly Teaching a Definitive Instruction that Enables Men to Leave Behind Timidity and Quickly to Enter Firm Faith.* Keep and treasure this sūtra under these names."[87]

The reference to a *Sūtra of the Six Faculty-Aggregates* may be to the *Ch'i-shih ching* (Scripture Concerning the Arising of the World),[88] or, more likely, to a *Sūtra of the Six Faculty-Aggregates* cited by title in the *Ratnagotravibhāga,* a late tathāgatagarbha treatise translated by Ratnamati. There, in commenting on a gāthā, this work is cited to show how the six faculties are grounded in the tathāgatagarbha:

[The tathāgatagarbha] is indivisible from the buddha's properties,
It has the essence of suchness,
The essence of dharmas is not illusory,
Its own nature is originally pure.

"World-honored One, from beginningless time, the six faculties have thus [assumed many forms] because [the tathāgatagarbha has attained] the ultimate essence of the various realities."[89]

Either way, the *CCC* had managed to mold complex currents in Mahāyāna philosophy together to fit the simpler needs of the pious. In the end, the *CCC*'s support for popular piety would be what redeemed this once banned work.

The Aftermath

The Canton penitence cult was banned in 593, but the *CCC* continued to circulate. The opinions of sūtra cataloguers, however, changed little throughout much of the seventh century. In 664, Tao-hsüan still considered the *CCC* to be a fabricated work.[90] But the cult of Kṣitigarbha grew unabated[91] and eventually helped to redeem the *CCC*. The 695 sūtra catalogue sponsored by the Chou empress Wu Tse-t'ien (r. 684–709) affirmed the authenticity of the *CCC*,[92] and the later *K'ai-yüan shih-chiao-lu*, compiled in 730, finally threw out all the old suspicions against it.[93] The *CCC* was introduced to Korea in 740 by Chinp'yo (b. 718), and its divination technique was in use at Mt. Hiei in Japan during the Edo period.[94] Yet it was not the subject of a Chinese commentary until we come to the eminent late Ming monk, Chih-hsü (1599–1655).[95]

Chih-hsü was the most ardent advocate of Kṣitigarbha devotion since Hsin-hsing, the founder of the Three Stages sect. Influenced by Chu-hung's (1535–1615) *Tzu-chih lu* (Record of Self-Knowledge), Chih-hsü turned for spiritual guidance and assurance to the *CCC* around the age of thirty-five. Initially attracted to Kṣitigarbha by the *Pen-yüan ching*'s message of the priority of filial piety,[96] he then adopted the *CCC* confessional. Chih-hsü saw the *CCC*'s divinatory method not as magic but as the most appropriate means of religious cultivation during the Final Age of the Dharma. Chih-hsü commented on the *CCC* as follows:

The three realms are mind-only, there being no dharmas outside the mind. As the principle is replete, phenomena will surely follow, since there is no duality between them. It is only when one is deluded that the three hindrances arise. Once enlightened, one sees how the three virtues are simply so. There is no substance to delusion or enlightenment. Following the mundane, [the mind] becomes false; adhering to the true, it reverts to its original state. The dual is nondual; the nondual is dual. Thus, too, delusion and

> enlightenment are only seemingly different. To be deluded is to be deluded about what is enlightened. To be enlightened is to be enlightened about what was once delusion. This *CCC* points at delusion but in principle returns to enlightenment. The "foretelling and observing" *(chan-ch'a)* is the wisdom that contemplates; the "good and evil" *(shan-o)* are the objects contemplated. The subject-wisdom is none other than the one mind in its three aspects; the object-viewed is the one realm with the three truths. To dispel doubts and hindrances, to make steadfast pure faith, to reveal expediencies in order to approximate the mystery, to comfort the weak-hearted [is the purpose of this scripture].[97]

However, what is most exemplary is how Chih-hsü took the teaching to heart:

> The sūtra says, "Those with much evil karma should not practice immediately samādhi or prajñā; they should first learn to confess. . . . "[98] It also says, "Even those seeking faith and understanding, practicing the *vipaśyanā* of mind and consciousness only or that of suchness as real, cannot make progress if their wholesome faculties *(kuśalamūla)* are shallow, or if the various defilements cannot be suppressed, or if their minds are unduly anxious, or if there are various kinds of obstacles. If so, they should chant ardently the name [of Kṣitigarbha]."[99]

So seriously did Chih-hsü take the signs divined by the tops that he waited for thirteen years, until the age of forty-eight, for the three wheels to yield "purity of body, speech, and mind" before he would take the monk's precepts:

> Diligently I revered the thousands and millions of buddhas and followed the *CCC* divination method. Gratefully, thanks to the compassion of the various buddhas and bodhisattvas, I was granted this past new year, on the fifteenth day of the first [lunar] month, the top-divination, [indicating] purity. Thus I may finally take heart a little [in my efforts].[100]

Chih-hsü, himself versed in the art of the *I ching,* would have been a good judge of the use and abuse of divination. Clearly separating the *CCC* divination from what he called other "crass divinations,"[101] he saw revealed through the *CCC* the reality of karmic burdens, a means by which to know these, a dire foreboding of the Final Age, and a legitimate hope for spiritual guidance. By maintaining in oneself a purified and sincere, ultimate mind, one could tread the karmic path of precepts and meditation leading to final enlightenment.

Conclusion

The *CCC* is a fortune-telling or karma-validating text to the novice and a nirvāṇic induction into the truth to the gnostic. As such, the *CCC* represents the medieval synthesis of what modern rationalists often presume to be the irreconcilable realities of élite and popular culture, or the Great and the Small Traditions. As noted in the introduction to this chapter, this two-tiered view of society is seldom true to reality in our times and was even less so in medieval ones. Prior to the "protestant" or "rational" purge of magic from religion, it was more the norm that the two were intertwined. During such times, the local villager was linked to spiritual wisdom through the medium of magic no less than the élite philosopher was tied to the miraculous in his knowledge of the mysteries.

To take a cue from Peter Brown,[102] medieval eras are also not so single-mindedly "otherworldly" as some might like to imagine. Nor does a text such as the *CCC,* by being apparently concerned with "this-worldly" benefits, betray the nirvāṇic impulse, as has been charged. Finally, it was the temper of reformation arising independently in both West and East that would eventually polarize these two spheres of concern. During the medieval era, however, there remained in the West the delightful gray area in between, which Brown calls the "upperworldly." In sixth-century China, this same area was represented by the many stages of rebirth that linked the lowest destiny to the highest. Medieval man lived harmoniously amid that semi-certainty, reconciled to the fact that there was a bridge between "this" and the "other" shore. It is on that threshold that we should place the *CCC.* Along that spectrum between magic and religion, chance and destiny, blind faith and profound wisdom, lay the *CCC* and the world that both created and derived from it. Perhaps this chapter has helped to part the veil of obscurity that has enveloped the text of the *CCC* so that we may catch a glimpse of that seemingly timeless drama of our own past.

NOTES

1. See David Hume, *Essays Moral, Political and Literary* (London: Longman, Green, 1875). For a powerful criticism of this view, see Peter Brown, *The Cult of the Saints: Its Rise and Function in Latin Christianity* (Chicago: University of Chicago Press, 1981), 12–22.

2. *CCC, T* 839.17.901c–910c (henceforth cited only by page, register, and line).

3. For a review of the judgment of the various sūtra catalogues on the *CCC,* see Makita Tairyō, *Gikyō kenkyū* (Kyoto: Jimbun kagaku kenkyūsho, 1976), 108–109.

4. Sometimes *teng* is given without the fire radical. No records of this monk or of other works translated by him exist.

5. *Li-tai san-pao chi* 12, *T* 2034.49.106c9–22. An interlinear note appears at the end: "The *CCC* is based on the *Sūtra of the Six Faculty-Aggregates.*" This is probably not part of the original record.

6. See Fa-ching's list of suspected sūtras in *Chung-ching mu-lu, T* 2146.55. 126b–c.

7. For secondary studies on the *CCC,* see Mochizuki Shinkō, *Jōdokyō no kigen oyobi hattatsu* (Tokyo: Kyōritsusha, 1930), 222–229, reprinted in his *Bukkyō kyōten seiritsu shiron* (Kyoto: Hōzōkan, 1946), 485–493; also Makita Tairyō, *Gikyō kenkyū,* pp. 108–116. The above dating is noted in Kashiwagi Hiroo, *Daijō kishinron no kenkyū: Daijō kishinron no seiritsu ni kansuru shiryōron teki kenkyū* (Tokyo: Shunjusha, 1981), 206, 211 n. 1. His complete analysis of the text appears on pp. 383–405. Robert Buswell also notes related secondary studies by Korean scholars: Kim Yŏngt'ae, "Silla ŭi Chŏmch'al pŏphoe kwa Chinp'yo ŭi kyobŏp yŏn'gu," *Pulgyo hakpo* 9 (1972):99–136, reprinted in Sungsan Pak Kilchin paksa hwagap kinyŏm saŏp hoe, ed., *Han'guk Pulgyo sasang sa,* Sungsan Pak Kilchin paksa hwagap kinyŏm (Iri: Wŏn Pulgyo sasang yŏn'gu wŏn, 1975), 383–405; Ch'ae Inhwan, *Shiragi Bukkyō kairitsu shisō kenkyū* (Tokyo: Kokusho kankōkai, 1977), 571–579.

8. Most of the works studied by Makita Tairyō in his *Gikyō kenkyū* are of northern origin.

9. The *Shih-lun ching* was crucial to Hsin-hsing's idea of a "universal teaching" applicable to the third of the Three Stages, and he became a zealous devotee of Kṣitigarbha. The *Shin-lun ching* is cited 128 times in Hsin-hsing's *San-chieh fo-fa,* leading all others (the *Nirvāṇa Sūtra* is second, with only 87); see Yabuki Keiki, *Sangaikyō no kenkyū* (Tokyo: Iwanami shoten, 1927), 595. On the *Shih-lun ching*'s history, see also Mochizuki, *Bukkyō kyōten,* pp. 488–489.

10. On Kṣitigarbha, see Manebe Kōsai, *Jizō bosatsu no kenkyū* (Kyoto: Sanmitsudo, 1960); Sawa Ryūken, "Jizō bosatsu no tenkai," *Bukkyō geijutsu* 87 (1974):3–24, esp. 6–7. Also, more generally, see Hayami Tasuku, *Jizō bosatsu* (Tokyo: Hanawa shobō, 1975). The *Shih-lun ching* has, however, been translated twice; the first version (predating the *CCC*) has since been lost. There is also a Sanskrit recension of a *Kṣitigarbha-sūtra,* quoted in the *Śikṣāsamuccaya* 13.7, which is, however, not identical to the Chinese apocryphal *Ti-tsang p'u-sa ching.*

11. *CCC,* p. 910c4. Takasaki Jikidō reconstructs the title as *Ṣaḍāyatana-sūtra* or *Ṣaḍindriyarāśī-sūtra;* see Takasaki, *A Study of the Ratnagotravibhāga (Uttaratantra): Being a Treatise on the Tathāgatagarbha Theory of Mahāyāna Buddhism,* Serie Orientale Roma, vol. 32 (Rome: Istituto Italiano per il Medio ed Estremo Oriente, 1966), 259–260, and 260 n. 457.

12. See *Chiu-ching i-sheng pao-hsing lun* 3, *T* 1611.31.835c1–2, and Mochizuki, *Bukkyō kyōten,* p. 491. The *CCC* is said to endorse Amitābha devotion. We generally associate the nascent Pure Land cult of Amitābha with the North; it was a faith shared by Ratnamati, Bodhiruci, and their followers, and is similarly included in the *AFM.* But I fail to find Amitābha mentioned in the *CCC;* the term *fa-tsang (dharmakara)* was used, but not as a designation of Bodhisattva Dharmakara, who later became the Buddha Amitābha.

13. Mochizuki saw a possible borrowing by the *CCC* in its discussion on the "eighteen *śūnyatās* (emptinesses)" (*CCC,* pp. 909c–910a), which comes from the *Shih-pa k'ung lun* (*T* 1616), attributed to Nāgārjuna and translated by Paramārtha; see Mochizuki, *Bukkyō kyōten,* p. 491, and the entry in his *Bukkyō daijiten* (Tokyo: Sakai shōten kankōkai, 1933), 2962. But the eighteen emptinesses is a standard set, which is found already in earlier translations of the *Prajñāpāramitā-sūtra.* See Kashiwagi, *Daijō kishinron,* pp. 216–217.

14. For a sampling of the more moderate forms of confession, see Tao-hsüan,

Kuang Hung-ming-chi 28, section 9, *T* 2103.52.330b29–335a24. However, this immoderation can be explained by the eschatological anxiety that began to plague the southern capital at the end of the Liang dynasty.

15. *CCC,* p. 901c13–16.

16. See the "Reasons for Writing" section of the *AFM* in Yoshito S. Hakeda, trans., *Awakening of Faith Attributed to Aśvaghosha* (New York: Columbia University Press, 1967), 25–27. Some scholars would prefer to translate *hsin* here as "conviction," but the usage by the text includes both "faith" for the undetermined type of person and "conviction" for the determined type. The *AFM* is, however, totally silent on the decline of the dharma; the *CCC,* in contrast, explicitly mentions the chaos and calamity of the Final Age. The *CCC* might thus have witnessed the Buddhist persecution of 574–576, whereas the *AFM* probably did not.

17. *CCC,* pp. 901c–902a.

18. Compared with the Kṣitigarbha corpus, the *CCC* is more this-worldly and karmatic than the *Pen-yüan ching,* which has Kṣitigarbha delivering men from hell to the Heaven of the Thirty-Three. The *Ti-tsang P'u-sa ching* offers the loftiest goal; it places Kṣitigarbha in his own Pure Land in the South.

19. *CCC,* p. 902b16–17.

20. Ibid., p. 902b24–28. The *Taishō* text gives "top" for the last word; but it should be "turn." See the alternative reading offered by the collation notes there.

21. Ibid., p. 902b28–902c.

22. Ibid., p. 902c3–7. The ten wholesome actions are (1) not to kill; (2) not to steal; (3) not to commit adultery; (4) not to lie; (5) not to use immoral language; (6) not to slander; (7) not to equivocate; (8) not to covet; (9) not to give way to anger; (10) not to hold false views. The ten unwholesome actions are their opposites.

23. Ibid., p. 903a13–17.

24. Ibid., p. 903b7–19.

25. Ibid., p. 905a15–19, 905b.

26. Ibid., pp. 905b–906c.

27. Buddhism in Northern Wei is often called "State Buddhism" *(kokka bukkyō).* In actual fact, it was more critical of the state than the label might suggest.

28. Makita, *Gikyō kenkyū,* pp. 113–115. The psychic thesis—that a sincere mind can somehow touch the heart of Heaven, such that it would respond perfectly—is assumed by the *I ching* and Han moral theory in general.

29. *CCC,* p. 902b22–23. Such clinging to worldly happiness would hinder the practice of the noble paths.

30. L. S. Yang, "Tao-chiao chih tzu-po yu Fo-chiao chih tzu-p'u," in *Bukkyō shigaku ronshū,* Tsukamoto Zenryū Festschrift (Kyoto: Kyoto University, Jimbun kagaku kenkyūsho, 1961), 962–969. Smiting oneself on the cheeks and kowtowing are still standard Chinese admissions of self-incrimination. A maid who says something amiss would strike herself on the mouth in anticipatory chastisement. A son would kowtow "until the forehead bleeds" to beg for forgiveness.

31. *Cheng-t'ung Tao-tsang,* fascicle III, pp. 7b, 75b, 76b. Smiting oneself on the cheek is found in the *Yün-chung yin-chung hsin-k'o chih chieh* (Articles of a New

Code to be Chanted to the Yin-Sung Musical Notation) that inspired K'ou Ch'ien-chih (d. 448) in the North, while in the South, Lu Hsiu ching (406–477) would endorse the "penance by smearing ashes" (actually mud)—rolling in the mud and smiting oneself.

32. See Yoshioka's response to Yang in his "Jibaku to jibaku ni tsuite," *Bukkyō shisō ronshū,* Sato Mitsuo Festschrift (Tokyo: Sankibō, 1972), 609–629. Yoshioka cites from Yang, who noted Hu Shih's private exchange with him.

33. This mode and metaphor is not found in the confessionals noted in the *Kuang Hung-ming-chi,* section 9 (see n. 14); however, the later Pure Land master Shan-tao would adopt this. See Yang, "Tao-chiao," p. 966.

34. Yang, "Tao-chiao," p. 967. This is still how Zen students bow upon entering the *dōjō.*

35. See the biography of Dharmakṣema in *Kao-seng chuan* 2, *T* 2059.50.335c–337a; it observes (pp. 336c29–337a2) that the *bodhisattvaśīla* practiced in China began in Liang-chou with this master and had flourished ever since.

36. *CCC,* p. 902b22–23. Divination was practiced in India, but Buddhists were told not to follow it; see *Fa-yüan chu-lin* 9, *T* 2122.53.346c–349c. Robert Buswell refers me also to the rejection of divination in Chinese apocryphal scriptures; see, for example, *Fan-wang ching, T* 1484.24.1007a24–26, 1007b16–19; and *Fo i-chiao ching, T* 389.12.1110c22–23.

37. Peasant women still use two crescent pieces to divine a simple "yes" or "no" to questions asked; the broken and unbroken lines in the *I ching* hexagram can also be constructed by throwing two coins.

38. Such use is not unknown elsewhere. Tibetans play a similar "rebirth" game by casting dice over a kind of "snakes and ladders" board of destinies; see Mark Tatz and Jody Kent, *Rebirth* (New York: Doubleday, 1977). The use of a spinning top as a way to "turn the wheel of dharma" may be compared to the pious use of prayer wheels in Tibet. These wind-activated prayer-wheels are only a justifiable extension of the accepted "speed-chanting" *(chuan-tu)* of scriptures.

39. Buddhas and cakravartins all have wheels. Kṣitigarbha has ten wheels. The *Shih-lun ching* praises the power of Kṣitigarbha in aiding those men who have committed the ten unwholesome deeds by turning them from evil to good (*T* 410.13.684c). However, except for the fact that one of the ten wheels has to do with saṃsāric fates—saṃsāra is itself often depicted as a wheel—this scripture knows of no spinning tops.

40. This is an apocryphal text; see Henri Maspero, "Sur la date et l'authenticité du Fou fa tsang yin yüan tchouan," *Mélanges d'Indianisme offers par ses éleves à M. Sylvain Levi* (Paris, 1911), 129–149. I am grateful to Robert Buswell for this reference. This text was compiled in China after the persecution to answer a charge made by Ts'ui Hao (381–450) that there was no record to verify that there was a Buddha or a living Buddhist tradition in India. The text listed a lineage of patriarchs terminated by a persecution, which might have some basis in history.

41. Morita Ryūsen, *Shaku makaenron no kenkyū* (Kyoto: Bunseido, 1935), 728–729. In the Ānanda episode, one marks one's every intention, whether wholesome or unwholesome, with white and black stones, thereby purifying the mind by actually changing the ratio of the colors. This is a contemplative use of indi-

cators for self-cultivation. Chinese Buddhists and later Neo-Confucians use beans to so purify their mind.

42. *CCC,* p. 903c6–10.

43. Ibid., pp. 903c16–904a24.

44. Ibid., p. 904a29–b13.

45. Ibid., pp. 904c–905a.

46. See above; the South picked up this tradition during the sixth century through a Mahāyāna preceptory text compiled in China, the *Fan-wang ching* (Book of Brahmā's Net; *T* 1484). This might also be indebted indirectly to the North, since the 446 persecution drove some northern monks to the South.

47. The term might be taken from the Pure Land tradition that insists on a *chih-hsin* or *chih-ch'eng-hsin* (mind of utter sincerity/truthfulness), as in the well-known formula of "transferring all of one's merits in utter sincerity" for the purpose of rebirth in the Pure Land. See under *shinjin* in Mochizuki Shinkō, ed., *Bukkyō daijiten,* p. 1788c.

48. *CCC,* p. 905a6–13.

49. Ibid., p. 905a19–28.

50. Wang Pi, like Plotinus, recognized that "one" is not a number (like other numbers) since it is also the all, i.e., the source of all numbers. This mystical one is represented by one of the fifty stalks, which is put aside before the other forty-nine are used to construct the hexagrams. The one that is useless *(wu-yung)* is the substance *(t'i),* as distinct from the function *(yung)* of the rest. See T'ang Yung-t'ung, "Wang Pi's New Interpretation of the *I ching* and *Lun-yu,*" *Harvard Journal of Asiatic Studies* 10 (1947):124–161.

51. *CCC,* p. 903a20–22.

52. If the first set of ten tops promise "good" for the body because the person has done good bodily deeds in the past, but the second set of three tops yield "evil" for the same, then this is a simple noncorrespondence and is to be ignored. A person nonviolent in a past life does not deserve to suffer bodily harm and should have no impulse toward violence, either; any indications to the contrary should be discarded. See *CCC,* p. 903b–c.

53. For a complete list of studies related to this issue, see Kashiwagi, *Daijō kishinron,* bibliographical section, pp. 498–501; for the history of the controversy, see pp. 61–182.

54. See Kashiwagi's doubts expressed in ibid., p. 182. I, and many other scholars, think Chinese authorship is possible. The reason Kashiwagi thinks it is impossible is that he reads the *AFM* not in terms of its original, sometimes problematical, simplicity, but in terms of a complicated structure "unearthed" in the text by the classic commentaries after they had struggled with and resolved some of the problems of the *AFM.* Furthermore, if the *AFM* were indeed of Indian origin, as alleged, and if its teaching were so universally profound, as claimed, we should expect some reference to it, directly or indirectly, in still later Indian and Tibetan materials. To date, we have none.

55. The whole exchange is found reported from both sides in Mochizuki, *Daijō kishinron no kenkyū* (Tokyo: Kanao bunendō, 1922), pt. 1, and Tokiwa Daijō, *Shina bukkyō no kenkyū* (Tokyo, 1943), 2:26–128.

56. This persecution was initiated in 574 in northwestern China by Northern Chou Emperor Wu and spread east by 576 when the emperor conquered Northern Ch'i. T'an-ch'ien was then in Ch'i.

57. The *She-ta-sheng lun* is a text considered superior to the *Daśabhūmikasūtropadeśa* as an introduction to Yogācāra. T'an-ch'ien would later introduce this southern She-lun (Saṃgraha) scholarship to the North.

58. Here Mochizuki took a cue from Tokiwa who, aiming to disprove one of Mochizuki's earlier speculations on authorship, had catalogued the viable candidates as simplified in the diagram above. See Tokiwa, *Shina bukkyō* 2:106–111.

59. For a summary of this hypothesis, see Kashiwagi, *Daijō kishinron,* pp. 151–155.

60. On those two points, Tokiwa refuted Mochizuki as follows (see note 55): it is one thing to say there were differences in interpretation and another to say that such differences were so glaring as to make reconciliation necessary. Tokiwa hit the mark when he noted that it was probably not until Tao-ni (d.u.), a direct disciple of Paramārtha, was invited in 591 to the Sui capital (probably by T'an-ch'ien) that the very problematical discrepancies between the *AFM* and the *She-ta-sheng lun* became evident. Compared with that, the discrepancy between the *She-lun* and the *Ti-lun*—which Hui-yüan knew—was minor and more easily resolved. In other words, the *AFM* could not have been the product of a conscious resolution of differences, because historically the *AFM* is what created the heated controversy that led to the charge in the seventh century that it was a forgery. Tao-ni's role was so critical in bringing the discrepancies to light that, at one point, he was picked by Murakami Sensho as the author of the *AFM;* see Kashiwagi, *Daijō kishinron,* p. 155. If, after all that, I continue to side with Mochizuki and trust in the northern genesis of this text, I am still, in a sense, following Tokiwa's lead. This is because it would not have been necessary for the author of the *AFM* to know the She-lun philosophy in order to derive his own reading of the *ālayavijñāna* and the trikāya. He could have derived it simply by knowing the *Laṅkāvatāra-sūtra.*

61. This charge is noted by Mochizuki in his *Bukkyō kyōten,* pp. 544–545; see also Kashiwagi, *Daijō kishinron,* pp. 92–93. The following is supplied by Robert Buswell. The Korean work in which this notice appears is the *T'amhyŏn'gi sagi,* a commentary on Fa-tsang's *T'an-hsüan-chi* (*T* 1733); the commentary is otherwise unknown and does not appear in any of the bibliographical catalogues. The only works known for Chinsung are: (1) *Hwaŏm kongmok-ki,* a commentary on a work of Chih-yen (*T* 1870), mentioned in the *Tōiki dentō mokuroku* (*T* 2183.55.1147a; the catalogue was compiled in 941 C.E.) and in *T* 2177.55.1134a; and (2) *Ilsŭng pŏpkyedo-ki,* in *Showa hōbō mokuroku* 3:911c (Japanese copy in Kanazawa Bunkō, dated 1120). Chinsung's works are outlined in Tongguk taehakkyo Pulgyo munhwa yŏn'guso, eds., *Han'guk Pulgyo ch'ansul munhŏn ch'ongnok* (Seoul: Tongguk taehakkyo ch'ulp'anbu, 1976), 86–87.

62. Mochizuki, *Daijō kishinron no kenkyū,* pp. 14–18.

63. See the omission of this point in the entry on this debate in Mochizuki, ed., *Bukkyō daijiten,* p. 2962; this dictionary was compiled after the dust had settled on the controversy.

64. *CCC,* p. 907b13–18. For the most detailed alignments of the two texts, see Morita, *Shaku makaenron,* pp. 720–723.

65. *AFM, T* 1666.32.576a5–13; Hakeda, trans., *Awakening of Faith,* pp. 31–48.

66. See the comments by Kashiwagi, *Daijō kishinron,* p. 228.

67. *Ta-sheng i-chang* 3, *T* 1851.44.528a.

68. Kashiwagi, *Daijō kishinron,* p. 228.

69. Ibid., p. 208, comparing two lines; the first is from the *CCC,* pp. 902b10 and 903a7, and the second is from p. 907a10.

70. *CCC,* p. 907a2–4. The expression "one real realm of dharma" is one of the preferred expressions in the *CCC.*

71. Ibid., p. 907a5–8.

72. Ibid., p. 907a26–b4.

73. See Hakeda, trans., *Awakening of Faith,* pp. 41, 55; 47–52.

74. Ibid., pp. 37–38; 29–30.

75. *CCC,* pp. 907c10–11, 907c28–908a1.

76. *Sheng-man shih-tzu-hu i-sheng ta-fang-pien fang-kuang ching, T* 353.12.222b5–28. See Alex and Hideko Wayman, *The Lion's Roar of Queen Śrīmālā* (New York: Columbia University Press, 1974), 104–106. The expression "pure yet impure; impure yet pure" is used by the Chinese commentators to summarize the point made here by the sūtra.

77. *CCC,* p. 408a3–10.

78. The first to note this was Murakami Sensho; see Kashiwagi, *Daijō kishinron,* p. 156. This debate over the idea of a mutual permeation of suchness and ignorance led critics to charge that the *AFM* was of northern origin, prompted Hsüan-tsang to go to India, and allowed Fa-tsang to claim the superiority of the *AFM* philosophy.

79. *CCC,* p. 908a13–15; 908b29–c7.

80. It does so by speaking of the "subtle" and "gross" defilements without however using the terms "inner" and "outer." See Hakeda, trans., *Awakening of Faith,* pp. 47–52.

81. Mind Only is supposedly superior because it knows the pure mind and the *dharmatā* as essence, while Consciousness Only knows only the deluded mind and the characteristics of dharmas as phenomena.

82. As far as I am able to ascertain, the *bhūmi* system employed in the *CCC* is selectively and freely constructed.

83. *CCC,* p. 909a25–b5.

84. See Hakeda, trans., *Awakening of Faith,* p. 80.

85. *CCC,* p. 909b5–27.

86. At that point a person cannot regress into the Two Vehicles, whereas during the first dhyāna he was so proud that he let himself be trapped again in the world, and in the second dhyāna he was so fearful of the pollutants of saṃsāra that he accepted the world-denying tendencies of the Hīnayāna.

87. *CCC,* p. 910c3–10.

88. The text appears in the *Dīgha-nikāya,* sections 18–22; Morita has tracked down this opinion of past monk-scholars in his *Shaku makaenron,* pp. 714–715. This sūtra could provide the basis for throwing the six tops thrice to effect the eighteen *dhātus.*

89. *Chiu-ching i-sheng pao-hsing lun* 3, *T* 1611.31.835b26–c2.

90. In Tao-hsüan's *Ta-T'ang nei-tien lu, T* 2149.55.335c and 279a–b.

91. Since we do not find comparable popularity for Kṣitigarbha in either India or Tibet, we have to assume that a Buddho-Taoist fusion of Kṣitigarbha and the old earth deity, T'u-ti, caused his popularity in China (and subsequently in Korea and Japan). T'u-ti happens also to have his own association with hell and judgment via his ties with T'ai-shan.

92. *Ta-Chou lu, T* 2153.55.379a.

93. *Ch'u-san-tsang chi-chi, T* 2154.55.551a.

94. Makita, *Gikyō kenkyū,* pp. 115–116; on the Korean importation, see *Samguk yusa* 4, *T* 2034.49.1007c.

95. In a *CCC hsüan-i* and a *CCC i-so;* see *ZZ* 1.35.1. Chih-hsü also wrote a commentary to the *AFM* (*T* 1850).

96. Noted by Chang Sheng-yen, *Minmatsu Chūgoku Bukkyō no kenkyū* (Kyoto: Hōzōkan, 1975), 190.

97. Cited by Makita, *Gikyō kenkyū,* p. 109, these laudatory remarks are not particularly original or attentive to specifics in my view.

98. *CCC,* p. 903c9.

99. Ibid., p. 908c7–12. The whole passage is taken from a verbatim Chinese citation by Chang, *Minmatsu,* p. 193, appearing in Chih-hsü's *Tsung-lun* (Complete Works).

100. Cited by Chang, *Minmatsu,* p. 221, from Chih-hsü, *Tsung-lun.*

101. Chih-hsü said that the *CCC* divination was "a far cry from the usual divination text"; see Chang, *Minmatsu,* p. 222, citing from *ZZ* 35.62b (Taiwan reissue vol. 35, p. 123b).

102. Brown, *The Cult of the Saints,* p. 2.

GLOSSARY

Chan-ch'a shan-o yeh-pao ching 占察善惡業報經
Chan-ch'a shan-o yeh-pao ching hsüan-i 占察善惡業報經玄義
Chan-ch'a shan-o yeh-pao ching i-shu 占察善惡業報經義疏
chen 真
chen-ju 真如
Chen-ti 真諦
Cheng-t'ung Tao-tsang 正統道藏
Ch'i-shih ching 起世經
Chien-ching-hsin 堅淨信
chien-wu 漸悟
chih-ch'eng-hsin 至誠心
Chih-chou 岐州
chih-hsin 至心
Chih-hsü 智旭
Chih-yen 智嚴
ching-chieh 境界
Ch'ing-chou 青州
Ching-ying Hui-yüan 淨影慧遠
Chiu-ching i-sheng pao-hsing lun 究竟一乘寶性論
chiu-ching p'u-sa ti 究竟菩薩地
Chu-hung 株宏
chuan-tu 轉讀
dōjō 道場
Fa-ching 法經
Fa-shang 法上
Fa-tsang 法藏
Fa-yüan chu-lin 法苑珠林
Fei Ch'ang-fang 費長房
Fu fa-tsang yin-yüan chuan 付法藏因緣傳
gense rieki 現世利益
hsin 信
hsin-chieh 信解
Hsin-hsing 信行
Hui-kuang 慧光
Hui-yüan 慧遠
I ching 易經
i-hsing san-mei 一行三昧
K'ai-huang 開皇
kokka bukkyō 国家仏教
Kuang Hung-ming chi 廣弘明集
Kuo I 郭宜
Li-tai san-pao chi 歷代三寶紀
Li Yüan-ts'ao 李元操
Liang-chou 梁州
Liu ken-chü ching 六根聚經
Lu Hsiu-ching 陸修靜

mieh-tsui 滅罪
mo-fa 末法
nei 內
Nei-shih shih-lang 內使侍郎
nien 念
Pa-shih lun 八識論
Pao-ch'ang ssu 寶昌寺
pen-chüeh 本覺
pu-chih-hsin 不至心
pu-hsiang-ying 不相應
pu-sheng pu-mieh 不生不滅
P'u-t'i-teng 菩提燈
San-chieh fo-fa 三階佛法
San-fa-hsin 三發心
She-lun 攝論
shih-chüeh 始覺
Shih-pa k'ung lun 十八空論
shomin kyōten 庶民経典
Ssu-ma 司馬
Ta-fang-kuang shih-lun ching 大方廣十輪經
Ta-sheng ch'i-hsin lun 大乘起信論
Ta-sheng i chang 大乘義章
T'ai-p'ing ching 太平經
T'ai-p'ing Tao 太平道
T'ai-shan 泰山
T'an-ch'ien 曇遷
T'an-tsun 曇遵
T'an-yen 曇延
Tao-hsüan 道宣
teng 燈/登
t'i 体
Ti-lun 地論
Ti-tsang p'u-sa ching 地藏菩薩經
Ti-tsang p'u-sa pen-yüan ching 地藏菩薩本願經
T'ien-shih Tao 天師道
tsu-po 自搏
Tsung-lun 宗論
Tu-ti 土地
tzu-p'u 自撲
wai 外
wang 妄
wang-hsin 妄心
wang-nien 妄念
Wang Pi 王弼
wei-hsin 唯心
wei-hsin-shih 唯心識
wei-shih 唯識
wu-ming 無明
wu-sheng wu-mieh 無生無滅
wu-so-teh 無所得
wu-yung 無用
Yu-p'o-sai chieh ching 優婆塞戒經

The Suppression of the Three Stages Sect: Apocrypha as a Political Issue

Mark Edward Lewis

It has long been recognized that literary texts played a central role in the imperial Chinese polity. The most familiar example of this is the examination system of late imperial China, where the primary road to honor, power, and wealth lay through the mastery of a prescribed body of texts. The link between literary attainments and political power, however, long antedated the formal system of awarding office through performance on written examinations. In fact it dated back to the beginning of the empire and remained, in varying forms and degrees, fundamental to the Chinese social and political order. As Buddhism developed in China, its texts became entangled in this linkage of letters and authority, and the questions of textual authenticity or validity became political issues. Consequently the study of Buddhist apocrypha in China cannot be separated from the broader questions of the relations of "scriptural" texts to political authority.

In this chapter I offer a new explanation of the suppression of the Three Stages sect (San-chieh chiao) based on a textual analysis of its teachings. This sect was one of the most important religious movements in China in the sixth and seventh centuries, but its writings were barred from the canon as "apocrypha" and the sect itself ultimately stamped out. Its very existence was virtually forgotten and all knowledge of its teachings vanished until the discovery of a large number of the banned texts among the manuscripts discovered at Tun-huang. The motives for the suppression and the means by which it was carried out provide a clear example of how the definition of a canon and the adjudication of the "authenticity" of texts became political concerns, and show how the use of the term "apocryphal" in reference to a text was often less a matter of textual origins and transmission than of the exigencies of power. They also suggest how the repeated promulgations of a clearly delimited canon were part of the broader struggle by the imperial court to create an "official" Buddhism that would define the forms and limits of religious expression.

Texts and Imperium

The link between texts and authority in China was embodied in the word *ching,* which has been rendered variously by such terms as "classic," "scripture," or "canon." Etymologically, this character referred to the warp of a fabric and, by extension, to that which provided order or structure. It was employed verbally in the sense of "to order" or "to regulate." In works of the Han and subsequent dynasties it was often glossed with a homophone meaning "path" (*ching*[a]), and was said to refer to the "constant Way that penetrated all things." During the Warring States and early Han periods this term came to be used as a rubric for a body of texts that supposedly preserved the teachings of the sage rulers of the early Chou and transmitted the fundamental "arts" *(i)* that constituted human civilization.[1]

The Western Han's "triumph of Confucianism" established the principle that the definition of a canon and the propagation of its truths was a central role of government. Chia I (201–169 B.C.E.) argued explicitly that the true purpose of political authority was to preserve and disseminate the social arts delineated in the canons. In his famous memorial proposing the institution of a state orthodoxy, Tung Chung-shu (176–104 B.C.E.) argued that whatever did not lie within the "six arts" and the teachings of Confucius, i.e., within the canons, would disrupt the Way of the true ruler and ought to be proscribed.[2] The Han theory of the "uncrowned king" held that the canons transmitted the Way of the former kings, men who had been both sages and rulers. This exemplary rulership had been lost in the world but was preserved through the scholarly labors of Confucius, who assembled the literary remains of the Chou state and thus became the heir of the kingly Way. As the master of this textual wisdom he was held to be the true king of his day, despite his low political rank. This idea expressed dramatically the link between texts and political authority, for the true understanding of certain texts made a common man a king.

By the end of the Western Han the unique status of canonical texts and their relation to political authority had become conventional notions. When Liu Hsin (d. 23 B.C.E.) compiled a bibliography of the imperial library, he listed the canons as a separate category of text and granted them the first and highest position in the empire of letters. This became the standard practice in all subsequent Chinese bibliographic works, and the study of the canons became an independent discipline with its own specialized methods and monographs.[3] Moreover, in the bibliographic chapter of the *Han shu* (History of the Former Han), Pan Ku (32–92 C.E.) identified every category of text with the work of specific political offices, thus asserting the inseparability of writing and government.

The idea that the key to good government lay in a certain body of texts began to be incorporated into the structure of the imperial government in the time of Kung-sun Hung (200–121 B.C.E.). He was both the first scholar to hold the office of chief minister *(ch'eng-hsiang)* and the primary architect of the government policy that made systematic literary training a prerequisite for holding office. The emperor appointed a group of erudites *(po-shih)* who were noted for their mastery of specific canonical texts. Men selected from the various localities of the empire by a system of recommendation became their students, and those who successfully completed their studies were placed in a pool from which official appointments were made. This "imperial university" established two important precedents. First, the government claimed the right to decide which texts constituted the canon to be studied by aspiring officials. Second, mastery of those texts was made a key path to government office and power. The sanctioning of texts and dissemination of their doctrines had become a positive function of government, and mastery of those texts an attribute of the emperor's servants.[4] The fall of the Han dynasty temporarily ended the direct, institutional link between texts and office, but one of the hallmarks of the "great families" that dominated high office in subsequent centuries was the familial transmission of canonical texts and scholarly traditions, and literary education remained an important element of political power and status throughout the Age of Disunion and the T'ang.[5]

As Buddhism developed in China, its sūtras, which were called *ching* in imitation of the indigenous Chinese canon, provided a new vision of the good society and the nature of political authority. Critics of Buddhism argued that these new texts and their principles challenged the truths and values of the existing canon, while Buddhist apologists asserted that they strengthened and extended them.[6] This polemic lasted for centuries and is important for any understanding of the history of Buddhism in China, but for the purposes of this chapter it is sufficient to note that when Buddhism became an important religion in China, its texts were drawn into the political realm through the received idea that the definition and defense of "scripture" was a fundamental role of the state.

In the wake of the collapse of the Han, many dynasts invoked the defense and propagation of Buddhist scriptures and doctrines as a basis for their authority. If one accepts the account in the *Kao-seng chuan* (Biographies of Eminent Monks), Yao Hsing (366–416), ruler of the proto-Tibetan Later Ch'in dynasty, launched an expedition to bring Kumārajīva (344–413, var. 409) to his capital at Ch'ang-an in order to sponsor the latter's activities as a translator of sūtras.[7] The rulers of the Northern Wei (386–534) claimed the status of tathāgata and were vigorous patrons of Buddhism. In the South, members of the imperial family of the Ch'i dynasty (479–502) engaged in the copying and exposition of sūtras for the explicit purpose of securing blessings for the ruling house and all subjects of the realm. For the same reason competitions between monks were held in the explication of sūtras, and honors were heaped on the victors. The rulers of the Ch'en dynasty (557–589) claimed to be bodhisattvas and propagated through regular public readings sūtras like the *Jen-wang ching* (Book of Benevolent Kings) and *Chin-kuang-ming ching* (Sūtra of Golden Light), which exalted the ruler as defender of the dharma.[8] Thus, by the time of the reunification of China under the Sui (581–618), Buddhism and its scriptures had become an integral part of the intellectual and textual underpinnings of the Chinese state, and the Three Stages sect's proclamation of the end of the Buddha's dharma constituted a direct challenge to the imperial government as well as to the ecclesiastical hierarchy it now supported.

The End of the Dharma

The argument that the teachings of the Buddha would inevitably disappear from the world of men has been the object of both general surveys and detailed studies of its various aspects.[9] In this section I will only note two points fundamental to my interpretation of the fate of the Three Stages sect. First, this doctrine was a theory of the decay of the Buddha's law and all its manifestations as they existed in the world; it was not a theory of the general decay of all social mores. In a Buddhist context this distinction was not significant, since a society without the truth of the Buddhist faith was by definition benighted and defiled. But China of the sixth through the eighth centuries was not a purely Buddhist realm, and there were alternative bases for the assertion of ethical norms and political authority. Second, as a theory of the decline of the Buddha's dharma in the world, the doctrine was primarily espoused by those who perceived the Buddhist Order to be in decline and who advocated either a renewal of monastic discipline or a reform of Buddhist praxis.

In Buddhism the dharma had a dual nature, and it was this duality that led to its inevitable disappearance.[10] "Dharma" referred, first and foremost, to the supreme sacred reality—the law that regulated the totality of existence and the eternal truth that enabled men to break free from the wheel of rebirth. Dharma in this sense was immutable and unchangeable. But "dharma" also referred to the teachings by which the Buddha introduced his truth into the world, and in this form it was embodied in the sacred texts, the monastic order, and the images of the Buddha. In this worldly aspect it was bound by the laws of inevitable flux and decay that prevail in the realm of contingent existence.[11] Thus the most fundamental principles of Buddhism stipulated its own inevitable demise.

The most ancient and widespread account of the end of the dharma asserted that the true dharma would have lasted for a thousand years, but because the Buddha allowed women to join the order it was reduced to five hundred. This already shows that the fundamental issue was the purity of the Saṃgha. Other versions fall under the Pali rubric *okkammaniye dhammo,* the "retractions of the dharma," in which the dharma would pass through five phases of declining religious practice. In the first stage men would achieve liberation *(vimokṣa),* in the second concentration (samādhi), in the third observation of the prohibitions *(śīladhara),* in the fourth erudition *(bahuśruta),* and in the last only charity *(dāna),* the religious practice of the layman. Here the object of decay was clearly the specifically Buddhist knowledge and practice embodied in the monastic order.[12]

These schematic models of decline were dramatized in narratives of the dharma's end that appeared in the *Abhidharmamahāvibhāṣā* (Extensive Commentary), the *Aśokāvadāna* (Legend of King Aśoka), and other texts. These stories prophesied attacks by alien kings hostile to Buddhism, their defeat by the Buddhists' patron king, the increased generosity of lay patrons, and the consequent corruption of monks, who would abandon all discipline and meditation in pursuit of study for worldly glory. On the day of the disappearance of the Law, the laity would denounce the assembled monks for failing in their religious duties despite the laymen's faithful performance of their own obligations. That evening the chief of the monastic order, who was thoroughly learned in doctrine *(bahuśruta-pāramitā),* would refuse to recite the complete *Prātimokṣa* because he could no longer observe all its injunctions. Surata, the last arhat, would step forward, declare that he could obey the entire *Prātimokṣa,* and then challenge the chief to recite the whole *Tripiṭaka.* This assertion of the superiority of a clearly defined code of discipline over the study of endless texts would outrage the followers of the chief monk, who would slay Surata. The latter's followers would kill the chief, and the dharma would thus disappear from the world.[13]

These stories clearly demonstrate the point of the theory of the dharma's end and its role in internal Buddhist polemics. First, they deal entirely with the corruption of the monastic order and the disappearance of Buddhism; the lay followers are explicitly exonerated. Second, the stories place the blame for the disappearance on those elements in the Order who intellectually master Buddhist doctrines for worldly glory but can no longer carry out a disciplined, religious praxis. This same preference for discipline and action over intellectual knowledge is also reflected in the standard ordering of the "retractions of the dharma," in which meditation and the observation of the prohibitions are granted pride of place over wide knowledge. Thus the idea of the decay of the dharma was invoked by those who perceived the Saṃgha to be in a state of decline produced by excessive scholasticism in the cause of worldly glory.

This division between an intellectual faith and a faith of praxis is deep-rooted in Buddhism, and it played a major role in the history of the doctrine of the disappearance of the dharma.[14] In his study of the attitudes toward this doctrine evinced by the leading Chinese Buddhists of the sixth and seventh centuries, Takao Giken has shown that, in general, those who were devoted to philosophical speculation and intellectual synthesis tended to ignore or actively deny the disappearance of the Buddha's law, whereas the advocates of the Disciplinary School (Lü tsung), the devotional Pure Land sect, and the radical Three Stages sect all spoke of the end of the dharma as imminent or as an achieved fact.[15]

The leading philosophical thinkers of the period, such as Ching-ying Hui-yüan (523–592), Chi-tsang (549–623), all the exegetes of the Hua-yen school, and the T'ien-t'ai's founder Chih-i (538–597) denied the actual or imminent end of the dharma.[16] The single prominent exception to this generalization was the Fa-hsiang school, which produced philosophical arguments of great sophistication but whose founder Hsüan-tsang (596–664) and his chief disciple K'uei-chi (632–682) believed in the imminent end of the dharma and cited evidence for it in their writings.[17] This apparent anomaly is explained by the fact that both these men were devout followers of the cult of the future buddha, Maitreya; indeed, some Japanese scholars have argued that the worship of Maitreya was the actual center of Fa-hsiang Buddhism.[18] Since the ultimate coming of Maitreya was necessarily preceded by the disappearance of the teachings of the historical buddha, Śākyamuni, those who hoped for the former were inclined to look for the signs of the latter. But barring a strong commitment to such millennial expectations, thinkers who were devoted to the interpretation and synthesis of the vast canon attributed to Śākyamuni were not inclined to deal with doctrines or evidence which suggested that those teachings were no longer of value.

In contrast with those of a philosophical bent, men who advocated a restoration of discipline or a new religious praxis generally argued that the dharma was on the brink of disappearing or had already done so. The founder of the Disciplinary School, Tao-hsüan (596–667), believed that the world had entered the fourth of five stages in the decline of the dharma, and that the Buddha's law could be preserved for a further two centuries only through rigorous practice of a revived monastic discipline.[19] Despite his belief in the continued existence of the dharma, his works on the *Vinaya* code contain numerous references to the present corruption of the monastic order, and he argued that meditation was no longer efficacious in his day.[20] These arguments clearly reflect his belief that the dharma was in an advanced state of decay and that its ultimate disappearance was only a matter of time.

Even more radical were those who proclaimed that the Final Age of the Dharma *(mo-fa)* had already begun. The most important of these were the Pure Land sect and the Three Stages sect (San-chieh chiao), both of whose followers believed that the religious order was corrupt, that the teachings of the historical Buddha had lost their efficacy, and that the men of their day required a new religious praxis to attain salvation.[21] However, the Pure Land sect did not carry the consequences of these beliefs to such an extreme as did the Three Stages sect. While agreeing that the saving power of the buddhas had waned, they excluded Amitābha. While concurring that the texts of the Buddha's teachings were no longer efficacious, they claimed a special hundred-year extension for the *Wu-liang-shou ching* (Sūtra of the Buddha of Limitless Life). While acknowledging that true meditation was no longer possible, Huai-kan (fl. seventh century), the leading spokesman for the Pure Land sect, argued that men could still obtain a shallow form of samādhi, and this made the chanting of Amitābha's name effective. Even in the twilight of the dharma the Pure Land sect still believed in the continued efficacy of at least one buddha, one sūtra, and one meditation technique.

Such half measures, however, were unacceptable to the adherents of the Three Stages sect, and during the seventh century an increasingly rancorous polemic developed between the two schools.[22] Convinced that the dharma had entered its terminal age, the Three Stages sect declared the bankruptcy of received Buddhism and called for a new form of religion to rescue men from the world of error and sin in which the Buddhist establishment itself was now also caught. It is to the nature of this new practice and their critique of traditional Buddhism that we must now turn our attention.

Buddhism in the Terminal Age

The core of the doctrine of the Three Stages sect was that the dharma declined through three stages, and the descent of the dharma into its terminal stage invalidated all distinctions and judgments of value. Cut off from the dharma's truth, men could no longer distinguish right from wrong, and so, to avoid the crime of slander and false judgments, they had no choice but to affirm and reverence all beings on the basis of their ultimate buddhahood. As Yabuki Keiki, the leading modern student of the sect, has pointed out, the central word in all the teachings of the school was "universal" *(p'u,* Skt. *viśva).*[23] The writings of the sect repeatedly proclaim such ideas as "universal buddhahood," "universal dharma," "universal reverence," "universal sagehood," "universal truth," and the "universal common man." The foundation of this call for the abandonment of distinctions and universal reverence of all beings was the belief that all existence shared the "buddha-nature" known as the tathāgatagarbha. Various passages in the texts of the Three Stages sect proclaimed that all the various buddhas and buddhadharmas spoken of in the sūtras were just different names for the universal buddha, which was the true nature and substance of all sentient beings. The relation of the buddha-nature to sentient creatures was variously compared to that of water to waves, clay or metal to the implements made from them, or an actor to the many roles he plays, for the true nature of all those beings who were not yet buddhas was actually the same as that of the Buddha himself.[24] Since all beings shared the buddha-nature, all were in truth buddhas.

The doctrine of a universal buddha-nature inherent in all beings is common to much of Mahāyāna Buddhism and would, of itself, merit little notice. The radical character of the Three Stages sect's position lay in the belief that because the disappearance of the dharma invalidated all distinctions or judgments, the "essential" or "potential" buddhahood of all things had to be treated as a reality in the world. This led them to adopt as their model the Bodhisattva Never-Disparaging (Pu ch'ing p'u-sa) described in the *Lotus Sūtra,* who bowed to everything he encountered and proclaimed its future buddhahood. It also led them to denounce all those who uniquely reverenced the buddhas, the Saṃgha, or the doctrines of the Buddhist canon at the cost of contempt or condemnation for other creatures. In contrast with their own self-proclaimed universalism, all other sects were censured for being "split" or "separate" *(pieh),* because they divided all doctrines into true and false, perceptions into correct and incorrect, conduct into good and bad, and men into sages and villains. Each sect proclaimed the correctness of its own teachings and practice, and thereby condemned the ideas and actions of others as wicked. Such divisions and distinctions had once been valid in terms of the true dharma, but with its disappearance they became destructive illusions. The impossibility of correct perception in the Final Age of the Dharma invalidated earlier Buddhist practices and necessitated the creation of the new, "universalist" Buddhism of the Three Stages sect.

The very first sentence of a central scripture of the sect, the *San-chieh fo-fa* (Buddhadharma of the Three Stages), proclaimed the impossibility of correct perception in the Final Age of the Dharma, and because correct perception was impossible, any judgment would be slander. Men of the first two ages were still capable of correct perceptions, so for them to study the teachings of the various sūtras and pass judgments of right and wrong was correct, but for men of the third stage to do so was a great crime. For men of the terminal age to make distinctions was, as one passage remarked, like a blind man shooting an arrow; they would not hit what they shot at, but only cause harm. Instead they should reverence all things universally, which was like a blind man shooting at the ground; they could not miss. Because of the centrality of this belief in the impossibility of correct judgments, the standard epithets used in the sect's texts to describe men in the terminal age were "born blind" *(sheng mang)*, "of perverse views" *(hsieh chien)*, "of broken precepts and views" *(p'o chieh p'o chien)*, or "inverting [the real and illusory]" *(tien-tao)*.

Given the impossibility of correct perceptions, all distinctions—such as those between sage and petty man, good and bad, correct and deviant, large and small, or monk and layman—had to be abandoned.[25] In all cases the man of the terminal age was enjoined to regard all around him positively, out of recognition of their buddha-nature, and to regard himself negatively *(jen o,* lit., "acknowledge evil"), in full cognizance of his own inadequacies. In addition, to meet these new conditions the Three Stages sect propounded new models of action, such as the demand that when securing the necessities of life—food, clothing, and shelter—the believer must always take the inferior role or portion for himself and grant the superior to others; the assertion that giving *(dāna)* was the only true religious practice; and the ideal of zealous self-denial through rigorous performance of the twelve ascetic practices *(dhūta)*. However, for the purposes of this chapter this new praxis is not so important as are the sect's judgments on the traditional Buddhism that it claimed to supplant. I shall divide this discussion into three parts dealing with the sect's assessments of the nature of each of the Three Jewels—the Buddha, the monastic order, and the canon—in the Final Age of the Dharma.

Because the sect's fundamental tenet was universality, which was defined through the negation of separation, its subsidiary doctrines always centered on the denial of distinctions. The case of the buddha-jewel offers an extreme example of this tendency for, as already noted, the premises of universal buddha-nature and universal blindness combined to lead the sect to propose that all creatures should be treated as the Buddha. A clear example of this is found in the biography of an unnamed master of the Three Stages sect collected by Paul Pelliot and now in the Bibliothèque Nationale in Paris (Pelliot no. 2550).[26] According to this text, such was the power of the master's devotions that even ants gathered around his dwelling like disciples, and asses and other beasts of the mountains also joined his worship. He said, "I clearly know that these are all incarnations of the Buddha who have entered into the practice [of the Way]. They ought to be deeply reverenced; one cannot disparage them."[27]

Nor did this new definition of the Buddha simply include the beasts of the fields and forests. An account of the various means of seeking salvation in each of the three stages includes a description of the changing definition of the Buddha. The Buddha of the terminal age included not only the universal buddha-nature, the buddhas (*chen shen* and *ying shen,* Skt. dharmakāya and nirmāṇakāya) of previous Buddhist doctrine, and the images of the Buddha, but also the gods and spirits worshiped by heterodox faiths, the demons employed in casting spells and curses, and even Māras and evil spirits.[28] The blind men of the third stage could only find the Buddha by worshiping him everywhere, even in evil demons and in the gods of alien faiths.

Just as the disappearance of the dharma obliterated the distinction between buddha and non-buddha, so it removed the separation between monk and layman. This change was already foreshadowed in the *Hsiang-fa chüeh-i ching* (Book of Resolving Doubts During the Semblance Dharma Age, i.e., the second stage of the decline), an officially apocryphal text that was accepted as genuine by followers of the Three Stages sect and frequently quoted in their writings. The central teaching of the *Hsiang-fa chüeh-i ching* was the idea that giving *(dāna)* was the highest of all the perfections (pāramitās) and the only true road to salvation.[29] To understand the significance of this teaching and the way in which it obliterated the distinction between monk and layman, we must note the relation of *dāna* to the other pāramitās: *śīla,* "prohibitions, moral conduct"; *vīrya,* "energy, devotion"; *kṣānti,* "patience, resolve"; dhyāna, "meditation"; and prajñā, "wisdom, knowledge."

In his study on Buddhism in Thai society, Stanley Tambiah described the "asymmetrical and symbiotic pattern" incumbent on monks and laymen. The actual cultivation of a distinctively "Buddhist way of life," i.e., observance of all precepts, meditation, and study, is reserved for the monks, while the laymen earn merit through financing the building and repair of temples and the daily feeding of the Saṃgha.[30] Thus merit-making through *dāna* is the classic lay form of religious action, and the monks consummate *dāna* by accepting the gifts of the laymen and thereby sharing with them the merit earned through the monks' devotions and study. The other five pāramitās constitute the distinctive praxis of the monk as a religious specialist, although they might be observed in reduced form by the laity, in such guises as taking lay vows or attending public lectures.

The *Hsiang-fa chüeh-i ching,* however, systematically dismantled this classic, asymmetrical structure in which the monk purified himself apart from the world while the layman earned merit by supporting the monastic order. The text accomplished this through three radical propositions. First, it asserted that the object of *dāna* was not to support the monastic order or the Buddha, but rather to save the poor, the orphaned, and the suffering creatures of the world. It is better, the text argued, to feed one mouthful of food to an animal than to nourish all the buddhas, bodhisattvas, and śrāvakas in the universe for innumerable lifetimes.[31] Second, it argued that both monks and laymen were obliged to give *dāna*. All men, it proclaimed, whether high or low, rich or poor, monk or layman, should gather all they could spare and distribute this to whoever was in need.[32] Finally, the text claimed that *dāna* was the only road to salvation and that the other five pāramitās were, at best, aspects or developments of *dāna*. All the buddhas of the universe had attained their status through lifetimes of giving, and the performance of the other pāramitās for "kalpas as numberless as the sands of the Ganges" would not lead to nirvāṇa if not based on *dāna*. Masters of monastic discipline, meditation, or study could only succeed in destroying the dharma and would "go to hell like an arrow shot from a bow."[33] Thus the *Hsiang-fa chüeh-i ching* argued that there was a single, true mode of religious action common to monks and laymen, whereas the explicitly "monastic" pāramitās were at best adjuncts to giving and at worst roads to perdition.

The major texts of the Three Stages sect also focus on *dāna* as the primary form of religious action. The *Tui-ken ch'i-hsing fa*'s (The Dharma of Setting Out [on the Way] in Accord with Capacity) discussion of the cultivation of good during the terminal age deals almost entirely with giving, linking the generosity of *dāna* with the self-denial of the *dhūta*. In contrast with earlier stages of the dharma, the "good" in the final stage was no longer separate from the "bad"; it was entirely "good within bad" or the "good gained in bitterness." The discussion of the "good gained in bitterness" is divided into twelve sections, but the last eleven appear only as rubrics and detailed discussion is devoted entirely to the first topic, "regularly begging for food" *(ch'ang ch'i shih)*. This thus becomes the central discussion of proper conduct in the Final Age of the Dharma.

The discussion is divided into eight sections, and the first one, which deals explicitly with *dāna,* makes four points. First, it argues that by giving away all good food obtained and eating only the bad, a man quells his own desires and benefits other creatures. Second, it stipulates that food received from begging should be divided into four parts: one part was to be eaten by the recipient, the second by his companions, the third to be given to the poor, and the fourth to hungry ghosts and domestic animals. Third, the text states that food received in the two daily meals at a monastery, as part of a vegetarian feast, or at the homes of wealthy patrons of the Buddhist Order should not be eaten but instead given to those in need. Fourth, in begging for all his food and regularly sharing it with the poor, the devotee was to serve as a model and lead other beings to enter the Way of begging and giving. Giving thus culminated in granting all sentient beings an entry into the path to salvation. This passage clearly follows the *Hsiang-fa chüeh-i ching* in asserting the centrality of *dāna* to all religious conduct, transferring the charity from the Buddhist Order to the poor, and insisting that monks must join laymen as givers of *dāna*.

The remaining seven sections on "regularly begging for food" list a variety of virtues and attainments, but these are all treated as aspects of the basic duty of denying oneself and giving all to the poor. Thus "patience" *(kṣānti),* originally one of the pāramitās, is explained as bearing one's hunger and not eating any food presented. "Compassion" and "pity" are both manifested by feeding or saving the poor, and "renunciation and self-sufficiency" are marked by denying oneself in order to give to others. "Concentration" (dhyāna), also one of the six pāramitās, is defined simply as a fixed tranquillity of mind that is not disturbed by the desire for good food. "Much profit and merit" are explained as the two benefits of regularly begging for food rather than relying on lay patronage. First, when a patron staged a vegetarian feast for monks, only his family benefited from the merit of the deed. However, when many men engaged in begging, begged from many houses, and then distributed what they received to the myriad creatures, the benefits were immense and widespread. Second, by causing all creatures to give *dāna* in an endless circuit, the beggar himself would ultimately obtain more food. Finally, the section on "liberation" describes how the rejection of the old ties of lay patron and monastic client freed the monk from the trammels of the world.[34] In this way all virtues and the cultivation of the good were identified solely with self-denial and charity. In this expanded form *dāna* was to become the unique form of religious praxis, one that was common to laymen and monks.

Not only were monks enjoined to be givers of *dāna,* but any reliance on lay patronage was specifically attacked. This point appears clearly in the biography of the anonymous master of the sect referred to earlier. After expounding to his pupils the doctrine of giving all good food to others and eating only what they left behind, he noted that for a monk to accept charity in exchange for preaching was to sell the dharma.[35] Here the monks' traditional role of sharing merit through receiving lay charity was explicitly attacked in the name of universal participation in giving. This critique of patronage was not only an attack on the distinction between Saṃgha and laity but also an assault on the corruption of the religious orders that resulted from regular lay patronage, a corruption that was both cause and consequence of the decline of the dharma in the classic accounts of its disappearance already cited.

In addition to the centrality of *dāna* in the teachings of the sect, its most famous institution, the Inexhaustible Treasury *(wu chin tsang),* was based on the model of charity outlined above. As advocated in the *Hsiang-fa chüeh-i ching,* the sect established a treasury at the Hua-tu Temple in Ch'ang-an where all men could give charity that would then be distributed to those in need. As the institution became more popular, branch treasuries were established by members of the sect in monasteries all over the empire, and it became an accepted practice for people throughout the empire to give donations to these treasuries on the fourth day of the first month and again at the time of the Hungry Ghost Festival in the middle of the seventh month. These donations were used to stage religious festivals, to maintain monasteries, and to give relief to the poor.[36] It was primarily through this practice of empire-wide, organized charity that the Three Stages sect became influential in T'ang society, and the practice itself was a direct extension of the new religious praxis for the terminal age outlined in the teachings of the sect.

The merging of lay and monastic modes of religious practice was to be accompanied by the dissolution of physical and institutional divisions between the Saṃgha and the laity. In its discussion of the places where one could attain salvation, the *Tui-ken ch'i-hsing fa* noted that in the first age of the dharma men could attain the Way anywhere, in the second age they could attain it only in still places removed from human settlements, but in the third age they could attain the Way only in the midst of other men; they could not be separated from lay society.[37] This was an explicit attack on the separation of the monastic order from the world at large, and many other passages in the writings of the sect made the same point.[38] In actual practice, the adherents of the Three Stages sect were noted for mixing with lay society in the course of begging and preaching, and their practice of living apart from other monks in special quarters might also have reflected their rejection of the conventional divisions between the monastic order and lay society.

Further evidence that the Three Stages sect preached the end of a distinct monastic order is found in the biography of the anonymous master. When a group of monks upbraided him for not encouraging a group of wealthy visitors to sponsor a vegetarian feast, he replied with a parable comparing the awesome solemnity of a vegetarian feast with the purifying fasts undertaken by a civil official in preparation for a public ritual. For the slightest error the official would be stripped of his rank and sent into exile, and the consequences of an error in sacred ritual for one who had left the world were infinitely greater. Since the men of the terminal age had lost the capacity to perceive the Buddha's truth and no longer knew how to perform rituals correctly, the food offered to monks by lay patrons was like the bait placed in traps to lure animals to their deaths. The other monks were so impressed with the gravity of accepting the *dāna* of lay patrons that they abandoned their vows and reverted to secular status.[39] Indeed, four times in his biography the result of the anonymous master's preaching was to lead monks to abandon monastic life and resume life as laymen.[40] Since the intent of the biography is clearly hagiographic, we must conclude that the Three Stages sect celebrated the reversion of monks to secular life as one expression of proper religiosity. Another text even tells of five hundred monks in the terminal age who reverted to lay status because they realized that they had broken their precepts; moreover, as a direct consequence of ceasing to be monks, they met the Buddha and were able to attain the Way.[41]

In addition to persuading monks to return to lay life, the anonymous master did not adopt the traditional accoutrements of one who had left the world. One of the conversations that led his interlocutors to revert to lay status dealt with the differences in practice between the anonymous master and Hsin-hsing (540–594), the founder of the Three Stages sect. When the master stated that he was no different from Hsin-hsing, the others objected that Hsin-hsing shaved his head and wore the *kaṣāya.* The master replied that it was not in accord with the Buddhist faith for common men with broken precepts, i.e., the men of the terminal age, to wear the clothing of a sage.[42] This clearly shows that many adherents of the sect rejected any distinctions in dress and tonsure between monks and laymen.

Not only did this master of the Three Stages sect denounce lay patronage of the Buddhist Order, refuse to shave his head and wear a *kaṣāya,* and persuade monks to return to lay life, but he also made laymen and -women the primary targets of religious instruction. The biography records that a monk criticized him for preaching only to the laity and not to monks. The master replied that if one wore the *kaṣāya* in the Final Age of the Dharma, all the buddhas would not appear and the consummation of giving would not be accomplished. This was because self-styled monks were all greedy for wealth from the gifts of patrons and enchanted with sensual pleasures, thus embodying that corruption of the religious order which brought about the decay of the dharma. The questioner then asked why the master taught only women, and he replied that the dharma ought to have been performed by monks, but that their failure had led to its disappearance. Laymen could not perform it, for they were bound to the service of the emperor. Consequently, only laywomen could now attain the Way.[43]

In yet another passage, the master observed that anyone who gave away his wealth would become a monk. His interlocutors objected that people who did not shave their heads could not leave the household and become monks, and they asked the master why he called laymen monks. The master cited examples in the *Vinaya* where monks were allowed to keep their hair, and he then quoted the *Fo-tsang ching* (Sūtra of the Buddha-Treasure):

> I did not say that those who shave their heads and wear the *kaṣāya* are monks. Those who obey my law are monks; they are my disciples, and I am their master. If they do not obey my law, then I am not their master.[44]

The true division was not between official monks and laymen, but between those who obeyed the buddhadharma and those who did not. And in the terminal age, the buddhadharma was synonymous with the teachings of the Three Stages sect.

In addition to this evidence from doctrinal and hagiographical texts, other sources also indicate the blurring of the distinctions between laymen and monks in the practices of the sect. Hsin-hsing's biography in the *Hsü kao-seng chuan* (Further Biographies of Eminent Monks) records, "At the Fa-tsang Monastery, he renounced the precepts and personally engaged in physical labor."[45] Hsin-hsing's private secretary and close colleague, P'ei Hsüan-cheng (d.u.), remained a layman even while controlling many of the affairs of the sect and its monasteries. Hsin-hsing's "last testament" records that as of his forty-eighth year there were only four men who shared his religious practices, and they had sworn an oath with him to renounce property and life itself to become buddhas. Two of these four sworn comrades were laymen.[46] Inscriptional evidence also indicates that the skeletons of monks of the sect and of lay followers, both male and female, were buried together.[47]

The final element to be considered is the fate of the dharma-jewel, in its narrow sense of doctrine and texts, during the terminal age. To a certain extent, the repudiation of a distinct monastic order with its own religious praxis based on discipline, meditation, and study also denied the significance of texts and scholastic study. In a world where prajñā was impossible and dhyāna meant simply the ability to keep one's mind off food, texts could not play an important role. Various texts argued explicitly that to speak of anything other than the dharma of the universal buddha, i.e., the teachings of the Three Stages sect, was to slander the Buddha and his law.[48] Moreover, numerous passages also stated that in the terminal age the Buddhist canon would cease to exist as a defined body of texts, and the study and dissemination of texts would no longer be an aspect of correct religious praxis.

In the section on "taking refuge in the dharma," the *Tui-ken ch'i-hsing fa* notes that during the second age there was one dharma: the *Sūtra, Vinaya,* and *Abhidharma* texts of the three vehicles. This "one dharma," therefore, meant all the texts in the conventional Buddhist canon. In the terminal age, however, the dharma was divided into eight sections, and only one of these—the sūtras—corresponded to an element of the official canon. The exclusion of the *Vinaya* codes and the philosophical elaborations of the *Abhidharma* reiterated the sect's denunciations, cited above, of traditional monastic discipline and academic speculation. In place of the vanished categories of *Vinaya* and *Abhidharma,* however, the canon of the terminal age also included the "dharma of the great vehicle of the perception of universality"—apparently the teachings of the Three Stages sect—as well as "the dharma of the lay world," the "buddhadharma which perverts the good," and other dharmas that included the various heterodox faiths and perverted perceptions adhered to by the blinded creatures of the terminal age.[49] Just as the universal buddha of this corrupted age expanded to include alien gods and evil demons, and the monastic order incorporated lay society, so the canon encompassed all religious teachings and texts save those of the corrupted, traditional Saṃgha.

Another discussion of the transformation of the canon appears in the *San-chieh fo-fa.* This passage cites a sentence in the *Ta-pan-nieh-p'an ching* (Nirvāṇa Sūtra) which said that eleven of the twelve sections of the canon would disappear, and only the *vaipulya (fang teng)* sūtras would survive.[50] It then explains that this would occur because the *vaipulya* texts were in accord with the dharma of the terminal age, whereas the rest of the canon was not.[51] Apart from their own texts it is not certain which works the Three Stages sect would have included under the rubric *vaipulya,* which was not a clearly fixed set of texts but a generic term applied to works of a "universalist" bent. Nevertheless, there is no doubt that this passage denied scriptural status to a significant portion of the traditional Buddhist canon.

Not only were significant elements of the Buddhist canon denied legitimacy and much non-Buddhist doctrine accepted—at least for the sake of polemics—by the Three Stages sect, but the study and preaching of conventional Buddhist doctrine was severely criticized by the school. The *San-chieh fo-fa mi-chi* (Secret Record of the Buddhadharma of the Three Stages) described the possibility of doctrinal knowledge and preaching in the terminal age, as follows:

> The position in the third age is one of completely perverted views, fixed and unalterable, and cannot be saved through any of the five ways [of salvation, the traditional pāramitās]. This is also called the completion of deviant understanding and conduct. The [*Ta-pan-*]*nieh-p'an ching* says, "The bhikṣu Shan-hsing recited, chanted, and expounded all twelve sections of the canon, and in meditation attained the Buddha-Way of the four dhyānas. But he did not comprehend the meaning of a single sentence or a single word, did not achieve the slightest good root *(kuśalamūla),* and could not avoid slandering the Buddha."[52]

Here again we see how the members of the sect insisted that the blind men of the third stage could not grasp the truth and that their preaching of doctrine would inevitably slander the Buddha and his law. True learning in the third stage was impossible, and the exposition of doctrine constituted a positive danger. As the *San-chieh fo-fa* stated, "The age of erudition *(bahuśruta)* is past, and we are now in the age of meritorious deeds *(puṇya)*. . . . All the creatures of acute faculties . . . will increase every kind of evil, because they are partial to study for erudition and wisdom (prajñā)."[53] The anonymous master likewise stated that a man who studied texts in the terminal age was like a blind bird with a bean in its beak; it could not understand what it had.[54]

Since the study and exposition of texts in the third stage was hazardous, the Three Stages sect cautioned its adherents against teaching and lauded the virtues of silence. The fifth section on "universal reverence" in the *Tui-ken ch'i-hsing fa* spoke of the "buddhadharma of cutting off all speech" thus:

> For all creatures we reverence their essence [buddha-nature] and do not speak of their good or evil. We use the same name for all six destinies of sentient beings [i.e., make no distinctions between spirits in hell, hungry ghosts, animals, men, demons, and gods].[55]

In the practice of universal reverence, no judgments about others could be made, and doctrines that made distinctions and assigned judgments had to be avoided, so the safest course was not to speak at all about religious matters. The importance of this proscription is shown by the fact that in the list of the twenty-six characteristic evils of the terminal age, the very first one was "impure discourse on the dharma" *(pu-ch'ing shuo fa)* and the third was "to praise or malign the strengths and weaknesses of the Three Jewels and the Three Vehicles."[56] All study and disputation in the third stage became slander against the Buddha.

This injunction to silence and the avoidance of doctrinal discussion or dispute appeared in many other forms. The section in the *Tui-ken ch'i-hsing fa* on "seeking spiritual masters" during the third stage listed three types of men of good knowledge: the " 'mute sheep monk' who understood neither words nor meaning," the " 'mute sheep monk' who understood the words but not the meaning," and the man of acute faculties who through recognizing the character of the age imitated the "mute sheep monk."[57] The model of the perfect spiritual master was a mute monk who could not understand the meaning of texts, and one who through study came to understand the needs of his own age could only hope to imitate this "mute sheep."

No surviving text explains the meaning of "mute sheep," but the biography of the unnamed master contains several passages pertaining to the virtues of muteness. The master placed tremendous stress on not speaking, and indeed taught that the mouth should not be opened:

> When the master presented the dharma and [rules of] conduct to his disciples, he forbade them all to open their mouths and had them remain silent like dead men. Even if it reached the point that they were beaten or killed,

> even if they passed through a thousand deaths, ten thousand deaths, or a million deaths, they could not speak to defend themselves. If subjected to all sorts of punishments, they could not speak to defend themselves. The only exception was that they could open their mouths to eat. This continued to the ends of their lives, and then they died like wild beasts.[58]

This teaching was so central that it was elaborated in full twice. Moreover, one disciple in the course of a confession remarked that in the three years since she had last seen the master she had opened her mouth not in wasteful speech but only to eat one meal a day.[59] A list of those things that disciples had to renounce as part of their beggar's existence included "all fine expositions," "all commentaries on texts and catechisms," and "all flowery knowledge and ornamented words."[60] These passages show that the reference to a "buddhadharma cutting off all speech" was not simply hyperbole.

Several other passages in the text show that this ban on speech was not simply a form of discipline but grew out of the aforementioned fear of all exposition of the Law in the terminal age. One typical story relates how a group of men came from the city and asked the master to talk about the deviant and correct dharmas. The master replied that men had different understandings and practices, and he could not say which were correct. When pressed to reply he offered a parable of a cock who saw that a fox had entered his shed and did not dare to call out lest he attract attention to himself and be eaten. The master compared himself to the cock; as a common man of no perception he could not speak on deviance and correctness without destroying himself.[61] People, the master argued, used their mouths to swear the oath to renounce body and life in order to accord with the dharma. He imposed silence on his disciples as a sign of these vows, and in doing so he also prevented them from harming the dharma.[62] This ideal of muteness clearly entailed a condemnation of all scholasticism and textual exposition.

The reference to "sheep" is less clear. At least one text often quoted in the works of the sect used sheep as the image of stupidity or ignorance, but a passage in the biography of the unnamed master suggests another line of argument.[63] Someone asked the master to explain the significance of wearing a sheepskin garment and carrying a single gourd, which was apparently the master's standard apparel, and he explained that it was useful to guard against the wind and rain.[64] Thus the "sheep" may refer to the humble but sturdy garb worn by the adherents of the sect in their travels and on begging rounds. Another passage tells of a man who wore only a tattered garment, carried a gourd, and would not speak with men. He would only shout loudly:

> I deeply reverence all of you and do not dare to disparage you. You are all walking the Way of the bodhisattvas and will become buddhas.[65]

This strange figure, who was clearly imitating the Bodhisattva Never-Disparaging and hence was a follower of the Three Stages sect, was perhaps the very image of the "mute sheep monk."

Other evidence indicating that the Three Stages sect denied the efficacy of the conventional canon comes from the writings of hostile schools. In one story, Hsiao-tz'u (d.u.), a preacher from the Three Stages sect, told a group of women lay devotees that they would go to hell if they studied the sūtras, especially the *Lotus Sūtra.* Many of the women agreed to give up this sūtra, but one had reservations about abandoning her studies and devotions. She declared that if to chant the sūtra was truly against Buddhism, may anyone who did so contract a terrible illness and be reborn in hell; but if it were not against Buddhism, then may the same happen to the preacher. As soon as she finished speaking, the preacher and his associates were struck dumb.[66]

A vigorous polemic against the Three Stages sect was also conducted by the followers of the Pure Land sect.[67] One of the chief issues of this debate was the continued efficacy of scriptures in the terminal age. The adherents of the Pure Land sect held that, through the special grace of the Buddha, the *Wu-liang-shou ching* still had spiritual potency in the first half of the third stage. This position was denounced by the Three Stages sect, and as a Pure Land spokesman pointed out, this denial of the efficacy of any scriptures led inevitably to the conclusion that "the subtle and wondrous canon of the Great Vehicle no longer circulated in the world".[68] Although one cannot place complete reliance on the polemics of rival schools, the accusation that the Three Stages sect denied the efficacy of studying or chanting scriptures closely matches the arguments in the texts of the sect itself.

Thus the Three Jewels, as recognized and invoked by traditional Buddhism, were all declared to be null and void in the terminal age. The ultimate expression of the Three Stages sect's rejection of traditional Buddhism was the doctrine that the beings of the third stage could not be saved by the five ways *(wu-chung pu-chiu).* These five roads to salvation were the Buddha, the dharma, the monastic order, the deliverance of other sentient beings, and the cultivation of good/removal of evil.[69] The inability of these five to save the sentient beings of the terminal age is proclaimed on the first page of the *San-chieh fo-fa* and recurs periodically throughout the text. This doctrine was nothing less than a declaration of the bankruptcy of traditional Buddhism as a path to salvation and as a source of religious power. In this manner the Three Stages sect proclaimed the end of the old order and the rise of a new form of religion, in which the official Saṃgha, with its codes of discipline, meditative practices, and scholastic pursuits, was to be replaced by a new religious body that joined monks and laymen in the mute practice of universal austerities, begging, and *dāna.*[70]

The Suppression of the Sect

In light of the foregoing, we can now reassess the reasons for the suppression of the school. The accepted explanation was first offered by Yabuki Keiki,[71] who argued that in declaring the corruption of human character and mores in the Final Age of the Dharma, the Three Stages sect challenged the efficacy and legitimacy of all government. Kenneth Ch'en offers a good summation of this position:

> Moreover, its contention that the contemporary age was one of decay, in which people were depraved, lawless, and blinded by folly, was entirely unacceptable to the rulers, who looked upon their dynasty as responsible for the prosperity and well-being of the people. In addition, they further alienated the sympathies of the rulers by stating that in the age of decay no government existed which was worthy of the respect of the people, and that the present dynasty was incapable of restoring the religion or leading the people to salvation.[72]

This argument, however, has several weaknesses. First, as already pointed out, the doctrine of the disappearance of the dharma was a theory of decay in religious practice and perceptions; it did not comment on the mores of society at large or the possibilities of secular law. In the classic Indian accounts of the end of the dharma (also discussed earlier), lay society and the state not only maintained proper order but even continued to perform their assigned religious functions; it was the monks who became lax and corrupt.

Assertions of the possibility and even the virtue of government in the third stage are not restricted to Indian texts. In several places the *Hsiang-fa chüeh-i ching* calls upon the ruler to punish the corrupt men who destroy the buddhadharma and to encourage those who do good. Thus the text urged the authorities in the terminal age to beat and exile all those who sold Buddhist images or scriptures to make money. Another passage says that in the third stage the ruler, his ministers, local officials, and elders had to encourage monks and laymen to pity and save all sentient creatures, and that they should use their powers to prevent evil men from doing harm. If they performed these roles, it states, they would gain "inexhaustible merit."[73] Clearly the authors of this text, which was often cited as authoritative by the Three Stages sect, did not believe that the passing of the dharma rendered impossible the legitimate rule of kings.

Another text, the *Te-hu chang-che ching* (Sūtra of Elder Śrīgupta; Śrīgupta was an elder of Rājagṛha who plotted to murder Śākyamuni with fire and poison but was then converted through the Buddha's miracles), even contained a prophecy that in the terminal age of the dharma a great king would arise who would lead all the creatures of his land into the Buddha's Way and thereby plant good seeds for their future lives.[74] References in other texts show that this story was widely known, and it was used to praise Emperor Wen of the Sui (r. 589–604) for his efforts to restore Buddhism after the suppression under the Northern Chou.[75] Once again, no necessary connection was perceived between the decay of the dharma and the possibility or quality of rule. Indeed, the king might actually become even more virtuous and religiously potent as he took on the role once assigned to the now decayed Saṃgha.

Moreover, the texts of the Three Stages sect themselves positively affirmed the efficacy of lordship in the terminal age. At the end of his testament, Hsin-hsing stated that his unceasing pursuit of buddhahood would both benefit the myriad creatures and also aid the king and state.[76] The *San-chieh fo-fa* likewise contains an extended discussion of proper kingship that deals primarily with the question of how the ruler's punishments ought to adapt to each stage in the decline of the dharma.[77] For example, in the second stage the king could force those monks who broke the precepts to return to lay life, but he could not beat or execute them. In the third stage, however, he could impose the five kinds of "light punishments," including expulsion from a monastery, a city, or even the state. He could also still inflict corporal punishment on the laity in the third stage.[78] One passage even provided an extended justification of the king's taking life in the course of wars to defend the state and the people in the Final Age of the Dharma.[79] In fact, the writings of the sect never questioned the need for a ruler to uphold the Law at any stage of the disappearance of the dharma, and such attacks on government as they made were devoted to criticism of the alliance of the state with an official monastic order.

Yet another weakness of the accepted interpretation of the suppression of the sect is that it does not account for what actually took place. The proscription of the Three Stages sect was not completed by a single act of government, nor was it the consistent policy of all rulers. The sect became prominent during the Sui, and it was first condemned in 600 by the founding ruler of that dynasty, the Emperor Wen (r. 581–604). However, this initial ban did not lead to the disappearance, or even the long-term decline, of the sect. In fact, both Yabuki Keiki and Tsukamoto Zenryū have identified the seventh century as the period in which the sect flourished and reached its apogee.[80] Between the decree of 600 and similar decrees in 695 and 699 under Wu Tse-t'ien (r. 690–705) declaring its writings to be apocryphal and banning all practices that differed from those of conventional monks, the Chinese government made no recorded moves against the sect. Several monasteries in the capital were dominated by the sect; its texts circulated and were cited in various Buddhist catalogues as well as in the usually hostile writings of other schools; and its Inexhaustible Treasury became the nexus of an empire-wide system of charity. It is difficult to believe that, for almost a century, a sect of such high visibility could have proclaimed a doctrine that was believed to deny the virtue or efficacy of all government without eliciting a response from a dynasty that was then at the peak of its military power and international prestige.

In fact, as Yabuki himself has noted, only three rulers carried out active policies to suppress the school and its teachings: Emperor Wen of the Sui, Empress Wu, and Emperor Hsüan-tsung of the T'ang (r. 712–756). To explain this phenomenon, Yabuki has suggested that these three were dynamic, aggressive rulers who resented the Three Stages sect's advocacy of the virtue of "drawing in the head" (*su t'ou,* i.e., refusing to act as a leader).[81] This suggestion, however, is highly implausible. First, it is unlikely that monastic calls for humility, any more than those for boundless charity or for ceasing to take life, would have elicited the rulers' notice, much less their active hostility. Second, *su t'ou* is neither a central teaching of the sect nor distinctive to it, and the standard Buddhist call for "withdrawal from the world" would have been far more threatening to rulers if they thought it applied to themselves. However, the strictures on *su t'ou* were explicitly applied only to householders and monks, while the necessity of having rulers, as noted above, was fully acknowledged.[82] Finally, this explanation would scarcely account for the indifference to the sect of the emperors Kao-tsu (r. 618–627) and T'ai-tsung (r. 627–650), who were also, by any standards, dynamic and aggressive rulers.

The single factor uniting Emperor Wen, Empress Wu, and Emperor Hsüan-tsung was that all three were patrons of the official Buddhist Order. They all established official, state-sponsored monasteries distributed in accord with the divisions of the empire, wherein official monks performed ceremonies, meditation, and prayers to mobilize the forces of the spirit world in support of the empire and the ruling house. They likewise sponsored the translation of texts and the production of official catalogues of the Buddhist canon that adjudicated their authenticity. The teachings of the Three Stages sect explicitly denied that the official monastic order and the teachings it preserved had any special spiritual potency or significance. Moreover, as Kaneko Hidetoshi has shown, many of the passages added to the *Hsiang-fa chüeh-i ching* by monks of the Three Stages sect to compose the *Fo-shuo shih so-fan-che yü-ch'ieh fa-ching ching* (Book Spoken by the Buddha on the Yoga Dharma Mirror that Exposes Transgressors; see the chapter by Forte in this volume) explicitly denounced monks who became the adherents of civil officials.[83] Finally, with its call for the negation of all distinctions, the Three Stages sect challenged the rulers' right to declare the supreme truth and to justify their rule through the defense of that truth and the honoring of its presumptive masters. Since the sect spoke from a Buddhist perspective and aimed its criticisms specifically at the Buddhist Saṃgha, this challenge was felt most clearly by monarchs who made the patronage of the traditional Buddhist Order a significant element in their claims to power.

Emperor Wen was just such a ruler. He repeated constantly that he owed his throne to the buddhadharma, and he strove to drape himself in the trappings of a bodhisattva and cakravartin king. With his bodhisattva vows, his sponsoring of state monasteries, his construction of stūpas in imitation of Aśoka, his mass ordination of monks, and his sponsorship of the copying of sūtras, Emperor Wen made Buddhist symbols and the Buddhist Order a fundamental part of his restored empire. Consequently, he could brook no challenges to them.

The early T'ang rulers, however, merely tolerated Buddhism and offered it limited patronage—largess to all varieties of subjects being part of the imperial role and the prestige of Buddhism at every level of society being impossible to ignore—but they granted priority in all religious matters to Taoism.[84] Some people have sought to claim the second T'ang emperor, T'ai-tsung, as a supporter of Buddhism on the basis of his generosity toward Hsüan-tsang (ca. 596–664) and claims in the biography of the latter for a near conversion of the aging emperor, but in fact throughout his reign he followed his father's policy of granting ritual priority and more generous patronage to Taoism. Moreover, in a decree that he wrote with his own hand to an ardent Buddhist descendant of the old Ch'en ruling house, T'ai-tsung derided the folly of those who supported a faith which had led every dynasty that adopted it—the Liang, Ch'en, and Sui—to rapid collapse.[85] From the founding of the T'ang to the establishment of the Chou dynasty by Empress Wu, Buddhism held an adjunct, secondary position in the spiritual hierarchy of the Chinese realm.

Empress Wu, however, granted unquestioned supremacy to Buddhism. Her attempt to rule in her own person rather than through a child emperor, a practice that violated every precept and precedent of the Chinese imperial tradition, found moral justification, intellectual support, and religious sanction only in Buddhism and the Buddhist Order. Consequently, her intellectual and textual claims to rule were founded solely on the Buddhist canon. In his study of the *Ta-yün ching* (Great Cloud Sūtra) and related documents, Antonino Forte has with great skill and impressive command of detail reconstructed Wu Tse-t'ien's textual campaign to claim for herself the titles of bodhisattva, cakravartin, and future buddha.[86] For such a ruler, any claims that the old dharma had passed, that the monastic order was hopelessly worldly and corrupt, and that the texts of the canon were no longer spiritually potent or authoritative constituted a mortal challenge. A cakravartin needed a dharma and a monastic order in order to fulfill his or her role:

> The Buddhist conception makes the universalistic assertion that dharma (in its manifold aspects as cosmic law that regulates the world totality and as the truth embodied in the Buddha's teaching that shows the path to liberation) is the absolutely encompassing norm and that the code of kingship embodying righteousness (dharma) has its source in this dharma and is ideally a concrete manifestation of it in the conduct of worldly affairs. . . . The Buddhist position is that dharma informs and suffuses the code of conduct of the righteous ruler and, moreover, that it is his ruling activities (in the domain of political economy) that give form to society. . . . The Buddhist slicing is in terms of two levels—the dharma, as cosmic law and as truth (the seeker of which is the renouncing *bhikkhu*), encompassing the dharma of the righteous ruler, which attempts to give order to this world. The former brackets the latter.[87]

The righteousness of the Buddhist ruler was encompassed by, and found its meaning only within, the higher dharma of the Buddhist Order. Although for most Chinese rulers the Buddhist ideal of the cakravartin king was only an adjunct to or expansion of the indigenous Chinese ideal of the cosmically potent sage-king, for Empress Wu it was absolutely crucial to her claims to rule.

For this reason, Empress Wu and her advisors were acutely aware of the danger posed by the doctrine of the disappearance of the dharma. This is shown by the fact that in one forgery they inserted a passage in which the Buddha predicted that Devaputra, i.e., Empress Wu, would be reborn in China shortly before the end of Śākyamuni's dharma. After restoring it to its full efficacy, she would rule through the true buddhadharma.[88]

In these circumstances it was impossible for Wu Tse-t'ien not to act against a heresy that undercut her claim to rulership, and the publication of a new comprehensive bibliography of scriptures in 695 provided her with the opportunity to strike. According to the editors of the *Ta Chou k'an-ting chung-ching mu-lu* (Catalogue of Scriptures, Authorized by the Great Chou Dynasty), they received a decree in 694 that all apocryphal writings and prophetic texts were to be sent to the Department of National Sacrifices and stored away. In fact, this decree was primarily employed to blacklist the writings of the Three Stages sect.[89] In 699 the members of the sect were also forbidden to engage in any practices except for begging for food, fasting, abstaining from grains, keeping the precepts, and sitting in meditation. All practices different from those of ordinary monks were banned.

The very form of this suppression demonstrates that the issue was not direct subversion of the ruler but denial of the monastic order, orthodox doctrine, and conventional Buddhist practice. It was carried out by "official Buddhists" and consisted entirely of banning texts deemed hostile to the official canon and practices deemed inimical to the traditional Way of the Buddhist Order. The sect was not treated as a rebel movement but as a heresy, for its only defiance of the ruler had taken the form of a spiritual challenge to her right to define the ultimate truth, to support official organs for the propagation of that truth, and to rule as the patron of and defender of the buddhadharma. The accusation levied against the writings was not that they were seditious but rather that they were apocryphal, not that they challenged the ruler but that they called into question the spiritual authority of the Saṃgha. However, for a would-be cakravartin or patron of official Buddhism, the questions of textual authenticity and orthodoxy of practice inevitably became political questions.

Emperor Hsüan-tsung essentially continued the policies of Empress Wu, although, as Professor Forte shows in his chapter in this volume, he may have had the added motive that a leader of the Three Stages sect was associated with the participants in a conspiracy to poison him at the beginning of his reign. In 713, the year after the conspiracy, he banned the Inexhaustible Treasury and the associated separate chambers for the monks of the Three Stages sect. This move both extended Empress Wu's ban on all distinctive practices by the sect and provided the new emperor with a huge financial windfall. In 730, a new imperial canon excluded the works of the sect, but this likewise simply carried forward the policies of Empress Wu. Although he was not an avid patron of Buddhism and restored the priority of Taoism, Hsüan-tsung continued the practice of supporting a network of official monasteries in the capital and provinces to earn merit and spiritual potency for the empire. Moreover, he became deeply interested in the use of the magical techniques of Esoteric Buddhism to secure and expand his power and that of his state. For this reason he patronized a coterie of monks at his court and supported the translation of numerous scriptures.[90] The hostile activities of the sect at the time of his accession, their attacks on the official Buddhism which he supported, and the precedent of Empress Wu are sufficient to account for his policy of suppression.

After the reign of Hsüan-tsung there are no further records of attempts to suppress the sect. As Yabuki Keiki has noted, the strongest evidence for the prestige and influence of the sect consists of the repeated government attempts to suppress it and the frequent hostile stories and polemics in the writings of other schools.[91] The cessation of these suppressions and attacks in the second half of the eighth century suggests that with the abolition of the Inexhaustible Treasury, the banning of all distinctive practices, and the decades-long suppression of their texts, the sect lost most of its importance and popular appeal. Although there are scattered records until the end of the T'ang of activities by adherents of the sect, it appears that they no longer posed a radical challenge to official Buddhism. Indeed, in 800 the writings of the sect were even temporarily included in a catalogue of the Buddhist canon prepared by a *Vinaya* master who apparently saw in their denunciations of monastic corruption a useful spur for a program of renewed discipline.[92] But such tentative gestures at reconciliation and absorption probably had more to do with the sect's decline than with any acceptance of its doctrine by official Buddhism, and within a century all traces of the sect's activity had vanished, just as its writings disappeared from later editions of the canon.

Conclusion

The fate of the Three Stages sect, and the political aspect of all adjudications of textual authenticity in Chinese Buddhism, can best be understood as one element in the project of a Buddhist empire in China. For several centuries, a series of monarchs attempted to renovate the Chinese political order by building an explicitly Buddhist state, a state that justified itself at least in part through its patronage of Buddhism. Central to these attempts was the creation of an official Buddhist establishment, housed in state temples, performing rituals for the benefit of the ruling house and the empire, and compiling massive, officially approved collections of canonical texts. As the chief patron of such an establishment, the Chinese sage-emperor added to his traditional cosmic role as the earthly double of Heaven a new aspect as cakravartin king, the supreme defender of the dharma.

In this context the Buddhist canon became charged with the same political character that infused the traditional Chinese classics; the sūtras joined the other sacred texts whose dictates offered the state its form and whose defense gave the state its purpose. This "politicization" of Buddhist texts was most intense in the reigns of those monarchs who craved or needed the trappings of the cakravartin, but it was a general tendency of the entire medieval period. As Erik Zürcher has noted, throughout these centuries all texts that might have been included in the canon were regularly scrutinized, and any doctrines that challenged the interpretations of the official monastic order and their imperial patrons were suppressed as "heretical."[93] When the Three Stages sect proclaimed the bankruptcy of traditional monastic Buddhism and suggested a new path to salvation, its adherents had not declared an explicitly political program. But for those who aspired to create a Buddhist empire and an imperial Buddhism, this was a political question. Since imperial authority was defined in part by adherence to and defense of a prescribed body of texts, the right to declare textual truth and authenticity was a fundamental aspect of government. In such a realm, the preaching of apocrypha became a form of treason.

NOTES

1. Honda Shigeyuki, *Shina keigaku shiron* (Kyoto: Kōbundō, 1947), 1–13; Hiraoka Takeo, *Keisho no seiritsu* (Osaka: Zenkoku, 1947), 16–30; Matsumoto Masaaki, "Koten no seiritsu," in *Iwanami kōza sekai rekishi,* vol. 4, *Kodai* (Tokyo: Iwanami, 1970), 101–103.

2. Ch'i Yu-chang, ed., *Chia-tzu hsin shu chiao-shih* (Taipei: self-published, 1974), 945–958; Pan Ku, *Han shu* (Beijing: Chung-hua, 1962), *ch.* 56, p. 2523.

3. P'i Hsi-jui, *Ching-hsüeh li-shih* (Beijing: Chung-hua, 1958).

4. *Han shu, ch.* 6, pp. 171–172; chap. 88, pp. 3589, 3593; Ssu-ma Ch'ien, *Shih chi* (Beijing: Chung-hua, 1959), chap. 121, pp. 3118–3120.

5. Patricia Buckley Ebrey, *The Aristocratic Families of Early Imperial China* (Cambridge: Cambridge University Press, 1978), 31, 39–42, 58, 78, 84, 87, 96, 104–105, 116–119; Yen Chih-t'ui, *Family Instructions for the Yen Clan: Yen-shih chia-hsün,* trans. Teng Ssu-yü (Leiden: E. J. Brill, 1968), 3–8, 52–84; David McMullen, *State and Scholars in T'ang China* (Cambridge: Cambridge University Press, 1988).

6. Kenneth Ch'en, *The Chinese Transformation of Buddhism* (Princeton: Princeton University Press, 1973), 14–124.

7. *Kao-seng chuan* 2, *T* 2059.50.332a16–25; cited in T'ang Yung-t'ung, *Han Wei Liang-Chin Nan-Pei-Ch'ao fo-chiao shih* (Beijing: Chung-hua, 1955), 290.

8. Ōchō Enichi, *Chūgoku bukkyō no kenkyū,* vol. 1 (Kyoto: Hōzōkan, 1958), 346, 259–260, 359–360.

9. David Chappell, "Early Forebodings of the Death of Buddhism," *Numen* 27:1 (1980):122–154; Étienne Lamotte, *Histoire du bouddhisme indien: Des origines a l'ère śaka* (Louvain: Universitaire de Louvain, 1958), 210–222; Jean Przyluski, *La légende de l'empereur Açoka* (Paris: P. Geuthner, 1923), 161–185; Erik Zürcher, "Prince Moonlight: Messianism and Eschatology in Early Medieval Chinese Buddhism," *T'oung Pao* 68:1–3 (1982):1–59; Tamura Enchō, "Mappō shisō no keisei," *Shien* 63 (1954):65–92; Kumoi Shōzen, "Hōmetsu shisō no genryū," in Ōchō Enichi, ed., *Hokugi bukkyō no kenkyū* (Kyoto: Heirakuji, 1970), 287–300; Maruyama Takao, "Chūgoku ni okeru mappō shisō," in Nomura Yōshō, ed., *Hokkekyō shinkō no sho keitai* (Kyoto: Heirakuji, 1976), 377–425; Yamada Ryūjō, "Mappō shisō ni tsuite—Daijikkyō no seiritsu mondai," *Indogaku bukkyōgaku kenkyū* (hereafter *IBK*) 4.2 (1957):54–63; Yuki Reimon, "Shina bukkyō ni okeru mappō shisō no kōki," *Tōhō gakuhō* (Kyoto) 6 (1936):205–216; Sasaki Kyōgo, "Indo bukkyō ni okeru shō zō niji no shisō ni tsuite," *Ōtani gakuhō* 37:1 (1957):83–84; Hashizume Kanshū, "Mappō shisō ni kansuru yuin," *IBK* 17.2 (1969):134–135; Kimura Nichiki, "Daijō kyōten ni arawareta mappō shisō no nijūsō," *IBK* 11.1 (1963):130–131.

10. Frank Reynolds, "The Two Wheels of the Dhamma: A Study of Early Buddhism," in Bardwell L. Smith, ed., *The Two Wheels of Dhamma,* AAR Studies in Religion, no. 3 (Chambersburg, Pennsylvania: American Academy of Religion, 1972), 15.

11. See, for example, Mrs. Rhys Davids, trans., *The Book of Kindred Sayings (saṃyuttanikāya) or grouped suttas,* vol. 2, assisted by F. H. Woodward (London: Oxford University Press for the Pali Text Society, Translation series vol. 10,

1922), 21; Leon Feer, ed., *The Saṃyuttanikāya of the Suttapiṭaka,* vol. 2 (London: H. Froude, 1884–1904), 25; E. B. Cowell, ed., *The Divyāvadāna* (Cambridge: Cambridge University Press, 1886), 27, 100, 486.

12. Kumoi Shōzen, "Hōmetsu shisō," pp. 290–292; Lamotte, *Histoire du bouddhisme indien,* pp. 217–222; Przyluski, *La légende de l'empereur Açoka,* pp. 161–185.

13. Lamotte, *Histoire du bouddhisme indien,* pp. 218–220.

14. Ōchō, *Chūgoku bukkyō no kenkyū,* vol. 1, pp. 256–289.

15. Takao Giken, "Mappō shisō to shoka no taido," *Shina bukkyō shigaku* 1:1 (1937):1–20, 1:3 (1937):47–70.

16. Ibid., 1:1 (1937):6, 8, 9–11; 1:3 (1937):47–50, 67–70; Maruyama, "Chūgoku ni okeru mappō shisō," pp. 377–425. This fact was particularly striking in the case of Chih-i, whose teacher Hui-ssu, a noted advocate of meditation and religious discipline, believed that the world had entered the Final Age of Dharma *(mo-fa)* and described events in terms of the eclipse of the Buddhist religion. Convinced of the corruption of the Saṃgha of his day, he vowed to make a copy of the *Mahāprajñāpāramitā-sūtra* in gold letters and store it in a gem-encrusted box to preserve the true teaching. This vow became the prototype for all those who sought to carve the Buddhist canon in stone to preserve it in anticipation of the coming of the future Buddha Maitreya. See Tsukamoto Zenryū, "Sekikyō unkyoji to sekikoku daizōkyō," *Tōhō gakuhō* (Kyoto) 5 supplement (1938):1–245; Michihata Ryōshū, *Chūgoku bukkyō shi* (Kyoto: Hōzōkan, 1944), 102–106. His student Chih-i, by contrast, systematically ignored the idea of *mo-fa,* and in his commentaries on works that mentioned the end of the dharma he deliberately distorted the sense of the relevant passages to avoid any mention of the doctrine.

17. Hori Kentoku, *Kaisetsu saiikiki* (Tokyo: Kokusho Kankōkai, 1970), 136–139.

18. Yabuki Keiki, *Sangai-kyō no kenkyū* (Tokyo: Iwanami, 1927), 547.

19. Takao, "Mappō," 1:1 (1937):12–16.

20. Ibid., 1:1 (1937):15, *Hsü kao-seng chuan* 20, *T* 2060.50.596a23–26ff.

21. On the shared historical background and beliefs of these two sects, see Tsukamoto Zenryū, "Shinkō no Sangai-kyōdan to mujinzō ni tsuite," in *Chūgoku chūsei bukkyō shi ronkō* (Tokyo: Daitō, 1975), 193–194; idem, *Tō chūki no Jōdokyō* (Kyoto: Hōzōkan, 1975), 71–77; idem, *Chūgoku Jōdokyō shi kenkyū* (Tokyo: Daitō, 1975), 134–175; idem, "Sangai-kyō shiryō zakki," in *Chūgoku chūsei bukkyō,* pp. 144–146; Yabuki, *Sangai-kyō no kenkyū,* pp. 203, 535–578; Tajima Tokuon, "Reiji sakuhō to sangaikyū to no kankei," *Taishō gakuhō* 30–31 (1940):188–199; Michihata Ryōshū, "Dōshaku zenshi to Sangai-kyō," *Ōtani gakuhō* 15:1 (1934):24–49; Yagi Kōkei, "Eshin kyōgaku ni okeru Sangai-kyō no kōsatsu," *Shina bukkyō shigaku* 6:2 (1942):38–58, 7:2 (1943):10–17; Tokiwa Daijō, "Sangai-kyō no botai toshite no Hōzanji," *Shūkyō kenkyū* 4:1 (1928):36–37.

22. Yabuki, *Sangai-kyō no kenkyū,* pp. 547–563.

23. Ibid., p. 284.

24. See, for example, *Tui-ken ch'i-hsing fa,* Yabuki, *Sangai-kyō no kenkyū, betsu hen* (hereafter *betsu hen*), pp. 131.12–.13, 139.13; *P'u-fa ssu fo,* ibid., pp. 201–206. On the identity of the "eight buddhadharmas" and the idea of universal buddhahood in the writings of the Three Stages sect, see Kimura Kiyotaka, "Chigon Hōzō to Sangai-kyō," *IBK* 27.1 (1978):102.

25. *San-chieh fo-fa,* Yabuki, *betsu hen,* pp. 257.1–.2; 333.14–334.2; *Tui-ken ch'i-hsing fa,* ibid., pp. 129.11–130.4; 133.10–.12; 149.11–150.2.
26. Ōtani Shōshin, "Sangai bōzenshi gyōjō shimatsu ni tsuite," in *Shigaku ronsō* no. 7, Keijō Teikoku Daigaku Bungakkai Ronsan (Tokyo: Iwanami, 1938), 247–302.
27. Ōtani, "Sangai bōzenshi," p. 284.21–.24.
28. *Tui-ken ch'i-hsing fa,* Yabuki, *betsu hen,* pp. 111.15–112.1, 113.8, 114.14–115.56.
29. Makita Tairyō, *Gikyō kenkyū* (Kyoto: Kyōto Daigaku Jinbun Kagaku Kenkyūsho, 1976), 310–313.
30. S. J. Tambiah, *Buddhism and the Spirit Cults in North-east Thailand* (Cambridge: Cambridge University Press, 1970), 141–149.
31. *Hsiang-fa chüeh-i ching, T* 2870.85.1336a24–26, a29–b2.
32. Ibid., *T* 2870.85.1336a27–29, b2–15.
33. Ibid., *T* 2870.85.1336b19–24, 1337a27–b1. The biography of the anonymous master of the sect also includes a denunciation of those who would practice monastic discipline and meditation in the age of the terminal dharma. See Ōtani, "Sangai bōzenshi," pp. 295.203–296.205.
34. *Tui-ken ch'i-hsing fa,* Yabuki, *betsu hen,* pp. 121.13–124.9.
35. Ōtani, "Sangai bōzenshi," p. 289.103.
36. Jacques Gernet, *Les aspects économiques du bouddhisme dans la société chinoise du Ve aux Xe siècle* (Paris: École Française d'Extrême-Orient, 1956), 205–212; James Bert Hubbard, "Salvation in the Final Period of the Dharma: The Inexhaustible Storehouse of the San-chieh-chiao" (Ph.D. diss., University of Wisconsin, 1986).
37. *Tui-ken ch'i-hsing fa,* Yabuki, *betsu hen,* pp. 125.4–.9.
38. For example, a discussion of "taking refuge in the monastic order" during the third age divided the monks into five types, only one of which was "those who shave their heads and wear the *kaṣāya,*" i.e., officially ordained monks (*Tui-ken ch'i-hsing fa,* Yabuki, *betsu hen,* p. 115.9–.10). One of the five dichotomies in a discussion of "universal conduct" was that between "those who have left the world" and "those who remain in the world." The text stipulates that regardless of whether or not a man has left the world to become a monk, he should think of himself as in the world, i.e., as a layman. In contrast, he should look upon all others, regardless of their status, as if they had left the world (ibid., pp. 130.14–131.1). One account of the world after the disappearance of the dharma says, "Creatures of the dullest faculties will exhort all to conversion and the management of the affairs of the monastic order; together with those who have left the household they will be preceptors *(ho-shang)* and ācāryas" (*San-chieh fo-fa,* Yabuki, *betsu hen,* p. 264.4–.5). Another passage says, "After the one thousand years during which the dharma is brilliant, the dharma of the Four Noble Truths will be extinguished, and the *kaṣāyas* will turn white and no longer take the color of the dye" (ibid., p. 74.2–.3). Since the saffron dye of the monks' robes distinguished them from the white-clothed laity, white *kaṣāyas* would mark the disappearance of a separate monastic order.
39. Ōtani, "Sangai bōzenshi," pp. 290.122–291.131.
40. Ibid., pp. 289.92, 291.131, 292.144, 296.212.
41. *San-chieh fo-fa,* Yabuki, *betsu hen,* p. 364.1–.5.
42. Ōtani, "Sangai bōzenshi," p. 292.141–.144.

43. Ibid., p. 287.70–.74.

44. Ibid., p. 295.192–.196. This passage does not appear in the version of the *Fo-tsang ching* in the *Taishō* edition of the *Tripiṭaka.*

45. *Hsü kao-seng chuan* 16, *T* 2060.50.560a9–10.

46. *Hsin-hsing i-wen,* Yabuki, *betsu hen,* p. 7.8–.10.

47. Tsukamoto, *Chūgoku chūsei bukkyō,* pp. 235–236.

48. *Tui-ken ch'i-hsing fa,* Yabuki, *betsu hen,* pp. 133.10–.12, 149.11–150.2.

49. Ibid., p. 115.6–.9.

50. *Ta-pan-nieh-p'an ching* 18, *T* 374.12.472b7–10.

51. *San-chieh fo-fa,* Yabuki, *betsu hen,* pp. 266.14–267.4.

52. Ibid., p. 75.4–.8; citing *Ta-pan-nieh-p'an ching* 33, *T* 374.12.561c10–13.

53. *San-chieh fo-fa,* Yabuki, *betsu hen,* pp. 263.14, 265.11–.13.

54. Ōtani, "Sangai bōzenshi," p. 300.269–.272.

55. *Tui-ken ch'i-hsing fa,* Yabuki, *betsu hen,* p. 132.13–.15.

56. Ibid., pp. 115.15–116.2.

57. Ibid., pp. 124.9–125.3.

58. Ōtani, "Sangai bōzenshi," p. 297.220–.223. "Died like wild beasts" may refer to dying in silence, or it could refer to the sect's practice of exposing corpses in the wild to allow animals to feed on them—in imitation of the Jātaka tale of the Buddha and the hungry tigers—and then retrieving the bones for burial.

59. Ōtani, "Sangai bōzenshi," p. 302.309.

60. Ibid., p. 301.284–.285.

61. Ibid., p. 290.111–.121.

62. Ibid., p. 298.237–.239. This passage is framed by two stories on the value of silence. One tells of a man who hid a pearl in his wife's mouth to keep it from a thief, but the thief hid under the bed, tricked the wife into speaking, and thus gained the pearl. The second tells of a disciple who studied the sūtras and *Abhidharma* for years without attaining enlightenment. He was about to ask the master for help, and in the moment of silence before speaking he suddenly perceived the truth.

63. *Fo-tsang ching* 1, *T* 653.15.789a12, 24.

64. Ōtani, "Sangai bōzenshi," p. 296.212–.213.

65. Ibid., p. 285.40–.43.

66. *Shih-men tzu-ching lu* 1, *T* 2083.51.806b3–23.

67. Yabuki, *Sangai-kyō no kenkyū,* pp. 547–582.

68. Ibid., p. 559, citing the *Ch'un i lun.*

69. *Tui-ken ch'i-hsing fa,* Yabuki, *betsu hen,* pp. 116.13, 134.10–135.3, 257.7ff.

70. Kaneko Hidetoshi, "Sangai-kyō no fuse kan," *Bukkyō shigaku* 7:4 (1959): 46–50.

71. Yabuki, "Sangai-kyō," *Shisō* 60 (1926):49–53.

72. Kenneth Ch'en, *Buddhism in China: A Historical Survey* (Princeton: Princeton University Press, 1964), 300.

73. *Hsiang-fa chüeh-i ching,* *T* 2870.85.1337c27–1338a2; 1338a10–20.

74. *Te-hu chang-che ching* 2, *T* 545.14.849b20–24.

75. Ōchō, *Chūgoku bukkyō no kenkyū,* 1:377–379.

76. *Hsin-hsing i-wen,* Yabuki, *betsu hen,* p. 7.11.

77. *San-chieh fo-fa,* ibid., pp. 273.7–283.3.

78. Ibid., p. 279.2–.9.

79. Ibid., pp. 283.1–285.1.

80. Yabuki, *Sangai-kyō no kenkyū,* pp. 62–63; Tsukamoto, *Chūgoku chūsei bukkyō,* p. 198.

81. Yabuki, "Sangai-kyō," p. 53.

82. The passage on "drawing in the head" states, "In the household you will not be head or take a government office . . . ; after leaving the household you will not be a master of men or a master of the dharma." See *Tui-ken ch'i-hsing fa,* Yabuki, *betsu hen,* p. 124.12–.14. Clearly neither of these strictures applied to rulers, who were neither simple "householders" nor monks.

83. Kaneko, "Fuse kan," p. 49.

84. Stanley Weinstein, "Imperial Patronage in the Formation of T'ang Buddhism," in Arthur F. Wright and Denis Twitchett, eds., *Perspectives on the T'ang* (New Haven: Yale University, 1973), 265–267; idem, *Buddhism under the T'ang* (Cambridge: Cambridge University Press, 1987), 5–37.

85. Ch'en Yin-k'e, "Wu-chao yü fo-chiao," in *Ch'en Yin-k'e Hsien-sheng lun chi* (Taipei: Chung-yang Yen-chiu-yüan Li-shih Yü-yen Yen-chiu-so, 1971), 306–307. For the argument that T'ai-tsung was not an active patron of the Buddhist Order, see also Arthur F. Wright, "T'ang T'ai-tsung and Buddhism," in *Perspectives on the T'ang,* pp. 247, 252–256, 258–263.

86. Antonino Forte, *Political Propaganda and Ideology in China at the End of the Seventh Century* (Naples: Istituto Universitario Orientale, 1976).

87. S. J. Tambiah, *World Conqueror and World Renouncer* (Cambridge: Cambridge University Press, 1976), 40.

88. Forte, *Political Propaganda,* p. 130.

89. Ibid., pp. 166–167.

90. Weinstein, *Buddhism under the T'ang,* pp. 51–57.

91. Yabuki, *Sangai-kyō no kenkyū,* p. 104.

92. Ibid., pp. 93–94.

93. E. Zürcher, "Perspectives in the Study of Chinese Buddhism," *Journal of the Royal Asiatic Society* (1982):163–164.

GLOSSARY

Ch'ang-an 長安
ch'ang ch'i shih 常乞食
chen shen 真身
ch'eng-hsiang 丞相
Chi-tsang 吉藏
Chia I 賈宜
Chih-i 智顗
Chin-kuang-ming ching 金光明經
ching 經
ching[a] 徑
Ching-ying Hui-yüan 淨影慧遠
Fa-hsiang 法相
fang teng 方等
Fo-tsang ching 佛藏經
Han shu 漢書
Hsiao-tz'u 孝慈
hsieh chien 邪見
Hsin-hsing 信行
Hsü kao-seng chuan 續高僧傳
Hsüan-tsang 玄奘
Hua-tu ssu 華度寺
Hua-yen 華嚴
Huai-kan 懷感
i 藝
jen o 任惡
Jen-wang ching 仁王經

Kao-seng chuan 高僧傳
K'uei-chi 窺基
Kung-sun Hung 公孫弘
Liu Hsin 劉歆
Lü tsung 律宗
mo-fa 末法
P'ei Hsüan-cheng 悲玄證
pieh 別
po-shih 博士
p'o chieh p'o chien 破戒破見
pu ch'ing p'u-sa 不輕菩薩
pu ch'ing shuo fa 不清說法
p'u 普
San-chieh fo-fa 三階佛法
San-chieh fo-fa mi-chi 三階佛法密記
Shan-hsing 善行
sheng mang 生盲
su t'ou 縮頭
Ta Chou k'an-ting chung-ching mu-lu 大周刊定衆經目錄
Ta-pan-nieh-p'an ching 大般涅槃經
Ta-yün ching 大雲經
Tao-hsüan 道宣
Te-hu chang-che ching 德護長者經
tien-tao 顛倒
T'ien-t'ai 天台
Tui-ken ch'i-hsing fa 對根起行法
Tung Chung-shu 董仲舒
wu chin tsang 無盡藏
wu-chung pu-chiu 五種不救
Wu-liang-shou ching 無量壽經
Yao Hsing 姚興
ying shen 應身

The Relativity of the Concept of Orthodoxy in Chinese Buddhism: Chih-sheng's Indictment of Shih-li and the Proscription of the *Dharma Mirror Sūtra*

ANTONINO FORTE

In 712 C.E., the master Shih-li (d.u.) of the Three Stages sect (San-chieh chiao) had the *Fo-shuo shih so-fan-che yü-ch'ieh fa-ching ching* (Book Spoken by the Buddha on the Yoga Dharma Mirror That Exposes Transgressors; hereafter *Dharma Mirror Sūtra*) included in the official canon of Buddhist works. While the scripture itself subsequently disappeared, a fragmentary manuscript was discovered at Tun-huang.[1] Although approximately the first half of the manuscript (including the preface; see below) is now lost, at the end of the extant fragment is a colophon that is important for two reasons. First, it provides the names of, and some basic information about, the translators—of whom Shih-li was one. Second, and most important, this colophon proves that this work was considered an authentic sūtra and was included in the *Tripiṭaka* in 712, although all later scriptural catalogues list the text as apocryphal. Another reason for the importance of the colophon is that it details the names, offices, and noble and honorary titles of all ten members of the imperial commission that was charged in the same year to examine the work carefully and fix the text that would be entered into the canon. All but one of these were scholars from the imperial College for the Glorification of Literature (Chao-wen kuan), and they included such famous personages as the poet Shen Ch'üan-ch'i (656?–714), the calligrapher and painter Hsüeh Chi (649–713), and the statesman Ts'ui Shih (671–713), who was chief minister at the time.[2] Ts'ui Shih and Hsüeh Chi, himself also a former chief minister, were to commit suicide the following year (713) after their participation in a failed plot, instigated by the political faction headed by Princess T'ai-p'ing, to poison Emperor Hsüan-tsung (r. 712–756).[3]

The relations between this group of ten eminent scholars and the Three Stages sect can be surmised also by the fact that, in 706, one of them, Hsüeh Chi, had written the calligraphy for a cenotaph of Hsin-hsing (540–594), the founder of that school. The text itself was written sometime before 688 by Li Chen (d. 688), prince of Yüeh and eighth son of Emperor T'ai-tsung, who in that year had committed suicide following his own botched coup attempt against the Empress Wu (r. 690–705).[4]

In that same year of 712, this imperial commission was also enjoined to examine and settle the text of seven works, the Sanskrit originals of which had been brought to China from Kashmir by the Tantric master Manicintana (Pao-ssu-wei; d. 721).[5]

Although the *Dharma Mirror Sūtra* was accorded canonical status by the commission, eighteen years later it was listed among the apocrypha in the *K'ai-yüan shih-chiao lu,* published in 730. The compiler of this catalogue, Chih-sheng (d.u.), did not limit himself to labeling the text apocryphal; he also appended a rather lengthy note, which is interesting not only for the information it gives on the scripture, but also because it is a good example of the relativity of the Chinese conceptions of "orthodox" and "apocryphal," as the definitions adapt to the vicissitudes of time and the vagaries of politics. In the case of this text, which was earlier assumed to be an authentic Indian scripture, we shall see how such traditional criteria as the presumed existence of an original Sanskrit manuscript—no matter how suspect that evidence might have been—were nonetheless accepted by the 730 catalogue as a valid means of certifying authenticity.

Chih-sheng is well reputed as a meticulous and reliable bibliographer and, accordingly, his statements concerning the *Dharma Mirror Sūtra* might be assumed to be credible. But there is something in Chih-sheng's attitude toward the text that makes us cautious and obliges us to examine the facts with attentive eyes—particularly Chih-sheng's surprising display of acrimony and bitterness toward Shih-li. For example, when speaking of Shih-li's misfortunes, he remarks with evident satisfaction: "How could it be that Shang-t'ien [Supreme Heaven] would shield this man from punishment? Moreover, approaching the time of his end, his paunch became swollen like a jar." Why did Chih-sheng have such a lack of human pity and kindness for a man who was either about to, or had already, died? The answer is simple: Shih-li was a heretic of the Three Stages sect and had published an apocryphal work that was a menace to the accepted orthodoxy of his time; hence he was an evil person who had to be exposed and for whom no mercy could be permitted. It is Chih-sheng's attitude toward the heretic Shih-li that must make us wary about his adjudication of this text. We must not forget that Chih-sheng's standards of objectivity, no matter how high they may have been, were nonetheless subordinated to the demands of orthodoxy as defined at that historical moment; even with the best of intentions, the two forces would often have been irreconcilable. At the same time, if

Chih-sheng's assertions concerning Shih-li prove to be suspect, this may suggest a certain reliability in some of Shih-li's statements in the preface to this sūtra—which, unfortunately is no longer extant, but which Chih-sheng himself quotes in his annotation.

I will first give a complete rendering of Chih-sheng's statements concerning the *Dharma Mirror Sūtra* and Shih-li, followed by a discussion of the implications of those statements. Problems concerning the formation and content of the suspect sūtra are, unfortunately, beyond the scope of this chapter. Instead, I will attempt to detail both Chih-sheng's attitude toward the San-chieh chiao heresy and the limits of his objectivity. This will also allow us to make some remarks on a field and period that are difficult to comprehend because of the harsh censorship imposed during Hsüan-tsung's reign.

Yü-ch'ieh fa-ching ching, in two *chüan.*

[Interlinear note:] Alternatively, in one *chüan;* it has, besides, a preface containing false statements *(wei-hsü).*

The above work has been made by combining the earlier text *(ch'ien-wen)* of the *Hsiang-fa chüeh-i ching* [Book of Resolving Doubts During the Semblance Dharma Age, which had been included] in the old list of apocrypha *(chiu wei-lu),* with the addition of two other *p'in* (*parivarta;* chapters). The first [of these added chapters] is the *Fo lin-nieh-p'an wei A-nan shuo fa-chu-mieh p'in* [Chapter on the Subsistence and Disappearance of the Dharma, Spoken to Ānanda by the Buddha (at the Time of His) Approaching Nirvāṇa]; this chapter, in fact, is the *Fo lin-nieh-p'an chi fa-chu ching* [Sūtra Recording the Subsistence of the Dharma (Spoken by the Buddha at the Time of His) Approaching Nirvāṇa],[6] translated by the dharma master [Hsüan]-tsang, which, [after having undergone] changes, alterations, additions, and deletions, was put at the beginning [of the text under consideration]. The next [added chapter] is the *Ti-tsang p'u-sa tsan-t'an fa-shen kuan-hsing p'in* [Chapter on the Contemplation Practice of Kṣitigarbha Bodhisattva Lauding the Dharmakāya]. The final [chapter] is the *Ch'ang-shih p'u-sa so-wen p'in* [Chapter on the Questions of the Bodhisattva Ch'ang-shih]; this is the chapter that coincides with the old book [the *Hsiang-fa chüeh-i ching*]. These texts were simply ordered one after another according to their persuasiveness, without any connection between one another.

In the first year of Ching-lung (5 October 707–27 January 708), [this scripture] was spuriously fabricated by Shih-li, a monk of the Three Stages [sect]. In his preface *(hsü),* he falsely states: "The Trepiṭaka Bodhiruci (572–727 [sic]),[7] the Trepiṭaka Manicintana (d. 721), and others have jointly translated it at Ch'ung-fu Monastery." Shih-li claimed that there was a Sanskrit manuscript *(fan-chia,* Skt. *pothī),*[8] but [Bodhi]ruci has neither seen nor heard of it.

Since the old compilation [of the *Hsiang-fa chüeh-i ching*] was included among the apocrypha, it was reworked in the hope that it would gain remission from the list of doubtful [works]. [Thus] falsity has been compounded by more falsity, and the deceptions are even more numerous. One can know this just by looking at [the text], and I need not bother to relate this in detail.

[Interlinear note: I, Chih-sheng,] compiler of the *Catalogue,* say: Previously, I asked the Trepiṭaka [Bodhi]ruci in person about this matter. The Trepiṭaka said with his own mouth,[9] "My frontier [region of southern India] has never had a Sanskrit text [of this sūtra], nor have I ever translated this work." The Trepiṭaka's disciple, Prajñāgupta (Po-jo-ch'iu-to),[10] who is intelligent, openminded, and sagacious, is completely familiar with these facts.

Being afraid that, with the passage of time, the error could confound the truth, I here have referred to and explained clearly [all this matter] in order to warn posterity.

As for that monk Shih-li, since [he engaged in] petty disputes and polemics, the Saintly Person [i.e., the Emperor] personally considered [the matter] and, through an ad hoc order *(t'eh-ling),*[11] returned him to secular status *(huan-su).* How could it be that Shang-t'ien [Supreme Heaven] would shield this man from punishment? Moreover, approaching the time of his end, his paunch became swollen like a jar; can one not be awestruck that such ominous portents promptly appeared?[12]

As a bibliographical cataloguer whose duty was to distinguish between authentic and spurious texts, Chih-sheng was the spokesman and guarantor of the proclaimed orthodoxy of his time. Indeed, it is clear from this account that the constraints of the status quo compelled Chih-sheng to place the *Dharma Mirror Sūtra* among the list of prohibited works. Accordingly, Chih-sheng adopts all possible means in order to support this judgment. These consisted primarily of (1) bibliographical proofs, (2) rejection of the claims made by Shih-li in his preface, and (3) imperial and celestial sanctions, which need not concern us here.

In his bibliographical proofs, Chih-sheng tries to show that the *Dharma Mirror Sūtra* cannot be an original translation because it contains both sections from the apocryphal *Hsiang-fa chüeh-i ching,* which had been condemned earlier, as well as parts of previously translated sūtras that had been cleverly adapted and manipulated for inclusion in this text. Certainly Chih-sheng did not invent all this, and we have no choice but to admit the truth of his observations and conclusions. However, behind such an apparently simple picture there is an extremely complex reality that can only be adumbrated here. His first piece of evidence, for example, is not faultless because the *Hsiang-fa chüeh-i ching* had not always been considered an apocryphal work. Second, Chih-sheng's appeal to the adaptation of previously translated works as proof of the text's spuriousness could be applied with equal validity to works such as the *Ratnakūṭa-sūtra* (Heap of Jewels Sūtra), which all cataloguers regarded as canonical. In addition, the insertion of spurious passages in a sūtra could have taken place before the translation itself had been done, as is probably the case with an interpolation added in 693 to the *Ratnamegha-sūtra* (Precious Clouds Sūtra).[13]

Chih-sheng's bibliographical proofs thus ran the risk of convincing nobody. He was probably well aware of this himself, since he realized that the author of this apocryphal text had adopted all the precautions necessary to ensure that the text would be considered an authentic translation from Sanskrit. In his preface, Shih-li goes so far as to claim that an original Sanskrit recension was extant and that it was that very text which was translated into Chinese with the participation of Bodhiruci and Manicintana. Moreover, the Tun-huang colophon makes clear that the certifier of the existence of the Sanskrit text was the Trepiṭaka Śrīmata (d.u.) (see below). In this wise, Shih-li had furnished the two elements most fundamental for verifying the authenticity of a foreign Buddhist work: the existence of a Sanskrit original, and the participation in the translation work of one or more learned masters from abroad.

I need not dwell on the importance assumed by a Sanskrit text as evidence for the authenticity of a translation. For centuries, the Chinese cultivated the illusion that the existence or absence of a corresponding Sanskrit text was sufficient to establish whether a specific work written in Chinese was authentic or apocryphal. Although convenient heuristically for rejecting many would-be sūtras produced in China—as, for example, in the 705 condemnation of the *Lao-tzu hua-hu ching* (Book of Lao-tzu Converting the Barbarians)[14]—such a criterion would have been of little help in determining falsifications made outside China. For this reason, the participation of foreign *Tripiṭaka* masters would have been essential, for only they would know whether a text was current outside of China and therefore "canonical." Hence it can be said with little exaggeration that these foreign teachers symbolized orthodoxy for the Chinese—to the point that they were considered the guarantors, if not the very source, of translated texts. It is for this reason that translated texts were attributed to such foreign Trepiṭakas, and certainly not because they had actually translated anything, for, as is well known, their often inadequate knowledge of the Chinese language, especially in the early years of their tenures in China, would not have permitted them to engage in any but a modicum of translation activities.

Obviously, not all the Trepiṭakas who came to China were privileged to represent the orthodoxy. One may readily assume that the official clergy and those who wielded political power would have had their own ideas on these matters and would have chosen as representative the monk most suitable to them from among the available stock. The case of Śrīmata shows quite clearly that the fortunes of the Trepiṭakas in China were subject to the whims of the politicians. Śrīmata seems to have had his fleeting moment of glory in 707–708. His name would appear today among the Trepiṭakas found in all the catalogues of Buddhist works if the *Dharma Mirror Sūtra,* which he certified, had continued to be included among the canonical works rather than being blacklisted in 730 by the *K'ai-yüan lu.*

Some of the *Tripiṭaka* masters were so famous throughout the Buddhist world that the court expressly invited them to China. This was the case with Bodhiruci, who was first invited to T'ang in 683. When he arrived at last in Lo-yang in 693, he was considered the representative of the orthodoxy, and whatever was sanctioned by him was not subject to suspicion. From the beginning of his stay, however, Bodhiruci was inextricably associated with the contemporary political leadership—so much so, in fact, that in many ways he was a living symbol of a conscientiously followed political line that aimed to make China a privileged place for Buddhism. Wu Chao (regent 684–690, r. 690–705), the woman then at the pinnacle of this leadership hierarchy, was the one to whom Bodhiruci was beholden for his livelihood and status; thus he would hardly have been a disinterested adjudicator of ecclesiastical controversies. It is easily surmised that Bodhiruci's initial invitation to come to China was issued by Wu Chao; hence Bodhiruci's destiny in China would have coincided closely with that of the Chou dynasty (690–705) and the political ideals represented by it. Bodhiruci was willing to commit the most unprejudiced actions in order to support Buddhism and the contemporary political group that had tied its fortunes to the religion. Given this set of circumstances, it would not be surprising if, around 707, he felt compelled to certify the authenticity of a work like the *Dharma Mirror Sūtra,* if that work were strongly supported by the government.

The same can be said for Manicintana. Although apparently of marginal influence in the contemporary Buddhist scene, he was undoubtedly the most important Tantric master of his time in China. I have discussed his activities and those of his group elsewhere.[15] What is important in the present context is that, by naming Bodhiruci and Manicintana in his preface, Shih-li intended to provide another irrefutable piece of evidence proving the authenticity of the *Dharma Mirror Sūtra;* and one can hardly imagine that Shih-li would have named these two eminent masters without their mutual consent.

Thus, it is not surprising that the *Dharma Mirror Sūtra* was included in the canon, as is conclusively demonstrated by the testimony of the Tun-huang colophon.[16] This colophon allows us to understand the difficulty faced by Chih-sheng in using bibliographical evidence to disprove the authenticity of the work. In actual fact, it was thanks to such evidence that the work had been considered canonical since 712; and because of these proofs, vague assertions to the contrary by Chih-sheng would not have been sufficient to show the apocryphal nature of the text. This is the reason for Chih-sheng's vehement attacks on Shih-li's preface—that is to say, he had to refute the very things that most contributed to proving the authenticity of this work: the existence of a Sanskrit original, and the participation of Bodhiruci and Manicintana in its translation.

Concerning the second point, Chih-sheng was also compelled to reject any role for Bodhiruci and Manicintana in the translation of the text, because he could not accept them as guarantors of the orthodoxy if he admitted that they had any connection with Shih-li and his associates.

Chih-sheng must have faced the same dilemma with Śrīmata, the Trepiṭaka whom the colophon states had certified the *Dharma Mirror Sūtra.* It must have seemed easiest to Chih-sheng to resolve this particular problem simply by ignoring Śrīmata throughout his *Catalogue* and by systematically eliminating all traces of him from the canon. The way in which Chih-sheng treats the question of the *Amoghapāśadhāraṇī-sūtra (Pu-k'ung-ch'üan-so t'o-lo-ni ching)*[17] is instructive in this regard. This work, consisting of seventeen chapters *(p'in),* was originally certified by Bodhiruci and included in the canon in 700. It continued to be attributed to Bodhiruci until 730, when Chih-sheng claimed that it was from the hand of Li Wu-ch'an (d.u.). This was done to expunge from the canon its final chapter which, in reality, had been translated by Śrīmata. Conveniently for Chih-sheng, this also concealed any evidence of collusion between Bodhiruci and Śrīmata—which would in turn have implied collusion between Bodhiruci and Shih-li himself.[18]

This effacement of Śrīmata was probably a fairly easy task for Chih-sheng, because apparently there were few traces of Śrīmata's activities. But this was not the case with Bodhiruci and Manicintana. How, then, could Chih-sheng attack the attributions made by Shih-li in his preface? Although he stated categorically that Shih-li's words were false, Chih-sheng knew that without substantiating evidence such a statement would not be irrefutable. Since Manicintana had died in 721, it was impossible to have him bear direct witness, but this was possible with Bodhiruci, who had been living in Ch'ung-fu ssu, the same monastery in Ch'ang-an where Chih-sheng resided, until three years before the publication of the *K'ai-yüan lu,* and who was still alive at the time of the suppression of the Three Stages sect in 725. According to Chih-sheng's account, Bodhiruci declared not only that he had had nothing whatsoever to do with the translation of the text, but also that he did not even know of a Sanskrit text of the *Dharma Mirror Sūtra.* Here, finally, was an unimpeachable witness to the mendacity of Shih-li's preface. However, since Bodhiruci had died in 727 and the catalogue was not published until 730, Chih-sheng did not yet feel completely assured about the credibility of his proof. To circumvent any possible accusations that he might have fabricated Bodhiruci's words, Chih-sheng took recourse in the corroboration of Prajñāgupta, a living disciple of Bodhiruci, who, more than any other person, could attest to the veracity of his master's statements.

There is no point today in exploring the questions of whether Chih-sheng really questioned Bodhiruci on the subject of the *Dharma Mirror*

Sūtra and, if so, whether Bodhiruci answered the way he did because he had been forced to recant. What is important is that Chih-sheng's thesis of the falsity of Shih-li's preface—which claimed the participation of Bodhiruci and Manicintana in the publication of the *Dharma Mirror Sūtra* —and the consequent conclusion that these two masters had not been associated with Shih-li and the Three Stages sect, become very shaky when compared with the reality obtained from the *Dharma Mirror Sūtra* colophon (Stein no. 2423) and other Tun-huang colophons. These records tell us (1) that Shih-li was not only a collaborator of Manicintana but was also instrumental in having Manicintana's translations included in the canon;[19] and (2) that Śrīmata, the certifier of the *Dharma Mirror Sūtra,* collaborated with the eminent traveler and Vinaya Master I-ching (635–713) as well as with Manicintana,[20] and that his translation of the seventeenth chapter of the *Amoghapāśadhāraṇī-sūtra* had also been validated and signed by Bodhiruci in 700. It would therefore be no surprise if Manicintana and Bodhiruci had participated in some way in the publication of the *Dharma Mirror Sūtra,* as Shih-li stated in his preface.

This does not mean, obviously, that the sūtra has then to be considered authentic. Because I have chosen not to discuss the content of the text, we are able to grasp with greater clarity the relativity of the concept of an "apocryphal work" in the Chinese context. In the case of the *Dharma Mirror Sūtra,* regardless of whether the text was fabricated inside or outside of China, directly in the Chinese language or previously in Sanskrit, the fact that, thanks to Shih-li, it was included in the canon on 8 July 712 (a little more than a month before Jui-tsung abdicated in favor of Hsüan-tsung), tells us only that Shih-li had become very influential at the time. Since he was a powerful monk, it is only normal that Manicintana and Bodhiruci, two masters of the *Tripiṭaka* who had come to China to contribute to the construction of the Buddhist state, would have thought it advisable to collaborate with him. Far from rejecting their collusion with Shih-li, as Chih-sheng tried so hard to do, we must accept it as a matter of fact and, in future research, try instead to understand why Shih-li and his sect had become so influential in that era.

We have seen that Hsüeh Chi and Ts'ui Shih, two of the members of the imperial commission charged with determining the authenticity both of Manicintana's translations and the *Dharma Mirror Sūtra,* were part of a conspiracy to poison Hsüan-tsung (who had become emperor on 8 September 712), and that they committed suicide after their failure. If Shih-li was closely associated with certain members of that conspiracy, it would not be surprising for Hsüan-tsung to take action against Shih-li and his sect once he had consolidated his power.

In conclusion, I think it is clear that Chih-sheng approached the *Dharma Mirror Sūtra* with two entirely different purposes in mind. On the one hand, Chih-sheng had to ensure that Manicintana and Bodhiruci would be free from any taint of heresy; accordingly, when writing of their activities, he had to avoid making any allusions to equivocal facts or to such personages as Shih-li, with whom they might have been too intimately associated. On the other hand, he also had to condemn Shih-li in no uncertain terms. The resulting tableau is falsified and purposely retouched in order to blur the much more complex reality of the years between the T'ang restoration in 705 and Hsüan-tsung's assumption of power in September of 712.

NOTES

1. *Fo-shuo shih so-fan-che yü-ch'ieh fa-ching ching,* Stein no. 2423; reprinted in *T* 2896.85.1416–1422.

2. This constitutes a supplement to the 708 listing of the literary establishment at the court, as used by Stephen Owen, *The Poetry of the Early T'ang* (New Haven: Yale University Press, 1977), 231–233.

3. See Denis Twitchett, *The Cambridge History of China* (Cambridge: Cambridge University Press, 1979), vol. 3, pt. 1:344–345.

4. On Li Chen, see *Chiu T'ang shu* 76.2661–2664; *Hsin T'ang shu* 80.3575–3577; *Ch'üan T'ang shih* 6.66; Chi Yu-kung (d. ca. 1161), *T'ang-shih chi-shih* (Peking: Chung-hua shu-chü, 1965), 3.29. Li Chen's tomb was excavated and a stele concerning him discovered; see *Wen-wu* 10 (1977):41–49. My friend Tonami Mamoru also brought to my attention that *Sung-shih* 491.14135 contains an interesting notice on a work by Li Chen brought to China from Japan by the monk Chōnen (938–1016).

5. This is shown by another translation colophon from Tun-huang (Stein no. 2926). I have studied and translated the two colophons in my article on Manicintana; the few references I have found to Shih-li are also found in that study. See Antonino Forte, "The Activities in China of the Tantric Master Manicintana (Pao-ssu-wei: ?–721 C.E.) from Kashmir and of his Northern Indian Collaborators," *East and West* 34 (1984):301–345.

6. *Fo lin-nieh-p'an chi fa-chu ching, T* 390.12.1112b–1113c.

7. I have rendered the Chinese term *san-tsang* as Trepiṭaka (Trepiṭakā in feminine gender) throughout this article, because it seems to me that this is the most solid Sanskrit form attested in epigraphy; see T. W. Rhys Davids, *Pali-English Dictionary* (London: Luzac and Co., 1966), 457b, s.v. *"piṭaka"*; Shizutani Masao, *Indo bukkyō himei mokuroku* (Catalogue of Indian Buddhist Inscriptions; Kyoto: Heirakuji shoten, 1979), nos. 572, 760, 1689 for Trepiṭaka, and nos. 530, 572, 1689 for Trepiṭakā. Another attested term is Tripiṭa (Tripiṭā for women). Franklin Edgerton (*Buddhist Hybrid Sanskrit Grammar and Dictionary,* vol. 2, *Dictionary* [New Haven: Yale University Press, 1953], 258a, s.v. "Tripiṭa") says that the term Tripiṭa means a monk or nun "who knows the three *piṭakas*"; a less common form is Tripiṭaka (ibid.). In Pali we find Tipeṭaka, Tipeṭakī, Tipeṭakin, Tepiṭaka, and Tipiṭaka-dhara. T. W. Rhys Davids says, "The knowledge of the three piṭakas as an accomplishment of the bhikkhu is stated in the term tepiṭaka, 'one who is familiar with the three piṭakas.' In Buddhist Sanskrit, we

find the term trepiṭaka in early inscriptions, . . . the term tripiṭaka in literary documents . . . as also tripiṭa . . . " (ibid.). See also Étienne Lamotte, *Le Traité de la grande vertu de sagesse*, vol. 2 (Louvain: Université de Louvain, Institut orientaliste, 1949), 879 n. 2, where some references are also given. It is possible that the form Tripiṭaka became more widespread in later times, but I prefer to use Trepiṭaka to distinguish it clearly from the use of the word *Tripiṭaka* to refer to the Buddhist canon. Concerning the Chinese usage, Chou Yi-liang ("Tantrism in China," *Harvard Journal of Asiatic Studies* 8 [1945]:257 n. 31) says that the earliest occurrence he was able to find of this title in Chinese was in the biography of Saṃghavarman, who arrived in China in 433 C.E. (see *T* 2059.50. 342b14, 19). I believe that Trepiṭaka was not a simple laudatory denomination; it is possible that it was the highest official title given to Buddhist doctors in the big Buddhist universities of India. This could account for the fact that the Chinese eagerly looked for such doctors to legitimate the orthodoxy of the works brought from foreign lands that were to be translated. Research is needed in this respect.

8. For this term, see *Hōbōgirin,* 2:120a.

9. At this point, the *Taishō* edition of the *K'ai-yüan shih-chiao lu* (*T* 2154.55. 672c12) gives the sign for a missing character; this is probably a mistake for the character *k'ou* (mouth), which appears in the parallel text of the *Chen-yüan hsin-ting shih-chiao mu-lu* 28, *T* 2157.55.1016c21.

10. He is probably identical to the Prajñāgupta (Po-jo-ch'ü-to) who is quoted in the 706 colophon to the *Ratnakūṭa-sūtra:* see the text of this colophon reproduced in Yōro Tetsujō, *Yakujō retsui,* first printed in 1863, which is included in *Kaidai sōsho* (Tokyo: Kokusho kankōkai, 1916), 375–401; see p. 388b for Prajñāgupta. There, he is said to have been a native of southern India, as was Bodhiruci.

11. The Sung, Yüan, and Ming editions of the *Tripiṭaka* read *shih-ling* (perhaps "contemporary order," or "timely order") instead of *t'eh-ling;* see *K'ai-yüan lu,* *T* 2154.55.672c12, collation note no. 13.

12. *K'ai-yüan lu* 18, *T* 2154.55.672b29–c14; cf. also *Chen-yüan lu* 28, *T* 2157.55. 1016c9–23, which omits the passage on Shih-li's swollen belly.

13. See discussion in Antonino Forte, *Political Propaganda and Ideology in China at the End of the Seventh Century* (Naples: Istituto Universitario Orientale, 1976), 135.

14. Ibid., p. 88ff.

15. Idem, "The Activities in China of the Tantric Master Manicintana."

16. For the colophon, see ibid., fig. 2; a translation of the colophon appears at pp. 341–342, 337–341. It is remarkable that Chih-sheng never once mentions that the *Dharma Mirror Sūtra* had been considered canonical since 712. Of course, he may simply have thought that there was no point in referring to something that everybody of his period would have known. For us, the fact that the text was accepted as canonical is important because it makes us understand why Chih-sheng tried so hard to prove that it was actually apocryphal.

17. *Pu-k'ung-ch'üan-so t'o-lo-ni ching,* *T* 1096.20.409c–421b.

18. Antonino Forte, "Brevi note sul testo kashmiro del *Dhāraṇī-sūtra di Avalokiteśvara dall'infallibile laccio* introdotto in Cina da Manicintana," in *Orientalia Iosephi Tucci memoriae dicata,* edited by Gherardo Gnoli and Lionello Lanciotti,

Serie Orientale Roma, vol. 56, no. 1 (Rome: Istituto Italiano per il Medio ed Estremo Oriente, 1985), 371–393.

19. Idem, "The Activities in China of the Tantric Master Manicintana," pp. 329–330.

20. Ibid., pp. 327–329.

GLOSSARY

Ch'ang-shih p'u-sa so-wen p'in 常施菩薩所問品
Chao-wen kuan 昭文館
Chen-yüan hsin-ting shih-chiao mu-lu 貞元新定釋教目錄
ch'ien-wen 前文
Chih-sheng 智昇
Ching-lung 景龍
chiu wei-lu 舊偽錄
Chōnen 奝然
chüan 卷
Ch'ung-fu ssu 崇福寺
fan-chia 梵夾
Fo lin-nieh-p'an chi fa-chu ching 佛臨涅槃記法住經
Fo lin-nieh-p'an wei A-nan shuo fa-chu-mieh p'in 佛臨涅槃為阿難說法住滅品
Fo-shuo shih so-fan-che yü-ch'ieh fa-ching ching 佛說所犯者瑜伽法鏡經
Hsiang-fa chüeh-i ching 像法決疑經
Hsin-hsing 信行
hsü 序
Hsüan-tsang 玄奘
Hsüan-tsung 玄宗
Hsüeh Chi 薛稷
huan-su 還俗
I-ching 義淨
K'ai-yüan shih-chiao lu 開元釋教錄
k'ou 口
Lao-tzu hua-hu ching 老子化胡經
Li Chen 李貞
Li Wu-ch'an 李無諂
Pao-ssu-wei 寶思惟
p'in 品
Po-jo-ch'iu-to 般若丘多
Po-jo-ch'ü-to 波若屈多
Pu-k'ung-ch'üan-so t'o-lo-ni ching 不空羂索陀羅尼經
San-chieh chiao 三階教
san-tsang 三藏
Shang-t'ien 上天
Shen Ch'üan-ch'i 沈佺期
Shih-li 師利
shih-ling 時令
T'ai-tsung 太宗
t'eh-ling 特令
Ti-tsang p'u-sa tsan-t'an fa-shen kuan-hsing p'in 地藏菩薩讚歎法身觀行品
Ts'ui Shih 崔湜
wei-hsü 偽序
Wu Chao 武曌
Yü-ch'ieh fa-ching ching 瑜伽法鏡經
Yüeh wang 越王

The *Fan-wang ching* and Monastic Discipline in Japanese Tendai: A Study of Annen's *Futsū jubosatsukai kōshaku*

Paul Groner

In almost all forms of Buddhism, religious practice begins with the cultivation of morality. Before a person can enter into deep meditative states, he is expected to be a moral person. The cultivation of morality for monks and nuns was traditionally based on a detailed set of rules or precepts, compiled during and shortly after the historical Buddha's lifetime, which concerned virtually every aspect of a monk's life, including food, clothing, and toilet habits. In most Buddhist traditions, these rules have been altered very little, even though they have not always been followed literally or have been supplemented with other sets of rules.

One of the distinguishing characteristics of Japanese Buddhism, particularly the Tendai school and several of the Kamakura schools that arose out of the Tendai tradition, has been an unusually liberal attitude toward monastic discipline. Japanese Tendai monks were ordained with a different set of precepts and applied them in ways that varied significantly from those adopted by monks in other Buddhist traditions. Instead of following the two-hundred fifty precepts of the *Ssu-fen lü* (*Dharmaguptaka-vinaya; T* 1428), which traditionally had been used by almost all East Asian Buddhists, Tendai monks were ordained with the fifty-eight precepts of an apocryphal Chinese work, the *Fan-wang ching* (Book of Brahmā's Net; *T* 1484). As a result, the *Fan-wang ching* played a major role in the development of uniquely Japanese views of religious practice.[1]

The adoption of the *Fan-wang* precepts as the primary guide to monastic discipline was proposed by the founder of the Tendai school, Saichō (767–822), and approved one week after his death. By arguing that the *Fan-wang ching* precepts should be the basis for Tendai ordinations, Saichō made the *Fan-wang ching* one of the most influential texts in Japanese Buddhism. Tendai monks could have used the *Fan-wang ching* as the basis of a new interpretation of Buddhist monastic discipline that would have been better suited to Japanese monks than the precepts of the *Ssu-fen lü* (*Vinaya* in four parts). Saichō had clearly hoped that the

Fan-wang precepts would provide Tendai monks with a more relevant guide for their behavior than the *Ssu-fen lü*. However, the *Fan-wang ching* did not prove to be an adequate basis for monastic discipline. Instead of developing new and more effective interpretations of the precepts, Japanese monks began to interpret the *Fan-wang* precepts so loosely that within two centuries after Saichō's death, virtually every major precept was frequently violated and the *Fan-wang* precepts had ceased to serve as an effective guide for the behavior of monks.

This decline in monastic discipline has been attributed to various social, economic, and political causes, such as the increasing numbers of nobles who became monks because political careers were closed to them, the vast landholdings that the monasteries accumulated, and the decline of governmental supervision of the schools. The structure and contents of the apocryphal *Fan-wang ching* and their interpretation by Tendai monks also played a key role in the emergence of looser requirements for monastic behavior. In particular, an ordination manual entitled the *Futsū jubosatsukai kōshaku* (Detailed Explanation of the Universal Bodhisattva Ordination; *T* 2381), written by a Tendai master of Esoteric Buddhism named Annen (841–889?), played a seminal role in the development of permissive interpretations of the precepts. As a result, after Annen's time it was extremely difficult for Tendai monks to reform their Order by calling for a revival of monastic discipline, although ineffectual attempts to do so were sometimes made.

The purpose of this study is to examine why the *Fan-wang* precepts proved to be an inadequate guide for monastic discipline and to investigate how Annen's interpretation of them decisively contributed to the decline of monastic discipline. The study is divided into three parts. In the first, the compilation of the *Fan-wang ching* is discussed and the contents of the text examined to demonstrate that the compilers of the *Fan-wang ching* never intended that it be used as the primary source of monastic discipline for monks and nuns. In the second part, Tendai views of the precepts after Saichō's death are surveyed. Because Saichō's successors were preoccupied with their campaign to develop a comprehensive interpretation of Esoteric Buddhism, they failed adequately to discuss problems concerning the interpretation of the *Fan-wang* precepts. The need for an authoritative interpretation of the precepts was finally met by Annen's *Futsū kōshaku*. In the third part, the ways in which Annen's view of the precepts led to permissive attitudes toward monastic discipline are analyzed.

The *Fan-wang ching*

The *Fan-wang ching* is an apocryphal text that was purportedly spoken by the Buddha and recorded in Sanskrit in India, but in fact was composed in China. Although a Tibetan translation of the text exists, it was almost certainly based on the Chinese version of the *Fan-wang ching.* The *Fan-wang ching* consists of two fascicles, but is said to have been only a small part of a Sanskrit text that was 112 (or 120) fascicles long. According to later commentators such as Ming-kuang (fl. late eighth century) and Fa-tsang (643–712), the original full Sanskrit text would have been 152 or 300 fascicles long if it had been translated into Chinese.[2] In fact, no conclusive evidence has been found that such a longer full text ever existed.

The first of the two fascicles concerns topics such as the stages of the bodhisattva path. Apocryphal texts compiled shortly after the *Fan-wang ching,* such as the *P'u-sa ying-lo pen-yeh ching* (Book of the Original Acts that Serve as Necklaces for the Bodhisattvas, hereafter *Ying-lo ching; T* 1485), included better organized and more comprehensive discussions of this topic.[3] As a result, the first fascicle of the *Fan-wang ching* has not played a major role in subsequent Buddhist history and was often omitted in commentaries on the text.[4] By the end of the fifth century, the second fascicle of the *Fan-wang ching* was circulating in China as an independent text on the precepts.[5]

The second fascicle of the *Fan-wang ching* contains a list of ten major precepts and forty-eight minor precepts. Most of the Tendai commentaries on the text concern only this fascicle, because it was often used as a *Prātimokṣa* (collection of rules) for the bodhisattva precepts in both China and Japan. However, the Fa-hsiang patriarch Chih-chou (556–622) commented on both fascicles. As a result, Hossō commentaries on the *Fan-wang* precepts frequently treated both fascicles, whereas Tendai commentaries focused on the second fascicle.[6]

The *Fan-wang ching* was traditionally said to have been translated into Chinese by Kumārajīva in 406, who then conferred its precepts on three hundred people. However, this account has long been questioned. The translation and the first *Fan-wang* ordination are described in three primary sources: two prefaces (one from the Korean canon and the other, attributed to Kumārajīva's disciple Seng-chao, from the Sung, Yüan, and Ming canons) and a postface to the sūtra that was included in the *Ch'u-san-tsang chi-chi* (A Compilation of Notices on the Translation of the *Tripiṭaka*). These three texts relate the same basic story, but differences in detail suggest that they were written as successive attempts at making the account conform with what was known about Kumārajīva's translating techniques. For example, in the *Fan-wang ching* preface from the Sung canon, Kumārajīva is said to have held the Sanskrit text of the *Fan-wang ching* and translated it orally. This account agrees with those from other sources concerning Kumārajīva's methods of translation. However, according to the other two descriptions of the translation of the text, both probably written earlier than the Sung preface, Kumārajīva translated the text from memory, a detail included to suggest Kumārajīva's devotion to the *Fan-wang ching* and perhaps to explain why no Sanskrit text was available. In addition, no mention of the *Fan-wang ching* is found in any of the early biographies of Kumārajīva; however, references to a bodhisattva prātimokṣa translated by Kumārajīva are found in historical works such as the *Kao-seng chuan* (Biographies of Eminent Monks).[7] Such references were probably based on the postface and prefaces to the *Fan-wang ching* and reflect the use of the second fascicle of the *Fan-wang ching* as an independent text. No text entitled *Fan-wang ching* is mentioned in the biographies of Kumārajīva's contemporaries. Finally, there are no early references for the first *Fan-wang* ordination, even though the precepts were said to have been conferred on more than three hundred people.[8]

Doubts about the authenticity of the *Fan-wang ching* began to surface early in Chinese history. The *Chung-ching mu-lu* (Catalogue of Scriptures), a catalogue of Buddhist texts compiled in 594 by Fa-ching, noted that many earlier catalogues had listed the *Fan-wang ching* as a work of questionable authenticity.[9] Although most later catalogues list the work as a translation by Kumārajīva, almost all the information about the text is taken from the two prefaces and postface mentioned above.[10]

The *Fan-wang ching* was probably compiled during the middle of the fifth century. It is closely related to several other apocryphal texts, including the *Jen-wang ching* (Book of Benevolent Kings; *T* 245) and the *Ying-lo ching*. Discussions of the stages of the bodhisattva path and the bodhisattva precepts are found in all three texts. An analysis of the development of these common themes indicates that the *Jen-wang ching* was probably compiled first, the *Fan-wang ching* next, and the *Ying-lo ching* last. Common technical terms in the texts also suggest a close relationship between the three works.

The compilers of the *Fan-wang ching* borrowed from a number of authentic Indian sources. The setting in which the sūtra was preached was so similar to that described in the *Hua-yen ching (Avataṃsaka-sūtra)* that Chih-i, the de facto founder of the T'ien-t'ai school, called the *Fan-wang ching* the capping sūtra of the *Avataṃsaka-sūtra*. The precepts were based on passages from a number of texts including the *Jen-wang ching, Nieh-p'an ching (Mahāparinirvāṇa-sūtra), Ti-ch'ih ching* (*Bodhisattvabhūmi,* Stages of the Bodhisattva's Practice), *Shan-chieh ching (Bodhisattvabhūmi),* and *Yu-p'o-sai chieh ching* (*Upāsakaśīla-sūtra,* Sūtra on Precepts for Lay Practitioners).[11] Of these, the last to be translated was the *Shan-chieh ching,* completed by Guṇavarman in 431. Thus the *Fan-wang ching* must have been compiled after that date. A copy of the text from Tun-huang has been reported with a date between 479 and 482, suggesting that the text must have been compiled by 480.[12] The *Fan-wang ching* first appears in historical documents during Emperor Liang Wu-ti's reign (r. 502–

549). Hui-chiao (497–554), author of the *Kao-seng chuan,* was said to have written the first commentary on it.[13] Apocryphal Buddhist works by anonymous Chinese monks usually were not accepted as authentic texts by Chinese Buddhists for several decades. Thus the *Fan-wang ching* was probably compiled sometime between 440 and 480.

This date would place its compilation several decades after the translation of the full *Vinayas* of the Mahīśāsaka, Dharmaguptaka, Sarvāstivāda, and Mahāsaṃghika schools. The translations of these texts were completed during the first three decades of the fourth century. Because they were the first complete versions of the full *Vinaya* translated in China, these texts were the object of much attention. Around this time Dharmarakṣa (384–433) and Guṇavarman (367–431) finished translating several texts on the bodhisattva precepts, including the *Bodhisattvabhūmi.* Interest in the precepts was at a peak. However, these newly translated texts that detailed Buddhist behavioral standards probably contributed to increased friction between Buddhism and Confucian ideology. The *Fan-wang ching* may well have been compiled with the hope of ameliorating some of these difficulties through the use of a new set of precepts.

Filial piety and obedience, two subjects of vital concern to Confucians, were stressed in the *Fan-wang ching:*

> You must obey parents, teachers, monks, and the Three Jewels. Filial piety and obedience are the ultimate path. Filial piety is called the precepts.[14]

Such statements might have served to assuage Confucian criticisms of Buddhist customs, such as celibacy and shaving the head, which were contrary to traditional Chinese views on filial piety. However, the compilers of the *Fan-wang ching* were not willing to compromise on certain issues that were judged to be vital to the Order in the fifth century, such as the claim that Buddhist monks should be autonomous from secular power. Eleven of the forty-eight minor vows were at least partially concerned with the relationship between the government and the Buddhist Order.[15] The fortieth minor precept forbade a monk from paying obeisance to his parents, any of his family, or the ruler. According to the forty-seventh minor precept, the government was not to establish officials to oversee the Order or to keep registers of monks. At the same time, monks and nuns were not to give the government cause for concern by becoming involved in politics. The forty-eighth minor precept prohibited a person from using Buddhism as a means of obtaining the trust of rulers and officials to benefit himself. In addition, the tenth and thirty-second minor precepts forbade the storing of arms. All these issues affected church-state relations during the Six Dynasties period.

The contents of the *Fan-wang* precepts also suggest that the compilers hoped to compose a set of precepts that would join monks, nuns, and lay believers in a common organization. Most of the precepts, such as the restrictions on killing, stealing, and illicit sexual activity, applied to both members of religious orders and lay believers.[16] A small number of the minor precepts applied primarily to monks and nuns, such as the restrictions on receiving special invitations from lay supporters and the requirement that monastic officials perform their duties in an unselfish manner.[17] A very small number, such as the major precept that prohibited selling liquor, were principally concerned with lay conduct.

Seating at assemblies and seniority in this new universal order were to be determined for all strictly on the basis of order of ordination. According to the thirty-eighth minor precept,

> those who were ordained first should be seated first, and those who were ordained later should sit below them. It does not matter whether one is young, old, a monk, nun, king, prince, or even a eunuch or a slave.

The leaders of such organizations were not necessarily monks. Lay believers might confer the precepts on others; in fact, according to the *Ying-lo ching,* a man or woman could confer them on his or her spouse. This position was adopted in a number of commentaries, including those by Chi-tsang and I-chi.[18]

In the fortieth minor precept, a long list of beings who are qualified for ordination is given, including deities, demons, lascivious men and women, hermaphrodites, and those without sexual organs. In addition, rulers and government officials were especially encouraged to accept the *Fan-wang* precepts as a part of their coronation or installation to office (minor precept no. 1). Thus secular officials were to follow Buddhist rules and serve as protectors of the Order rather than as its oppressors. In both China and Japan, the ordination of rulers with the bodhisattva precepts was often used as a means of attempting to encourage rulers to be sympathetic to Buddhist concerns.[19]

The *Fan-wang* precepts were not always used in the way that their compilers had intended. Although many Chinese and Japanese rulers received *Fan-wang* ordinations, they usually did so to make merit and did not observe the precepts they found inconvenient. And while members of the Buddhist Order and lay believers were sometimes ordained at the same time, there is little indication that they actually practiced together. The focus of a universal organization for monastics and laity based on the *Fan-wang* precepts would probably have been fortnightly assemblies for chanting the precepts. In fact, *Fan-wang* fortnightly assemblies for lay believers were apparently held in China. For short periods in Japan, *Fan-wang* fortnightly assemblies for monks were held at Tōdaiji and later at Enryakuji. However, it is not clear that the universal assembly of people of all social classes envisioned in the *Fan-wang ching* ever existed.[20]

The compilers of the *Fan-wang* precepts probably did not intend to use them as the sole guide for monastic discipline. The presence of terms such as "monk" and "nun" within the text suggests that the compilers recognized that recipients might observe other sets of precepts that were suitable to their positions. Although the *Fan-wang ching* included several statements critical of Hīnayāna precepts and teachings, almost all Chinese commentators on the text argued that a person should observe the *Ssu-fen lü* precepts with Mahāyāna attitudes. Adherence to the *Fan-wang* precepts did not entail the rejection of the *Ssu-fen lü* precepts. Rather, in most cases commentators followed the *Bodhisattvabhūmi* explanation, which stated that a monk should receive the precepts for laymen, novices, and monks before being ordained with the bodhisattva precepts.[21] Although Chinese commentators had the option of following the explanation found in *Ying-lo ching,* which justified using the *Fan-wang* precepts alone, most chose to ignore that option. Thus Chinese monks used the *Fan-wang* precepts to supplement the *Ssu-fen lü* precepts, not as a set of independent precepts.[22]

When the Japanese Tendai school began ordaining monks with the *Fan-wang* precepts, it was clearly using the *Fan-wang ching* in a new way: as the primary guide for monastic discipline. The *Fan-wang* precepts had neither been compiled principally for monks nor been used in that manner in China. In the next section, early Japanese Tendai interpretations of the text are examined.

The *Fan-wang* Precepts after Saichō's Death: Problems of Administration and Esoteric Buddhism

If the *Fan-wang* precepts were to provide Japanese Tendai monks with an effective guide to monastic discipline, a number of important issues concerning the text would have to be discussed by Saichō's followers. The emphasis of the *Fan-wang* precepts was on correct intentions rather than on actions. The precepts themselves were general statements that gave little attention either to mitigating circumstances that might excuse violations or to how monks could judge the severity of violations of the precepts. For example, the first major precept prohibits knowingly killing any sentient being. However, for the precept to be used effectively, a distinction would have to be made between killing an insect and killing a human being. Other issues also had to be discussed, including that of whether a bodhisattva might take the life of an evil murderer to save other sentient beings and prevent the murderer from accumulating additional bad karma. These problems had been raised in Chinese commentaries, but since the commentaries were not in agreement, Tendai monks needed to determine which interpretations they would follow.[23] In addition, the first major precept required that a bodhisattva always act with compassion, filial piety, and obedience in order to protect sentient beings. If a person failed to maintain the required attitude, had he violated a major precept?

The *Fan-wang ching* lacked detailed instructions concerning the ceremonies and procedures that were to be followed at meetings of monks. Instructions concerning ordinations, rainy season retreats, and other monastic events were crucial if the Order were to function smoothly. If the *Fan-wang* precepts were to be an effective guide for monastic behavior, a detailed explanation of the *Fan-wang ching* was clearly required. Saichō had died before he could explain his views on the interpretation of the *Fan-wang ching*. For example, major problems such as which set of precepts were to be used in initiating novices within the Tendai Order were still not resolved at the time of Saichō's death.[24] Unfortunately, Saichō's immediate disciples were more interested in developing a form of Tendai Esoteric Buddhism that could effectively compete with the Shingon school founded by Kūkai (774–835) than in discussing the proper interpretation of the *Fan-wang ching*.

During the decades following Saichō's death, factionalism and a decline in monastic discipline emerged as serious problems within the Tendai school. Tendai leaders attempted to limit abuses by compiling sets of rules for Tendai monks. However, most of these early sets of rules made little direct reference to the *Fan-wang ching*, probably because the authors realized that there were numerous problems of interpretation to resolve before the precepts could be effectively used to administer the Order.[25] Comments in Tendai works from this period reflect the concern that the leaders of the school felt over the growing problem of regulating the activities of the monks on Mt. Hiei. In 888, the head of the Tendai school, Enchin (814–891), complained bitterly that Tendai monks ignored the basic rules of monastic deportment and did not attend the rainy season retreats or go to the hall for the fortnightly assemblies. Their robes were the wrong colors and too ornate. When they attended assemblies, Tendai monks and novices violated the rule that seating should be according to seniority. Monastic discipline had declined so much that Nara monks visiting Mt. Hiei ridiculed the Tendai monks' ignorance of monastic procedures.[26]

The two most prominent figures within the Tendai school during the middle and late ninth century, Ennin (794–864) and Enchin (814–891), both made attempts to reform the Order. Late in his life, Ennin began compiling a work of quotations concerning the precepts, the *Ken'yō daikairon* (Treatise Clarifying and Extolling the Mahāyāna Precepts; *T* 2380), but died before he could complete the work. As a result, the text contained few comments by Ennin and lacked both the structure and coherence to make it an effective interpretation of the *Fan-wang* precepts. Enchin attempted to introduce procedures and requirements from the *Ssu-fen lü* in order to tighten the application of the *Fan-wang* precepts, but did not write the comprehensive commentary on the *Fan-wang ching* that was needed if the Tendai school were to be able to effectively use the *Fan-wang* precepts for monastic discipline. In addition, Saichō's bitter denunciation of the *Ssu-fen lü* precepts as Hīnayānist hindered Enchin's efforts to utilize *Ssu-fen lü* procedures.[27]

Both Ennin and Enchin were among the most noted Japanese masters of Esoteric Buddhism during their lifetimes. However, neither of them discussed the precepts in terms of Esoteric Buddhist teachings, perhaps because Esoteric texts included passages that seemed to question the validity and importance of observance of the precepts.[28] In fact, with the sole exception of a short and difficult discussion by Kōjō (779–859), Tendai monks ignored the relationship between Esoteric Buddhism and monastic precepts until Annen's time. However, with the burgeoning of Tendai interest in Esoteric Buddhism, this issue could not be neglected for long. In the course of analyzing the relationship between Perfect exoteric teachings and Esoteric teachings, Tendai monks had begun to argue that although both were equal in terms of theory, Esoteric texts included superior practices. A brief survey of some of the passages concerning monastic discipline from Esoteric texts reveals the challenge that the growing Tendai interest in Esoteric Buddhism posed for a strict interpretation of the precepts.

Many of the Esoteric texts being circulated in Japan during the ninth century contained passages which maintained that the spirit or the intention of the practitioner was much more important than rigid observance of the precepts. Statements in authoritative Esoteric sūtras and their commentaries noted that rigid adherence to the precepts was not necessary. According to the Hīnayāna *Vinayas, pārājika* offenses (sexual intercourse, theft, killing, and lying about spiritual achievements) were to be punished by immediate, lifelong expulsion from the Order and would result in the loss of any possibility of significant spiritual gains in that lifetime. However, in the *Ta-jih ching su,* a commentary on the *Ta-jih ching (Mahāvairocana-sūtra),* such violations were considered to be attempted *(sthūlātyaya)* offenses that resulted in obstacles on the practitioner's path but did not necessarily have a disastrous effect on his spiritual endeavors.[29] In some Esoteric texts, the ideal practitioner seemed to be described as a layman rather than a monk. The buddhas and bodhisattvas portrayed in East Asian Esoteric scriptures and art were often portrayed as lay bodhisattvas. For example, Mahāvairocana was depicted with a crown.

Some of the rituals found in Esoteric texts contained elements that would have been unacceptable to any monk who carefully observed the *Vinaya.* A survey of the rituals described in Chinese translations of Esoteric texts available in Japan around the middle of the ninth century includes some that involved the use of animal and human flesh or illicit sex.[30] Although the correct interpretation of such descriptions involves difficult scholarly problems, it is clear that some of the passages are symbolic and that a qualified teacher must be present to interpret them. For example, according to some of the major Esoteric texts and commentaries that were circulating in China by the end of the eighth century, killing is permitted as an expedient to eliminate those who would destroy Buddhism, to save sentient beings, or to prevent the victim from accumulating additional bad karma. In such cases, a Buddhist must have no thought of maliciousness or hate when he takes life. In addition, the taking of life was said to refer to the destruction of one's own wrong states of mind rather than actual killing.[31] Thorough research on such rituals would require the investigation of how non-Buddhist ritual and magical elements were incorporated into the rituals and interpreted through Buddhist doctrine.[32]

An apocryphal eleventh century tale about a patriarch of Esoteric Buddhism, Śubhakarasiṃha (637–735), and the most authoritative commentator on monastic discipline in China, Tao-hsüan (596–667), dramatizes the differences in attitude between Esoteric Buddhism and the *Vinaya* tradition.[33] According to the story, Śubhakarasiṃha was once staying at the Hsi-ming Temple, where Tao-hsüan lived. While he was there, Śubhakarasiṃha ate meat, drank liquor, became intoxicated, and caused a commotion. Tao-hsüan was quite disturbed by Śubhakarasiṃha's actions. Later, in the middle of the night, just as Tao-hsüan was about to crush a bug and throw it to the ground, Śubhakarasiṃha called out from another room, "*Vinaya* master, why are you about to kill one of the children of the Buddha?" Tao-hsüan realized that Śubhakarasiṃha was no ordinary person and honored him as a teacher. The tale is obviously apocryphal since Śubhakarasiṃha came to China forty-nine years after Tao-hsüan's death, but it does illustrate the tension between the rigid adherence to the precepts advocated by some monks and the emphasis on attitude found in some Esoteric Buddhist writings.

Annen's *Futsū kōshaku* and Monastic Discipline

Annen's writings were the first within the Japanese Tendai tradition to consider the relationship between Esoteric Buddhism and monastic discipline in a comprehensive manner. In addition, the *Futsū kōshaku* was the first comprehensive and persuasive work to discuss the significance of the *Fan-wang* precepts for monastic discipline in Japan. Annen's positions on the precepts weakened monastic discipline and therefore differed substantially from those of Ennin and Enchin. Annen's arguments ultimately were much more influential than those of Ennin and Enchin and decisively affected subsequent works on the precepts by

Tendai monks, partly because Annen's positions suggested approaches to monastic discipline that were more attractive to the growing numbers of monks who entered the Order for political and economic reasons.[34]

Annen wrote about the precepts in a number of works. His most detailed explanation of the Perfect precepts *(enkai)* is found in the *Futsū kōshaku,* but he also discussed the Esoteric (J. *sanmaya,* Skt. *samaya*) precepts in the *Kyōjigi* and compared the Perfect and the Esoteric precepts in the *Taikon gushi kanjōki.*

The *Futsū kōshaku* is a detailed commentary on the ordination ceremony. Like the ordination manuals written by Chan-jan and attributed to Saichō, Annen's text is divided into the following twelve parts, which correspond to the divisions of the Tendai *Fan-wang* ordination ceremony:[35]

1. Introduction
2. Three refuges
3. Invitation to the teachers
4. Confession
5. Aspiration for supreme enlightenment
6. Questioning about hindrances to ordination
7. Conferral of the precepts
8. Witnessing the ceremony
9. Signs from the Buddha confirming the ceremony
10. Explanation of the precepts
11. Exhortation to observe the precepts
12. Dedication of the merit from the ceremony to all sentient beings

Annen's text is more detailed than any earlier *Fan-wang* ordination manual and is much more than a simple set of instructions about the performance of ordinations. Extensive discussions of the significance of the precepts, their relation to Esoteric teachings, the circumstances under which the precepts may be justifiably violated, and the role of confession in expiating wrongdoing are found in the text. Many of Annen's most innovative ideas were included in the introductory section of the *Futsū kōshaku,* which was much longer than the introduction of any previous *Fan-wang* ordination manual. Annen's introduction occupies the entire first fascicle of the text, more than one-third of the work. Since Annen was not required to discuss specific sections of the ceremony in the introduction, he could express his views freely.

Annen's decision to use the format of an ordination manual for his major work on the precepts is significant. Two basic types of works on the bodhisattva precepts were found in the Chinese T'ien-t'ai tradition at the time Annen wrote: (1) commentaries on the *Fan-wang ching* or subcommentaries on the *Fan-wang ching* commentary attributed to Chih-i

(*T* 1811), and (2) ordination manuals. Writing a commentary on the precepts themselves would have seemed to be the most logical choice for Annen or his predecessors. Such a commentary might have clarified many of the obscure points about how the *Fan-wang* precepts were to be used as the primary basis for monastic discipline. However, such a commentary was not written by a Japanese Tendai monk until the thirteenth century, when Hōjibō Shōshin (fl. 1153–1213) wrote a subcommentary for the commentary on the *Fan-wang ching* attributed to Chih-i.[36] Although monks from other Japanese schools wrote commentaries on the *Fan-wang ching,* Tendai monks were clearly more interested in extolling the virtues of the ordination ceremony than they were in discussing the details of actual observance of the *Fan-wang* precepts. In fact, even in the sets of monastery rules written by Ennin and Enchin, no appeal is made for monks to obey the *Fan-wang* precepts. Discussions of Tendai monastic discipline during the Heian period were found primarily in sets of monastery rules, not in texts on the precepts.

Annen's permissive attitudes toward monastic discipline are evident throughout the *Futsū kōshaku.* Annen's views on the precepts are surveyed below under five main categories: Esoteric Buddhism and the precepts; the buddha-nature and the precepts; confession ceremonies and the expiation of wrongdoing; rationales for the observance and violation of the precepts; and Annen's view of the Hīnayāna precepts.

Annen's Use of Esoteric Buddhism in the Interpretation of the Precepts

Saichō, Ennin, and Enchin almost never mentioned Esoteric texts in their discussions of the precepts. Annen, however, often referred to Esoteric Buddhist teachings in his interpretation of the precepts. In fact, he argued that all forms of Buddhism were ultimately expressions of Esoteric doctrines and practices. In the following passage from the *Futsū kōshaku,* Annen explained how the *Fan-wang* precepts were related to Esoteric teachings:

> If we follow an Esoteric commentary, then the *Fan-wang* precepts belong to the elementary level *(senryaku)* of the Diamond-realm. There are also separate precepts from the bodhisattva canon *(bosatsu daizōkyō)* that are called the *sanmaya* precepts of all the buddhas. A full list of the precepts would include the four *pārājikas* [of the Hīnayāna canon], the ten major precepts [of the *Fan-wang ching*], the four grave sins, and the ten expedient practices *(jū hōben gakusho)* [of the *Ta-jih ching*].
>
> Long ago, when the bodhisattva Śākyamuni had completed six years of austerities, he sat under the bodhi tree but was unable to realize enlightenment. All the buddhas came and conferred the *sanmaya* precepts and the five-part meditation resulting in enlightenment *(gosō jōbutsu).* Thus the World-honored One suddenly entered the realm of the buddhas through the direct path *(jikidō).*[37]

Although Annen mentioned both the Esoteric and exoteric precepts in the above passage, their exact relationship was not specified, perhaps because the *Futsū kōshaku* was intended to be a commentary on the exoteric Buddhist ordination. However, he was more explicit in the following passage from the *Kyōji mondō* (Questions and Answers on Classifying Teachings and Periods):

> According to the *Ta-jih ching i-shih* [I-hsing's commentary on the *Mahāvairocana-sūtra*], "A bodhisattava precepts ordination is described in the Diamond *(Chin-kang-ting,* Skt. *Vajraśekhara)* tradition. The four grave precepts, the ten grave precepts, the precepts without hindrances of the three periods *(sanze mushōgekai),* and the *sanmaya* precepts are found in the *Mahāvairocana-sūtra.* Since the four *pārājika* precepts for śrāvakas are based on the four grave precepts of the *Mahāvairocana-sūtra,* they should be considered as precepts concerning attempted *(sthūlātyaya)* offenses. All of the precepts of the three vehicles or the five vehicles are expedient rules used by bodhisattvas of the Esoteric tradition to benefit sentient beings."
>
> In addition, according to the *Chin-kang-ting i-chüeh,* "The *Fan-wang* Prātimokṣa is taken from the elementary level of the *Chin-kang-ting (ching).*" Each of the figures of the four-part maṇḍala has precepts that he maintains. Those of the first level, the central hall, observe the four basic secrets and the ten grave [Esoteric] precepts. Those in the second level observe the ten major and forty-eight minor precepts [of the *Fan-wang ching*], the four or six major precepts, and the twenty-eight minor precepts. Those in the third level observe the two-hundred fifty precepts for monks, the five-hundred precepts for nuns, the five lay precepts of men and gods, or the ten good precepts *(jūzen[kai]).*[38]

In this passage, Annen made several important points. He argued that all of the precepts are ultimately derived from several basic sets of Esoteric precepts. Esoteric precepts were classified into two basic types: the unhindered precepts, which a person always possessed, and the *sanmaya* precepts, which were conferred. The four secrets and ten grave precepts were both versions of the *sanmaya* precepts. The bodhisattva precepts found in various Mahāyāna sūtras, including the *Fan-wang ching,* were derived from the Esoteric precepts and classified in the second level of the maṇḍala. The Hīnayāna precepts and the ten good precepts were classified as belonging to the third level. Annen's treatment of the Hīnayāna and bodhisattva precepts suggested that both were expedients for the Esoteric practitioner. The precepts of both the *Ssu-fen lü* and the *Fan-wang ching* would thus be expedient practices designed to benefit sentient beings. Their observance would not be central to the individual practitioner's spiritual progress. Violation of a major precept or a *pārājika* was an attempted offense and did not necessarily lead to the expulsion of a person from the Order, or even to an obstacle on the spiritual path of the practitioner.

Annen often called the *Fan-wang* precepts the "Perfect precepts" *(enkai)* in the *Futsū kōshaku,* suggesting that they were the rules for those who followed the Buddha's ultimate teaching; however, his statement that the *Fan-wang ching* was the "elementary form of the Diamond-realm teaching" clearly indicated that the *Fan-wang* precepts were supreme only in the exoteric realm and were superceded by the *sanmaya* precepts when Esoteric teachings were considered.

The Esoteric precepts. To explain Annen's use of Esoteric Buddhist teachings in the *Futsū kōshaku,* the *sanmaya* precepts must be mentioned. In the previously quoted passage from the *Futsū kōshaku,* Annen mentioned the story of Śākyamuni's enlightenment related in the *Chin-kang-ting ching* (*Vajraśekhara-sūtra,* Diamond Peak Sūtra). The story, one of the most famous episodes in Esoteric Buddhist literature, was an interpretation of Śākyamuni's enlightenment in terms which clearly suggested that Esoteric Buddhism was both superior to and the culmination of exoteric Buddhism. According to the story, Śākyamuni Buddha had been unable to realize supreme enlightenment through exoteric teachings. Only after the various buddhas had conferred the *sanmaya* precepts and special meditative techniques on him was Śākyamuni able to realize supreme enlightenment. The story is historically important because it is one of the first clear declarations of the superiority of Esoteric Buddhism over exoteric Buddhism. Annen's citation of the story reinforced his position that the *sanmaya* precepts were the source and basis of all other precepts.[39]

The precepts that Śākyamuni received were the *sanmaya* precepts. The term *"sanmaya"* has a number of meanings. Four of them are relevant in the explanation of the *sanmaya* precepts. First, it has the meaning of "equal" *(byōdō).* Although there are differences in the profundity of the Buddha's teachings, the precepts remain the same for all. In addition, even though sentient beings have a variety of spiritual attainments, the essence of the precepts *(kaitai)* is the same for all. Thus a person who has the essence of the precepts is equal to a buddha even though his religious practices have not yet enabled him to realize enlightenment.

Second, *sanmaya* has the meaning of "primordial vow" *(honzei)* and is used primarily in reference to the bodhisattva vows in which the practitioner pledges to realize enlightenment for him/herself and to help others realize it. The term *"sanmaya"* may also refer to vows concerning the observance of the precepts. Third, *sanmaya* means "removal of obstacles" *(jōshō).* In this sense, it refers to the power of the *sanmaya* precepts ordination to remove delusion. Finally, *sanmaya* is said to refer to the "awakening" *(kyōgaku)* of people from the slumber of ignorance to the aspiration for supreme enlightenment *(bodaishin).*[40]

The fourfold definition of the term *"sanmaya"* suggests that the *sanmaya* precepts were intended to provide a practitioner with the basic attitudes that guided his actions and thoughts. They were not a series of specific prohibitions as were the *Ssu-fen lü* precepts.

The *sanmaya* precepts have traditionally been conferred just before a person received an Esoteric consecration (Skt. *abhiṣeka;* J. *kanjō*). Although the *sanmaya* precepts could be conferred at both elementary and advanced consecration ceremonies, in some lineages of the Shingon school, the *sanmaya* were conferred only for elementary *(kechien)* consecrations. In the Tendai school, the *sanmaya* precepts were conferred before advanced initiations; but in elementary consecrations for laymen, the simpler Three Refuges might sometimes have replaced the *sanmaya* precepts.[41] When Enchin studied in China, he received the *sanmaya* precepts from his teacher Fa-ju just before the advanced consecration.[42]

The *sanmaya* precepts generally used in the Tendai school consist of four general principles that may never be violated. The canonical source of the *sanmaya* precepts is the *Ta-jih ching (Mahāvairocana-sūtra):*

1. Not to abandon the true dharma.
2. Never to abandon the aspiration to enlightenment.
3. Never to refuse to confer Buddhist teachings on someone who sincerely wishes to study them.
4. To benefit sentient beings.[43]

An expanded list of ten *sanmaya* precepts, based on the four from the *Ta-jih ching,* was developed by Śubhakarasiṃha and used by Shingon monks. Annen also referred to this list.[44]

The relationship between the *sanmaya* precepts and the full *(upasampadā)* precepts was described in several ways. The *sanmaya* precepts could be said to embody the essential purport of the full precepts. Monks, therefore, were expected to observe the traditional precepts. Kūkai maintained a position close to this.[45]

Annen, in contrast, argued that the *sanmaya* precepts should never be violated but that other precepts, such as the *Fan-wang* or Hīnayāna precepts, were expedients and could be readily violated if one were complying with the spirit of the *sanmaya* precepts. Tendai monks consequently had no set of rules that they were absolutely required to follow other than the idealistic and vague principles of the *sanmaya* precepts. When Annen explained his position in a commentary on an ordination manual, the clear implication was that monks need not concern themselves with the close observance of the full set of *Fan-wang* precepts. If Annen's explanation had been made in another context, with the provision that it applied only to advanced practitioners, it might not have seriously undermined monastic discipline. Such a presentation would have been consistent with the more restrained treatments by Chinese monks of topics, such as confession and the nonsubstantiality of karma, that might have contributed to a decline in monastic discipline.

After Annen's time, many Tendai monks came to accept the primacy of the *sanmaya* or other idealistic and vague sets of precepts over the *Fan-wang* precepts. In the middle of the eleventh century, the Tendai temple, Miidera, attempted to proclaim its independence from the Mt. Hiei branch of the Tendai school by establishing a precepts platform. The Miidera monks first attempted to establish a platform for the conferral of the *Fan-wang* precepts, but when the monks from Mt. Hiei blocked their plans, the Miidera monks proposed using a *sanmaya* precepts platform.[46]

The *sanmaya* precepts also gradually supplanted exoteric ordinations in parts of the Shingon school. The monk Ninjitsu, in a set of rules *(okibumi)* for his followers in 1317, asked that seniority at the Shingon Kongō Temple be primarily based on *sanmaya* ordinations, rather than on full exoteric ordinations *(kenkai)*. Thus a monk who had received both the full *(upasampadā)* and *sanmaya* ordinations was to be seated in a position superior to all monks who had received the full but not the *sanmaya* ordination. The *sanmaya* ordination was clearly considered to be the more significant ceremony. However, when all the monks in question had received the *sanmaya* precepts, then seniority was to be based upon their full ordination *(upasampadā)*.[47]

The Bodhisattva Precepts and the Realization of Buddhahood with This Very Body

Annen followed Saichō by using such terms as "Perfect teaching" *(engyō)* and "Sudden teaching" *(tongyō)* when referring to the *Fan-wang* precepts. These terms suggested that the *Fan-wang* precepts occupied the highest place in the Tendai classification of exoteric teachings, even if they were not among the most profound of Esoteric teachings. Saichō often used the term "Perfect precepts" *(enkai)* in his discussions of the *Fan-wang* precepts because it suggested that the precepts had the same purport and profundity as the Buddha's ultimate teaching expressed in the *Lotus Sūtra*.[48]

Although Annen used some of the same terminology as Saichō, Annen's discussion of the function of *Fan-wang* ordinations in the "realization of buddhahood with this very body" *(sokushin jōbutsu)* suggests that Annen did not regard the *Fan-wang ching* to be as profound as the *Lotus Sūtra,* the highest exoteric teaching. Saichō had written about the realization of buddhahood with this very body in several of his works, but had never clearly defined the concept. After his death, several of his successors had discussed the concept, but it was not given its classical Tendai definition until Annen analyzed it in several of his works. The concept was particularly important in Tendai thought during the ninth century, as Tendai monks strove to develop Esoteric Buddhist teachings and rituals that would enable them to compete with the Shingon school.

For Annen, "the realization of buddhahood with this very body" meant that a person could realize supreme enlightenment *(myōkaku)* on the sole basis of the practices in his current lifetime. Moreover, the realization of buddhahood was not only a mental transformation, but a physical transformation through which one no longer need fear harm from external forces and could preach to sentient beings in other realms. In contrast, most earlier Chinese and Japanese Tendai thinkers had maintained more conservative positions, arguing that more than one lifetime of practice was required for the realization of buddhahood and that terms such as *sokushin jōbutsu* referred to the development of the aspiration to enlightenment and the attainment of the first abode *(shojū),* not to the realization of supreme enlightenment.[49]

In the *Futsū kōshaku,* Annen listed the desire to realize buddhahood with this very body as the first of ten motivations for receiving the *Fan-wang* ordination, thereby implying that *sokushin jōbutsu* was closely related to the ordination.[50] Later in the text, however, he discussed passages from exoteric texts that justified *sokushin jōbutsu* and arranged these passages in accordance with a Tendai classification system based on the premise that because sentient beings possess the buddha-nature, they are essentially identical to buddhas. However, sentient beings must still perform religious practices in order to realize that identity. The Tendai "six degrees of the [realization of] identity" *(rokusoku)* classifies the religious practitioner's spiritual progress as he strives to realize that basic identity.[51] In addition, Annen classified exoteric texts according to which of nine grades of religious practitioner the texts might be appropriate.

> The *Ta yüan-chüeh* (Book of Consummate Enlightenment) states, "All sentient beings are originally Buddhas." This is the principle of identification *(risoku).* The *Fan-wang ching* states, "When sentient beings receive the precepts of the Buddha, they enter the ranks of the buddhas." Thus in this very existence, they hear that they are identical [to buddhas] in name *(myōji).* This stage is for those whose faculties are the very lowest *(gege).* . . .
>
> The *Lotus Sūtra* states that "the instant one hears this, he will realize supreme enlightenment." Thus in this very existence he realizes [the highest stage] of wondrous enlightenment. This is for those whose faculties are the most advanced *(jōjō).* Thus you should realize that precepts of the Perfect Vehicle only yield [good fruit]; there is no retribution for breaking them.[52]

According to Annen, the *Fan-wang ching* is appropriate for those who have the lowest of the nine grades of religious faculties, and is suitable for those in the second lowest of the *rokusoku.* The first stage of the *rokusoku* refers to the principle that buddhas and all sentient beings are identical because sentient beings possess the buddha-nature. However, people at the first stage have not yet begun the religious practices necessary to realize this truth. In the second stage, they hear or read about this truth. The second stage thus represents the beginning of religious practice. Practitioners then advance through various stages on the path to the realization of supreme enlightenment. Thus according to Annen's formulation, the *Fan-wang* ordination represented the beginning of the practices that lead to the realization of buddhahood in this existence and is for people with the lowest grade of religious faculties. Those people with higher grades of religious faculties could probably omit the *Fan-wang* ordination.[53] In his other works on the realization of buddhahood with this very body, such as the *Sokushin jōbutsu shiki* (Personal Record of Teachings on Realization of Buddhahood with This Very Body), Annen did not mention the role of the *Fan-wang* ordination.[54] Since the *Fan-wang* ordination was a necessary requirement for anyone who wished to become a Tendai monk, Annen could not ignore it; but he probably did not believe that it was indispensable for a person's spiritual progress.

The Precepts and the Buddha-nature

Both the *Fan-wang ching* and texts on the *sanmaya* precepts include statements that the precepts are based on the buddha-nature.[55] The buddha-nature and the precepts are the main topics in the *Ta-pan-nieh-p'an ching (Mahāparinirvāṇa-sūtra),* a text traditionally considered to be representative of the Perfect Teaching by Tendai monks. The relationship between the buddha-nature and the precepts has been described in terms of a tension between the unchanging nature *(shō)* of sentient beings and the requirement of religious practice *(shu).*[56] Anyone can observe the precepts, practice religious austerities, and realize buddhahood because everyone has the buddha-nature; in other words, all possess the potential to realize buddhahood. Consequently, the existence of beings who can never realize buddhahood *(icchantika)* is denied in the *Nieh-p'an ching.* Even the most evil person always has the potential to reform himself, practice religious austerities, and realize buddhahood. The realization of buddhahood (the full possibilities presented by the buddha-nature) can occur only through religious practice. Thus the universal presence of the buddha-nature does not free a person from the obligation to receive and observe the precepts.

If the universal and absolute qualities of the buddha-nature are overemphasized and the importance of practice overlooked, the ordination ceremony may be considered to be an initiation that confers a special spiritual power on the recipient but does not necessarily obligate him to observe the precepts. Annen's treatment of the ordination suggests this type of interpretation. Annen's emphasis on the buddha-nature *(shō)* can be clearly seen in his discussion of the type of precepts conferred in the ordination, the subject of the seventh section of his manual, "The Conferral of the Precepts" *(jukai).* This section marks the climax of the ordination, since it describes the way in which the candidate for ordination actually receives the precepts. The preceding discussions of the *Futsū kōshaku* all lead up to the conferral of the precepts, while the subsequent sections concern lesser matters, such as teaching the newly ordained monk the precepts or confirming that the buddhas and bodhisattvas will serve as witnesses to the ceremony.

In the Tendai bodhisattva ordination manuals written by Chan-jan (711–782) and Saichō, the section on the conferral of the precepts was not developed very much. Chan-jan and Saichō noted that the candidate was about to receive the Three Collections of Pure Precepts *(sanju jōkai):* (1) the precepts that prevent evil, (2) the precepts that promote good, and (3) the precepts that benefit sentient beings. These precepts were to be interpreted in accordance with the Perfect Teachings of Tendai. The master of ceremonies *(kaishi)* then asked the candidate three times whether he would observe the precepts. Each time the candidate answered that he would observe them, the master of ceremonies stated that the precepts were coming closer to him and were about to enter his body.[57] After the candidate had answered that he would observe the precepts for the third time, the master of ceremonies stated, "You are now a bodhisattva and should be called a true son of the Buddha. Thus the *Mahāparinirvāṇa-sūtra (Daikyō)* states that the arising of the aspiration to realize enlightenment and the realization of supreme enlightenment are not distinct."[58]

Annen's treatment of this section of the ordination ceremony is much more developed and reflects his efforts to argue for a more relaxed view of monastic discipline. In particular, Annen emphasized the importance of identifying the bodhisattva precepts with the buddha-nature and the idea that the bodhisattva precepts could never be lost.

Annen argued that three types of precepts were actually involved in the Tendai ordination ceremony. Although Annen did not identify the source for his classification of the precepts into three types, it was apparently derived from a passage in the *Yogācārabhūmi-śāstra.*[59]

The first type was the precepts that are transmitted through a lineage of teachers *(denjukai)*. An example of this type is the *Fan-wang* precepts, which have been transmitted through a lineage beginning with Rushana Nyorai (Vairocana Buddha) and continuing through a series of bodhisattvas and teachers in India, China, and Japan. This type of ordination is equivalent to that described in earlier ordination manuals and mentioned by Saichō in his work on lineages, the *Kechimyakufu.*[60]

The second type was the precepts that are called forth from within the candidate through the ordination ceremony *(hottokukai)*. These arise at the instant the candidate states for the third and final time that he will observe the precepts, thereby completing the conferral of the precepts. Annen noted that "once these precepts have been called forth, they are eternal and indestructible."[61]

The third type is called the precepts that are innate and based on one's unchanging nature *(shōtokukai).* This is the most subtle type of precepts. These precepts are not received through the ceremonial actions of another person. Rather, those who receive the precepts are "awakened within their own minds to the precepts which are an aspect of their original five-part body *(gobun kaishin).*"[62] In this passage, Annen referred to a tradition which maintained that the buddha-nature had five aspects *(gobun hosshin):* morality, meditation, wisdom, emancipation, and the knowledge of emancipation. Thus the ordination was the occasion of awakening a person to that aspect of his own nature which gave him the ability to be moral.

The tradition that the precepts were not lost at death was mentioned in texts on the bodhisattva precepts, such as the *Bodhisattvabhūmi* and the *Ying-lo ching.*[63] Only when the practitioner lost the aspiration for supreme enlightenment or violated a major precept without remorse were they lost. Although earlier Tendai masters had been aware of the tradition, they had not emphasized it as much as Annen did in the *Futsū kōshaku,* perhaps because they were concerned about whether such statements might lead to a decline in monastic discipline. Usually this type of passage was quoted in arguments concerning the superiority of the bodhisattva precepts, rather than in discussions of the conferral of the precepts. In addition, passages concerning the buddha-nature and the precepts were found in a number of works before Annen's time, but Annen was probably the first thinker to discuss the relationship in terms of a clearly articulated three-part classification. His classification system suggested that the second and third types of precepts, which could never be lost, were more profound and more important than the first type. Once Annen had made the distinction between the three types of precepts, he could explore the implications of the system. Annen's interest in precepts identified with the buddha-nature clearly had important implications for monastic discipline, as is evident in Annen's statements that

> for the person [who has realized his] Perfect precepts body, all actions are the Buddha's actions. Since the precepts are never violated through the Buddha's actions, these precepts are eternal.
>
> For the precepts of the Perfect Vehicle, there are only rewards and no [karmic] retribution for violations.[64]

Expiation of Transgressions and the Confession Ceremony

If the *Fan-wang* precepts were to serve as an effective guide to monastic discipline, they would have to be enforced through a series of measures to ensure that monks strove to follow them. According to the *Ssu-fen lü,* violations of the precepts generally were to be expiated through a carefully graduated series of confessions before the entire Order, a small group of monks, or by oneself. When major rules were violated, a monk was permanently expelled or temporarily suspended from the Order. Although this system often was not rigidly followed in China and Japan, it did provide a model toward which monks could aspire. The *Fan-wang* precepts, however, had never been used as the primary guide for monastic discipline. As a result, the requirements for expiation were not specified in detail. In this section, Annen's discussion of the moral requirements for ordination and the expiation of violations of the precepts is considered.

When a person was ordained as a monk with the *Ssu-fen lü* precepts, he was expected to meet certain requirements. Some of these requirements concerned the candidate's social or physical condition: he could not be a debtor, a slave, a hermaphrodite, or a eunuch. Other requirements were moral: the candidate must not have violated a *pārājika* precept, had sexual intercourse with a nun, killed his mother, father, or teacher, or caused a schism in the Buddhist Order. The requirements for a *Fan-wang* ordination were not as stringent. Candidates for ordination could be eunuchs, hermaphrodites, or slaves as well as royalty, monks, or nuns. According to the fortieth and forty-first minor precepts, anyone who had not committed any of seven heinous crimes or broken a major precept could be ordained. The seven heinous crimes were:

1. Shedding the blood of the Buddha
2. Patricide
3. Matricide
4. Killing one's preceptor
5. Killing one's teacher
6. Killing the director of a Buddhist ceremony
7. Killing a sage

The list of seven heinous crimes was unique to the *Fan-wang ching,* but was based on an early Buddhist list of five heinous crimes (nos. 1–3, 6–7) that resulted in a person dropping into the depths of Avīci Hell for all time. The *Fan-wang ching* softened the onus of these crimes by requiring that a person not have committed them during his current lifetime in order to be ordained. In addition, commission of a heinous crime no longer condemned a person to hell for all time, a doctrinal position in accord with many Mahāyāna teachings on the buddha-nature.

Annen further liberalized the restrictions on ordinations by arguing that even a person who had committed one of the seven heinous crimes during his current lifetime could be ordained if he confessed his wrongdoing. Although support for this position was not found in the *Fan-wang ching,* Annen cited a number of other sources that discussed the power of confession. He was particularly interested in practices based on the position that all karma was nonsubstantial, and that if a practitioner realized this truth, he could eliminate the karmic consequences of any wrongdoing. Finally, Annen cited a passage from the *Chi fa-yüeh* (Collection Resulting in Happiness at Hearing the Dharma), which stated that a certain dhāraṇī could eliminate the karmic consequences of the five heinous crimes. Annen concluded that the same dhāraṇī would be equally effective against the seven heinous crimes.[65]

Precedents for Annen's views on the power of confession can be found in the writings of a number of thinkers. For example, both T'ien-t'ai and Lü-tsung (Vinaya school) commentators had discussed the effect of confession ceremonies based on the principle that karma was nonsubstantial. However, these commentators had differed from Annen in one noteworthy way: they had generally noted that such ceremonies were for advanced practitioners only. They had warned that in the hands of beginners, the use of such practices could lead to gross immorality. For example, Chih-i (538–597) had warned against such problems in his discussion of the "neither walking nor sitting samādhi" *(higyō hiza zanmai),* in which the practitioner was allowed to meditate on the nonsubstantiality of evil. Chih-i had also been vitally concerned with confession ceremonies and had argued that confessions based on the principle *(risen)* of perceiving the true nature of wrongdoing were particularly effective at destroying evil karma. Moreover, for the practitioner of the Perfect Teaching, the precepts might not apply under special circumstances. For example, even killing might be justified to protect Buddhism and to prevent the intended victim from accumulating additional bad karma.[66] In all these cases, Chih-i had warned his followers against misunderstanding the teaching of the nonsubstantiality of evil and using it as a justification for the commission of wrongdoing. Tao-hsüan (596–667), the de facto founder of the Nan-shan Lü-tsung, noted that confession ceremonies based on the principle of nonsubstantiality *(risen)* of wrongdoing and karma were the most effective types of expiation and had the power to permanently destroy bad karma *(metsuzai),* whereas confessions based on repentance for a particular deed *(jisen)* were less effective and could only temporarily suppress bad karma *(bukuzai).* Confessions based on the principle of nonsubstantiality could be performed only by those practitioners with superior faculties, presumably because such confession could easily be misinterpreted by those with immature religious faculties.[67]

Annen's permissive attitudes toward violations of the precepts are also evident in his discussion of the expiation of wrongdoing. According to the forty-first minor precept, if a person who had been ordained with the *Fan-wang* precepts violated any of the major precepts, he lost the precepts. However, if he confessed his transgression and received a supernatural sign from the Buddha, such as a touch on his head or a vision of flowers, his precepts would be restored. Commentators noted that such signs could be perceived while the practitioner was either awake or dreaming. However, if the practitioner did not perceive such a sign, his precepts were not restored. Expiation of a major violation of the precepts required concerted effort and a sincere desire to reform.

If confession failed, a person who had broken a major precept could also receive the precepts again in a new ordination. Although the passage in the *Fan-wang ching* that permitted this option was subject to several interpretations, Annen cited passages from other texts such as the *Ying-lo ching* and *P'u-sa ti-ch'ih ching (Bodhisattvabhūmi)* that clearly allowed a person who had violated one of the major precepts to be ordained again. This position was adopted in commentaries by Fa-tsang (643–712) and I-chi (fl. late seventh century) and subsequently followed by Annen.[68] However, the effect of Annen's arguments was quite different from that of the two Chinese commentators. Both Fa-tsang and I-chi assumed that a monastic recipient of the *Fan-wang* precepts had also taken the *Ssu-fen lü* precepts, and that the latter were operative. Although the commentators might be forgiving about violations of the *Fan-wang* precepts, they could depend on the *Ssu-fen lü* precepts for the maintenance of monastic discipline. Receiving a new ordination was clearly a much easier alternative than undergoing confession until a special sign from the Buddha was received.

Violation of a major *Fan-wang* precept resulted in the loss of the precepts until the violation was expiated. However, Annen did not discuss the procedures by which the Order might have expelled monks who had violated major precepts. Since *Fan-wang* ordinations were said to be conferred by the Buddha and confession for major wrongdoing was performed in front of an image of the Buddha, Annen was able to ignore the role of the Order of monks in his discussion of the administration of the precepts.[69] The practical problems of adopting the *Fan-wang* precepts as the foundation of monastic behavior were not considered in any detail.

Rationales for the Observance and the Violation of the Precepts

At several points in the *Futsū kōshaku,* Annen suggested rationales that excused violations of the precepts. Annen insisted that a person's attitudes were far more important than adherence to the full set of precepts. In fact, for a bodhisattva, the observance of one precept was sufficient for ordination. For Annen, since the *Fan-wang* ordination qualified a person to become a monk, it could not be ignored. However, the ordination was significant to a person's spiritual progress because it instilled the attitudes of a bodhisattva within him, not because the recipient was obliged to observe the precepts. Annen cited the *Ying-lo ching* as canonical support for his position:

> The [*P'u-sa ying-lo*] *pen-yeh ching* states that if a person receives one precept, then he should be called a "one-part bodhisattva." If he receives the full set of precepts, then he should be called a "full bodhisattva." Thus we should realize that it is better to be ordained and not observe the precepts than it is to be without an ordination and observe the precepts. Even if a person [who has been ordained] breaks the precepts, he is still called a bodhisattva. However, a person who [has not been ordained and] does not break the precepts is called a follower of heterodox religions. How much more so is it with the precepts of the Perfect Vehicle? If a person observes even one precept, then he encompasses all the precepts.[70]

For Annen, the most important aspects of ordination were the development of the aspiration to realize enlightenment and the resolve to help sentient beings. If the practitioner developed these attitudes, then the issue of whether he literally observed every precept was of little importance. In fact, as long as the practitioner was motivated by such attitudes, he was not bound to observe any of the precepts. To demonstrate this point, Annen collected a number of traditional Buddhist tales in which virtually all the most important precepts of the *Ssu-fen lü* and *Fan-wang ching* are broken:

> Long ago, there was a man named Shih-chien-hsien who was taught by his teacher that he must kill a thousand people in order to demonstrate his loyalty. He set out to kill a thousand people and to string their fingers into a garland for his head. Consequently, he was known as Aṅgulimālya, which means "finger garland." However, because he killed out of devotion for his teacher, Aṅgulimālya's actions should not be considered violations of the precepts on taking life.[71]
>
> Long ago, King Virūdhaka killed countless numbers of people. This was because the people of his country were evil, stubborn, and difficult to teach. Only when they were faced with imminent death did they develop the aspiration for enlightenment. Thus King Virūdhaka's killings were called "entering the dharma realm" and did not constitute violations of the precept on taking life.[72]
>
> Long ago, Vasumitrā made the following vow in order to benefit sentient beings: "May anyone who kisses my mouth be able to speak eloquently. May anyone who embraces me receive great wisdom. May anyone who takes my hand accumulate great merit. May anyone who marries me realize supreme enlightenment." Thus illicit sexual activities served as her precepts, and her actions should not be considered violations of the precepts on illicit sexual conduct. . . .[73]
>
> You should understand that the ten evil acts and the three poisons can all serve as precepts. Ajātaśatru injured and killed his father and mother, but

> ignorance was his father and lust his mother. By performing such deeds, he made great progress in Buddhism. Although Devadatta committed three of the heinous sins *(sangyaku)* and is now in hell, it is like the pleasures of the third meditation heaven *(sanzen)* to him. Long ago he was Śākyamuni Buddha's teacher; now he is Śākyamuni's disciple. . . . Thus you should understand that the five heinous crimes and three evils are all like precepts [under the correct circumstances].[74]

Annen also cited the examples of the layman Vimalakīrti and the laywoman Mallikā to make the point that laypeople could be profoundly versed in Buddhist doctrine and not be hindered by their failure to remain chaste, be truthful, or refrain from alcohol.[75]

Annen did not completely ignore the traditional exhortations to observe the precepts. *Fan-wang* ordination manuals usually concluded with a section that encouraged the newly ordained person to adhere to the precepts. This section of the ordination ceremony is discussed in the eleventh section of the *Futsū kōshaku,* which consists of ten rationales for observing the precepts. Annen began by urging monks to adhere to all of the precepts, including those for Hīnayāna practitioners. However, the last nine rationales in his discussion are analyses of selective adherence to the precepts—in other words, treatments of the circumstances under which all or some of the precepts may be violated. For example, a distinction is drawn between true wrongdoing *(shōkai),* such as killing, and actions that are not necessarily morally wrong but that are prohibited in the precepts *(shakai),* often out of the need to conform to social convention. Restrictions concerning clothing and alcoholic beverages are considered to be examples of the latter type of precept. A practitioner could ignore precepts that were based on custom rather than moral standards. Such distinctions could be utilized by monks to select which rules they would observe. Monastic discipline would thus reflect the actual practices of ninth century Japan instead of India or China many centuries in the past. However, Annen went even further and maintained that precepts concerning taking life could be broken in order to benefit others or as expedients to draw others toward Buddhist teachings.

Annen also noted that if ordained monks were required to follow the precepts too rigidly, the passions that they were attempting to control, particularly their sexual desire, might become even stronger. Rather than be too strict, it was better to take a lax approach to monastic discipline. Annen compared the situation to fishing. If a fisherman pulled too strongly on his line when a fish took the bait, he might lose both the hook and the fish. But if he allowed the fish to have some freedom, he would eventually land it.

Finally, Annen argued that a true Mahāyāna practitioner violated the precepts only when he discriminated between objects: "You should realize that for a bodhisattva of the Perfect Vehicle all phenomena have the mark of suchness. If such a person has no thought of male and female, self and other, observing and breaking the precepts, then he truly observes the precepts."[76]

Annen's views on the precepts were not entirely new. He repeatedly cited passages from a variety of sūtras and śāstras to support his argument. However, when he did so, he often gave the texts new significance. Although these texts had originally been concerned with issues such as the effectiveness of sincere confession, the power of faith in the Buddha, the purity of the buddha-nature, the nonsubstantiality of good and evil, and use of expedient teachings, Annen now cited them for their relevance to the precepts. The main point of the texts had not been to foster a lax attitude toward monastic discipline, but to make doctrinal points. In fact, some of the texts contained passages that warned against misuse of the teachings that might seem to justify wrongdoing. However, when Annen repeatedly cited examples of violations of precepts in an ordination manual, he gave the impression that those who had just been ordained need not concern themselves with strict adherence to the precepts. The various cases of those who had broken the precepts were not treated as exceptional but as stories with general significance for anyone who had been ordained.

Annen's discussion of the ten rationales for observing the precepts concluded with an analysis of the three collections of pure precepts *(sanju jōkai):* (1) the precepts that prevent evil, (2) the precepts that promote good, and (3) the precepts that benefit sentient beings. Although these three categories originally referred to different aspects of the same precepts, they had long been used to rank different sets of precepts in a hierarchy that had the precepts preventing evil as the lowest level. The precepts preventing evil encompassed the various sets of precepts mentioned in the ten rationales, including those from the *Fan-wang ching;* the precepts promoting good were equated with the four *sanmaya* precepts; and the precepts that benefited sentient beings consisted of helping four groups to whom the practitioner owed debts of gratitude: his parents, all sentient beings, the ruler, and the Three Jewels. This list was based on a passage in a text, the *Hsin-ti kuan ching* (Sūtra on the Discernment of the Mind-Ground), which included many additions by Chinese monks.[77] Annen's emphasis on a person's obligations to help others was also based on a passage in the *Fan-wang ching* that identified filial piety with the precepts.[78] Thus any actions that were consistent with the goals of promoting good and benefiting sentient beings constituted observance of the precepts, even if they violated the literal meaning of some of the precepts preventing evil.

Annen did not pardon violations of the precepts that occurred out of selfish motives. However, he effectively argued for an interpretation of the precepts which was so permissive that it easily resulted in serious lapses in monastic discipline.

Annen's Position on the Hīnayāna Precepts

Annen's position on the Hīnayāna precepts differed from that of most of his Tendai predecessors. In the *Shijōshiki* (Rules in Four Articles), Saichō had stated that Tendai monks were to be permitted to go to Nara to receive a Hīnayāna *Ssu-fen lü* ordination after they had completed twelve years of training on Mt. Hiei. After Saichō's death, the expedient Hīnayāna ordination was abandoned by his disciples. Almost all subsequent Tendai thinkers were critical of the *Ssu-fen lü* precepts.[79] Even when Enchin adopted some of the procedures of the *Ssu-fen lü* to supplement the *Fan-wang ching,* there was never any suggestion that Tendai monks would be ordained with the *Ssu-fen lü* precepts.

Annen, however, seems to have had a much more favorable attitude toward the Hīnayāna precepts than any of the other early Tendai masters. Annen's clearest statement concerning the Hīnayāna precepts is found in the first of the ten "exhortations" to observe the precepts in the eleventh section of the *Futsū kōshaku:*

> 1. On observing all the precepts: According to the *Fan-wang ching,* as for the ten major and forty-eight minor precepts, "a person should not break a single one of them." Whether one wishes to be a monk, nun, male novice, female novice, layman, laywoman, or a probationary nun, one should follow all the ten major and forty-eight minor precepts. The *Yü-ch'ieh lun* (*Yogācārabhūmi-śāstra,* Stages of the Follower of Yoga Practice) states that although śrāvakas are concerned with benefiting themselves and with the opinions of others, bodhisattvas should make benefiting others their primary concern. Consequently, bodhisattvas should observe all the precepts that were formulated to accord with public opinion and custom *(kigenkai),* even if those precepts are not an integral part of the ultimate teaching. Bodhisattvas must observe all the precepts of the expedient teachings of the Hīnayāna, as well as those precepts that lead to rebirth as men or deities. If we do not observe them, we will not have done our utmost to help others. People will slander us and fall into bad rebirths as a result.[80]

At first, Annen might seem to be advocating that Tendai monks adhere to both the *Fan-wang* and *Ssu-fen lü* precepts, a position that would have strengthened monastic discipline in the Tendai school. However, his tolerance for the *Ssu-fen lü* precepts was probably motivated by other factors. First, since the autonomy of the Tendai school from the control of the Nara schools had already been clearly established, the conferral of *Ssu-fen lü* ordinations on Tendai monks did not threaten Tendai independence. Some Tendai monks, such as Annen's teacher Henjō, had permitted their disciples to study in Nara as a means of reducing tensions between the Tendai and Nara schools and facilitating the appointment of Tendai monks to the Office of Monastic Affairs (Sōgō). Second, some of the nobility had begun to seek initiations on the precepts platforms both at Tōdaiji and at Mt. Hiei. Annen's position on the Hīnayāna precepts provided a Tendai rationale for receiving both ordinations. Consequently, his tolerance of the Hīnayāna precepts must be viewed as a shrewd political move rather than as an attempt to strengthen monastic discipline in the Tendai school.[81]

Conclusion

The *Fan-wang ching* was composed late in the fifth century in China, a time when Chinese interest in the precepts was high because Hīnayāna and Mahāyāna texts on morality had just been translated. The contents of the *Fan-wang ching* reflected Chinese interests at the time. Such topics as filial piety and relations between Buddhism and the state are mentioned prominently in it. Within one or two centuries of its compilation, the text had come to play an important role in Chinese Buddhist life. Commentaries on it were written by some of the leading monks of the T'ang dynasty. A close reading of their interpretations of the *Fan-wang ching* demonstrates that the text was used in a variety of ways in China, often depending on the texts used in its interpretation.[82] The *Fan-wang ching* also played a major role in Korean Buddhism.[83]

The focus of this chapter was early Japanese Tendai interpretations of the *Fan-wang ching,* a text that has been one of the most influential apocryphal texts in Japanese religious history since the Nara period. With the approval of Saichō's proposal making it the basis of Tendai ordinations in 822, the *Fan-wang ching* could have become the basic text for monastic discipline in the Japanese Tendai school. Before this could occur, however, basic problems concerning the administration of the *Fan-wang* precepts had to be resolved. Saichō's disciples, instead of applying themselves to this task, devoted most of their time and energy to the mastery of Esoteric Buddhism. Although Ennin and Enchin attempted to supplement the *Fan-wang* precepts with passages from the *Ssu-fen lü* and from texts on the Mahāyāna precepts, they did not write a consistent and comprehensive work that solved the practical problems of administering the *Fan-wang ching.* In addition, they studiously ignored the issue of whether the burgeoning Tendai interest in Esoteric Buddhism had any implications for monastic discipline. Finally, sixty years after Saichō's death, Annen's *Futsū kōshaku* resolved many of these issues, but in a manner that probably would not have been satisfactory to Saichō, Ennin, or Enchin.

Annen was the first Tendai monk since Kōjō to seriously consider the implications that Esoteric Buddhism posed for monastic discipline. For

Annen, the attitudes specified in the idealistic and abstract Esoteric *(sanmaya)* precepts served as the basis of religious behavior. If the precepts of the *Fan-wang ching* or *Ssu-fen lü* were violated as part of a practitioner's efforts to act in accordance with the attitudes of the *sanmaya* precepts, such transgressions were a regrettable necessity. Moreover, even if the precepts were violated without such a lofty justification, a person could avail himself of powerful confession ceremonies or simply be ordained again. With such a free interpretation of the precepts, it no longer seemed so important to resolve the many practical problems of interpreting the *Fan-wang* precepts so that they could serve as an effective guide for monastic discipline. Most Tendai administrators resorted to writing sets of monastery regulations to control monastic behavior. In most of these monastery codes, little or no reference was made to the *Fan-wang* precepts.

Since Annen never served as the head *(zasu)* of the Tendai school, his interpretation of the *Fan-wang* precepts may not have been very influential during his lifetime. However, during the following centuries his interpretation of the precepts was adopted by many monks. Annen had presented a forceful and compelling argument with numerous scriptural citations. In addition, social and economic conditions in Japanese society had resulted in the ordination of many men who were not seriously interested in pursuing the religious austerities that had appealed to earlier Tendai monks.

After Annen's time, other interpretations of the precepts were advanced. Many of these also resulted in liberal interpretations of the precepts. For example, instead of being interpreted in terms of Esoteric Buddhism, the *Fan-wang* precepts were often considered in terms of the *Lotus Sūtra,* a text that contained general instructions about behavior but no specific rules concerning monastic discipline. Individual precepts could thus be violated if the general purport of the *Lotus Sūtra* was observed. The term "Perfect-Sudden precepts" *(endonkai),* by which the Tendai precepts are generally known today, came into common use as the *Fan-wang* rules were being subordinated to the general principles of the *Lotus Sūtra.*[84]

The precepts were also identified with other practices. Within Tendai, the Eshin-ryū and Danna-ryū factions maintained that practices such as the cultivation of the three truths were identical to observance of the precepts. Consequently, rigid adherence to the specific rules of the *Fan-wang ching* was not necessary. For those who maintained this view, keeping a lineage of the precepts was no longer necessary and ordinations were not regarded as very important. By the end of the Heian period, ordinations played a small role in the Tendai and other schools, and in some cases may not even have been performed.[85]

Other traditions, such as the Seizan sect of the Jōdo school and the

Shinsei sect of Tendai, argued that the performance of Pure Land practices, especially the chanting of Amida's name, were identical to observance of the precepts. Although these traditions recognized the importance of ordination, rigid adherence to the *Fan-wang* precepts was not necessarily required since the chanting of the *nenbutsu* could eliminate a practitioner's accumulated sins.[86]

Although the contents of the argument varied, the final result was that the actual rules of the *Fan-wang ching* were generally ignored for a seemingly higher principle. Periodically, attempts were made to reform a particular school by reviving the *Fan-wang* precepts or by calling for the renewed use of the *Ssu-fen lü* precepts, but most of these failed after a short time.

The history of the *Fan-wang ching* in Japanese Tendai reveals the immensely important role that some apocryphal works played in East Asian Buddhism. In this case, the text was interpreted so that it freed Japanese Tendai practitioners from some of the constraints of both Indian and Chinese models of behavior and thought. The use of the *Fan-wang ching* by Tendai monks also demonstrates that the interpretation of these texts constantly changed, often varying dramatically from the original intention of the compilers.

NOTES

1. The *Fan-wang ching* has been translated into French by J. J. M. De Groot, *Le Code du Mahayana en Chine: Son influence sur la vie monacal et sur le monde monacal* (Amsterdam: Verhider Kon. Ak. van Wetensch, 1893), 14–88.

2. *Ch'u-san-tsang chi-chi, T* 2145.55.79b, and *Fan-wang ching, T* 1484.24.997a–b; Ming-kuang, *T'ien-t'ai p'u-sa-chieh su, T* 1812.40.580c; Fa-tsang, *Fan-wang ching p'u-sa-chieh pen su, T* 1813.40.605a.

3. The *Ying-lo ching* was probably compiled slightly later than the *Fan-wang ching* and is closely related to it. Both texts mention the same set of ten major precepts. The compilation of the *Ying-lo ching* and its relationship to other texts has been extensively discussed by Satō Tetsuei in *Zoku Tendai Daishi no kenkyū* (Kyoto: Hyakkaen, 1981), 72–112.

4. Most commentaries on the *Fan-wang ching* discuss only the precepts in the second fascicle, although several Hossō commentaries are concerned with both fascicles. See Shirato Waka, "*Bonmōkyō* kenkyū josetsu," *Ōtani daigaku kenkyū nenpō* 22 (1970):119–121, for a survey of commentaries.

5. Shirato has noted that four different formats for the *Fan-wang* Prātimokṣa were used by commentators ("Kenkyū josetsu," pp. 111–114).

6. Although Chih-i, the de facto founder of the T'ien-t'ai school, is said to have written a commentary (*T* no. 1811) on the precepts of the *Fan-wang ching,* when he discussed the stages of practice of the bodhisattva path in his other works, he ignored the *Fan-wang ching* and relied on the *Ying-lo ching,* an apocryphal text that was better organized and had a more complete discussion of the

stages of practice. Chih-i and other Chinese scholars were willing to refer to texts that they knew were apocryphal when they believed that the passage under discussion was in accord with the basic purport of Buddhism (see Makita Tairyō, "Tendai Daishi no gikyōkan," *Shikan no kenkyū* [Tokyo: Iwanami shoten, 1975], 201–215).

7. *Kao-seng chuan, T* 2059.50.332b, 362b.

8. The postface of the *Fan-wang ching* is found in *T* 2145.55.79b; the prefaces are found in *T* 1484.24.997a–b. The postface and prefaces are analyzed in Mochizuki Shinkō, *Bukkyō kyōten seiritsushiron* (Kyoto: Hōzōkan, 1978), 442–449. The postface and prefaces have been translated into English and discussed by Leo Pruden, "Some Notes on the *Fan-wang-ching,*" *Indogaku bukkyōgaku kenkyū* (hereafter *IBK*) 15.2 (1967):915–925.

9. *Chung-ching mu-lu, T* 2146.55.140a.

10. Mochizuki, *Bukkyō kyōten,* pp. 442–450. Mochizuki's argument for the Chinese compilation of the text is also found in his *Jōdokyō no kigen oyobi hattatsu* (Tokyo: Sankibō Busshorin, 1972), 155–184. A number of other scholars have also argued that the *Fan-wang ching* was compiled in China. See Ōno Hōdo, *Daijō kaikyō no kenkyū* (Tokyo: Risōsha, 1954), 252–284; Ishida Mizumaro, *Bonmōkyō* (Tokyo: Daizō shuppansha, 1971), 11–15; Shirato, "Kenkyū josetsu"; and idem, "*Bonmōkyō* no keitai," *Ōtani daigaku bukkyōgaku seminā* 16 (1972):30–42. Hirakawa Akira has noted that although the text may have been compiled in China, much of its content is borrowed directly from Indian sources (Hirakawa's opinion is recorded in Ch'ae Inhwan, *Shiragi bukkyō kairitsu shisō kenkyū* [Tokyo: Kokusho kankōkai, 1977], 396).

11. *T* nos. 245, 374, 1581, 1582, 1488, respectively. Aspects of some of these texts are discussed in Groner, "The Ordination Ritual in the *Platform Sūtra* within the Context of the East Asian Vinaya Tradition," in Proceedings of the International Conference on the *Platform Sūtra* (Kaohsiung, Taiwan: Fo-kuang shan, forthcoming). Useful charts demonstrating how the *Fan-wang precepts* were probably based on passages from other texts are found in Ōno, *Daijō kaikyō,* pp. 267, 271–273.

12. Mochizuki Shinkō, *Bukkyō kyōten,* p. 446.

13. *Hsü kao-seng chuan, T* 2060.50.471b; *Li-tai san-pao chi, T* 2034.49.100a.

14. *Fan-wang ching, T* 1484.24.1004a–b.

15. Minor precepts nos. 13, 17, 21, 37, 38, 39, 40, 42, 43, 47, 48. The major precepts are found in *T* 1484.24.1004b–1005a, and the minor precepts are listed in 1005a–1009b. Rather than give page numbers for each precept cited, I have referred to them by number.

16. Major precepts nos. 1–3. Sakaino Kōyō has analyzed Chinese commentaries on the *Fan-wang ching* and argued that the ten major and thirty-six of the forty-eight minor precepts were usually said to apply to lay believers, monks, and nuns (*Shina bukkyō seishi* [Tokyo: Kokusho kankōkai, 1972], 842–843). However, individual commentators differed on the range of people to whom they applied the precepts. Fa-tsang interpreted the *Fan-wang* precepts as being appropriate for virtually anyone, but Chih-i interpreted them as suitable only for advanced bodhisattvas (Yoshizu Yoshihide, "Hōzō no *Bonmōkyō bosatsu kaihon sho,*" in Kamata Shigeo hakase kanreki kinen ronshū kankōkai, ed., *Chūgoku no bukkyō to bunka* [Tokyo: Daizō shuppansha, 1988], 273–274).

17. Special invitations are mentioned in three of the minor precepts (nos. 26–28). The *Fan-wang ching* takes a much stricter position on the issue than either the *Ssu-fen lü* or the *Yü-ch'ieh shih-ti lun (Yogācārabhūmi-śāstra),* both of which permitted special invitations to monks under certain circumstances. Since completely prohibiting special invitations was impractical, most commentators permitted them at times. Requirements for monastic officials are mentioned in minor precept no. 25.

18. Satō Tatsugen, "*Bonmōkyō* ni okeru shingaku bosatsu no kairitsu," *Komazawa daigaku bukkyōgakubu kenkyū kiyō* 41 (1983):111.

19. Tōdō Kyōshun ("Kōnan to Kōhoku no bukkyō: Bosatsukai deshi kōtei to kōtei soku nyorai," *Bukkyō shisō* 4 [1981]:1–18) has contrasted Buddhism in southern China, where a ruler was often treated as a disciple who followed the bodhisattva precepts, with Buddhism in northern China, where rulers were sometimes identified with the Buddha. Tsuchihashi Shūkō ("Kairitsu to ōron: Bonmōkai ni tsuite," *Ryūkoku daigaku ronshū* 404 [1974]:20–54) has suggested that one of the objectives of the compilers of the *Fan-wang ching* was to influence rulers to act in accordance with Mahāyāna ideals of a bodhisattva. Annen was aware of how often bodhisattva precepts had been conferred on rulers and discussed the subject in the *Futsū kōshaku, T* 2381.74.760b–c.

20. Satō, "*Bonmōkyō* ni okeru shingaku bosatsu," p. 116; Ishida Mizumaro, *Ganjin: sono kairitsu shisō* (Tokyo: Daizō shuppansha, 1974), 253–267.

21. For a full discussion of this tradition, see Tsuchihashi Shūkō, *Kairitsu no kenkyū* (Kyoto: Nagata bunshōdō, 1980), pp. 1033–1046; and Groner, "The Ordination Ritual in the *Platform Sūtra.*"

22. For a discussion of the differences between the positions of the *Bodhisattvabhūmi* and the *Ying-lo ching* on the "Hīnayāna" precepts, see Groner, *Saichō: The Establishment of the Japanese Tendai School* (Berkeley: Berkeley Buddhist Series, 1984), 215.

23. For a survey of Chinese views on the first major precept, see Ishida, *Bonmōkyō,* pp. 75–82.

24. Groner, *Saichō,* p. 119.

25. For a list of the monastery rules compiled by Tendai monks, see Ogami Kanchū, "Tendaishū ni okeru kyōdan goji no shomondai," *Nihon bukkyō gakkai nenpō* 39 (1973):151–171.

26. Enchin, *Fugen bosatsu gyōhōgyō monku gōki, Dainihon bukkyō zensho* (Tokyo: Bussho kankōkai, 1912–1930), 26:508a–b.

27. Groner, "Annen, Tankei and Henjō and Monastic Discipline in the Tendai School: The Background of the *Futsū jubosatsukai kōshaku,*" *Japanese Journal of Religious Studies* 14.2–3 (1987):133; and idem, *Saichō,* pp. 301–302.

28. Asai Endō, *Jōko Nihon Tendai honmon shisōshi* (Kyoto: Heirakuji shoten, 1973), 370–371. The views of Kōjō, Ennin, and Enchin on the precepts are discussed in Groner, *Saichō,* pp. 292–306. For a useful discussion of the interaction between Esoteric Buddhism and the precepts in early Tendai, see Ishida Mizumaro, "Enkai to mikkyō to no kōshō," *IBK* 9.1 (1961):277–280.

29. *Ta-jih ching su, T* 1796.39.757c; this principle was also applied to the Esoteric *sanmaya* precepts at times. In the Tendai tradition, violation of one of the ten major *sanmaya* precepts is sometimes said to be a *sthūlātyaya* offense (*Sanmayakai shiki,* in Ōmori Shin'ō, ed., *Kokuyaku seikyō taikei:* Taimitsu-bu [Tokyo:

Kokusho kankōkai, 1975] 4:3). *Sthūlātyaya* offenses can be described as failed attempts to commit *pārājika* or *saṅghādisesa* offenses (offenses punished respectively with expulsion and suspension). Among the examples that have been given are attempted murder in which the wrong person is killed. Since the monk did not intend to kill the person who died, his or her death would not be grounds for charging the monk with committing a *pārājika* offense. The *sthūlātyaya* would usually be expiated by confessing the wrongdoing. The type of confession required varied according to the severity of the offense (Hirakawa Akira, *Genshi bukkyō no kenkyū* [Tokyo: Shunjūsha, 1964], 283–288).

30. Ōmura Seigai discusses Esoteric texts in the order in which they were translated in his monumental *Mikkyō hattatsushi* (Tokyo: Bukkyō kankōkai, 1918). Although the number of references to rituals involving activities prohibited by the *Vinaya* increases in later texts, many references to such activities are found by the time of Amoghavajra (ibid., pp. 540–542, 677–678, 680, 684, 690).

31. *Ta-p'i-lu-che-na ch'eng-fo shen-pien chia-ch'ih ching, T* 848.18.39b; *Ta-lo chin-kang pu-k'ung chen-shih san-mei-yeh ching po-jo po-lo-mi-to li-ch'ü shih, T* 1003.19.616c; *Ta-p'i-lu-che-na ch'eng-fo ching su, T* 1796.39.759a.

32. For a discussion of some of the moral issues associated with Esoteric Buddhism, see Matsunaga Yūkei, *Mikkyō kyōten seiritsushi ron* (Kyoto: Hōzōkan, 1980), pp. 64–82.

33. *Ta-jih ching i-shih yen-mi ch'ao, ZZ* 1.37.1–2; also see *Sung kao-seng chuan, T* 2061.50.715c, 791a–b; the text was compiled in the eleventh century by the Chinese monk Chüeh-yüan. Japanese Taimitsu scholars are said to have been attracted by its position that both the Perfect and Esoteric teachings belonged to the One-vehicle (Ono Genmyō, ed., *Bussho kaisetsu daijiten* [Tokyo: Daitō shuppansha, 1964], 7:387a).

34. The important role of the *Futsū kōshaku* in medieval Tendai is mentioned in the early-fourteenth-century text, the *Keiranshūyōshū* (*T* 76.692b). Many modern scholars have argued that Annen's views on the precepts decisively influenced later Japanese attitudes toward monastic discipline. Among them are: Tsukamoto Zenryū, ed., *Jōdoshū daijiten* (Tokyo: Sankibō, 1974), 1:141c; Takagi Yutaka, *Kamakura bukkyōshi kenkyū* (Tokyo: Yoshikawa kōbunkan, 1982), 55; Taga Munehaya, *Eisai* (Tokyo: Yoshikawa kōbunkan, 1965), 236–237; Fujita Kairyū, "Endonkai shisō shijō ni okeru Godaiin Annen no ichi," in Buttan nisen gohyaku nen kinen gakkai, ed., *Buttan nisen gohyaku nen gakkai kiyō* (Tokyo: 1935), 57–62; Tonegawa Hiroyuki, "Shoki Nihon Tendai no enkai," *Tendai gakuhō* 27 (1984):75–79.

35. Chan-jan's manual, the *Shou p'u-sa-chieh i* (*ZZ* 2.10.1), established the twelve-part format followed by most subsequent manuals; for a discussion of it, see Groner, "The Ordination Ritual in the *Platform Sūtra.*" For example, the *Jubosatsukaigi* (*T* 2378, called the *Wakokubon* [Japanese manual] by Annen), is a manual written for the Japanese Tendai school by Saichō or one of his immediate disciples that closely follows Chan-jan's manual.

36. Shōshin's subcommentary has not survived; however, it is quoted approximately fifty times in the *Bosatsu kaigishoshō* (*Dainihon bukkyō zensho* [Tokyo: Suzuki gakujutsu zaidan, 1971] 16:1–65) by Enrin (b. 1174?). Shōshin, with the support of the Tendai head monk *(zasu)* Jien, hoped to discourage Japanese Tendai monks from subordinating Chih-i's teachings to Esoteric Bud-

dhism and *hongaku* (original enlightenment) thought. To revive the study of traditional Chinese exoteric T'ien-t'ai studies, Shōshin wrote extensive commentaries on Chih-i's major works. Shōshin's desire to revive observance of the precepts was probably closely connected to his critical attitude toward Esoteric Buddhism. For more on Shōshin's subcommentary on the *Fan-wang ching,* see: Nakao Ryōshin, "Enrinshō ni okeru Shōshin no in'yō," *Komazawa daigakuin bukkyō kenkyūkai nenpō* 13 (1979):66–73; Kotera Bun'ei, "Hōjibō Shōshin no *Jike bosatsukai ryakusahō,*" *IBK* 18.2 (1970):30.

37. *Futsū kōshaku, T* 2381.74.764b. The ten expedient precepts *(hōben gakusho)* are identical to the ten virtuous precepts *(jūzenkai)* and are found in the *Ta-jih ching* (*T* 848.18.39a–c). The four grave sins *(shōzai)* are wrongdoings that are intrinsically immoral regardless of the circumstances under which they are committed. They consist of killing, stealing, illicit sexual behavior, and lying.

38. *Kyōji mondō, T* 2396.75.400a–b. The four major precepts are probably those mentioned in the *Bodhisattvabhūmi.* The six major and twenty-eight minor precepts are found in the *Yu-p'o-sai chieh ching* (*T* 1488). The five vehicles mentioned in the text are discussed in Groner, *Saichō,* pp. 183–186. The maṇḍala to which Annen refers is the Taizōkai (Womb-realm) maṇḍala.

Both the *Chin-kang-ting ching* and the *Fan-wang ching* were said to have been only a small part of much larger texts, thus suggesting to commentators that the two texts might have been related (*T* 1798.39.808a). The *Chin-kang-ting i-chüeh* is said to be a record of Vajrabodhi's comments on the *Chin-kang-ting ching,* which was written down by Amoghavajra in 723. If this account is correct, it would be the earliest and one of the most important commentaries on the *Chin-kang-ting ching.* The text was said to have originally been three fascicles long, but the last two fascicles were lost by the time Enchin brought the text to Japan. Although the text clearly dates from the T'ang dynasty, Ōmura Seigai has questioned the traditional story of how it was recorded by Amoghavajra, thus casting doubt on its authenticity (Ōmura, *Mikkyō hattatsushi,* pp. 507–508; Ono, *Bussho kaisetsu daijiten* 3:480).

Annen's comment that the *Fan-wang ching* was an elementary level of the *Chin-kang-ting ching* referred to a four-part system of interpreting teachings *(shijūhishaku)* used by Esoteric thinkers: (1) elementary *(senryakushaku)* refers to superficial interpretations; (2) profound *(shinpishaku)* refers to exoteric Buddhist interpretations; (3) the secret within the profound *(hichū shinpishaku)* refers to Esoteric teachings that explain issues unexplained in exoteric Buddhism; and (4) the most secret within the profound *(hihichū shinpishaku)* refers to the most profound level of Esoteric explanation. In the *Kanjō gusokushibun,* Annen argued that Vajrabodhi probably classified the *Fan-wang ching* as elementary because of its restrictions on ordinations for those who had committed the seven heinous crimes (*T* 2393.75.234a). In other writings, Annen noted that the *Fan-wang ching* is the capping sūtra for the *Hua-yen ching (Avataṃsaka-sūtra)* and that both are elementary teachings of the *Chin-kang-ting ching* (*T* 2397.75.513a).

39. *Chin-kang-ting i-ch'ieh ju-lai chen-shih she ta-sheng hsien-cheng ta-chiao wang-ching, T* 865.18.207c–208a. For a discussion of the significance of the reformulation of the story of Śākyamuni's enlightenment in Esoteric terms, see Hirakawa Akira, *Indo bukkyōshi* (Tokyo: Shunjūsha, 1979) 2:343. Annen treated this story as the model upon which Tendai ordinations were based (*Futsū kōshaku, T*

2381.74.775a). For a discussion of Annen's views of the *sanmaya* precepts based on sources other than the *Futsū kōshaku,* see Kubota Tessei, "Annen no sanmayakai setsu ni tsuite," *IBK* 35.1 (1986):150–153.

40. The four-part definition of *sanmaya* is based on a passage in the *Ta-p'i-lu-che-na ch'eng-fo ching su* (*T* 1796.39.674c), a commentary on the *Mahāvairocana-sūtra* by Śubhakarasiṃha and I-hsing which is one of the most influential texts in East Asian Esoteric Buddhism. This definition was later adopted in both Tōmitsu and Taimitsu works. See, for example, Ōmori Shin'ō, *Kokuyaku seikyō taikei: Taimitsu-bu* (Tokyo: Kokusho kankōkai, 1975), 4:3. Almost all of the modern research on the *sanmaya* precepts has been based on Shingon (Tōmitsu) interpretations. For information on Taimitsu interpretations, the best sources are the notes in the *Sanmayakai shiki, Kokuyaku seikyō taikei: Taimitsu-bu* 4:1–79, and Shibutani Jigai, ed., *Kandō kyōchū kanjō shikimon* (1938), 1–33. The texts included in these two works were compiled after Annen's time. Also see *Asabashō, T (Zuzō)* 8:779–787.

41. Conversation with Professor Kiuchi Gyōō of Taishō University on 15 June 1983. Toganoo Shōun noted that in the Shingon school, the *sanmaya* precepts were conferred in a variety of ceremonies. However, depending on the monk's lineage, *sanmaya* ordinations were used in two general ways: (1) solely for elementary *(kechien)* initiations, and (2) for both elementary and advanced *(denbō)* initiations (*Mikkyō jisō no kenkyū* [Tokyo: Rinsen shoten, 1982], 113).

42. Ono Katsutoshi, *Nittō guhō gyōreki: Chishō Daishi Enchin hen* (Kyoto: Hōzōkan, 1982), 214.

43. *Ta-jih ching, T* 848.18.40a; also see 12b.

44. *Wu-wei san-ts'ang ch'an-yao, T* 917.18.943c–944a. Śubhakarasiṃha's list played an important role in Kūkai's view of the *sanmaya* precepts (*Himitsu sanmaya butsukaigi,* in Katsumata Shunkyō, ed., *Kōbō Daishi chosaku zenshū* (Tokyo: Sankibō Busshorin, 1970) 2:159–160.

45. Kūkai generally maintained a position on the precepts that was acceptable to the monks of Nara. One way in which he differed, however, was in following the Mūlasarvāstivādin *Vinaya* instead of the Dharmaguptaka *Vinaya.* Among the reasons that have been suggested for Kūkai's preference have been: (1) Amoghavajra and other Chinese Esoteric masters followed the Mūlasarvāstivādin precepts, (2) Saichō had discredited the Dharmaguptaka *Vinaya,* and (3) the stories *(avadāna)* in the Mūlasarvāstivāda *Vinaya* contained a number of Mahāyāna elements (Takagi Shingen, "Kūkai no kai to fuhō ni tsuite," in Wada Shūjō and Takagi Shingen, eds., *Kūkai: Nihon meisō ronshū* [Tokyo: Yoshikawa kōbunkan, 1982] 3:112–121; Hirakawa Akira, "Kairitsu to mikkyō," *Mikkyōgaku kenkyū* 18 [1986]:2–5; and Katsumata Shunkyō, *Mikkyō no Nihonteki tenkai* [Tokyo: Shunjūsha, 1970], 65–104, in which Kūkai's view of the *Ssu-fen lü* precepts is discussed on pp. 94–95.

46. For good accounts of the controversy, see Ishida Mizumaro, "Onjōji kaidan," in idem, *Nihon shisō kenkyū* (Kyoto: Hōzōkan, 1986) 2:145–196; and Tsuji Zennosuke, *Nihon bukkyōshi* (Tokyo: Iwanami shoten, 1944), 1:824–842.

47. *Kongōji monjo,* no. 105, quoted in Hirata Toshiharu, *Heian jidai no kenkyū* (Tokyo: San'ichi shobō, 1943), 12–14.

48. For a discussion of the significance of the term "Perfect precepts" in Chinese T'ien-t'ai, see Groner, *Saichō,* pp. 220–236.

49. For studies of Tendai views of *sokushin jōbutsu,* see Groner's articles: "The *Lotus Sūtra* and Saichō's Interpretation of the Realization of Buddhahood with This Very Body *(sokushin jōbutsu),*" in George J. Tanabe, Jr., and Willa Jane Tanabe, eds., *The Lotus Sūtra in Japanese Culture* (Honolulu: University of Hawaii Press, 1989); "Tendai Interpretations of the Realization of Buddhahood with This Very Body *(sokushin jōbutsu)* after the Death of Saichō: Sources and Preliminary Considerations," in David Chappell, ed., *Studies in Tendai/T'ien-t'ai* (forthcoming); "Shortening the Path: The Interpretation of the Realization of Buddhahood in This Very Existence in the Early Tendai School," in Robert Buswell and Robert Gimello, eds., *Paths to Liberation: The Mārga and Its Transmutations in Buddhist Thought* (Honolulu: University of Hawaii Press, 1991).

50. *Futsū kōshaku, T* 2381.74.758a.

51. For a fuller discussion of the *rokusoku,* see Groner, *Saichō,* pp. 28n–29n; and idem, "The *Lotus Sūtra* and Saichō's Interpretation of the Realization of Buddhahood with This Very Body."

52. *Futsū kōshaku, T* 2381.74.765b. The quotations are found in *Ta yüan-chüeh ching, T* 842.17.915; *Fan-wang ching, T* 1484.24.10004a; *Miao-fa lien-hua ching, T* 262.9.31a (Leon Hurvitz, trans., *Scripture of the Lotus Blossom of the Supreme Dharma* [New York: Columbia University Press, 1976], 176). The teaching of *Ta yüan-chüeh ching* is summarized rather than quoted literally.

53. See Ishida Mizumaro, *Nihon bukkyō ni okeru kairitsu no kenkyū* (Tokyo: Zaike bukkyō kyōkai, 1963), 414–415.

54. *Dainihon bukkyō zensho* (Suzuki gakujutsu zaidan, ed.), 41:68a–84a.

55. *Fan-wang ching, T* 1484.24.1003c, 1006b. In discussions of the definition of *sanmaya* as meaning "equal," the relationship of the *sanmaya* precepts to the buddha-nature is often raised.

56. This approach is based on Tsuchihashi Shūkō, "Shō to shu no mondai: *Nehangyō* ni okeru tenkai," *Kairitsu no kenkyū,* pp. 193–213.

57. For a discussion of some of the reasons why the essence of the precepts was regarded as being a "quasi-physical" entity that entered the person, see Hirakawa Akira, *A History of Indian Buddhism* (Honolulu: University of Hawaii Press, 1990), chap. 12.

58. Saichō, *Jubosatsukaigi, T* 2378.74.628b. Chan-jan, *Shou p'u-sa-chieh i, Jōdo-shū zensho* (Tokyo: Sankibō Busshorin, 1971), 15:876–877. Examples of passages from the *Mahāparinirvāṇa-sūtra* that are paraphrased in the ordination manuals are found in *T* 374.12.511a, 533b; 375.12.755a, 778a.

59. *Yü-ch'ieh shih-ti lun, T* 1579.30.522a. Both Etani Ryūkai ("Annen no *Futsū kōshaku* ni mirareru enkai shisō," *Okuda Jiō Sensei kiju kinen: Bukkyō shisō ronshū* [Kyoto: Heirakuji shoten, 1976], 317) and Kotera Bun'ei, ("Annen oshō to enkai," *Annen oshō no kenkyū* [Kyoto: Dōhōsha, 1979], pt. 1, pp. 90–91) argue that the threefold division was probably devised by Annen. The passage in the *Yogācārabhūmi-śāstra,* ignored by most commentators, lists four types of precepts.

60. See Groner, *Saichō,* p. 259, for the *Fan-wang* lineage.

61. *Futsū kōshaku, T* 2381.74.773c.

62. Ibid., 774a.

63. *Yü-ch'ieh shih-ti lun, T* 1579.30.515c; *P'u-sa ti-ch'ih ching, T* 1581.30.913b; *P'u-sa ying-lo pen-yeh ching, T* 1485.24.1024b.

64. *Futsū kōshaku, T* 2381.74.764c, 765b.

65. Ibid., 759b, 773b. This position is mentioned in T'ai-hsien's commentary on the *Fan-wang* precepts as one of a number of positions held by exegetes (*T* 1815.40.716b). The *Chi fa-yüeh* dhāraṇī is mentioned in the *Chi fo pa p'u-sa so-shuo ta t'o-lo-ni shen-chou ching* (*T* 1332.21.544b–c) and the *T'o-lo-ni tsa-chi* (*T* 1336.21.631a–b). The *Chi fa-yüeh* is listed in Nara-period bibliographies (Ishida Mosaku, *Shakyō yori mitaru Narachō bukkyō no kenkyū* [Tokyo: Hara shobō, 1982], bibliography, no. 1795). Debates arose in the twelfth and thirteenth centuries about whether a person who had committed any of the seven heinous sins could confess the wrongdoing and be ordained (Kubota Tessei, "Enkai ni okeru shichigyaku jukai no mondai," *IBK* 32.2 [1984]:750–753).

66. For comments on Chih-i's view of meditation on evil, see Tamura Yoshirō, *Bukkyō no shisō: Zettai no shinri* (Tokyo: Kadokawa shoten, 1970), 163–165; and Neal Donner, "Chih-i's Meditation on Evil," in David Chappell, ed., *Buddhist and Taoist Practice in Medieval Chinese Society* (Honolulu: University of Hawaii Press, 1987), 49–64. Chih-i's views on confession and justified instances of killing are discussed in Fukushima Kōsai, "Chigi no kairitsu shisō," in Sasaki Kyōgo, ed., *Kairitsu shisō no kenkyū* (Kyoto: Heirakuji shoten, 1981), 343–366.

67. For studies of Tao-hsüan's views on confession, see Satō Tatsugen, "*Gyōjishō* ni okeru sangehō," *Komazawa daigaku bukkyō gakubu kenkyū kiyō* 39 (1981):37–58; and Tokuda Myōhon, *Risshū gairon* (Kyoto: Hyakkaen, 1969), 313–327.

68. *T* 2381.74.772b. Annen claims that the quotation is from the *P'u-sa ti-(ch'ih ching)*, but it is actually from the *Yü-ch'ieh-shih ti lun* (*T* 1579.30.521a–b). A related text is found in the *P'u-sa ti-ch'ih ching* (*T* 1581.30.917a). The relevant passages from the commentaries by Fa-tsang and I-chi are found in *T* 1813.40.652c–653a and *T* 1814.40.685c.

69. The Tendai *Fan-wang* ordination was based, in part, on a passage from the *Kuan P'u-hsien p'u-sa hsing-fa ching* (*T* 277.9.393c) which stated that the candidate for ordination was to ask Śākyamuni to serve as his preceptor, Mañjuśrī to serve as the master of ceremonies, Maitreya to serve as the teacher who questioned the candidate about his qualifications, the buddhas of the ten directions to serve as witnesses, and the bodhisattvas of the ten directions to be his fellow students. The human teacher did not confer the precepts; rather, he was said to "transmit" *(den)* the precepts while the Buddha "conferred" *(ju)* them. In his comments on the type of person qualified to transmit the precepts, Annen noted that holding correct views was much more important than blind adherence to the precepts, since any violation of the precepts can be atoned for through confession (*Futsū kōshaku, T* 2381.74.762b; also see 767a–770b).

70. *Futsū kōshaku, T* 2381.74.777b. The quotation from the *Ying-lo ching* is located in *T* 1484.24.1021b.

71. Shih-chien-hsien is one of the Chinese translations of the name Aṅgulimālya (*Bukkyō daijii* [Tokyo: Fūzanbō, 1935], 433b). Aṅgulimālya was chosen as the subject of a text (*T* 120) on tathāgatagarbha theory, probably to illustrate that his buddha-nature remained pure despite his numerous murders. In the text, the Buddha argues that tathāgatagarbha teachings should not be taken as an excuse for wrongdoing. See Takasaki Jikidō's extensive analysis of the text (*Nyoraizō shisō no keisei* [Tokyo: Shunjūsha, 1974], 191–233).

72. Virūdhaka was the king of Kosalā. Because he had been insulted by the

Śākyas, he attacked their country and destroyed it, massacring many of them in the process. In early sources, he is said to have dropped into Avīci Hell.

73. Vasumitrā, a prostitute, appears in the *Hua-yen ching (Avataṃsaka-sūtra)* as the twenty-sixth of the fifty-five teachers visited by the youth Sudhana, who is in search of Buddhist teachings.

74. *Futsū kōshaku, T* 2381.74.765c–766a. Ajātaśatru killed his father in order to seize the throne. He is the subject of a number of Buddhist texts. In Mahāyāna scriptures, he serves to illustrate how faith in the Buddha and confession enable a person to expiate even the worst wrongdoing. For an analysis of the ways in which Ajātaśatru has been treated in the Buddhist canon, see Hirakawa Akira, "Daijō kyōten no hattatsu to Ajaseō setsuwa," *IBK* 39 (1971):1–12. Devadatta was the Buddha's cousin and Ānanda's brother. His three heinous crimes were purposefully shedding the Buddha's blood, causing a schism in the Order, and killing a sage (the nun Utpalavarnā). Although in early sources Devadatta is said to have dropped into hell for these crimes, in the *Lotus Sūtra* he is said to have been the Buddha's teacher in an earlier life and the prediction is made that he will eventually become a Buddha (Hurvitz, trans., *Scripture of the Lotus Blossom,* pp. 196–197).

75. Vimalakīrti's activities are described in the *Vimalakīrtinirdeśa-sūtra* (*T* 474–476), which has been translated into English several times. Mallikā violated the precepts against lying and alcoholic beverages as a stratagem to teach others about Buddhism (*Wei-ts'eng-yu yin-yüan ching, T* 754.17.585b–587b).

76. *Futsū kōshaku, T* 2381.74.777b–778b. The quotation is found on 778a.

77. For the four debts of gratitude, see the *Hsin-ti kuan ching* (*T* 159.3.297b–c), which was translated in 811. Its references to the *Fan-wang* precepts and emphasis on filial piety have led to questions about the authenticity of the text. Ōno Hōdō (*Daijō kaikyō no kenkyū,* p. 286) has suggested that the text must have been altered in China. Other modern scholars have been more reluctant to question its authenticity (e.g., Katsumata Shunkyō, *Kōbō Daishi no shisō to sono genryū* [Tokyo: Sankibō Busshorin, 1981], 209–239). The passage cited by Annen was also cited by Ennin in the *Ken'yō daikairon* (*T* 2380.74.705c). In addition, Kūkai discussed the four debts of gratitude in a number of his writings, and mentioned them once in a discussion of the *Fan-wang ching* (*Shōryōshū,* in Katsumata Shunkyō, ed., *Kōbō Daishi chosaku zenshū* [Tokyo: Sankibō Busshorin, 1973] 3: 347–352).

78. *Fan-wang ching ching, T* 1484.24.1004a; *Futsū kōshaku, T* 2381.74.766a.

79. For a discussion of the provisional Hīnayāna ordination, see Groner, *Saichō,* pp. 195–205.

80. *Futsū kōshaku, T* 2381.74.777b. The quotation from the *Fan-wang ching* is located at *T* 1484.24.1005a. The reference to the *Yü-ch'ieh lun* is probably a paraphrase of *T* 1579.30.517a.

81. For Henjō's attitude toward the Nara schools and the Sōgō, see Groner, *Saichō,* pp. 283–284; and idem, "Annen, Tankei and Henjō and Monastic Discipline in the Tendai School, pp. 148–150.

82. The complex history of the precepts in China deserves detailed study. Chinese bodhisattva ordinations are discussed in Groner, "The Ordination Ritual in the *Platform Sūtra.*" References to some of the Japanese scholarship on this topic can be found in that paper.

83. Ch'ae Inhwan has composed an exhaustive study of Korean views of the precepts *(Shiragi bukkyō kairitsu shisō kenkyū).*

84. One of the earliest texts with this interpretation is the *Gakushōshiki mondō* (*Dengyō Daishi zenshū,* 1:335–414), which is attributed to Saichō but was probably written around the thirteenth century; also see Etani Ryūkai, "Endonkai no konpon mondai," *Ōtani daigaku bukkyōgaku seminā* 15 (1972):75–80.

85. Hirata (*Heian jidai no kenkyū,* p. 10) suggested that ordinations were completely ignored by some traditions. A recent book by Matsuo Kenji, however, demonstrates that ordinations remained important as initiation ceremonies throughout the Heian and Kamakura periods (*Kamakura shin bukkyō no kenkyū: nyūmon girei to shoshi shinwa* [Tokyo: Yoshikawa kōbunkan, 1988]).

86. Etani, "Endonkai no konpon mondai," pp. 83–85.

GLOSSARY

Annen 安然
bodaishin 菩提心
Bosatsu daizōkyō 菩薩大蔵経
bukuzai 伏罪
byōdō 平等
Chan-jan 湛然
Chi-fa yüeh 集法悦
Chi-tsang 吉蔵
Chih-chou 智周
Chih-i 智顗
Chin-kang-ting ching 金剛頂経
Chin-kang-ting i-chüeh 金剛頂義決
Ch'u san-tsang chi chi 出三蔵記集
Daikyō 大経
Danna-ryū 檀那流
den 伝
denjukai 伝受戒
Enchin 円珍
endonkai 円頓戒
engyō 円教
enkai 円戒
Ennin 円仁
Enryakuji 延暦寺
Eshin-ryū 恵心流
Fa-ching lu 法経録
Fa-hsiang 法相
Fa-tsang 法蔵
Fan-wang ching 梵網経
Futsū jubosatsukai kōshaku 普痛授菩薩戒広釈
gege 下下
gobun hosshin 五分法身
gobun kaishin 五分戒身
gosō jōbutsu 五相成仏
higyō hiza zanmai 非行非坐三昧
hōben gakusho 方便学処
Hōjibō Shōshin 宝地房証真
honzei 本誓
hottokukai 発得戒
Hsin-ti kuan ching 心地観経
Hua-yen ching 華厳経
Hui-chiao 慧皎
I-chi 義寂
I-hsing 一行
Jen-wang ching 仁王経
jikidō 直道
jōjō 上上
joshō 除障
ju 授
jukai 授戒
kaishi 戒師
kaitai 戒体
kanjō 灌頂
Kao-seng chuan 高僧伝
Ken'yō daikairon 顕揚大戒論
kigenkai 譏謙戒
Kōjō 光定
kōngō 金剛
Kūkai 空海
kyōgaku 警覚
kyōjigi 教時義
Liang Wu-ti 梁武帝
metsuzai 滅罪
Miidera 三井寺

Ming-kuang 明曠
myōji 名字
myōkaku 妙覚
nenbutsu 念仏
Ninjitsu 忍実
Nieh-p'an ching 涅槃経
okibumi 置文
P'u-sa ti-ch'ih ching 菩薩地持経
P'u-sa ying-lo pen-yeh ching 菩薩瓔珞本業経
risen 理懺
risoku 理即
rokusoku 六即
Saichō 最澄
sangyaku 三逆
sanju jōkai 三聚浄戒
sanmaya 三昧耶
sanze mushōgekai 三世無障礙戒
sanzen 三禅
Seizan 西山
senryaku 浅略
shakai 遮戒
Shan-chieh ching 善戒経
Shih-chien-hsien 世間現
Shijōshiki 四条式
Shingon 真言
Shinzei 真盛
shō 性
shoju 初住
shōkai 性戒
shōtokukai 性徳戒
shū 修
sōgō 僧綱
sokushin jōbutsu 即身成仏
Sokushin jōbutsu shiki 即身成仏私記
Ssu-fen lü 四分律
Ta-jih ching 大日経
Ta-jih-ching i-shih 大日経義釈
Ta-jih-ching i-shih yen-mi ch'ao 大日経義釈演密鈔
Ta-jih-ching su 大日経疏
Ta-yüan chüeh 大円覚
Tendai 天台
Ti-ch'ih ching 地持経
T'ien-t'ai 天台
Tōdaiji 東大寺
tongyō 頓教
Ying-lo ching 瓔珞経
Yü-ch' ieh lun 瑜迦論
Yu-p'o-sai chieh ching 優婆塞戒経

Appendix
An Introduction to the Standards of Scriptural Authenticity in Indian Buddhism

RONALD M. DAVIDSON

The Buddhist traditions in India found themselves, at one time or another, inundated with a morass of material that passed under the rubric of the "word of the Buddha" *(buddhavacana).* As a result, during the course of its approximately seventeen hundred years in the land of its origin, Indian Buddhist communities constantly found themselves encountering the tension between the more conservative masters of Buddhist doctrine and those who, either tacitly or not, were open to the prospect of the reinterpretation and recodification of the dharma preached by the Tathāgata. The dynamics of this tension and the institutional and doctrinal modifications of the system as a whole represent some of the most fascinating facets of Indian Buddhist history.

With the rise of apocryphal literature in East Asia, the literati, within both the orthodox and reform communities, must have kept an eye on the practices of literary verification coming from the Indian source, even if they had to modify these for their own purposes. Thus, to assess properly the Buddhist intellectual orientation of East Asian masters toward apocryphal scripture, the historian should have access to the values and polemics espoused by the Indian missionaries who brought them the dharma.

It is my intention to examine certain specific aspects of the development of standards of scriptural authenticity in India: (1) the method of scriptural transmission of the early Saṃgha and the general attitudes that contributed to the early scriptural and doctrinal elaboration; (2) the role of the councils in the compilation of a canon and the codified standards of authenticity established to effect scriptural purity; (3) the claim to authority of the Ābhidharmika masters as a model of development and the response of their critics; (4) the mythology and apologetics for the Mahāyāna; and (5) the steps taken by the Vajrācāryas to establish the authority of the Vajrayāna.

Early Saṃgha

Like all such societies of individuals, the early Buddhist brotherhood developed and was subject to certain kinds of dynamics that became representative of the manner in which the Saṃgha addressed itself to the problem of scriptural transmittal, a concern central to its survival and expansion. Two modes of these complex dynamics concern us the most: (1) the formal ways in which scriptural transmission was effected within communities and between communities, and (2) the attitudes that evolved in the larger Indian Buddhist community toward the sources and goals of that transmission.

(1) From the beginning, there were formal factors in the transmission of the Buddhist dispensation which virtually assured that the early Saṃgha would modify the literal content of the sayings of the Buddha. I will consider two of the most significant: the early denial of a standard linguistic basis for the recitation of the sayings of the Buddha, and the ease of scriptural cross-pollination.

That the early Saṃgha accepted different dialects in the recitation of the *Sūtra* and the *Vinaya* is virtually assured. A now very familiar story tells of two monks requesting the Buddha to allow them to render his sermons into some formal language *(chandas).*[1] They were disturbed that the other members of the community were corrupting the Buddha's words by rendering them into their own dialects *(sakāya niruttiyā).* The Buddha forbade the two from doing so, saying that anyone who did would be committing an infraction and that it was correct for the community to learn his words in their own dialects. The Pāli tradition, following the opinion of their most respected commentator, Buddhaghosa, has unilaterally maintained that the Bhagavān was indicating that his sermons should not be translated into some formal language but retained in his own dialect, Pāli.[2] However, the most persuasive position, set forth with such eloquence by Franklin Edgerton, is that the Buddha did not speak in one but in many dialects.[3] He undoubtedly tailored his language to the area in which he was teaching, and this circumstance may be a basis for the myth that the Buddha was understood by each listener in his own language.[4] Conversely, the prohibition, ascribed to the Buddha, against formalizing the dialect of his doctrine provided the medium for its elaboration in other phonemic and idiomatic constructions, including the eventual "transposition" of the doctrine into Sanskrit.[5]

Over and above this linguistic latitude, the circumstances of the Buddha's teaching and the condition of the Saṃgha during the Buddha's life must be the focal point for understanding the later elaboration of the "word of the Buddha." It seems clear that, as soon as they became "worthy men" (arhats), the Buddha sent his disciples out to propagate his dharma.[6] While they were engaged in this enterprise, he continued to teach elsewhere, constantly endorsing the realization of new arhats. Thus, during the more than forty years of the Buddha's teaching career, there were many monks acting as authoritative teachers of the doctrine throughout the kingdom of Magadha and its border areas. They would cross paths with the master from time to time and receive new information as his doctrine and teaching style developed. They would also receive new information from one another during the fortnightly congregations, the summer rains retreat, and whenever they met as their mendicant paths crossed. After forty years of their obtaining new information through such contact, we may be certain that, by the death of the Buddha, the process of receiving new "teachings of the teacher" *(śāstuḥ śāsanaṃ)* had become a well-accepted practice. The network of instruction was thus established, and doubtless most of the monks realized that much of what the Buddha had said during his lengthy career remained unknown to them personally. They therefore kept the network alive to obtain instruction committed to other bhikṣus. In my opinion, this was the beginning of the continuing cross-fertilization of scripture and doctrine which was the hallmark of Indian Buddhism.

Erich Frauwallner has pointed out that there appears to have been a reification of language in the various sūtras that treat related topics.[7] When a sūtra in the *Dīrghāgama,* for example, discusses a certain topic, virtually the same wording is found in the *Saṃyuktāgama* and the *Ekottarāgama.* The natural result is a formalization that forfeits the more complex, rounded view of the topic as it was taught at different times and in different places. This is the sort of formalization that is to be expected from an oral tradition, and Frauwallner maintains that it was a tool, like the ubiquitous mnemonic verse *(uddāna),* useful in stretching the capacity of memory. Once the initial phrase is met in a sūtra, the entire succeeding block of text can be reeled off almost effortlessly, since the same material would already have been memorized in another sūtra.

(2) Certainly, these two processes of elaboration and consolidation must have begun during the life of the Buddha, and they continued to occur throughout the tenure of Buddhism in India. They cannot, of course, account for all the eventual alterations in doctrinal and scriptural basis that the tradition experienced, but they did serve to keep the institutional doors of vitality open. If the Buddha or the early Saṃgha had decided to put linguistic strictures on his sayings, or if there had been a thoroughgoing movement during the life of the Buddha to codify his sermons, then the diversity of material classed under the rubric of the "word of the Buddha" might not have obtained its present extent. Two extremely important values, however, effectively precluded movement in that direction: the perceived nature of truth or reality, and the

factors effecting access to that truth. These two values were probably the deciding elements in the continuing development of Buddhism in all its stages, right through that of Vajrayāna.

With the parameters of the "doctrine of the teacher" amorphous and ill-defined, the church elders *(sthavira)* were compelled to address the problem of the relationship between the Buddha and the dharma preached by him. Characteristically, the dharma was defined as that which was discovered by the Buddha, but it was neither invented by him, nor indeed was he the first of the buddhas.[8] Therefore, the speech of the Buddha embodied the dharma, yet the dharma went beyond the speech of the Buddha. Thus words other than those of the Buddha himself may accurately represent the dharma. This worked in three ways.[9] First, the dharma could be learned from a disciple's preaching of the word of the Buddha. The characteristic introduction to this teaching would most typically be the phrase *(nidāna)* that starts the sūtras: "Thus have I heard at one time . . ." *(evaṃ mayā śrutam ekasmin samaye),* apparently intended to reflect the idea that this discourse came from one who had heard (śrāvaka) it from the Buddha himself. Second, a person in the presence of the Buddha could be inspired *(pratibhāti)* by the power of the presence of the Buddha *(buddhānubhāvena)* to speak the dharma in his own words. Usually a sūtra spoken thus by a third party concludes with phrases of approval by the Tathāgata. As we shall see, this variety of sūtra was recognized by many of the traditions and was to play a great part in the development of Indian Buddhism. Finally, the rubric of dharma was very early extended to the teaching of the immediate disciples of the Buddha, the Ārya Śrāvakas, whether or not the presence of the Buddha inspired their preaching. From them it was extended to others, and both the Dharmaguptaka and Theravāda *Vinayas* broadened the list considerably:

> That which is called dharma is that spoken by the Buddha, spoken by the śrāvakas, spoken by the sages *(ṛṣi),* or spoken by divinities, when significant *(atthūpasaṃhita)* and when endowed with doctrinal principle *(dhammupasamhito).*[10]

For these traditions, then, the definition of dharma can be applied to the speech of those who somehow represent a superior kind of knowledge, obtained by themselves or with the help of the Buddha.

Over and above these definitions of dharma, the functional orientation of the Buddhist masters led to a shift in perspective: the perception of a kind of circularity between the Buddha, his dharma, the reality discovered by him, and the cognition of that reality. For example, in the later Vaibhāṣika tradition, according to the *Abhidharmadīpa,* the dharma spoken by the Buddha served to define the Tathāgata's omniscience:

> Those [determinate words, statements, and phonemes] not established by human agency *(apauruṣeya)*, illuminating the elements *(dhātu)*, doors of perception *(āyatana)*, and aggregates *(skandha)*, etc., are first within the sphere of cognition of the buddhas. Because he awakens to these, the Lord is designated "omniscient."[11]

While the dharma, or more precisely the dharma spoken by the Buddha, could define the enlightenment of the Buddha, its primary goal was to develop the same quality of realization in others. In the Pāli Nikāyas this characteristic of the dharma is called its ability to generate the fruit of mendicancy *(sāmaññaphala)* and is considered to be unique to the buddhadharma.[12] This characteristic is concomitant with the unique value of the buddhadharma—the single flavor of liberation:

> In that same manner, Pahārāda, as the great ocean has one taste, the taste of salt, even thus, Pahārāda, this Dhammavinaya has one taste, the taste of final release.[13]

This unique ability of the dharma was both its ultimate benefit and its final touchstone. That which does not confer liberation could not be considered dharma. Therefore the teaching of the Buddha had to be tested for this unique flavor, a regular theme in Indian Buddhism. Primacy is given those who have not merely accepted what the teacher has said *(śraddhānusārin)* but have explored and continually reexamined the dharma until they have arrived at certainty of its meaning *(dharmānusārin)*.[14] Thus we see that the dharma, as instruction, depends both on the Buddha for the revelation of its words and phrases as well as on the bhikṣu for the testing of its potency. Likewise, when the dharma is preached by a third person, that person must conform to the dharma if he is really to be considered a "teacher of dharma."[15] In the *Mahāvagga*, too, the requisites for one to become an *upādhyāya*, a preceptor, are that he be possessed of the five aggregates of the dharma: moral conduct, concentration, insight, liberation, and the vision of the gnosis of liberation. The correct conditions for teaching the dharma must therefore be met with in the individual bhikṣu, and this requirement was to be maintained throughout the course of Buddhism in India.[16]

The circular dependence of the dharma as instruction and the monk as instructor is ultimately grounded in the nature of reality *(dharmatā)* toward which both are oriented, and which in turn is not even dependent on the Buddha:

> Whether there is the arising of tathāgatas or there is the nonarising of tathāgatas, this mode *(dharmatā)* of the elements of existence remains fixed.[17]

I bring up the question of *dharmatā*, here in its most basic environment of dependent origination *(pratītyasamutpāda)*, because we can observe, through time, not only circularity but also a sense of increasing permeability between the four conceptual structures mentioned above: the reality discovered by the Buddha *(dharmatā),* his insight into that reality (*prajñā* or *jñāna*), the words of the Buddha as a expression of that insight *(buddhavacana),* and the significant message of the Buddha (dharma). For example, the *Śālistamba-sūtra* equates insight toward one of these with insight toward others:

> Whoever, O monks, perceives dependent origination, he perceives the dharma. Whoever sees the dharma, sees the Buddha.[18]

These various factors were therefore seen to overlap one another. Gnosis or insight developed by a monk through the teaching provided access both to reality and the Buddha on one hand, and to a position as teacher on the other.

So far, the extension of authority has been from the word of the master toward the words of his representatives by means of the dharma. The Ārya Śrāvakas could speak for the Buddha, either in his own words, in his presence, or through their own insight. This extended authority, however, came to work in the reverse direction as well: the teaching of the śrāvakas, because it was dharma, could conceivably be considered the word of the Buddha. This appears to have been a primary mechanism of scriptural and doctrinal elaboration—truth, applicable universally and cognizable by the Buddha's lineal successors, may be assigned to him, though spoken by them, in much the same way that the truth initially spoken by him was eventually internalized and passed on by them. Likewise, that which assists in the attainment of the "fruit of mendicancy" *(śrāmaṇyaphala)* must, by nature, be dharma. Since he was omniscient, the Buddha must have had this or that particular doctrine (method, statement, etc.) in mind. Elaborating what must have been the Buddha's idea is merely liberating his intention from the bonds of extreme literalism *(saṃdhinirmocana).*[19]

In my opinion, these were the major attitudinal factors governing the development of the Indian Buddhist elaboration of the word of the master. These attitudes served to augment and elaborate the Buddhist oral tradition in striking contrast with one other major Indian oral lineage—the Vedic. The Vedic sayings, so well preserved for us, were the focus of almost precisely the opposite orientation toward their preservation. They enjoyed a very effective series of checks and balances in the manner of their several recitations, which ensured little textual variation. It was the duty of the *brāhmaṇas* to recite the text exactly as received, and this precision was ensured by a series of accents and the memorization of the same text in different sequences.[20] Furthermore, the linguistic model, as opposed to the content model, was the basis for Vedic recitation: as long as correct recitation of the phonemes was maintained, content comprehension was optional. Finally, the position of the individual was paramount for the verification of the dharma among Buddhists. For Kumārila, however, the *Vedas* had self-validity *(svataḥprāmāṇyam)* and were independent of the individual revealing or reciting them, factors that he felt substantiated his claim of the superiority of the *Vedas* over the sayings of the Buddha.[21]

It is certainly not my intention here to demonstrate that the above attitudinal factors, present at one time or another in Buddhist India, were fully developed from the earliest period. Still, the sources I have cited all point to an earlier, less well-developed common orientation of the leading members of the early Buddhist Saṃgha: the unique experience that the word of the master embodied must be kept as vital and alive as possible. If some amount of distortion in the discourses occurred, that was understandable, particularly where this involved slightly altered pronunciations or idiomatic interpolations necessary to transplant the message into a new region. The early missionary bhikṣus especially—losing day-to-day contact with the Buddha and having to rely on their own resources—must have been responsible for the initial modifications, particularly since their understanding had undoubtedly received the Buddha's own seal of approval, and since they were sent with his authorization.

Councils and Standards

Given these trends of thought within Buddhist India, it is not surprising that they should become codified in accordance with certain rules of criticism that were to be applied during the discussions of whether or not a text or interpretation was to be considered authoritative. But now we must, in this context, consider the problem, so far put aside, of the compilation of the sayings of the Buddha, the codification of a canon, and the role of the councils in establishing scriptural and doctrinal authenticity.

According to well-entrenched tradition, the compilation of the Buddhist canon, the *Tripiṭaka,* occurred during the First Council, convened at Rājagṛha, the capital of Magadha, during the first rains retreat immediately following the demise of the Buddha.[22] According to the standard account contained in the various *Vinayas,* the precipitating event was a perceived threat to the discipline of the Order. In this narrative, while most of the monks are mourning the passing of the Tathāgata, one of the monks has the audacity to declare the death of the Buddha to be their release from his exacting disciplinary standards. Mahākāśyapa, alarmed at the direction events are taking, calls the monks together to recite all the sayings of the Buddha: Ānanda reciting the *Sūtra* and Upāli, the *Vinaya.* Again according to the *Vinaya* sources, the Second Council of Vaiśālī, held approximately one hundred years after the *parinirvāṇa* of the Buddha, is convened because of some infractions of the Vṛjiputraka monks, the most important being their acceptance of silver and gold for their needs.[23] Yaśas, staying with the monks, precipitates the council, which draws the most important monks from all over central India. The Vṛjiputraka monks are declared in the wrong, the *Vinaya* is recodified, and the council is dispersed. This council is followed closely by a split over the so-called five theses of Mahādeva, most of them having to do with the fallibility of an arhat.[24] At Pāṭaliputra a council is convened under the aegis of the king, Kālāśoka, but the rift is irreparable, resulting in the appearance of the two traditions—the Sthaviravādas on the side of the arhats, and the Mahāsāṃghikas on the side of the theses of Mahādeva. Factional disputes proliferate and the two sectarian councils follow: that of the Sthaviravādas at Pāṭaliputra under Dharmāśoka, which produced that masterpiece of polemics, the *Kathāvatthu;* and, much later, that of the Sarvāstivādas in Kaśmīra under Kaniṣka, which produced the magnificent compendium of Sarvāstivāda doctrines, the *Mahāvibhāṣā.*[25]

This account does not reflect the extreme variations of narrative that are found in the different *Vinaya* collections. These variations have sometimes led those researching the councils to an impasse, admitting that nothing can be known for or against the historicity of the councils. We need not adopt this extreme approach to the accounts, and André Bareau, in his remarkable work, *Les Premiers conciles bouddhiques,* has demonstrated satisfactorily that historical probability can be maintained if a judicious approach is taken.[26]

It is, of course, impossible to accept the general position adopted by the Buddhist apologists concerning the recitation *(saṃgīti)* or collection of the scriptures at Rājagṛha. Every version of the *Tripiṭaka* contains texts that, by their own admission, are later than the earliest stratum of Buddhist literature. We need look no further than the accounts of the councils themselves—included, as they are, in the canon—to be confident that not everything passing under the rubric of "word of the Buddha" *(buddhavacana)* was compiled at an early date. However, the First Council was ostensibly convened during the first rains retreat following the death of the Buddha. No doubt a retreat during the rainy season took place that year, and the death of the Buddha is generally understood to have occurred during Vaiśākha, which comes a month before the rains. The Saṃgha was probably, on its own, assembled for the cremation of the Tathāgata and the distribution of his relics. It is thus likely that many of the elders spent their rains retreat together, since, with the death of the master, the very existence of the Order was in jeopardy. This being the case, the question is not whether there was a council of Rājagṛha, but rather what occurred during the rains retreat following the passing of the Buddha, which was later recorded as "the Council of Rājagṛha." Now we are on solid ground, since the word for "council" was *saṃgīti,* which indicates recitation, even if Tibetan translators have rendered the term as "collection" *(bsdus-pa)* in their histories and translation of the *Mūlasarvāstivāda-vinaya.*[27]

Perhaps the following scenario could be considered the most likely course of events. After the *parinirvāṇa* of the Buddha, the elders of the Saṃgha found themselves for the first time without the fully awakened one. During the first rains retreat, the younger monks, many of whom may never have heard the Buddha preach, wanted further information about the teaching of the master. The elders, too, doubtless wished to increase their understanding of the fine points of specific doctrines, and certainly there would have been a movement to establish the *Prātimokṣa* so that a uniform recitation of the rules of order could be performed.[28] Thus the first rains retreat became a forum for the discussion and elaboration of the legend and doctrine of the Tathāgata. Perhaps some rules of order were brought toward codification, some of the teachings of the master were recited, and some verses were standardized, but it is highly unlikely that there was any formal collection or literary distinction of the various types of the master's teachings.

During the hundred years following that first rains retreat, this same process must have taken place all over Buddhist India, particularly in the area of Magadha—the discussion, acceptance, and rejection of teachings as the word of the Buddha, or perhaps we should say as the teachings of the teacher, since the terms "word of the Buddha" *(buddhavacana)* and "spoken by the Buddha" *(buddhabhāṣita),* both indicating the speech of the Buddha, appear to be later than the terms *buddhānuśāsanam* and *śāstuḥ śāsanam,* meaning the dispensation of the Buddha or the doctrine of the teacher.[29] Finally, when the legend of the Council of Rājagṛha became established—perhaps toward the end of the first century following the *parinirvāṇa*—along with it became codified a ritual exclamation of authenticity by which a teacher or local Saṃgha declared a certain body of material to be valid: "This is the dharma, this is the *Vinaya,* this is the teaching of the teacher" *(eṣa dharma eṣa vinaya idaṃ śāstuḥ śāsanam).* Certain standards of authenticity, however, had to accompany this phrase, since the natural reaction of one not accepting this declaration is: how has it been ascertained?

Within the *Bhikkhunīkkhandakam* of the *Cullavagga,* a discourse occurs that appears to show a subsequent phase in the elaboration of this initial exclamation.[30] Mahāpajāpatī Gotamī is depicted as asking the Buddha to expound a teaching *(dhamma)* by which she might remain in solitude, practicing with vigor. The Bhagavān answers that whatever teachings she might know which lead to dispassion, dissociation from the passions, lack of further accumulation, contentment, satisfaction, seclusion, the application of effort, and ease of development, but not their opposites—all those teachings she should unequivocally bear in mind for "that is the dharma, that is the *Vinaya,* that is the teaching of the teacher."[31]

Such a loose formulation, however, could not satisfy those attempting to establish critical guidelines for authenticity within the broad milieu of the early Buddhist Saṃgha. The guidelines that came to be established were set in the context of the means by which a monk might receive a text that others in a tradition claimed to be the teaching of the Buddha. These circumstances are the well-known four references to authority *(caturmahāpadeśa),* which have received much attention.[32] Four specific situations were designated as normative in the transmission of the dharma. A bhikṣu might claim that certain teachings were the dharma, the *Vinaya,* the teaching of the teacher, as they were heard from:

1. the mouth of the Buddha,
2. a Saṃgha of elders,
3. a group of bhikṣus who were
   —specialists in the dharma *(dharmadhara),*
   —specialists in the *Vinaya (vinayadhara),* or
   —specialists in the proto-*abhidharma* lists *(mātṛkādhara),* or,
4. a single bhikṣu who was such a specialist.

The response prescribed for the other monks to these claims is instructive of what must have been going on during the first centuries following the demise of the Buddha. The following is the manner of approval for the first of the circumstances just listed, as demonstrated in the *Mūlasarvāstivāda-vinaya:*

(24.24.52) Therefore, O Ānanda, bhikṣus are to follow the transmitted discourses *(sūtrānta)* and not to follow individuals.
(27) Moreover, O Ānanda, a bhikṣu might come and say,
(28) "Directly from the Bhagavān, this dharma, this *Vinaya,* this teaching of the teacher was heard and grasped by me."
(29) Now, O bhikṣus, that doctrine of his should not be praised or disparaged, but, having heard and grasped its statements and sounds, one should see if it conforms to the *Sūtra* and compare it with the *Vinaya.* If in doing so,
a. it conforms to the *Sūtra,* and
b. is reflected in the *Vinaya,* and
c. does not contradict reality *(dharmatā),*
then let this be said [to that bhikṣu]:
(30) "Truly, O Noble One, these dharmas have been spoken by the Bhagavān. O Noble One, these dharmas have been well grasped by

you. Put against the *Sūtra* and compared with the *Vinaya,* these dharmas conform to the *Sūtra* and are reflected in the *Vinaya* and do not contradict reality *(dharmatā).*

(31) "Therefore, this is dharma; this is *Vinaya;* this is the teaching of the teacher. Having comprehended it, let it be carried aloft in the mind."[33]

Much is worthy of note in these "references to authority." As both Lamotte and Jaini have observed, the third *(c)* of the threefold criteria in (29)—that the teachings not contradict reality *(dharmatāñ ca na vilomayanti)*—is absent in the versions found in the *Dīgha-nikāya* and the *Aṅguttara-nikāya* but is found in the extracanonical *Nettipakaraṇa* of the Theravādas.[34] Apparently the older form of the criteria stressed the precise textual environment, whereas the Mūlasarvāstivādas were additionally concerned that nothing pass under the rubric of the "teaching of the teacher" that contradicted apparent reality. Certainly the meaning of *dharmatā* in this context does not have the ontological overtones that its translation by some scholars as "the nature of dharmas" suggest. Rather, as Wapola Rahula has shown in his classic article on *dharmatā,* the term indicates the "way of things," the natural progress of the elements of reality, identified in many contexts as the general formulation of dependent origination: this being, that occurs, etc.[35] Its presence as one of the three criteria of acceptance in the *Mūlasarvāstivāda-vinaya* and other texts indicates both the developing fascination with dependent origination and the desire that the Buddha's teaching remain acceptable to the perceptive observer. Its presence also indicates the intrusion, for the first time, of a philosophical argument into the criteria —the other two criteria (*a* and *b* in 29) being almost critical in their philological concern for conformity to what we might call "style."[36] Virtually all later textual justifications, particularly those of the Mahāyāna, would be conducted on the basis of philosophical argument.

Although these four circumstances—from 1. the mouth of the Buddha, etc.—are known as such in other Sanskrit texts, the *Mūlasarvāstivāda-vinaya* does not refer to them as the *mahāpadeśa,* the four "references to authority." Instead, this *Vinaya* focuses on the three criteria (*a, b,* and *c* in 29) as demonstrating the way in which the bhikṣu is to follow the transmitted discourses *(sūtrānta)* rather than individuals. The Mūlasarvāstivāda reference here seems to allude to an early development of a doctrinal structure missing in Theravāda texts: the four bases—or "refuges"—of comprehension *(catuḥpratisaraṇa).* The standard form of these, as given in other, much later texts, is that one is to have recourse:

i. to dharma but not to individuals,
ii. to the meaning but not to the letter,

iii. to the sūtras of definitive meaning *(nītārtha)* but not to those of provisional meaning *(neyārtha),* and
iv. to gnosis *(jñāna)* but not to perceptual consciousness *(vijñāna).*[37]

It appears to me most likely that the first of the four rules of interpretation—*i.* following dharma and not individuals—came directly out of the circumstance depicted here: the early Saṃgha's decision to take the rules of behavior as its primary focus in lieu of any individual. The *Gopakamoggallāna-sutta* relates a conversation between Ānanda and Vassakāra, a minister for Ajātasattu, set shortly after the passing of the Buddha.[38] Vassakāra asks Ānanda if the Buddha has nominated any bhikkhu as his successor or if the Saṃgha has appointed any bhikkhu as its leader in his place. Upon receiving a negative reply to both questions, Vassakāra then asks Ānanda to explain the cause for the continued unity *(samaggiyā)* among the members of the Order. Ānanda replies that the basis for this unity is the fact that all take refuge in *Dhamma (dhammappaṭisaraṇa).* Asked to elaborate, Ānanda identifies this as the maintenance of the rules of order, the *Prātimokṣa.*

Given the orientation toward content and personal validation, it might be seen as quite remarkable that the thrust of Buddhist monastic life did not exhibit more vicissitudes than it did. This stability can be attributed to the continuing concern for the basic rules of order. In a society like India, where the proclivity of the group is to surround an individual assuming a position of authority, the cult of personality can quickly displace all other standards. When the early tradition isolated the rules of behavior as the center of gravity, it selected group conduct over individual leadership. All the other criteria reinforce the individual's position as a functioning member of a subculture, rather than as a leader or follower. The model of authority is not the strictly vertical teacher-disciple relationship so built into the Vedic system of recitation, however. Instead, the empowerment for decisions was toward a broad spectrum of the community and was grounded in monastic decorum. This decorum was to be the backbone of the Buddhist tradition, right through the period of Vajrayāna monasticism.

According to Bareau, the development of the separate canons of the various sects began immediately following the first council of Pāṭaliputra, in the first half of the second century following the Buddha's nirvāṇa.[39] That canons began to be formed at this time, however, does not indicate that they were completed or even titled as such.[40] Whenever the initial formation of the canon, be it only under the general title of "teaching of the teacher" *(śāstuḥ śāsanam),* we must concur with Étienne Lamotte's assessment that no Buddhist sect, as long as it remained vital and alive with the inspiration of the teaching, completely closed its canon.[41] For the duration of a sect's appearance in Buddhist India, it continued to include later material in its canon as the "teaching of the teacher."

Abhidharma: The Model of Development

Despite the initial division of the Order following the incident at Pāṭaliputra, the actual differences between the Mahāsāṃghikas and the Sthaviravādas were quite negligible. A much more far-reaching change was quietly taking place among the masters of the *mātṛkā,* the numbered lists of elements of reality that were initially abstracted from the sūtras. In the oldest forms available to us now—such as the binary *(duka)* and ternary *(tika)* lists at the beginning of the *Dhammasaṅganī*—the lists are themselves quite innocuous, being little more than mnemonic devices facilitating the memorization of certain groups of psycho-physical elements.[42] In this capacity, they appear to be developments of an older form of mnemonic device *(uddāna),* a list summarizing the content of this or that section of the *Sūtra* or the *Vinaya.* The *mātṛkās,* however, became the focus of an intense scholastic movement that aspired to remove any doubt about the functional relation of any element of reality to any other element, the sūtras being neither exhaustive on all points of doctrine nor written with a clear structural layout. With this in mind, the Ābhidharmika masters wished to construct a "definitive" *(lākṣaṇika)* statement about which no doubt could be harbored, since they maintained that the sūtras were "intentional" *(ābhiprāyika)* in their content, being spoken by the Buddha for a certain audience in a specific frame of mind.[43]

Having thus exhaustively constructed these pithy phrases, these scholiasts must certainly have wished to endow the *mātṛkās* with authority equal to that of the *Sūtra* and *Vinaya,* so that the specialists in these would enjoy the same doctrinal, monastic, and social privilege as the specialists in the other two literary genres.[44] We have seen, in the context of the *Mūlasarvāstivāda-vinaya* passage cited above, that the third and fourth members of the lines of authority (3 and 4) included those who were specialists in the numbered lists *(mātṛkādhara),* but the criteria of authenticity in (29) only included the *Sūtra* and the *Vinaya.* For the then-emerging *Abhidharma* to obtain the same gravity as these two, it had to be classed as the word of the Buddha. To establish this desideratum, the differing Abhidharma schools went about the process in their several ways. We will examine the methods of the two dominant Abhidharma traditions, those of the Sarvāstivādas and of the Theravādas.

It seems that the Sarvāstivādas wished to pursue the already well-defined channels of authenticity to legitimatize the seven works of their *Abhidharma-piṭaka* as Śākyamuni's own statements. To do this they had to determine that the Buddha preached the system, that it was collected by someone, and that it was recited at the First Council. To establish the first two items, they relied on two other circumstances.[45] First, they utilized the doctrine that whatever discourse or treatise was approved by the Buddha became the "doctrine of the teacher" and, by extension, the word of the Buddha. Second, they used the similarity of names between Kātyāyanīputra—the putative author of the *Jñānaprasthāna,* the core of the *Sarvāstivāda-abhidharma,* composed perhaps in the second century B.C.E.—and [Mahā]Kātyāyana, one of the disciples of the Buddha who was considered to have been present at the First Council.[46] Evidently developing associations already current among his (or their) predecessors, the author(s) of the *Vibhāṣa,* a commentary on the *Jñānaprasthāna,* maintained that Kātyāyanīputra collected various sayings of the Buddha into a volume of *Abhidharma* that constituted the *Jñānaprasthāna.*[47] This text was then approved by the Tathāgata as *buddhavacana.* The other six works of the *Sarvāstivāda-abhidharma*—considered by the Sarvāstivādas to be the six limbs *(pada)* of the *Jñānaprasthāna*—were likewise collections of the word of the Buddha, arranged systematically.[48]

Taking another tack, the Theravādas attempted to establish an elaborate mythology surrounding the discovery, propagation, and dissemination of their *Abhidhamma-piṭaka.* First, they tried to show that the Buddha's attainment of awakening *(mahābodhi)* involved the realization of the *Abhidhamma.* To this end, Buddhaghosa elaborates a scenario in which the Buddha contemplates the literal contents of the seven works of the *Theravāda-abhidhamma,* one book after another.[49] The next difficulty was showing that the Buddha had personally preached this material. Not resorting to the expedient of collection by a disciple, as had the Sarvāstivādas, the Theravādas adapted an old story about the Tathāgata traveling to the Trayatriṃśa heaven during a rains retreat to preach the dharma to his mother, Mahāmāyā, who had passed away shortly after the bodhisattva's birth. The story is mentioned in the *Divyāvadāna,* without elucidation of the contents of the lecture tour except to say that he taught dharma.[50] The Theravādas utilized this popular filial legend as a basis for identifying the first teaching of their *Abhidhamma-piṭaka.* There was still the problem of the manner of its transmission to one of the śrāvakas, since Mahāmāyā had remained in heaven. The story goes that the Buddha, having completed his teaching in heaven, returned by way of Anavatapta Lake, sometimes located in the Himalayas, where he taught the entire *Abhidhamma* to Sāriputta, the most insightful of his disciples.[51] During the First Council, the *Abhidhamma-piṭaka* was recited by Ānanda, and an extemporaneous commentary on all seven books was given by Mahākassapa at that time. This commentary was said to serve as the basis of the orthodox (Mahāvihāra) understanding of the *Theravāda-abhidhamma.*[52]

The *Abhidhamma* became so important for the Theravāda tradition that they based the transmission of their system on those upholding its study. Buddhaghosa singles out for special mention the obscure passage in the *Mahāvagga* where the ability to impart the *Abhidhamma*—whatever it means in this early context—is identified as one element in several lists of requisites to be possessed before a bhikkhu can take part in the ordination of a new disciple.[53] In the *Aṭṭhasālinī,* he further declares that one preaching the dharma *(dhammakathika)* is not a true preacher unless he has intimate knowledge of the *Abhidhamma.* Otherwise he will confuse the various kinds of ethical action and their maturation, and will be unable to discuss correctly the differences between those elements of reality which are material *(rūpa)* and those which are not *(arūpa).*[54] Thus knowledge of the *Abhidhamma* supplanted a more specifically meditative orientation, seen in the earlier literature, as the criterion for validation as a "preacher of Dhamma." To be fair, the Theravādas in all honesty considered the *Abhidhamma* to be the supreme statement of all Buddhist values and the unique means of obtaining stainless insight. Buddhaghosa even goes so far as to maintain that one rejecting the *Abhidhamma* is guilty of striking a blow against the wheel of the Victor's doctrine and is culpable of dividing the Saṃgha, one of the sins requiring expulsion.[55]

Internal inconsistencies in their mythologies did not give either the Sarvāstivādas or the Theravādas pause, for both of them had Ānanda recite their *Abhidharmas* at the First Council, while neither made much provision for Ānanda to learn the *Abhidharma* from either Mahākātyāyana or Sāriputta. Ānanda's name, for example, does not occur in the formal lineage list given in the *Aṭṭhasālinī.*[56] Nonetheless, in both cases the apologists were relatively efficient in obtaining their goal: the general acceptance of *Abhidharma* as a scriptural member and as the sole intellectual standard to be met by succeeding developments. *Abhidharma* was the first wholly new form of literature to arise in Buddhist India claiming status as scripture. Its methodologies, both intellectual and apologetic, were to set much of the stage for the Mahāyāna.

Mahāyāna

With the rise of the Mahāyāna, the field of polemics expanded greatly. Again, the circumstances governing authenticity were different both from the early sectarian sūtras of the various Nikāyas and from the *Abhidharma.* Most of the *Mahāyāna-sūtras* were authored much later than the previous literature and, particularly as time went on, their content was decidedly different. The milieu from which they arose has not yet been defined with sufficient accuracy, and certain theories place excessive importance both on the theme of faith and on the laity. These were important factors, of course, but hardly the exclusive property and primary orientation of the Mahāyāna. Fortunately, the origins of the Mahāyāna have recently been subjected to intense scrutiny, and the dominant conclusion of this research has been that of organic development from the earlier tradition rather than "revolutionary" breaks with the past.[57]

Whatever the source of Mahāyāna, by the time its apologetic works appeared, the organization of its defense was certainly in the hands of some of the greatest monastic intellects that India has produced. Facing many of the same objections that had confronted the Ābhidharmikas, the Mahāyānists adopted a similar approach: the enlightenment of the Buddha, his preaching of the dharma, and its collection by his disciples all had to be reconstructed in Mahāyāna terms. Furthermore, criteria of authenticity had to be maintained, along with proofs that the Mahāyāna scriptures met these criteria. These latter arguments were almost solely philosophico-legalistic in nature, lacking the more critical approach prevalent during the first centuries following the Buddha's nirvāṇa. Finally, we must note that the apologists of the new tradition tended to identify Mahāyāna in the abstract with Mahāyāna in the particular: a vindication of the theory of the bodhisattva career implied that the scriptures of the Great Vehicle were the word of the Buddha.

It appears that the mythology and the apologetic were, in general, constructed long after the formation of the Mahāyāna, and mostly stem from around the third or fourth centuries C.E. The exception to this was the initial Mahāyānist formulation of the enlightenment of Śākyamuni as found in the *Saddharmapuṇḍarīka (Lotus Sūtra).* Chapter 15 of the received Sanskrit text depicts Śākyamuni revealing to the assembled śrāvakas that he had not in fact obtained enlightenment under the bodhi tree in this life but had already secured awakening incalculable aeons in the past.[58] The acts undertaken by him as Siddhārtha were merely a show for the sake of his disciples. Building on this model, later scriptures like the *Daśabhūmika* describe the way in which a bodhisattva generally obtains his goal; the process was envisioned as common to all buddhas, including Śākyamuni.[59]

In the *Daśabhūmika* account, a bodhisattva ascending to the tenth and final level of the path obtains the level of consecration with the gnosis of universal omniscience *(sarvākārasarvajñajñānābhiṣekabhūmi-prāpta).*[60] Then he passes through a million levels of concentration (samādhi) until he confronts the samādhi specific to the gnosis of omniscience. Enlarging his body, the bodhisattva takes his place in the middle of a great miraculous lotus, while other lotuses are filled with innumerable bodhisattvas, all of whom face the bodhisattva and enter into a hundred thousand samādhis. Then all the tathāgatas of the ten directions respond with rays of light coming from the circles of hair in their foreheads. These rays consecrate the bodhisattva into the range of accomplishment of the complete Buddha *(saṃyaksambuddhaviṣaya).* He thus obtains all of the powers and qualities of the Buddha and reaches the level of the "cloud of the dharma" since, like a vast rain cloud, he spontaneously sends down the rain of the Saddharma.

While one of the earliest Mahāyāna scriptures, the *Śūraṃgamasamādhi-sūtra,* mentions the consecration at the tenth level of the bodhisattva, the *Prajñāpāramitā-sūtras* do not seem to recognize such an achievement.[61] Apparently derived from the Mahāsāṃghika-Lokottaravāda tradition, consecration is explicitly described by means of the simile of a young prince *(kumāra)* obtaining the position of crown prince *(yauvarājya).*[62] The epithet "having obtained his consecration" *(abhiṣekaprāpta)* is applied to Maitreya in the *Gaṇḍavyūha,* and the term may have initially indicated Maitreya's anointment as the successor to Śākyamuni.[63] In any event, by the second half of the Gupta period the consecration of a bodhisattva who is obtaining the stage of the Buddha was a relatively well-accepted doctrine.[64]

As the doctrines and mythology of the enlightenment developed, the later sūtras, such as the *Laṅkāvatāra,* no longer maintained that the bodhisattva obtained his release under the tree at Vajrāsana, but instead in Akaniṣṭha, the highest heaven of the world of form.[65] Other Mahāyānists, however, evidently did not wish to define enlightenment in any worldly way whatsoever, and so the realm of "Dense Array" (Ghanavyūha), as described in the *Ghanavyūha-sūtra,* was identified as the locus of final emancipation.[66] Ghanavyūha is the perfect realm wherein the real *(maula)* Buddha resides, while his emanations *(nairmāṇika)* proceed out into the various world systems to work for the benefit of beings. It is not physical and is made entirely of uncompounded matter *(asaṃskṛtaparamāṇu).*[67] Only tathāgatas and bodhisattvas on the tenth stage may reside there, and they provided the setting for the coronation of Śākyamuni when he obtained enlightenment so long before. There he too resided, sending his emanation into this Sāha world system to go through the twelve acts of the Buddha for the benefit of those bound into the cycle of existence.

Traditions concerning both the teaching and the recitation of the *Mahāyāna-sūtras* remained problematic throughout the duration of Indian Mahāyāna. The author of the *Ta chih-tu lun* (Treatise on Perfect Insight), ascribed incorrectly to the great Mādhyamika Nāgārjuna, maintained that the Mahāyāna scriptures were never taught to the śrāvakas.[68] This statement is difficult since many of the "entrusting" *(parīndanā)* chapters of the Mahāyāna materials have the Buddha commit the text of the sūtra to the care of Subhūti, Ānanda, Mahākāśyapa, or another of the śrāvakas.[69] The *Saṃdhinirmocana-sūtra* sought to solve the chronological and territorial difficulties of Śākyamuni's preaching of the dharma by use of its famous "three turnings of the Wheel of the

Dharma."[70] According to this doctrine, the Buddha first elaborated the sūtras of the Śrāvakayāna at Vārāṇasī, in Mṛgadāva. Elsewhere, he later taught the doctrine of the lack of intrinsic nature in all elements of existence *(sarvadharmaniḥsvabhāvatā)* and their emptiness. Finally, he taught the well-discriminating sūtras of definitive significance *(nītārtha),* which maintain the doctrines espoused by the Yogācāra masters. The *Saddharma-puṇḍarīka,* in contrast, could not admit that the Buddha preached any doctrine at all and declared that all the dharma was spoken by means of just a single sound *(ekasvara).*[71] Surpassing even this point of view, the *Tathāgataguhyaka-sūtra*—in its elaboration of the mythology of the acts of the Buddha—maintained that, from the time of his enlightenment until his final nirvāṇa, the Tathāgata does not preach even a single word.[72] All the doctrines and all the scriptures simply arise in the hearing of those around the Buddha, each according to his own proclivities.

Allied to the mythology of the preaching of the dharma is the problem of the recitation of the Mahāyāna scriptures immediately after the demise of the Buddha. Bhāvaviveka, in his *Tarkajvālā,* merely maintained that the various bodhisattvas severally collected the Mahāyāna scriptures.[73] A more pervasive tradition is found in sūtra commentaries ascribed to Vasubandhu and in the *Abhisamayālaṃkārāloka* of Haribhadra: Vajrapāṇi (Mahāvajradhara) recited the *Prajñāpāramitā* when the other bodhisattvas, with Maitreya at their head, inquired about the sūtra.[74] For the *Aṣṭasāhasrikā-Prajñāpāramitā-sūtra,* Haribhadra seems to prefer another view based on the entrusting chapter *(parīndanā),* in which Ānanda is entrusted with the spread of the sūtra.[75] He therefore spoke the "Thus have I heard at one time" formula at the beginning of the sūtra, and it must have been Ānanda who collected the sūtra. An objection is raised that Ānanda, being a śrāvaka, could not possibly have comprehended the deep significance of the sūtra, so how could he have recollected and recited it? In response Haribhadra declares that as long as the sūtra has been accurately heard directly from the Lord just as he spoke it, there is no fault if it is recited by one who has not totally realized its contents. Thus it is correct that Ānanda and the other śrāvakas have recited the *Mahāyāna-sūtras,* permitted, as they were, by the Tathāgata in the *Dharmasaṃgīti-sūtra.* Finally, it appears that the later Mahāyāna tradition took the convenient step of inventing another council ostensibly coincident with that held at Rājagṛha. According to the Tibetan historians bSod-nams rtse-mo and Bu-ston, some ācāryas claim that, while the śrāvakas were reciting the *Tripiṭaka* at Rājagṛha, one (or 900) million bodhisattvas assembled in the cave Vimalasvabhāva (variant: Vimalasaṃbhava) in the south of India. There, Mañjuśrī recited the *Mahāyāna-abhidharma,* Maitreya the *Mahāyāna-vinaya,* and Vajrapāṇi the *Mahāyāna-sūtras.*[76]

Unfortunately for the Mahāyānācāryas, establishing the Vimalasvabhāva mythology was easier than getting the *Mahāyāna-sūtras* accepted as the word of the Buddha. Indeed, if we can judge by the increasing intensity of polemics from the fourth to sixth centuries C.E., it appears that the Mahāyāna met with opposition in proportion to its popularity. As long as it was still a small, ill-defined movement, it evidently was not seen as a threat to the stability of Indian Buddhism as a whole—such a perception came only with wider acceptance. The Mahāyāna apologists responded in kind, utilizing some of the same arguments already elaborated by the Ābhidharmikas and creating more of their own. The general outline for the Mahāyāna apology was established by the author of the *Mahāyānasūtrālaṃkāra;* most later authors echoed or elaborated the same concerns.[77]

Verse I.7 contains eight reasons that the author of the *Mahāyānasūtrālaṃkāra* considers definitive in determining that the Mahāyāna is the word of the Buddha:[78]

(1) The Buddha did not prophesy the rise of the Mahāyāna as a false dharma. If the Mahāyāna were a threat to the true dharma, then it would have been foreseen by the Buddha in the same way that he is recorded as making prophecies *(vyākaraṇa)* concerning the ultimate demise of the dharma.[79]

(2) In response to the charge that the Mahāyāna came later, the author of the *Mahāyānasūtrālaṃkāra* declares that the Mahāyāna and the Śrāvakayāna have simultaneous origins. While the Buddha was preaching the Śrāvakayāna to his disciples at Śrāvastī and elsewhere, he was also teaching the Mahāyāna.[80]

(3) The opponent has maintained that some sophists or some heretics, declaring themselves learned and wishing to deceive the world, wrote all the texts of the *Prajñāpāramitā* and so forth. The author replies that the profound and extensive teachings, such as those of the levels *(bhūmi)* and the perfections *(pāramitā),* are not practices of the heretics, so how could they have devised them? In fact, these terms do not occur in the śāstras of the sophists and the heretics, and even if one were to explain these doctrines to them, they would not be interested and would develop no confidence in them.[81]

(4) Some śrāvakas maintain that the Mahāyāna was not spoken by Śākyamuni but by another who passed through the stages and, realizing *saṃyaksambodhi,* became a buddha. But this would still prove that the Mahāyāna was the word of the Buddha, even if not the word of Śākyamuni, since this is the very definition of the "word of the Buddha" accepted by all.[82]

(5) Concerning the *prima facie* argument for the existence of the Mahāyāna, there can be no arising of buddhas without the vehicle of the Buddha *(buddhayāna).* If, therefore, it is agreed that some sort of

Mahāyāna exists (i.e., the *buddhayāna*), that existent Mahāyāna is precisely the Mahāyāna that we espouse, for there can be no other Mahāyāna.[83] Thus the Mahāyāna is *buddhavacana* describing the path of the Buddha.

(6) By the same token, if the Mahāyāna did not exist, there could be no Śrāvakayāna, since there would have been no Buddha to preach the Śrāvakayāna. Furthermore, if the Śrāvakayāna were preached without the Mahāyāna—that is, without the presence of the Buddha—then the Śrāvakayāna would not be the word of the Buddha. Thus the Śrāvakayāna's standing as *buddhavacana* is wholly dependent on the Mahāyāna's standing as *buddhavacana.*

(7) Moreover, when this Mahāyāna is cultivated, it becomes the antidote for the various defilements *(kleśa)* by virtue of its status as the basis for the arising of all nonconceptual gnosis *(sarvanirvikalpajñānāśrayatvena).*[84] Thus it must be the word of the Buddha since only the Buddha's word can serve as the proper antidote. This argument is also reflected in the second of three criteria listed in the *Śrutamayī Bhūmi* section of the *Yogācārabhūmi,* whereby material may be considered as representing trustworthy authority *(āptāgama):* a statement may be considered trustworthy (*āptāgama* = *buddhavacana*) because it acts as an antidote to the defilements *(saṃkleśapratipakṣatas).*[85]

Both these formulations work on the rationale that all statements which serve as a solid basis for eliminating defilements and for obtaining awakening must be considered the word of the Buddha. This is certainly not an innovation of the Mahāyāna, and we have already seen that both the Mahāsāṃghikas and the Theravādins maintain substantially the same point of view. Within the Mahāyāna, the logical extension of this was produced in the *Adhyāśaya-sañcodana-sūtra,*[86] which maintains that all "inspired speech" *(pratibhāna)* may be considered the word of the Buddha if it fulfills four criteria: (a) if it is significant *(arthopasaṃhita)* and not nonsense, (b) if it is endowed with doctrinal principle *(dharmopasaṃhita)* and not its opposite, (c) if it destroys the defilements *(kleśahāpaka)* and does not cause their increase, and (d) if it illuminates the benefits of nirvāṇa and does not increase the faults of saṃsāra. If endowed with these four criteria, all that is well said *(subhāṣita)* is the speech of the Buddha. It is interesting that the first two of these four criteria—endowment with significance and doctrinal principle—are precisely the same as the criteria given in the *Mahāvagga* definition of the dharma quoted above in the section on the early Saṃgha. We have already seen that the theme of the destruction of the defilements was a meaningful thread running throughout all the definitions of the "teaching of the teacher," and certainly the desideratum of showing the benefits of nirvāṇa cannot be considered revolutionary. Moreover, we have seen that both the early Nikāyas and the Ābhidharmikas accepted as authentic sūtras inspired *(pratibhāti)* by the Buddha and approved by him. The final clause of the sūtra section in question is a twist of the phrase found in both the *Aṅguttara-nikāya* and Aśoka's Bhābrū rock edict, "All that the Buddha has said is well-spoken."[87]

(8) Finally, one cannot determine merely by the literal meaning of the words alone that the Mahāyāna is not the word of the Buddha. For example, one may maintain that, because the Tathāgata declared the aggregates and so forth to be existent, the *Prajñāpāramitā-sūtras* are therefore not the word of the Buddha because they declare these same things to be nonexistent. Likewise, one may incorrectly conclude that these same sūtras declare the total nonexistence of the Buddha, the dharma, the Saṃgha, and all wholesome activity, and therefore must have been written by Māra. Such misconceptions arise from an improper application of the mind *(ayoniśomanasikāra)* coupled with one's own preconceptions arising from not studying the sūtras with learned masters.

The argument concerning literalness is especially pertinent to the Mahāyāna and, in the form given in these materials, constitutes the Yogācāra vindication of the Mahāyāna scriptures as the "middle path" *(madhyamā pratipad)*. According to this line of reasoning, the Mahāyāna steers a course between the total affirmation of existence found in the Śrāvakayāna and the total negation of the elements of reality that some Yogācāra masters claim is the perspective of the Mādhyamika school.[88] Therefore, to establish the Mahāyāna as the "middle way," the Yogācāra masters adapted the traditional division of scripture: some sūtras are of definitive significance *(nītārtha)* in their literal statements (for instance, the *Saṃdhinirmocana*), whereas the real meaning of others must be adjusted *(neyārtha)* according to the context, the intention of the Buddha, and so forth.[89]

Following these eight arguments, in verse I.11 the author of the *Mahāyānasūtrālaṃkāra* takes up the criteria established in the context of the "references to authority" *(mahāpadeśas)*—already examined in the section on councils and standards—and turns them into a ninth argument. Some may retort to the first eight arguments that the characteristics of the word of the Buddha *(buddhavacana-lakṣaṇa)* have already been set forth in the *Dīrghāgama* and elsewhere: if a statement conforms to the sūtras, is reflected in the *Vinaya,* and does not contradict reality *(dharmatā),* then it is the word of the Buddha. They will then maintain that since the major Mahāyāna statement that all dharmas are without any self-nature *(sarvadharmaniḥsvabhāvatā)* does not fulfill any of these three criteria, it cannot be considered the word of the Buddha. The reply to this criticism is that the Mahāyāna is true to itself in these areas. The Śrāvaka schools cannot claim to meet the criteria any better than this because none of the Śrāvaka sects agree with each other. Each has its own *Sūtra-piṭaka, Vinaya-piṭaka,* and definition of reality, all mutually contradictory. The *Mahāyāna-sūtras* are as internally consistent and externally inconsistent as those of any of the eighteen sects. As regards the *Vinaya,* the *Mahāyāna-sūtras* maintain that its purpose is to eliminate defilement *(kleśa),* and for a bodhisattva the only real defilement is conceptualization *(vikalpa).* Since the elimination of this conceptualization occurs through nonconceptual gnosis arising by means of the practices found in the Mahāyāna scriptures, the Mahāyāna is reflected in this *Vinaya* of nonconceptual gnosis. Finally, reality *(dharmatā)* is that which effects the attainment of the great enlightenment *(mahābodhi).* The sublimity and profundity of the Mahāyāna constitute its reality, since they are the characteristics whereby the Mahāyāna leads to that state. Therefore, the *Mahāyāna-sūtras* qualify as the word of the Buddha if the sūtras of any of the sects qualify.[90]

As his final analysis of the problem of communication between the Śrāvakayānists and the Mahāyānists, the author of the *Mahāyānasūtrālaṃkāra* complains that his opponents will not even listen to the sūtras of the Great Vehicle and give them a fair and impartial hearing; they are afraid of the doctrine and prejudiced against the sūtras (vv. I.14–15, 17–19, 21). He also maintains that the only way one could definitively ascertain that these texts were not spoken by the Buddha would be to possess omniscience (v. I.16).[91]

It is both ironic and telling that the difficulties of definition that surrounded the generation and codification of the sūtras throughout the history of Indian Buddhism finally caused Śāntideva to define the doctrine of the Buddha as that which has its basis in the condition of the fully ordained monk *(śāsanaṃ bhikṣutāmūlam).*[92] This is certainly very close to the consensual definition of the Buddha's teaching, which, as we have seen, held the earliest communities together.[93]

Vajrayāna

Very little of the genesis of the elements later known as Mantrayāna or Vajrayāna has been adequately explained. Moreover, the extremely close relationship that this tradition in its maturity had with normative Mahāyāna in the monastic setting has been largely ignored. Fortunately, David Snellgrove's recent *Indo-Tibetan Buddhism* has done much to redress the problem, being the most balanced assessment of the system in light of the available evidence.[94]

Space prevents me from attempting to impart anything more than a flavor of the Mantrayāna legends surrounding the discovery, propagation, and collection of the dharma. This tradition appears to have pursued this class of myths almost for its own sake, much as the earlier traditions did with the *Jātaka* and *Avadāna* literature, but for very different reasons. Still, the legend of the Buddha's enlightenment most often recognized in the literature of the Vajrayāna was the story found in the first chapter of the *Sarvatathāgata-tattvasaṃgraha-kalpa.*[95] In this text, the Bodhisattva Sarvārthasiddhi, while attempting to obtain enlightenment, was instructed by all the tathāgatas and led through the five stages of realization *(pañcābhisambodhi),* after which he emerged as a fully enlightened buddha. It is clear from the context and the exegetical material relating to it that, unlike the discussions addressed above, this delineation of the process of enlightenment was not intended as a justification of a certain class of literature, but rather as a model for meditation.[96] Thus the stages of his visualization were described in detail, but the philosophical *(darśana)* content of his realization has been largely ignored in the *Tattvasaṃgraha.* This was in effective contrast to the *Aṭṭhasālinī,* where Buddhaghosa had Śākyamuni review the contents of the seven books of the *Abhidhamma-piṭaka.*

According to the *Tattvasaṃgraha,* Sarvārthasiddhi was given the name Vajradhātu upon his enlightenment, but many commentators assumed that this bodhisattva was identical with Śākyamuni. Śākyamitra, basing himself on a line occurring toward the end of the *Tattvasaṃgraha,* assumed that this buddha went through the acts of the Tathāgata as the Buddha Śākyamuni shortly after obtaining enlightenment in this manner.[97] Others, however, referred to the time period delineated in the *Saddharma-puṇḍarīka-sūtra* and maintained that Śākyamuni had been Sarvārthasiddhi long before. Both factions agreed, though, that between the time of obtaining enlightenment and the demonstration of the acts of the Buddha under the name of Śākyamuni, this buddha preached the tantras from the top of Mt. Sumeru.[98] In terms of time, this means that the tantras were not initially preached by the Buddha during his lifetime, and there arose discussions as to just when the different tantras were initially spoken, and whether or not they passed out of existence during the interim. For example, the *Vajrapāṇyabhiṣeka-tantra* was putatively spoken first by Mahāvairocana in Aḍakāvatī and later, after an interval, repeated by Śākyamuni, who some considered to be identical with Mahāvairocana.[99] Yet the claim that a specific tantra was initially spoken by Śākyamuni in a prior time did not ensure that he repeated it later, and *Bhavyakīrti was known for maintaining that the *Laghucakrasaṃvara-tantra* was never lost after its initial exposition, since it continued to be utilized by male and female divine meditators *(vira/virā)* even during the destruction of the universe between the aeons.[100] The *Guhyasamāja-tantra* maintained a different scenario, claiming that it was always spoken by buddhas but was not preached during the period between Dīpaṃkara and Kāśyapa, since there were no worthy individuals living then to receive the tantra.[101] This entire line of thought was really an extension of the doctrine found in some *Mahāyāna-sūtras* that the buddhas of the three times always preach this or that individual sūtra.[102] Ultimately, it appears that such discussions relied on the model of the definition of truth or reality *(dharmatā)* as existing whether or not tathāgatas arise to discover it. We have seen in the quote from the *Abhidharmadīpa,* given in the section on the early Saṃgha above, that the later Vaibhāṣikas considered the Tathāgata to have discovered statements (dharma) which were not of human origin *(apauruṣeya).* Here, too, the Mantrayāna must have been making some effort at claiming that the Buddhist scriptures were as permanent as the Vedas, which purportedly remain when the world is destroyed.

The story associated with the *Tattvasaṃgraha* of the tantric preaching at the peak of Mt. Sumeru was by no means the only legend about the propagation of Vajrayāna circulating in India. One other major tradition concerned the mythical sojourn of the Buddha to the land of Uḍḍiyāna at the request of the King Indrabhūti.[103] According to this legend, Indrabhūti, upon seeing a group of bhikṣus flying through space, inquired of the Uḍḍiyāna citizens about the nature of these individuals. Upon learning that they were members of the Buddha's Saṃgha, he offered a flower in the direction of Śrāvastī and obtained a vision of the Buddha and his retinue. Beseeched by Indrabhūti, the Buddha and his attendants paid a visit to Uḍḍiyāna the following day. The king then requested that the Buddha explain the method for liberation from saṃsāra, and the Buddha replied that it was necessary to abandon family life first. Indrabhūti, however, asked the Buddha to develop a method whereby those addicted to the five sense objects might yet obtain liberation. The Buddha, having taken up residence in the *bhagas*—normally meaning "vagina," but made problematic by the plural—of the adamantine women, bestowed on Indrabhūti the proper consecration (abhiṣeka) and preached to him the tantras.[104] From Indrabhūti, the tantras spread through India.

This story was evidently developed by the tradition to unify a number of dissociated elements: the early presence of dhāraṇī practices in Uḍḍiyāna, attested by Hsüan-tsang in the seventh century; the local traditions concerning the visit of the Buddha to Uḍḍiyāna and elsewhere in the upper Indus drainage; the continued fascination of Indian storytellers with the figure of Indrabhūti, there being three separate Indrabhūtis by the twelfth century; and the need to incorporate the erotic imagery of the most commonly found introductory lines *(nidāna)* of the tantras into a format to account for the preaching of the tantras.[105]

The pursuit of legendary embellishment was perhaps done at the expense of polemics, for I have found no significant polemical arguments developed in defense of the Mantrayāna in India. This may be contrasted to Tibet, where the twelfth to the fourteenth centuries saw both bSod-nams rtse-mo and Bu-ston defending the system with arguments largely developed from the first chapter of the *Mahāyānasūtrālaṃkāra.*[106] The only Indic references for the defense of Vajrayāna that these two authors cited are almost totally expository and nonpolemical in nature, even if, as in the case of the *Tattvasiddhi* ascribed to Śāntarakṣita, the exposition is highly intellectual and designed to withstand the attacks of one versed in the logical forms of the day.[107] The *Tattvasiddhi,* however, does not conduct its argument in the standard *pūrvapakṣa-/siddhānta* format; its primary thrust is to vindicate the proposition that there is no inherent connection between sensory enjoyment and defilement. Perhaps even more significantly, Bhāvaviveka defends the use of mantras in the normative context of the Mahāyāna.[108] I can only assume that Mantrayāna, developing as a system from the seventh century on, received no serious challenge from the Buddhist community in India.

An apparent inference from the lack of polemics is that the Mantrayāna took its epithet of "secret" *(guhya)* seriously, so many of its methods were not widely publicized, unlike the Mahāyāna. Its lack of argumentation then begins to become comprehensible, for attacks on one Buddhist tradition by another mainly occurred, as we have inferred in the case of the Mahāyāna, when the new tradition achieved some degree of widespread popularity as a separate, new tradition. Neither the Mahāyānists nor the Vajrayānists appeared aware that this was the case, since the Vajrayāna still maintained the ideal of the bodhisattva (even if slightly offset as bodhisattva-cum-mahāsiddha), the path structure of the Mahāyāna, and the perspective *(darśana)* developed by the later Mādhyamikas, such as Śāntarakṣita. Both the *Prātimokṣa* and the bodhisattvaśīla were generally observed by Vajrayānists, since the *Vajraśekhara-tantra* had established the doctrine of the *trisaṃvara,* the triple discipline of Śrāvakayāna, Mahāyāna, and Vajrayāna, all undertaken by a single individual.[109] Primarily the methods of Vajrayāna and its time frame—enlightenment in this life—were the elements touted as dissimilar.[110]

Concluding Remarks

In the above discussion, I have tried to introduce the most pervasive attitudes and concerns, the dominant standards, and the normative mythologies of Indian Buddhism toward the development of its scriptures. It is clear that, for the majority of Buddhist traditions, scriptural authenticity was minimally defined as the claim that their materials had been cognized by the (or a) Buddha, recited or approved by him, preached to his disciples, and recited by them in a convocation called for that purpose. The values accepted in the validating process include the following:

a. Śākyamuni discovered the truth (dharma) but did not exhaust it—others could speak the truth for him.
b. The content of the scriptures was paramount; precise phonemic conservation was of less concern.
c. The individual was empowered to verify—textually or experientially—the word of the Buddha.
d. Orthopraxy (prātimokṣa) was considered the "essence" of the tradition, not orthodoxy.

In four particular instances, however, I may have neglected my task: the role of non-Buddhist literature in the formation of new genres of scripture, the classification systems of the scriptures, the lack of centralized authority, and the proliferation of the various sects.

The role of non-Buddhist literature was of concern to apologists. Yet the relationship between Buddhist literature and any one of the literary trends in India is often difficult to determine, partially because Buddhist texts frequently enjoy a more accurate chronology than some other branches of Indian writing. Moreover, the influences tend to be item-specific and text-specific—such as the borrowing of the four Buddhist views on time and the definition of avidyā by the author of the *Yogabhāṣya.*[111] At times, particularly in the early era, the non-Buddhist text is lost and the Buddhist text survives only in Chinese or Tibetan translation. All these circumstances present difficulties which, if not insurmountable, remain problematic and must await thorough investigation.

Scriptural classification systems, in contrast, have been subject to considerable research, although their position in the development and validation of various kinds of literature appears to be ad hoc and after the fact. When it has appeared to me to be significant, I have included it without elaboration.

Another factor that I have not considered directly, and that has been cited as a cause for the relatively quick fragmentation of the early Saṃgha into the various schools, is that of the lack of a strong centralized authority, such as that of the Pope in Christendom. This is a difficult proposal to assess since the theological and social values of the Semitic religions—not to mention the lines of authority stemming from those values—are so different from those in force in India. Certainly the decentralization of the Buddhist Order and the investiture of authority within the individual Saṃghas had much to do with the generation of alternative forms of the *Prātimokṣa,* which, as we have seen, was considered the unifying force *(samaggiyā)* within the early tradition. Over and above the *Prātimokṣa,* though, the individual Saṃgha, consisting of twenty or more *sthaviras,* is the basic legal unit in Buddhism, probably the case from virtually the inception of the Order. Authority invested in this manner cannot tolerate total subservience to external sovereignty because the basic model of authority is defined in terms of the small community. Charles Drekmeier has already shown that Buddhist communities lacked the dramatization of authority provided by the eternality and divinity of the Vedas in India or God in the Semitic religions.[112] The Vedic tradition maintained the dramatic model and, despite its lack of a strong centralized authority figure, preserved its homogeneity in a way unknown to the Buddhists. The example is significant because it provides the standard of scriptural and doctrinal stability without centralization.

Certainly the decentralization of the Saṃgha, the proliferation into sects *(nikāyas),* and the generation of variant redactions of the *Prātimokṣa* left an indelible imprint on subsequent modes of literary development and justification. The formation of the canon, the generation of new texts, the disputes of rules of order—all occurred in the monastic context where politics and pettiness were juxtaposed with astonishingly heroic discipline. Individual bhikṣus worked in common with other individual bhikṣus to interpret their task as disciples of the Buddha. When a sufficient number of monks agreed on their enterprise in a common manner, they formed a sect. If I have ignored the voluminous literature and many central questions concerning the sects, it is because I wished to focus on the problems of literary standards that concerned all the sects.

NOTES

Due to limitations of space, I have omitted some of the material presented in the original version of this essay, including several essential proofs, for which I beg the reader's indulgence.

1. Franklin Edgerton, *Buddhist Hybrid Sanskrit Grammar* (Delhi: Motilal Banarsidass, 1972), 1; Étienne Lamotte, *Histoire du bouddhisme indien,* Bibliothèque du *Muséon,* vol. 43 (Louvain: Université de Louvain Institut Orientaliste, 1958), 610–614; Herman Oldenberg, *Vinaya Piṭakam* (London: Williams and Norgate, 1879), 2:139; Heinz Bechert, ed., *Die Sprache der ältesten buddhistischen Überlieferung,* Symposien zur Buddhismusforschung, vol. 2 (Göttingen: Vandenhoeck & Ruprecht, 1980), passim.

2. Lamotte, *Histoire,* pp. 614–617; K. R. Norman, "The Dialects in Which the Buddha Preached," in Bechert, ed., *Sprache,* pp. 75–77; Wilhelm Geiger, *Pāli Literatur und Sprache* (Strassburg, 1916), 3–4.

3. Edgerton, *Grammar,* pp. 2–3.

4. Lamotte, *Histoire,* pp. 607–610; Edgerton, *Grammar,* p. 3 n. 8; Jiryo Masuda, *Origin and Doctrines of Early Indian Buddhist Schools* (Leipzig: Asia Major Verlag, 1925), 19; H. Kern and B. Nanjio, eds., *Saddharmapuṇḍarīka-sūtra,* Bibliotheca Buddhica, vol. 10 (St. Petersburg, 1914), vv. V.17–22.

5. Lamotte, *Histoire,* pp. 607ff., 645ff.; Bechert, ed., *Sprache,* pp. 11–16, 24–34.

6. Oldenberg, *Vinaya,* 1:20–21 (= *Mahāvagga* I.11).

7. Erich Frauwallner, *Geschichte der indischen Philosophie* (Salzburg: Otto Muller, 1953) 1:151.

8. Étienne Lamotte, "La Critique d'authenticité dans le Bouddhisme," *India Antiqua* (Vogel Festschrift) (Leyden: E. J. Brill, 1947), 213–222.

9. Adapted from the most useful division of Bu-ston. See Lokesh Chandra, ed., *The Collected Works of Bu-ston,* Śata-piṭaka Series, vol. 64 (New Delhi: International Academy of Indian Culture, 1971), pt. 25, pp. 662.7–663.5; E. Obermiller, *History of Buddhism,* Materialien zur Kunde des Buddhismus, vol. 18 (Heidelberg: O. Harrassowitz, 1931), pt. 1, pp. 40–41.

10. Oldenberg, *Vinaya,* 4:15; Lamotte, "La Critique d'authenticité," p. 216: *dhammo nāma buddhabhāsito sāvakabhāsito isibhāsito devatābhāsito atthūpasañhito dhammūpasañhito.*

11. Padmanabh S. Jaini, ed., *Abhidharmadīpa with Vibhāṣā-prabhāvṛtti,* Tibetan Sanskrit Works Series, vol. 4 (Patna: K. P. Jayaswal Research Institute, 1977), 113.15–19, 109.8, 393.7–8.

12. See *Sāmaññaphalasuttam* in T. W. Rhys Davids and J. E. Carpenter, eds., *Dīghanikāya* (London: P.T.S., 1890–1911), 1:47–86, esp. 56–85. A similar shortened statement is found at the end of the *Mahāparinirvāṇa-sutta, Dīgha-nikāya,* 2: 151–152; Ernst Waldschmidt, *Das Mahāparinirvāṇasūtra,* Abhandlungen der Deutschen Akademie der Wissenschaften zu Berlin, vols. 2–3 (Berlin: Akademie der Wissenschaften, 1951), 3:376–378.

13. R. Morris, E. Hardy, and M. Hunt, *Aṅguttaranikāya* (London: P.T.S., 1885–1910), 4:203. Also P. Steinthal, *Udāna* (London: P.T.S., 1885), p. 56; Oldenberg, *Vinaya,* 2:239; Lamotte, *Histoire,* p. 156.

14. See Dwarikadas Shastri, *Abhidharmakośa* (Varanasi: Bhauddha Bharati, 1970), 3:933 (= *Kośa* VI.29a–b).

15. L. Feer and C. A. F. Rhys Davids, *Saṃyuttanikāya* (London: P.T.S., 1884–1904), 3:163–164; cf. I. B. Horner, "The Teachings of the Elders," in Edward Conze, ed., *Buddhist Texts through the Ages* (Oxford: Bruno Cassirer, 1954), 93.

16. See, for example, Atīśa's discussion in verse 23 of his *Bodhipathapradīpa* and his autocommentary the *Bodhimārgadīpa-pañjikā;* Ui et al., eds., *A Complete Catalogue of the Tibetan Buddhist Canons* (Sendai: Tōhoku Imperial University, 1934), Tohoku nos. (hereafter To.) 3947, 3948; in D. T. Suzuki, ed., *Peking Tibetan Tripiṭaka* (Tokyo: Tibetan Tripiṭaka Research Institute, 1957), 103:21.1.3–4, 32.5.2–33.2.3 (Peking 5243, 5244).

17. Louis de la Vallée Poussin, *Mūlamadhyamakakārikās de Nāgārjuna avec la Prasannapadā,* Bibliotheca Buddhica, vol. 4 (St. Petersburg: Academy of Sciences, 1903–1913; rpt. ed., Osnabrück: Biblio Verlag, 1970), p. 40 and n. 1 for references.

18. Idem, *Bouddhisme, Études et Matériaux, Théorie des douze causes* (Gand: Librairie Scientifique E. van Goethem, 1913), p. 70 and n. 2.

19. Unrai Wogihara, ed., *Bodhisattvabhūmi* (Tokyo: Sankibō Buddhist Bookstore, 1971), 303; Étienne Lamotte, *Saṃdhinirmocana-sūtra,* Université de Louvain recueil de travaux publié par les membres de Conférences d'Histoire et de Philologie, 2e Serie, 34e Fascicule (Louvain: Bibliothèque de l'Université, 1935), 12–13.

20. For the method of this phonemic conservation, see J. F. Staal, *Nambudiri Veda Recitation* (The Hague: Mouton, 1961).

21. *Ślokavārtika* II.95–172; K. Sambasiva Sastri, ed., *The Mimamsaslokavartika with the Commentary Kasika,* Trivandrum Sanskrit Series, no. 90 (Trivandrum: Government Press, 1926), pt. 1, 109–149.

22. Excellent summaries of the first recitation are found in: André Bareau, *Les Premiers conciles bouddhiques,* Annales du Musée Guimet, Bibliothèque d'Études, vol. 60 (Paris: Presses Universitaires de France, 1955), 1–30; Erich Frauwallner, "Die buddhistischen Konzile," *Zeitschrift der Deutschen Morgenländischen Gesellschaft* 102 (1952): 240–296; Lamotte, *Histoire,* pp. 136–153.

23. M. Hofinger, *Étude sur le Concile de Vaiśālī,* Université de Louvain, Institut Orientaliste, Bibliothèque du *Muséon,* vol. 20 (Louvain: Bureau du *Muséon,* 1946), 31–87.

24. See Lamotte, *Histoire,* pp. 300–312; Louis de la Vallée Poussin, "The Five Points of Mahādeva and the *Kathāvatthu,*" *J.R.A.S.* 1910:413–423; André Bareau, *Les Sects bouddhiques du petit vehicule,* Publications de l'École Française d'Extrême-Orient, vol. 38 (Saigon: École Française d'Extrême-Orient, 1955), 64–65. See also Charles Prebish and Janine Nattier, "Mahāsāṃghika Origins: The Beginnings of Buddhist Sectarianism," *History of Religions* 16 (1977): 237–272.

25. Lamotte, *Histoire,* pp. 297–300, 648; J. Filliozat, *L'Inde classique* (Paris: École Française d'Extrême-Orient, 1953), 2:502–504; Bareau, *Premiers conciles,* pp. 112–133.

26. Bareau, *Premiers conciles,* pp. 84–87.

27. Paul Demiéville, "A propos du councile de Vaisali," *T'oung Pao* (1951): 239–296, esp. 239 n. 2.

28. Heinz Bechert, "Notes on the Formation of Buddhist Sects and the Origins of the Mahayana," in *German Scholars on India* (Varanasi: Chowkhamba Sanskrit Series Office, 1973), 7; Akira Hirakawa, *A Study of the Vinaya-piṭaka* (Tokyo: Sankibō-Busshorin, 1960), 4, 15–18; Nalinaksa Dutt, *Buddhist Monks and Monasteries of India* (London: George Allen and Unwin, 1962), 69–74.

29. See L. Finot and E. Huber, eds., "Le Prātimokṣasūtra des Sarvāstivādins," *Journal Asiatique* 1913:542; W. Pachow and Shri Ramakanta Mishra, "The Text of the Prātimokṣa Sūtra of the Mahāsāṃghikas," *Journal of the Ganganatha Jha Research Institute* 10 (1952–1953): appendix pp. 1–48, esp. 43; Anukul Chandra Banerjee, *Prātimokṣa-sūtram (Mūlasarvāstivāda)* (Calcutta: J. C. Sarkhel at the Calcutta Oriental Press Ltd., 1954), p. 37, verse 8. All these verses closely follow *Dhammapada* 183, a verse not found in the *prākṛta Dharmapada;* see John Brough, *The Gāndhārī Dharmapada,* London Oriental Series, vol. 7 (London: Oxford University Press, 1962), 287–290. Cf. Raniero Gnoli, *The Gilgit Manuscript of the Saṃghabhedavastu,* S.O.R. 49 (Rome: I.S.M.E.O., 1977), 1:141.10.

30. Oldenberg, *Vinaya,* 2:258–259.

31. A similar episode occurs in the Lokottaravādin tradition; see Gustav Roth, ed., *Bhikṣuṇī-vinaya—Manual of Discipline for Buddhist Nuns,* Tibetan Sanskrit Works Series, vol. 12 (Patna: K. P. Jayaswal Research Institute, 1970), 83, 99, 145.

32. Jaini, ed., *Abhidharmadīpa,* introduction, pp. 22–29, 48, text pp. 197–199 and notes; Lamotte, "La Critique d'authenticité," pp. 218–222; Louis de la Vallée Poussin, "Buddhica," *Harvard Journal of Asiatic Studies* 3 (1938): 137–160.

33. Waldschmidt, *Das Mahāparinirvāṇasūtra,* 2:238–250.

34. Rhys Davids and Carpenter, *Dīghanikāya,* 2:123–126; Morris and Hardy, *Aṅguttaranikāya,* 2:167–170; Lamotte, "La Critique d'authenticité," p. 220; Jaini, ed., *Abhidharmadīpa,* pp. 26–27; E. Hardy, *Nettipakaraṇa* (London: P.T.S., 1902), 21–22; Ñāṇamoli, *The Guide,* Pali Text Society Translations Series, no. 33 (London: Luzac, 1962), 37–38.

35. Walpola Rahula, "Wrong Notions of *Dhammatā (Dharmatā),*" in L. Cousins et al., eds., *Buddhist Studies in Honour of I. B. Horner* (Dordrecht, Holland: D. Reidel Pub. Co., 1974), 181–191.

36. Edward J. Kenney, *The Classical Text* (Berkeley: University of California Press, 1974), 41.

37. Étienne Lamotte, "La critique d'interpretation dans le bouddhisme," *Annuaire de l'Institut de Philologie et d'Histoire Orientales et Slaves IX [Mélanges Henri Gregorie]* (1949): 341–361, for references.

38. Dutt, *Buddhist Monks,* pp. 70–72; V. Trenckner, R. Chalmers, and C. A. F. Rhys Davids, eds., *Majjhimanikāya* (London: P.T.S., 1888–1925), 3:9–12.

39. Bareau, *Les Premiers conciles,* pp. 107–108.

40. Lamotte, *Histoire,* pp. 258–259.

41. Idem, "La critique d'authenticite," p. 217.

42. Jaini, *Abhidharmadīpa,* pp. 50–68.

43. Ibid., p. 51; Shastri, *Abhidharmakośa,* 1:254.

44. Gnoli, *Saṃghabhedavastu,* 2:51–52, 66–67; Dutt, *Buddhist Monks,* p. 249; Lamotte, *Histoire,* pp. 197–209.

45. Lamotte, *Histoire,* pp. 197–209.

46. Przyluski, *Rājagṛha,* pp. 201, 78, 303; Senart, *Mahāvastu,* 1:70ff.

47. Lamotte, *Histoire,* pp. 204–205; Junjiro Takasusu, "On the Abhidharma Literature of the Sarvāstivādins," *Journal of the Pali Text Society* 1904–1905:67–146.

48. Takasusu, "Abhidharma Literature," pp. 99–118.

49. P. V. Bapat and R. D. Vadekar, eds., *Aṭṭhasālinī,* Bhandarkar Oriental Series, no. 3 (Poona: Bhandarkar Oriental Research Institute, 1942), 12–14, 27, 30; Pe Maung Tin, *The Expositor,* Pali Text Society Translation Series, no. 8 (London: Luzac, 1958), 1:16–19, 40, 43.

50. P. L. Vaidya, ed., *Divyāvadāna,* Buddhist Sanskrit Texts, no. 20 (Darbhanga: Mithila Institute, 1959), 258.

51. Bapat and Vadekar, *Aṭṭhasālinī,* pp. 1 [v.9], 14–15; Pe Maung Tin, *The Expositor,* 1:1, 20.

52. *Aṭṭhasālinī,* p. 2, vv. 13–16; *The Expositor,* 1:2–3.

53. Oldenberg, *Vinaya,* pp. xii n. 2, 64; Birbal Sharma, *The Samanta-pāsādikā* (Patna: Nava Nālandā Mahāvihāra, 1967), 3:1034.

54. Bapat and Vadekar, *Aṭṭhasālinī,* p. 25; Pe Maung Tin, *The Expositor,* 1:37.

55. *Aṭṭhasālinī,* p. 25; *The Expositor,* p. 37.

56. *Aṭṭhasālinī,* p. 27; *The Expositor,* p. 40.

57. Lewis R. Lancaster, "The Oldest Mahāyāna Sūtra: Its Significance for the Study of Buddhist Development," *The Eastern Buddhist,* n.s. 8 (1975): 30–41; Andrew Rawlinson, "The Position of the *Aṣṭasāhasrikā Prajñāpāramitā* in the Development of Early Mahāyāna," in Lewis Lancaster and Luis O. Gómez, eds., *Prajñāpāramitā and Related Systems: Studies in Honor of Edward Conze,* Berkeley

Buddhist Studies Series, no. 1 (Berkeley: University of California and the Institute of Buddhist Studies, 1977), 3–34; Bechert, "Notes on the Formation," pp. 11–18; Paul M. Harrison, "Buddhānusmṛti in the Pratyutpanna-Buddha-Saṃmukhāvasthita-Samādhi-sūtra," *Journal of Indian Philosophy* 6 (1978): 35–57; Fujita Kotatsu, "One Vehicle or Three?" Leon Hurvitz, trans., *Journal of Indian Philosophy* 3 (1975): 79–166; Luis O. Gómez, "Proto-Mādhyamika in the Pāli Canon," *Philosophy East and West* 26 (1976): 137–165; Gregory Schopen, "The Phrase *'sa pṛthivīpradeśaś caityabhūto bhavet'* in the *Vajracchedikā:* Notes on the Cult of the Book in Mahāyāna," *Indo-Iranian Journal* 17 (1975): 147–181; idem, "Sukhāvatī as a Generalized Religious Goal in Sanskrit Mahāyāna Sūtra Literature," *Indo-Iranian Journal* 19 (1977): 177–210.

58. Kern and Nanjio, *Saddharmapuṇḍarīka,* pp. 323–326.

59. Rhys Davids and Carpenter, *Dīghanikāya,* 2:1–54; E. Waldschmidt, *Mahāvadāna-sūtra,* Abhandlungen der Deutschen Akademie der Wissenschaften zu Berlin, 1952 Nr. 8, 1954 Nr. 3 (Berlin: Akademie Verlag, 1953–1956), 2 vols.; *Ārya-Bhadrakalpika-nāma-Mahāyāna-sūtra,* To. 94, *mdo-sde,* vol. *ka,* especially fols. 102a7–287b5. See Yamada, *Karuṇāpuṇḍarīka,* 1:136–139, 154–159.

60. Ryuko Kondo, *Daśabhūmīśvaro nāma Mahāyānasūtra,* Rinsen Buddhist Text Series II (Kyoto: Ronsen Book Co., 1983), 178.10–189.2; followed closely by Candrakīrti in Louis de la Vallée Poussin, ed., *Madhyamakāvatāra par Candrakīrti,* Bibliotheca Buddhica, vol. 9 (St. Petersburg: Imperial Academy of Sciences, 1912), 349–350.

61. Étienne Lamotte, *La Concentration de La Marche Héroïque, MCB* vol. 12 (Brussels: Institut Belge des Hautes Études Chinoises, 1965), 158 n. 6, 166 n. 125, 258, 265. Nalinaksa Dutt, ed., *Pañcaviṃśatisāhasrikā-Prajñāpāramitā,* Calcutta Oriental Series, vol. 28 (Calcutta: Thacker, Spink & Co., 1934), 225; Edward Conze, *The Large Sūtra on Perfect Wisdom* (London: Luzac & Co. Ltd., 1961), 163. I assume that the nonrevised version of the *Pañcaviṃśati* also does not mention directly the abhiṣeka on the tenth *bhūmi.*

62. Kondo, *Daśabhūmīśvaro,* pp. 183.12–184.6; Senart, *Mahāvastu,* 1:76, 124. Cf. J. C. Heesterman, *The Ancient Indian Royal Consecration* (The Hague: Mouton, 1957).

63. Vaidya, ed., *Gaṇḍavyūha,* Buddhist Sanskrit Texts, no. 5 (Darbhanga: Mithila Institute, 1960), 372, and cf. pp. 74, 409; I have found, however, no evidence of this in the *Mahāvastu* or other early works.

64. Gadjin M. Nagao, ed., *Madhyāntavibhāga-Bhāṣya* (Tokyo: Suzuki Research Foundation, 1964), 56 (IV.14 and *Bhāṣya*); R. C. Pandeya, ed., *Madhyānta-Vibhāga-Śāstra* (Delhi: Motilal Banarsidass, 1971), 140–144; La Vallée Poussin, *Madhyamakāvatāra,* 349.

65. Vaidya, ed., *Saddharmalaṅkāvatāra,* Buddhist Sanskrit Texts, no. 3 (Dharbhanga: Mithila Institute, 1963), 13, 16, 23, 25, 87, 109; Daisetz T. Suzuki, *Studies in the Laṅkāvatāra Sūtra* (London: Routledge & Kegan Paul Ltd., 1968), 375–376.

66. To. 110, Peking 778; Suzuki, ed., *Peking Tibetan Tripiṭaka,* 29:132–157.

67. Suzuki, ed., *Peking Tibetan Tripiṭaka,* 29:133.2.5–6, 135.4.6f. I have not seen this extraordinary term elsewhere in Mahāyāna literature.

68. Lamotte, *Le Traité,* 1:4, 2:940 n. 1. A similar note is struct by Bhāvaviveka in his *Tarkajvālā,* To. 3856, sDe-dge bsTan-'gyur, *dbU-ma,* vol. *dza,* fol. 166a5–6, but with respect to the actual collection and recitation.

69. Vaidya, ed., *Samādhirājasūtra,* Buddhist Sanskrit Texts, no. 2 (Dharbhanga: Mithila Institute, 1961), 303; idem, ed., *Aṣṭa-sāhasrikā Prajñāpāramitā,* Buddhist Sanskrit Texts, no. 4 (Dharbhanga: Mithila Institute, 1960), pp. 227, 260–261; von Staël-Holstein, *Kāçyapaparivarta,* p. 223.

70. Lamotte, *Saṃdhinirmocana,* pp. 12–14, 85, 206–207; E. Obermiller, "The Doctrine of Prajñā-pāramitā as exposed in the Abhisamayālaṃkāra of Maitreya," *Acta Orientalia* 11 (1932): 1–131, esp. 91–93; Th. Stcherbatsky, "Die drei Richtungen in der Philosophie des Buddhismus," *Rocznik Orjentalistyczny* 10 (1934): 1–37.

71. Kern and Nanjio, *Saddharma-puṇḍarīka,* pp. 127–128 [V.17–22]. Contrast with the other theory of teaching in the *Saddharma-puṇḍarīka* [vv. III.89–91], in which the Buddha speaks to each differently according to their proclivities; ibid., p. 90.

72. To. 47, Peking 760/3; Suzuki, ed., *Peking Tibetan Tripiṭaka,* 22:62.5.5–63.1.1, 73.4.8–75.4.3.

73. To. 3856, sDe-dge bsTan-'gyur, *dBu-ma,* vol. *dza,* fol. 166a4–5; Chandra, *Collected Works of Bu-ston,* 24:812.3–7; Obermiller, *History of Buddhism,* 2:101.

74. Obermiller, *History of Buddhism,* 1:94–97, 2:101; Chandra, ed., *Collected Works of Bu-ston,* 24:705.4–708.2, 812.5; Vaidya, ed., *Aṣṭa,* p. 270; Étienne Lamotte, "Vajrapāṇi en Inde," in Mélanges de Sinologie offerts à Monsieur Paul Demiéville, Bibliothèque de l'Institut des Hautes Études Chinoises, vol. 20 (Paris: Presses Universitaires de France, 1966), 1:113–159, esp. 140–144.

75. Vaidya, ed., *Aṣṭa,* p. 270.

76. Bsod Nams Rgya Mtsho, ed., *The Complete Works of the Great Masters of the Sa Skya Sect of the Tibetan Buddhism,* Bibliotheca Tibetica I-2 (Tokyo: Tōyō Bunko, 1968), 2:28.1.5; Chandra, ed., *Collected Works of Bu-ston,* 24:812.3; Obermiller, *History of Buddhism,* 2:101; Lamotte, *Le Traité,* 2:939–942 n. 1.

77. Sylvain Lévi, ed., *Mahāyānasūtrālaṃkāra,* Bibliothèque de l'École des Hautes Études, Sciences historiques et philologiques, fasc. 159 (Paris: Librairie Honoré Champion, 1907), 3–8; corrections in Gadjin M. Nagao, *Index to the Mahāyānasūtrālaṃkāra* (Tokyo: Nippon Gakujutsu Khinko-Kai, 1958), xii–xxii; French trans. Sylvain Lévi, *Mahāyāna-Sūtrālaṃkāra,* Bibliothèque de l'École des Hautes Études, fasc. 190 (Paris: Librairie Honoré Champion, 1911), 6–18.

78. The arguments, reproduced from the *Sūtrālaṃkāra,* have been dealt with by La Vallée Poussin in his treatment of Hsüan-tsang's *Ch'eng Wei-shih Lun:* Louis de la Vallée Poussin, trans., *Vijñaptimātratāsiddhi: La Siddhi de Hiuan-Tsang,* Buddhica, vol. 1 (Paris: Librairie Orientaliste Paul Geuthner, 1928), 176–178. I have followed the Valabhī system of Sthiramati in the *Sūtrālaṃkāravṛttibhāṣya,* To. 4034, *sems-tsam* vol. *mi,* fols. 17a1–30a2.

79. Lamotte, *Histoire,* pp. 210–222; La Vallée Poussin, *Siddhi,* pp. 176–177; idem, *L'Abhidharmakośa,* 5:220–222; Jean Przyluski, *The Legend of Emperor Aśoka,* D. Kumar Biswas, trans., (Calcutta: Firma K. L. Mukhopadhyay, 1967), 167–189. Specifically mentioned by Sthiramati (fol. 17b4) are the legends surrounding the ten dreams of King Kṛkin, related in full in Yutaka Iwamoto, ed. and trans., *Sumāgadhāvadāna,* Studien zur Buddhistischen Erzählungs-literatur, vol. 2 (Kyoto: Hōzōkan, 1968).

80. Sthiramati, *Sūtrālaṃkāravṛttibhāṣya,* fols. 17b6–18a1, does not elaborate; La Vallée Poussin, *Siddhi,* p. 177.

81. Sthiramati, *Sūtrālaṃkāravṛttibhāṣya,* fols. 18a1–5, 19a3–6; the latter occurrence appears to be an afterthought by Sthiramati or a textual corruption. La Vallée Poussin, *Siddhi,* p. 177, perhaps relying on information in K'uei-chi's commentary, to which I do not have access, has misconstrued *tadadhimukteḥ* as if it were to agree with a *śrāvakānām,* whereas it certainly agrees with *tīrthikatārkikānām* of the text. See Sthiramati, *Sūtrālaṃkāravṛttibhāṣya,* fol. 18a4–5. The *Mahāyānasūtrālaṃkāra* continues with six arguments to demonstrate that the Mahāyāna is not within the purview of the sophists; cf. Sthiramati, fols. 23a7–24a3.

82. Sthiramati, *Sūtrālaṃkāravṛttibhāṣya,* fol. 18a5–7.

83. Arguments five and six are both derived by Sthiramati, *Sūtrālaṃkāravṛttibhāṣya,* fols. 17b1–2, 18a7–b5, from the phrase *bhāvābhāve 'bhāvāt,* (Lévi, p. 3.6,13–16). La Vallée Poussin, *Siddhi,* p. 177, has misunderstood this phrase; see Sthiramati, fol. 18a7–b5.

84. Sthiramati, *Sūtrālaṃkāravṛttibhāṣya,* fol. 18b5–7.

85. Alex Wayman, "The Rules of Debate According to Asaṅga," *Journal of the American Oriental Society* 78 (1958): 29–40, esp. 35.

86. P. L. Vaidya, ed., *The Śikṣāsamuccaya of Śāntideva,* Buddhist Sanskrit Texts, no. 11 (Darbhanga: Mithila Institute, 1961), 12; idem, ed., *Bodhicaryāvatāra of Śāntideva,* Buddhist Sanskrit Texts, no. 12 (Darbhanga: Mithila Institute, 1960), 205. David Snellgrove, "Note on the *Adhyāśayasaṃcodanasūtra,*" *Bulletin of the School of Oriental and African Studies* 21 (1958): 620–623, has given the best discussion and edition to date.

87. Lamotte, *Histoire,* pp. 255–260; Radhakumud Mookerji, *Aśoka* (Delhi: Motilal Banarsidass, 1972), 117–119, 217–218.

88. *Madhyāntavibhāga* I.2, V.23–24; Nagao, *Bhāṣya,* pp. 18, 69–73; Pandey, *Madhyānta-Vibhāga,* pp. 13, 173–178.

89. Lamotte, *Saṃdhinirmocana,* pp. 83–84, 205–206; idem, "La critique d'interpretation," pp. 354–359; idem, *La Traité,* 1:539–540. See the definition of *nītārtha* and *neyārtha* quoted from the *Bodhisattvapiṭaka* (To. 56) by bSod-nams rtse-mo in Bsod Nams Rgya Mtsho, ed., *Complete Works of the Great Masters,* 2: 10.2.3–3.1.

90. Cf. the rather specious argument concerning this topic in Vaidya, ed., *Bodhicaryāvatāra,* pp. 204–206 [vv. IX.42–44].

91. Sthiramati, *Sūtrālaṃkāravṛttibhāṣya,* fol. 27a4–6. In I.21, the author of the *Mahāyānasūtrālaṃkāra* recommends equanimity *(upekṣā)* as the only way to approach the problem. This recommendation was evidently the inspiration for Bu-ston's statement of equanimity when he decided to leave the rNying-ma tantras out of the Tibetan canon, and may be considered roughly similar to "suspension of judgement." David S. Ruegg, *The Life of Bu Ston Rin Po Che,* Serie Orientale Roma, vol. 34 (Rome: Istituto Italiano per il Medio ed Estremo Oriente, 1966), 27.

92. Vaidya, ed., *Bodhicaryāvatāra,* p. 206 [IX.45a].

93. Constatin Regamey, "Le problème du bouddhisme primitif et les dernier travaux de Stanislaw Schayer," *Rocznik Orjentalistyczny* 21 (1957): 38–58; Bechert, "Notes on the Formation," p. 12; Hirakawa, *A Study of the Vinaya-Piṭaka,* English summary, pp. 15–26.

94. David L. Snellgrove, *Indo-Tibetan Buddhism: Indian Buddhists and their*

Tibetan Successors (Boston: Shambhala, 1987), 2 vols.; idem, *The Hevajra Tantra,* London Oriental Series, vol. 6 (London: Oxford University Press, 1976), 2 parts.

95. For an introduction into the confusing mass of legendary material surrounding the Buddha and his preaching of the tantras according to the standard divisions of *kriya, carya, yoga,* and *anuttarayoga,* see Bu-ston's *rGyud sde spyi rnam rgyas pa rGyud sde rin po che'i mdzes rgyan,* in Chandra, ed., *Collected Works of Bu-ston,* vol. 15, pp. 128ff. The most useful text of the *Tattvasaṃgraha* is that prepared by Isshi Yamada, *Sarva-tathāgata-tattva-saṃgraha nāma Mahāyāna-sūtra,* Śata-piṭaka Series, vol. 262 (New Delhi: Sharada Rani, 1981). Complementary are Snellgrove's very informative "Introduction" and the facsimile reproduction of the ms. in Lokesh Chandra and David L. Snellgrove, *Sarva-tathāgata-tattva-saṅgraha—Facsimile Reproduction of a Tenth Century Sanskrit Manuscript from Nepal,* Śata-piṭaka Series, vol. 269 (New Delhi: Sharada Rani, 1981).

96. See Ronald M. Davidson, "The *Litany of Names of Mañjuśrī*—Text and Translation of the *Mañjuśrīnāmasaṃgīti,*" *Mélanges chinois et bouddhiques* 20 *(Mélanges Rolf Stein)* (1982): 1–69, esp. 2–4; Yamada, *Tattva-saṃgraha,* pp. 7–10; Chandra and Snellgrove, *Sarva-tathāgata,* pp. 15–16; Ferdinand D. Lessing and Alex Waymen, *Mkhas Grub Rje's Fundamentals of the Buddhist Tantras,* Indo-Iranian Monographs, vol. 8 (The Hague: Mouton, 1968), 24–35.

97. Quoted in bSod-nams rtse-mo's *rGyud sde spyi'i rnam par gzhag pa,* in Bsod Nams Rgya Mtsho, ed., *Complete Works of the Great Masters,* 2:20.4.6–21.1.1. See Yamada, *Tattvasaṃgraha,* p. 556.

98. Yamada, *Tattvasaṃgraha,* p. 556; bSod-nams rtse-mo, *rGyud sde spyi'i rnam par gzhag pa,* p. 23.3.1–2. Note that bSod-nams rtse-mo only agrees that this is true for the *yoga-tantras,* of which the *Tattvasaṃgraha* is one of the chief representatives.

99. bSod-nams rtse-mo, *rGyud sde spyi'i rnam par gzhag pa,* pp. 26.2.6–28.1.3.

100. Ibid., p. 26.4.1.

101. Yukei Matsunaga, *The Guhyasamāja Tantra* (Osaka: Toho Shuppan, Inc., 1978), 109.3–7.

102. See, e.g., Kern and Nanjio, *Saddharma-puṇḍarīka,* pp. 17–22. Cf. Davidson, "*Litany of Names,*" p. 14 [*Nāmasaṃgīti* 14].

103. bSod-nams rtse-mo lists the *gSang ba'i sgron ma zhes bya ba rnal 'byor ma'i rgyud* as his canonical source, in *rGyud sde spyi'i rnam par gzhag pa,* pp. 27.1.2–2.3, 28.3.6–29.3.3.

104. Chintaharan Chakravarti, ed., *Guhyasamājatantra-Pradīpodyotanaṭīkā-Ṣaṭkoṭivyākhyā* (Patna: K. P. Jayaswal Research Institute, 1984), 12–16; Snellgrove, *Hevajra Tantra,* pt. 2, p. 103.

105. Beal, *Records of the Western Countries,* 1:119–124; three Indrabhūtis are mentioned in the *sLob dpon mtsho skyes kyi lo rgyus* of Sa-chen Kun-dga' snying-po, found in Bsod Nams Rgya Mtsho, ed., *Complete Works of the Great Masters,* 1: 381.1.4.

106. Chandra, ed., *Collected Works of Bu-ston,* 15:106.5–127.7; Bsod Nams Rgya Mtsho, ed., *Complete Works of the Great Masters,* 2:9.1.2–14.1.1.

107. To. 3708; Peking 4531, vol. 81, pp. 119.3.6–125.2.1.

108. *Tarkajvālā,* To. 3856, fols. 183aff.; I wish to thank Matthew Kapstein for drawing my attention to this section.

109. A verse ascribed to the *Vajraśekhara* (To. 480) is quoted in 'Jam dbyang bLo-gter dbang-po's *gSung ngag rin po che lam 'bras bu dang bcas pa ngor lugs thun min slob bshad dang/ thun mong tshogs bshad tha dad kyi smin grol yan lag dang bcas pa'i brgyud yig gser gyi phreng ba byin zab 'od brgya 'bar ba,* fol. 39a1:

so sor thar dang byang chub sems |
rig 'dzin sngags kyi sdom pa'o ||

"There are the disciplines *(saṃvara)* of
the Prātimokṣa, the Bodhisattva, and that
of the [Guhya]mantra, the Vidyādhara.

Blo-gter dbang-po's work is found in vol. *Tsa* of the sDe-dge edition of the *Lam-'bras slob-bshad* collection. I have not attempted to trace the verse.

110. *Nayatrayapradīpa* (To. 3707, Peking 4530) of Tripiṭakamāla. See bSod-nams rtse-mo, *rGyud sda spyi'i rnam par gzhag pa,* p. 9.1.3; Chandra, ed., *Collected Works of Bu-ston,* 15:6.1.

111. Louis de la Vallée Poussin, "Le bouddhisme et le Yoga de Patañjali," *Mélanges chinois et bouddhiques* 5 (1937): 223–242.

112. Charles Drekmeier, *Kingship and Community in Early India* (Stanford: Stanford University Press, 1962), 101.

Contributors

Stephen R. Bokenkamp is an assistant professor in the Department of East Asian Languages and Cultures at Indiana University. He received his doctorate in Classical Chinese from the University of California, Berkeley, in 1986. Since 1983 he has written a number of articles on Taoism and, in particular, the *Ling-pao* scriptures. He is currently completing a book, entitled *The Celestial Masters,* on the origins of the Taoist church in the second century C.E.

Robert E. Buswell, Jr. is an associate professor in the Department of East Asian Languages and Cultures at the University of California, Los Angeles. His first publication, *The Korean Approach to Zen: The Collected Works of Chinul,* was a translation and study of the writings of the founder of the Korean Sŏn school. His most recent book, *The Formation of Ch'an Ideology in China and Korea: The Vajrasamādhi-Sūtra, a Buddhist Apocryphon,* explores the connections between a sinitic apocryphal scripture and the Ch'an school. He is presently writing books on the practice of *k'an-hua* Ch'an in Yüan-dynasty China and contemporary Buddhist monasticism in Korea, and coediting a volume on the Buddhist mārga.

Ronald M. Davidson is an assistant professor of religious studies at Fairfield University. He received his Ph.D. in Buddhist Studies from the University of California, Berkeley, in 1985 for the dissertation "Buddhist Systems of Transformation: *Āśraya-parivṛtti/-parāvṛtti* Among the Yogācāra." He has published several articles on the Yogācāra and Vajrayāna traditions in India and Tibet and is currently preparing a volume on the *Saphalamārga tradition in India and Tibet.

Antonino Forte is professor of East Asian religions and thought at the Istituto Universitario Orientale, Naples, and is concurrently director of the Italian School of East Asian Studies in Kyoto. He was a member of the École Française d'Extrême-Orient between 1976 and 1985. He is the author of *Political Propaganda and Ideology in China at the End of the Seventh Century* and *Mingtang and Buddhist Utopias in the History of the Astronomical Clock,* and the editor of *Tang China and Beyond.* His current research focuses on East Asian Buddhist philosophies of history and the historical relevance of the "borderland complex" in East Asian countries.

Kōtatsu Fujita is professor of Indian philosophy and Buddhism at Hokkaido University in Sapporo, Japan. His major publication, *Genshi Jōdo shisō no kenkyū* (Studies in Early Pure Land Thought), is a standard resource in the field. Professor Fujita is editor of the *Hokkaido Journal of Indological and Buddhist Studies*.

Paul Groner is associate professor of religious studies at the University of Virginia, Charlottesville. A specialist in the Japanese Tendai school, his major work to date is *Saichō: The Establishment of the Japanese Tendai School*.

Whalen Lai is professor and chair of the Program in Religious Studies at the University of California, Davis. A specialist in Six Dynasties and T'ang Buddhism, he has published extensively in a wide range of areas in Buddhism and comparative religious thought, including several articles on the *Awakening of Faith*.

Mark Edward Lewis, who received his doctorate from the University of Chicago in 1985, is currently university lecturer in Chinese Studies at Cambridge University. He is the author of *Sanctioned Violence in Early China* and is currently researching the origins in China of the idea of the "classic" *(ching)* and its impact on the theories of writing and genre.

Michel Strickmann studied in Leiden and Paris (1962–1972) and carried out fieldwork in Kyoto from 1972 to 1978. Since 1978 he has lived in Berkeley. He has published *Le Taoïsme de Mao-chan; chronique d'une révélation* and is editor of *Tantric and Taoist Studies in Honour of R. A. Stein,* to be completed in four volumes. Forthcoming works are *Chinesische Zaubermedizin; therapeutische Rituale im mittelalterlichen China; Mantras et mandarins: le bouddhisme tantrique en Chine;* and an edited volume, *Classical Asian Rituals and the Theory of Ritual.* From 1983 to 1985 he was a fellow at the Wissenschaftskolleg (Institute for Advanced Study) in Berlin.

Kenneth K. Tanaka is assistant professor of Buddhist Studies and assistant dean at the Institute of Buddhist Studies, an affiliate of the Graduate Theological Union, Berkeley. He is the editor of *The Pacific World: Journal of the Institute of Buddhist Studies* and the author of *The Dawn of Chinese Pure Land Buddhist Doctrine: Ching-ying Hui-yüan's Commentary on the Visualization Sūtra*.

Kyoko Tokuno is a doctoral candidate in Buddhist Studies at the University of California, Berkeley. Her dissertation is a study of Chinese popular religion as reflected in the apocryphal *T'i-wei Po-li ching*.

General Index

Index of Texts

[redacted]